Bolshevik Festivals, 1917–1920

Studies on the History of Society and Culture
Victoria E. Bonnell and Lynn Hunt, Editors

1. *Politics, Culture, and Class in the French Revolution*, by Lynn Hunt
2. *The People of Paris: An Essay in Popular Culture in the Eighteenth Century*, by Daniel Roche
3. *Pont-St-Pierre, 1398–1789: Lordship, Community, and Capitalism in Early Modern France*, by Jonathan Dewald
4. *The Wedding of the Dead: Ritual, Poetics, and Popular Culture in Transylvania*, by Gail Kligman
5. *Students, Professors, and the State in Tsarist Russia*, by Samuel D. Kassow
6. *The New Cultural History*, edited by Lynn Hunt
7. *Art Nouveau in Fin-de-Siècle France: Politics, Psychology, and Style*, by Debora L. Silverman
8. *Histories of a Plague Year: The Social and the Imaginary in Baroque Florence*, by Giulia Calvi
9. *Culture of the Future: The Proletkult Movement in Revolutionary Russia*, by Lynn Mally
10. *Bread and Authority in Russia, 1914–1921*, by Lars T. Lih
11. *Territories of Grace: Cultural Change in the Seventeenth-Century Diocese of Grenoble*, by Keith P. Luria
12. *Publishing and Cultural Politics in Revolutionary Paris, 1789–1810*, by Carla Hesse
13. *Limited Livelihoods: Gender and Class in Nineteenth-Century England*, by Sonya O. Rose
14. *Moral Communities: The Culture of Class Relations in the Russian Printing Industry, 1867–1907*, by Mark Steinberg
15. *Bolshevik Festivals, 1917–1920*, by James von Geldern

Bolshevik Festivals, 1917–1920

James von Geldern

UNIVERSITY OF CALIFORNIA PRESS

Berkeley / Los Angeles / London

University of California Press
Berkeley and Los Angeles, California

University of California Press, Ltd.
London, England

© 1993 by
The Regents of the University of California

Library of Congress Cataloging-in-Publication Data
Von Geldern, James.
    Bolshevik festivals, 1917–1920 / James von Geldern.
        p.   cm. — (Studies on the history of society and culture ; 15)
    Includes bibliographical references and index.
    ISBN 0-520-07690-7 (alk. paper)
    1. Theater—Soviet Union—History—20th century. 2. Soviet Union—History—Revolution, 1917–1921—Theater and the revolution. 3. Festivals—Soviet Union. I. Title. II. Series.
PN2724.V636 1993
792′.0947′09041—dc20   92-9074
                                                                                  CIP

Printed in the United States of America
9 8 7 6 5 4 3 2 1

The paper used in this publication meets the minimum requirements of American National Standard for Information Sciences—Permanence of Paper for Printed Library Materials, ANSI Z39.48-1984. ∞

To Anita,
with love and affection

O hushed October morning mild,
Thy leaves have ripened to the fall;
Tomorrow's wind, if it be wild,
Shall waste them all.
                    Robert Frost, *October*

Contents

LIST OF ILLUSTRATIONS	xi
ACKNOWLEDGMENTS	xiii
INTRODUCTION	1

1
The Precursors: *Tsars, Socialists, and Poets* — 15

2
Revolution and Festivity — 40

3
The Politics of Meaning and Style — 72

4
New Uses for Popular Culture — 103

5
Transformation by Festival: *Mass Festivals as Performance* — 134

6
Marking the Center: *Festivals and Legitimacy* — 175

EPILOGUE	208
LIST OF ABBREVIATIONS	221
NOTES	223
BIBLIOGRAPHY	259
INDEX	305

List of Illustrations

FIGURES

1. L. Petukhov, poster, May Day 1917.   19
2. E. Kruglikova, poster, Liberty Bond Campaign, May 1917.   20
3. Circus arena-stage for a production of *Macbeth* in Petrograd, 1918.   24
4. Cover of Kerzhentsev's *Creative Theater*, 1923.   29
5. V. Fidman, *Smolny*, engraving.   47
6. Poster for Meyerhold's production of *Mystery-Bouffe*, 1918.   67
7. Mayakovsky's costume sketches for the "clean" and the "unclean," *Mystery-Bouffe*, 1918.   69
8. Monument to Taras Shevchenko, Moscow, built as part of Lenin's monumental plan.   87
9. Grigory Zinoviev addressing the May Day 1918 parade on the Field of Mars, Petrograd.   92
10. Emblem of the Mobile-Popular Theater, Petrograd.   120
11. Mikhail Blokh, *The Metalworker*, monumental sculpture, Petrograd, July 1920.   170
12. Amphitheater, Rock Island, Petrograd.   171
13. Stereotypical Polish nobleman of Civil War posters.   173

14. Poster claiming the heritage of the Paris Commune for the Bolsheviks, 1921.	179
15. Graphic representations of the Third International, 1919 and 1920.	182
16. Maria Lebedeva, commemorative plate for the Second Congress of the Third International.	184
17. Layout of Palace Square, Petrograd, for the November 1920 mass spectacle.	202

PLATES

Following page 133

1. Holiday fireworks display, Moscow, 1744.
2. Lithograph of the carnival on St. Petersburg's Field of Mars, 1825.
3. Mariinsky Palace, Petrograd, November 7, 1918.
4. Demonstration in Red Square, November 7, 1918.
5. Decoration of Hunters' Row, Moscow, November 1918.
6. Tribune covering Pavel Trubetskoi's equestrian statue, Uprising Square, Petrograd, May Day 1919.
7. Boris Kustodiev, *Celebration for the Second Congress of the Third International,* Petrograd, July 1920.
8. *Toward a World Commune,* mass spectacle, Stock Exchange, Petrograd, July 1920.
9. Vladimir Tatlin, *Monument to the Third International,* Petrograd, 1920.
10. The Red stage, *Storming of the Winter Palace,* mass spectacle, Petrograd, November 1920.
11. Liubov Popov and Alexander Vesnin, design for a theatricalized mass maneuver in honor of the Third International, Moscow, 1921.

Acknowledgments

I have been gratified during the writing of this book by the interest I have met with on the part of my colleagues. Studying mass festivals nudged me into new and unanticipated fields, where my knowledge and skills were often minimal; and I cannot thank enough those scholars whose advice has guided my first steps. My appreciation goes to Victor Terras, Sam Driver, and Patricia Arant, who encouraged me when I chose an untraditional dissertation topic and continued to support my work. I would also like to thank Albin Konechnyi, Lewis Siegelbaum, Lynn Mally, and Hubertus Jahn for lending me their knowledge of topics beyond my ken. Alma Law gave me great joy by showing me the film of a mass spectacle, one that I had given up for lost, finally allowing me to see this thing I had studied so many years in print. Richard Stites offered essential assistance throughout the writing period, ranging from simple encouragement and fertile brainstorming to suggestions for the more mundane matter of bibliography. Victoria Bonnell and others who remain anonymous read the manuscript several times—fortitude enough already—and offered me far-reaching guidance and criticism. I thank them particularly for their commitment and diplomacy.

Important institutional support has come from IREX, the U.S. Department of Education in the form of a Fulbright-Hayes grant, a Mellon Fellowship from Stanford University's Center for Soviet and East European Studies, and a summer grant from the University of Illinois's Center for Russian and East European Studies. I would also like to thank my anonymous friends, advisors, and aides in Russia, particularly those in Leningrad's Theater Institute and the Lunacharsky Theater Library and Theater Museum.

Most of all, I thank my wife, Anita, who read the manuscript more times than anyone should have to, provided persistent and conscientious criticism, and endured a year in Russia. This book, which would never have been completed without her help, is dedicated to her.

Introduction

Finding a Focus for Memory and Experience

The people's army takes up position. Orders are telephoned. Movement in the streets... *The Red Army encloses the Winter Palace in a ring of steel.* ... A demand for surrender to avoid bloodshed is written and carried to the Winter Palace by messengers with a white flag. A woman soldier receives it and passes it into the building. Waiting...

Agitators from Smolny penetrate into the Winter Palace. They enter through cellars, past electric cables, up stairways, along elaborate galleries with chandeliers.... The agitators reach the Cossacks in the inner courtyard and begin talking to them.... A sailor in the gallery of the Winter Palace throws a grenade among the cadets. The Cossack artillery gallops out of the Palace, deserting the Government. But *still no answer* to the ultimatum.

The envoys with the white flag return from the Palace and firing begins.... The cruiser *Aurora* opens fire on the Winter Palace. The Mayor of Petrograd at the head of the bourgeois Committee of Salvation crosses a bridge to parley with the workers and is held up by pickets of sailors.... While the Mensheviks are still protesting, midnight strikes, and the Bolsheviks set the people's army on the attack of the Winter Palace. The attack begins....

The people pour up through the palace... and drive out the women soldiers, who surrender with the other troops.... The Ministers are arrested in their council room. By 2 a.m.... the Provisional Government is overthrown and Lenin announces the news.[1]

Many of us know the storming of the Winter Palace from the enactment in Sergei Eisenstein's *Ten Days That Shook the World,* which is summarized above. The great event began with a salvo from the battleship *Aurora*—the shot heard round the world—and by the time it was over the world had been transformed by revolution. The account, which is filled with a human drama and historical sweep that have fired the imaginations of generations, is no less gripping for its being imprecise. The historical storming was something of a letdown. The palace housed a powerless and ineffectual cabinet; it was seized a day after the Bolsheviks had taken power; and it was never really stormed. Eisenstein was not in Petrograd for the October Revolution and can be excused for the embellishments. Far from detracting from the event, he improved on it, focused it, and, for many contemporaries, made it seem more truthful than before.

The inspiration for Eisenstein's film was, in fact, a mass spectacle performed at a festival on the third anniversary of the event. If he seemed unduly inspired by the battle, it was because the spectacle was as thrilling as history claimed the storming to have been. Thousands of angry Red Guardsmen, led by Lenin and whipped on by centuries of oppression, charged across the vast square and seized the destiny that history decreed was theirs. There were more soldiers struggling, more ammunition fired, and probably as many injuries suffered during the theatrical re-creation as during the historical event. A hundred thousand spectators witnessed it from the square. It occurred at the stroke of midnight—a much more dramatic setting than the drizzly, gray, typically dreary Petrograd morn of 1917—and banks of floodlights illuminated the progress of the battle.

Bold, colorful, and striking, mass dramatizations were memorable features of the culture of the Russian Revolution, and they came to symbolize the era to many contemporaries. Yet why, one might ask, did the regime make such an investment? Politicians sacrificed valuable time to organize and participate in the festivals; the press gave them central coverage, even when the Civil War hung in the balance. The festivals were deemed so important that essential funds and manpower were diverted to them during a time of economic disaster. In the midst of famine, valuable foodstuffs were distributed almost freely; and during a housing and heating crisis, lumber and fuel were appropriated for decorations and parade floats. And why did the festivals prove so memorable? Revolutionaries, Comintern delegates, foreign dignitaries, and incidental bystanders all remembered the celebrations years afterward. Yet these were minor incidents in an axial era: a world war divided the nation; three hundred years of Romanov rule were overthrown; the October Revolution swept the country and launched it into civil war. Social, economic, and political life were shaken to the core; still, everyone remembered the holidays. The impression was often so strong, as in the case of the Winter Palace spectacle, that the recollections of original participants were overridden. Nikolai Podvoisky, a member of the troika that commanded the Palace Square attack in 1917, was so enamored with the dramatic version that he sponsored Eisenstein's 1927 film and incorporated its dramatism into his memoirs. His enthusiasm was testimony to the plasticity of human memory.

This book describes the mass festivals and spectacles celebrated by revolutionary Russia in the years 1917–20 and their impact on the memory and experience of revolution. Experience is a welter of chaotic, often conflicting impressions, which require sorting and interpretation. We are guided in this task by our culture, which provides clues as to what should be perceived as "real," what should be ignored, and how the acknowledged impressions should be arranged in a construction of reality. The revolutions of 1917 shook Russian political culture to the foundation and discredited the alternatives that appeared. A hoary tradition of discourse on political power and legitimacy, revolving around religion, bloodlines, and fealty, was effaced; the democratic language spawned by the February Revolution was discredited by hunger, disorder, and continuing war; the Marxist idiom remained incomprehensible and alien to most of the population. Mass festivals helped fill the vacuum of public debate that ensued. Public spectacles were a medium that allowed for the enactment of revolutionary stories. Recent and remote history could be picked through and molded to reflect the most attractive sides of the Bolshevik uprising and to animate the historical vision that lay at its center.

The Bolsheviks were fortunate, though not always pleased, to have some of the century's most talented artists eager to help them. The festivals were often aesthetic triumphs. Artists were given entire cities as their canvases: Marc Chagall covered Vitebsk buildings with murals; Nathan Altman redesigned Petrograd's Palace Square. Theater directors were given thousands of actors and vast urban expanses for mass spectacles, which culminated in the Winter Palace spectacle of 1920. The festivals realized artists' wildest dreams: they had the trust of the state, almost unlimited funds, and audiences that could approach one hundred thousand people. Art once again mattered, and artists met the challenge with verve and creativity.

The spectacles generated considerable scholarly excitement in their own day, with fortunate and unfortunate results. Our good fortune is that the firsthand accounts of many perceptive witnesses were recorded, which give a rich and variegated picture of how the spectacles were made and perceived. However, these impassioned critics were often themselves directors, whose observations were skewed by subjective involvement. Detailed descriptions were often prejudiced by partisan judgment and aesthetic evaluations influenced by political considerations. Although the spectacles purported to speak with the people's voice, accounts of spectator reaction usually reflected the tastes of the commentator, not the audience. This bias made the rare dispassionate observer, like the Hungarian journalist René Fülöp-Miller, even more valuable.

Dispassionate analysis was rarely the aim of critics during the Revolution. Nevertheless, almost everyone—Formalists, Marxists, advocates of proletarian culture, materialist sociologists, refined aesthetes, and cultural activists, even foreign visitors—found mass festivals and spectacles worthy of attention. All, including the most discerning, were impressed. Some of the finest critics, who were situated in Leningrad's State Institute of Art History (GIII), produced a series of rich monographs on mass festivals that are still among the best sources available.[2] With deep erudition they traced the origins of public spectacles and festivals back through the Renaissance, Middle Ages, and classical world. Although they saw the Russian Revolution as the start of a new epoch, they did not believe it unique in world history, and they examined parallels in all civilizations. Perhaps for political reasons, they neglected two important precedents, Russian dynastic celebrations and popular festivals; and they often found in ancient festivals a class consciousness that was not there. Yet their learning and perception led to essential insights on why festivals are celebrated and how they shape culture. Of particular import was the critics' broadening of the notion of theater to include other performative activities like rituals, game playing, parades, and demonstrations. Many of the critics, notably Adrian Piotrovsky, a young poet, translator, playwright, and director, were artists in their own right, and they provided invaluable information on how the mass spectacles were made.

Fêtes, as well as criticism on the subject, suffered a precipitous decline under Stalin. Vast outdoor entertainments were celebrated throughout the 1930s in Moscow, but they lacked all spontaneity.[3] The Great War and postwar reconstruction made festivals a distant memory. Few authors wrote on the Civil War festivals for thirty years, and those who did were too busy apologizing for revolutionary excess to say much of value.[4]

Interest did not revive until the Thaw of the mid-1950s. The moderate reforms initiated by Khrushchev compelled propagandists to develop forms of political education that enlisted citizen compliance through means other than force. They looked to the Revolution as a model; and cultural forms like festivals associated with the Revolution experienced a revival that continued through the Brezhnev years. Leading directors like Georgy Tovstonogov produced mass spectacles; the Krupskaia Institute of Culture in Leningrad established a curriculum for mass-festival cadres. New celebrations and rituals for weddings, induction into the army, and granting internal passports were developed, and old holidays like the winter solstice were revived. There were several objectives for the new festivals and rituals. They were meant to reinvigorate popular support for Soviet socialism; as one festival organizer said, "Mass festivals reflect the unity of the Soviet people and their support for the Communist Party and Soviet government."[5] Religious sentiment was growing among the population, and socialist festivals were thought to counterbalance the compelling beauty of the Russian Orthodox service.[6] The festivals also fed on nostalgia for the Revolution's spontaneous enthusiasm, something long absent from Soviet public life.

The rebirth of festivals has led to a salutary revival of scholarship on the subject. Collections of materials have been published;[7] the memoirs of survivors of the revolutionary years have been published;[8] a large critical and theoretical literature on the subject has developed.[9] There is controversy in Russia over what festivals accomplish and how they should be conducted, yet several general themes emerge, all of which underscore the educational role of festivals rather than their immediate political context. Festivals enable citizens to celebrate and experience the values of society in ways that other forms of discourse do not allow. They are spontaneous civic manifestations, and citizens understand their message directly. Political orthodoxy has often led commentators to overstate claims of spontaneity and political-education impact, but some, notably A. I. Mazaev, are capable of subtle commentary. Mazaev notes the unique features of the festival world, and he is aware that festivals have served many purposes in many societies.

Western scholars, led by anthropologists, have arrived at the topic of mass celebration along a somewhat different route—through an interest in culture and symbolic analysis. Festivals have proved a particularly fertile topic. They demonstrate how a system of beliefs can mobilize a population, either to support the status quo or to undermine the present social structure.[10] Public celebrations become particularly meaningful during times of revolutionary change, when societies not only must project themselves into the future but must grapple with the legacy of their past. Historians of the French Revolution, which the Russians saw as a model for their own, have produced fascinating accounts of how festivals and symbols were used to replace the old regime's hierarchical culture with an egalitarian, revolutionary culture.[11]

An erosion of the totalitarian model of the socialist state and society has also led those who study Russia to a shift in focus that makes festivals a fertile topic. The belief that the Soviet system rested solely on institutions of power and that its foundation was a systematic ideology has been shaken, allowing historians to reach a more layered and nuanced understanding. Cultural studies have contributed to the revision; revolutionary Russia has come to be seen as a participatory, if not democratic, society, where competing myths and ideas were exchanged by the population and leaders. Official culture used to be dismissed as political hackwork, yet under scrutiny it has yielded many insights into the society that produced it.[12] Attention has been devoted to the revolutionary propaganda and utopian enthusiasm that underlay popular support for the Bolsheviks during the war;[13] the flexible application of the "cult of Lenin," which guided the party through various phases of its development;[14] and the traditions, tastes, and myths that constituted socialist realism.[15] There has been considerable interest in Soviet festivals: scholars have examined them as a theatrical phenomenon,[16] as a source of the emerging Soviet culture,[17] and as a means of cultural management in post-Stalinist Russia.[18]

The purpose of this book is to provide an overview of mass festivals during the Civil War (1917–20) and to discuss some of the theoretical issues raised by their study. The intended audience is broad: it includes specialists in the history and culture of the country; lovers of the theater, particularly the rich Russian theater of this century's first quarter; historians interested in revolutionary cultures and cultures undergoing rapid change; anthropologists and sociologists interested in symbolic performance and communication.

Combining the roles of historian and theoretician has been difficult; the chapters are arranged chronologically but with the intent of building a theoretical argument at the same time. The narrative begins not with the Marxist ideology that inspired the Revolution, not with the needs and aims of the Bolshevik regime, but with the legacy of mass celebration active in 1918. The tradition, which seemed democratic back then, was in parts authoritarian and often contrary to Bolshevik doctrine. Its sources included the French Revolution, the Russian autocratic tradition, and the February Revolution. Festivals were integral to the utopian tradition that animated Bolshevism; ideas were borrowed from Tommaso Campanella, Thomas More, Jean-Jacques Rousseau. Festivals had been a centerpiece of the French Revolution;[19] and they were deemed a supreme art form by continental reformers of theater and society such as Richard Wagner, Friedrich Nietzsche, and Romain Rolland. The Russian symbolists Viacheslav Ivanov and Andrei Bely had devoted considerable attention to the topic, as had the Bolsheviks Anatoly Lunacharsky, Vladimir Friche, Platon Kerzhentsev, and Aleksandr Bogdanov. Holidays were, in fact, instrumental to revolutionary history. The February Revolution was sparked by an International Women's Day demonstration; and later in 1917 the Bolsheviks used Petrograd Soviet Day, declared by themselves on October 22, as a dry run for taking power.

After the Revolution, the regime created a new holiday calendar of its own, which for several years coexisted and competed with the extensive calendar of Orthodox religious holidays. The Bolshevik celebrations combined tradition with innovation. A demonstration was usually the central moment. In prerevolutionary times, working-class demonstrations were an expression of animosity toward the rich and powerful; they were illegal and thus an act of civil disobedience. After the February Revolution they became legal, and after the October Revolution they received full state sponsorship. Grim manifestations became celebratory parades; days of struggle became holidays. Festival participants carried brightly colored banners through decorated streets and squares; they were greeted from tribunes by local and national leaders. Puppet booths were set up on sidewalks; wandering actors performed skits about revolution and class struggle; party orators addressed marchers from impromptu platforms. The banners were usually made by workers in their factories, and the artwork was prepared only days before the celebration; thus, alongside works that have entered art history, much was crude and amateurish. This only contributed to the mood of spontaneity that enlivened the earliest festivals. After the demonstrations, theaters and variety houses were thrown open at discount prices; tickets were distributed in Soviet enterprises, but it was easy enough to buy a ticket from a scalper. On occasion, restaurants and cafés offered cheap hot meals to the starving population (they often shut down again the next day). If money was available and the local authorities were so inclined, the celebration could be crowned by a fireworks display or even a mass spectacle.

Many traditions brought together in the revolutionary festivals were transformed by new social purposes. The most important factor in remaking celebrations was a new function: propaganda. The use of public spectacles to explain intricate political principles moved the Bolsheviks into a dialogue with a cultural tradition that was in many ways alien to their goals. Drawing an idiom from traditional popular culture, liturgical rites, and even tsarist ceremonies was expedient because that vocabulary was most familiar to the people. Yet these symbols and spectacles shifted attention away from ideology, the Bolsheviks' fundamental claim to power.

The spectacles had a tangled, and surprisingly unrevolutionary, genealogy. Before the Revolution, many Bolsheviks were fascinated by the prospect of socialist mass celebrations; and several of them, most prominently Lunacharsky, held sufficient power after 1917 to sponsor festivals. Yet, oddly, these enthusiasts could take little credit for revolutionary festivals, particularly after 1919. Responsibility for the festivals—for their shape, content, and the message they conveyed to spectators—belonged more to artists and directors than to politician/sponsors, who offered little concrete guidance. The directors sifted the Bolshevik program, ideology, and history for elements that would fit the festive tradition and suit dramatic presentation. They selected what was appropriate for a revolutionary celebration; in doing so, they reshaped the Revolution. This is not to say that the festivals were nonpolitical. Rather, it confirms the substantial influence of two outside factors: the aesthetics of festivity and the Russian artistic tradition.

What makes a festival festive is not its politics but the fact that it stands apart from everyday existence. Festive time can be compressed or expanded; the setting can be universalized or minutely compacted. Festivals can be celebrated by deists and atheists, conservatives and revolutionaries, the rich and the poor; but they must, above all, feel different. Frequent attempts have been made to associate aspects of the festival aesthetic with certain messages and certain social groupings. Carnivals, which offer a compact, immediate experience of reversed hierarchy, have been associated with the lower classes and their aspirations. Stately rites, which span breathtaking expanses of time to commemorate the past, have been ascribed to ruling orders and their dominant ideologies. But this theory has flown in the face of the evidence, particularly in Russia. Revolutionaries observed rites as solemn and pompous—if not as sumptuous—as the Romanovs; and Russia's merriest urban carnivals were sponsored by the imperial dynasty on the square right next to the palace. Rather than forcing festivity into the straitjacket of ideology or class and asking how certain groups celebrated certain ideas, it is more productive to reverse the question and ask what happened to ideas when they were celebrated.

The festive environment is segregated from surrounding time and place by decorative markings. The marking system—an artistic style—informs and shapes the content of the festival. Some artistic styles decorate better than others. The realism dominant in late nineteenth-century Russia was uniquely inappropriate to the task. Realists drew or wrote about things, they filled their work with ideas, they frowned on playfulness—all of which are designed to spoil a festival. The fin-de-siècle symbolist movement reacted to realism with consternation. How, the symbolists asked, can truth be depicted realistically, when it is intangible, objectless, ethereal? Eventually, with the arrival of a second generation of symbolists, the antirealist impulse bred an interest in older styles of theater associated with festivals and fairgrounds. These forms included medieval mystery plays, Italian commedia dell'arte, and eventually even Russian fairground entertainments. The analogy proved fertile; from these experiments, prerevolutionary directors, most prominently Vsevolod Meyerhold and Nikolai Evreinov, learned the rudiments of what would become mass theatrical art after the Revolution.

One aspect of symbolism's philosophical heritage that proved durable was the belief that theater could remedy the ills of modern society. The thread ran back at least to Wagner, whose dramatic vision was inspired by the social upheaval of 1848. Wagner believed that theater and society had been fragmented by industrialization. Nineteenth-century theater was divided: actors were separated from spectators by the proscenium arch, and patrons were segregated by ticket price. Reformers strove to return the theater to its festive origins: the audience, chosen from all levels of society, would celebrate its most cherished myths and find respite from the alienation of modern life. Participants and spectators could then transport the experience outside the theater walls and reform society.

The vision was both naive and dictatorial, and augured terrible consequences under state patronage. A desire for social harmony was commendable, but the quest for unanimity hid a distrust of diversity. The unforeseen repercussions were later represented by the bone-chilling Festival of Unanimity in Evgeny Zamiatin's dystopian novel *We:*

At the beginning all arose, and the Hymn, like a solemn mantle, slowly waved above our heads. Hundreds of tubes of the Musical Tower, and millions of human voices . . . All eyes were directed upward; in the pure morning blue, still moist with the tears of night, a small dark spot appeared. Now it was dark, now bathed in the rays of the sun. It was He, descending to us from the sky, He—the new Jehovah—in an aero, He, as wise and as lovingly cruel as the Jehovah of the ancients. Nearer and nearer He came, and higher toward Him were drawn millions of hearts.[20]

Festivals, as Zamiatin notes, are a powerful tool of social manipulation. They engage spectators in a symbolic, yet highly tangible, vision of reality. Clearly, the Bolsheviks invested valuable resources in festivals for the purpose of indoctrinating the population with new ideas and legitimizing the October Revolution. Subsequent commentators have taken the intention as the result. A 1981 book by a western sociologist calls the Soviet festivals part of "the arsenal of means to exert social control employed by political elites," "a means to structure and maintain power relations," and "the behavioral dimension of ideology."[21] Intention, though, should not be mistaken for execution; that position presupposes a systemic consistency never present in Russian society, certainly not during the Revolution. It assumes the existence of a single, monolithic ideology; a knowledge of that ideology by local festival makers; the willingness of artists to transmit the message objectively; the capacity of festivity to convey a political ideology without distortion; the absence of alternative interpretations of the message; the ability or willingness of the spectators to understand it.

All these assumptions ignore the vagaries of symbolic communication, the subjectivity injected into the process by the audience, and the chaos and confusion of Civil War Russia. Propaganda was a dialogue, with the audience as the silent interlocutor. It was a living interaction in which audience and maker were in constant communication. Agitators read the latest decree from a rostrum; newspapers were read aloud to a group or performed in skits; pamphlets were delivered by "agit-trains" that penetrated the dark corners of the country. Each new presentation faced a new audience; and the messages that reached deepest into the people's consciousness were those that targeted the audience best. The interaction was idiosyncratic, fluid, elusive; propaganda rarely conveyed a single message but offered potential messages on many levels. Sometimes they were contradictory. Spectators rejected and distorted particular symbols and ideas; and their stubborn habits of misinterpretation often thwarted understanding between state and people.

The frustration that confronted the Bolsheviks in their quest to reform their country and the measures taken to bridge the communication gap speak eloquently about the dynamics of state/society communications and the popular dimension of the Revolution. Though the need to understand these dynamics makes the lack of reliable sources on popular reception even more regrettable, information is available with a bit of decoding. Popular reaction was rarely recorded in the press, yet its imprint was discernible in the lengths to which organizers went to control audience response. The struggle to shape spectator impressions often was waged over words and symbols: newspapers provided acceptable reactions, while alternative interpretations were suppressed; photos were cropped to draw the proper focus; old icons were forcibly reinterpreted.

Ultimately, the conventions and rules of the performance conditioned audience response, providing clues to the role of popular participation. Commentators then and now have acquired the habit of calling all the celebrations *rituals,* but that term is perilously inexact. Ritual is only a single form of festive performance, one employing hieratic, hermetic symbols that allow for compact communication and encourage interpretative unanimity among spectators. This language is highly conventionalized; because its interpretive code exists prior to the performance, it addresses an exclusive audience. In revolutionary times, when the regime was presenting its program to new and unfamiliar people with whom it shared no political language, ritual was of limited utility. Forums in which many people of different classes and opinions could be addressed and in which the dynamism and intrigue of revolution could be conveyed offered greater advantage. Performance modes like drama and play, which were native to the festive environment and offered communicative properties unavailable in rituals, became increasingly popular as the Revolution progressed and the ambitions of directors expanded. Directors eschewed several constricting properties of ritual—audience participation, narrative disjunction—and cultivated dramatic properties that could project powerful myths to hundreds of thousands of citizens. Revolutionary commentators often claimed to recognize rituals in the mass spectacles, but they were likely incorrect. The misperception was telling; it indicated an unfamiliarity with popular spectators and a failure to recognize their autonomy.

The urge to dramatize the Revolution, represented by the shift away from ritualism, inspired a new mythology of revolution that was enacted in the mass spectacles. Each spectacle presented a new understanding of the revolutionary past, which suggested new needs in the present and new paths into the future. To label the festivals mere propaganda, and point out that the history in them was distorted, is to miss the point. Historical drama usually "distorts" history, and it is always partisan: Sophocles, Shakespeare, Schiller, as well as their predecessors and successors, turned to the past not to discover precisely what happened but to draw from it a message for the present. This was also the design of revolutionary spectacles; the past was probed to define who, precisely, were the ancestors of the Bolshevik revolution. The fact that Marx was rarely mentioned, while Stepan Razin, the Cossack rebel, was frequently brought up, reveals an evolution of the Bolsheviks' public image and perhaps even of their self-conception. Mass dramas grouped the Bolsheviks at one time or another with Spartacus, the French Revolution, the Cossack rebels Razin and Emelian Pugachev, the Paris Commune, even the Decembrists. Each association threw a different light on the Revolution and suggested a different destination.

In the process of communicating their program to the people, the Bolsheviks shaped and changed themselves. The myths created and projected in mass festivals were constantly changing, and the party program was rarely, if ever, the central theme. It would therefore be wiser to concentrate less on what the message or myth was and more on how it came into being, what context it appeared in, and to what uses it was put. The cultural process was dynamic and creative, like the revolution it sought to represent. New socialist practices sprang to life in celebrations; and the Bolshevik mythos continually evolved. Festivals, along with the other propaganda media, allowed the party to develop new identities that would legitimize its rule and assist its difficult transition from a revolutionary underground inspired by ideology to a ruling power.

In many ways, the Bolsheviks' ideology impeded their consolidation of power. To undermine the legitimacy of the monarchy and then of the Provisional Government, the Bolsheviks had rejected the old culture and spoken of the redistribution of power and a social order that would transcend national boundaries. In doing so, they weakened the legitimacy of all authority. Festivals countered this tendency by shaping the past into a myth of destiny. The Bolsheviks were associated with the most progressive elements of Russian and world history, which created a hierarchy of events. The October Revolution stood at its summit. History was a highly political issue. To make the October Revolution the sole heir of progressive history was to legitimize Bolshevik power.

When the Bolsheviks celebrated their revolution, they did not seem to be a party emerging from the underground and split by ideological conflicts; they were united by a clear historical mission stretching from the beginnings of civilization to its culmination in communism. The process was not simply a matter of propagandists choosing a new identity and foisting it on the population. The decision was hardly conscious, and it was not made by the party alone. Artists, directors, marchers, actors, and political sponsors all took part; give-and-take, not command from above, was the norm. This interaction involved a complicated and often frustrating dialogue between the sponsors' needs and the artists' abilities; factors as varied as the Russian festival tradition, artistic and dramatic form, audience comprehension—as well, of course, as socialist ideology—had to be taken into account. The result was that the Bolsheviks joined the tradition of fledgling regimes using festivals to propagate legitimizing genealogies. Pharaohs of the Middle Kingdom had to establish their descent from the gods; the Stuarts and Medicis claimed an ancient royal bloodline. What is remarkable about the Bolsheviks is not that they pursued this time-honored practice, but that the mythic past was for them only several years prior.

The immediate past was, during the Revolution, undergoing constant change as it was asked to reflect the present. As our understanding of the October Revolution and of abrupt historical transformation becomes ever more intricate and as the historical tapestry is increasingly woven together from politics, society, and culture, we must question the primacy of politics. If the revolutionary festivals did ultimately serve to strengthen Bolshevik power—which is not at all clear—they did so because artists displayed their magic according to their own rules. Politicians did not make the festivals, just as the artists could not have run the state. What is fascinating is to observe their interaction and their influence on one another. Artists were given opportunities that they could not have dreamed of before and that would soon cease to exist; politicians saw their program and movement imagined in new, often salutory, ways. The Revolution was not, contrary to the Marxism current during that time, a historically determined occurrence; it underwent constant redefinition, and the leading actors were not always aware of the script. In that sense, the mass festivals were, as leading proponents fancied, vast improvisations, where revolutionaries, artists, soldiers, and simple citizens reenacted the past in the hope it might yield images of the future.

ONE

The Precursors

Tsars, Socialists, and Poets

> *I am convinced that awful magistrate my Lord Mayor contracts a good deal of that reverence which attends him through the year by the several pageants which precede his pomp.*
>
> Henry Fielding, *Tom Jones*

By the summer of 1918, Soviet power in Voronezh was six months old, and local Bolsheviks had already formed a municipal theater department. One evening the department invited four thousand spectators to a natural amphitheater on the sloping banks of the River Voronezh for a re-creation of the city's greatest moment in history: the taking of Azov from the Turks by Peter the Great's navy, built under his supervision at the town wharves. The actors were foot soldiers of the new Red Army, stunt men from the touring Cinizelli Circus, and local yachtsmen.

The presentation lasted two hours and consisted of five scenes: "The Turks in Azov," "The Battle of the Russian and Turkish Navies near Azov," "The Siege of Azov," and "The Taking of Azov by the Russians," topped off by a "Parade of the Victors." The scope of action necessitated a certain compression of dramatic time and space. An island in the middle of the river represented the Azov Fortress; prop fortifications and cannons were built over the ruins of Peter's wharves; the river was the Gulf of Taganrog. Because the gap between audience and stage precluded spoken dialogue, a brass band of ninety played throughout

16   THE PRECURSORS

the production, interspersed with commentary from onshore megaphones. The result was similar to a silent movie. Artillery battles were effected by illuminations and Bengal fire, hand-to-hand fighting by the circus stunt men, and naval engagements by the yacht club. The aquatic "Parade of Victors" gave the yachtsmen a chance to flaunt their skill, and it was accompanied by circus numbers performed on deck and by fireworks. At the show's conclusion, spectators were ferried to the island for a carnival that lasted until two in the morning.

For even the best of times there is a spoilsport, and here the *Voronezhskii telegraf* (*Voronezh Telegraph*), a paper soon shut down for its "bourgeois tendencies," complained that "in conditions of starvation and the general uncertainty of human existence the Bolsheviks decided to organize a mass festival needed by nobody." But according to the organizer—not an unbiased observer—the spectators enjoyed themselves and the yachtsmen put on an unmatched show.[1] Whether the yacht club was bourgeois or proletarian is unknown.

Though this was the first mass spectacle in Bolshevik Russia, such things were not new in 1918. They were popular under the Romanovs, particularly during the patriotic years of the Great War. One of the most spectacular had been *The Taking of Azov,* performed in St. Petersburg's Petrovsky Park under the direction of Aleksei Alekseev-Iakovlev.[2] During the war, battle programs were a specialty of Petrograd circuses, and the Cinizelli group on tour from that city provided practical experience to the Voronezh production.[3]

The Autocratic Tradition

Mass dramas require a sponsor, a duty that has more often than not devolved on the state or the church. The Roman state held the masses' fickle loyalty with extravagant spectacles, and the medieval Catholic church gave birth to the mass liturgical drama (mystery play). In Romanov Russia, rituals and spectacles were an essential channel of communication between the autocracy and its subjects; for many years, the Lenten festival allowed tsars to mingle with common folk. Imperial sponsorship did not, of course, guarantee artistic success; nineteenth-century mass dramas attracted few talented actors or directors. The reign of Nicholas II was marked by many sumptuous celebrations: two hundred years since the founding of St. Petersburg (1903); fifty years since the defense of Sebastopol (1906); one hundred years since the Battle of Borodino (1912); and, the greatest of all, the tercentenary of the Romanov dynasty in 1913.[4] For the 1913 anniversary in Kostroma, home of the dynasty, a grand ceremony was followed by a carnival and fireworks;[5] and similar programs were sponsored in cities and provinces. But artistic participation was limited to some crude historical films, one them starring the young Mikhail Chekhov as Fedor Mikhailovich, founder of the dynasty.[6]

Artists had once willingly contributed to state celebrations. Eighteenth-century poets had considered it the highest honor to compose verses for an imperial procession or coronation, architects to construct allegorical floats. Peter the Great was himself an enthusiast of carnivals. On the occasion of the Treaty of Nystad (1723), the whole of St. Petersburg was treated to a three-day masquerade, followed by a carnival procession. The merriment halted only once, for a memorial service, which most of the celebrants attended in costume. Peter and his circle of friends, the Most Drunken Council of Fools and Jesters, headed the procession, dressed as anything from the Pope to a slave; ethnic costumes were also popular.[7] Catherine the Great laid claim to Peter's tradition in her coronation ceremony. Fedor Volkov, founder of the Russian theater, arranged an allegorical tribute, *Minerva Triumphant*, for the occasion, with verses by the poets Aleksandr Sumarokov and Mikhail Kheraskov celebrating reason's ascendancy over the elements (the elements were triumphant in the end, for Volkov soon died of pneumonia contracted during the march).[8]

The procession closed out an era, though later artists would occasionally decorate royal ceremonies. For the June 1883 coronation of Alexander III, Mikhail Lentovsky, renowned for his fairground theater (*balagan*), arranged a carnival on Moscow's Khodynka Field. Four theaters, a circus, puppet shows, choirs, and orchestras all competed for the spectators' attention; and the day was capped by an allegorical procession, *Spring Is Beautiful*.[9] The coronation of the last Romanov, Nicholas II, in May 1896, saw an ominous end to the tradition. A sumptuous service in Moscow's Kremlin was followed by a carnival on the Khodynka. As the tsar distributed gifts to his people, the crowd surged toward the platform, crushing women and children; and when boards covering a ditch collapsed, thousands perished in a panicked stampede.

The February Revolution

The February Revolution, which swept away the hated autocracy, let artists consider cooperation with the state honorable. On March 4, 1917, the Arts Commission (Komissiia po delam iskusstva) was established; its leading members were the renowned author Maxim Gorky and Aleksandr Benois, Nikolai Roerich, and Mstislav Dobuzhinsky, who were connected with the World of Art movement. Two days later the commission, which was a private organization, established contact with the Petrograd Workers' and Soldiers' Soviets, and, on March 13, the same group under the name Special Conference for Matters of Art (Osoboe soveshchanie po delam iskusstva) met in response to overtures from the Provisional Government. Although the group devoted some discussion to an arts program—including mass spectacles—it focused on the more pressing need to save art from the ravages of war and revolution.[10] Other artists in Petrograd banded together to form the All-Arts Union (Soiuz deiatelei vsekh iskusstv). The union, covering everything from futurism to traditional realism, proved an odd coalition. Artists were organized, if not entirely united; at least organized enough to help the government create two very different mass festivals: May Day and Liberty Bond Day (May 26).

Festivals and commemorations in autocratic Russia were a projection of power; only the tsarist state commanded the financial resources and legal authority to sponsor them. Demonstrations were illegal, and May Day observances were met by severe countermeasures. The only legal processions were funerals, which often served as pretexts for political manifestations. The prohibition was not exclusive to socialists; the radical right, even monarchists, often had their marches outlawed, despite their carrying religious and nationalistic banners and chanting antiworker slogans. Left and right shared the marching color red.[11]

Russia's first legal May Day was declared by the Provisional Government in 1917. Revolution had changed the nature of the day; it could no longer be a demonstration against the autocracy and begged a new celebratory style.[12] Planners felt May Day should celebrate the fresh revolution, and to mark its optimism and unity they suggested a great *Social Mystery-Play*.[13] In the end, though, a more traditional street demonstration was preferred. *Social Mystery-Play*, with its liturgical overtones of oneness, implied a camaraderie absent in Russian society. Workers had rid themselves of the tsars, but the factory owners and an unpopular war

Figure 1. L. Petukhov, poster, May Day 1917 (V. P. Lapshin, *Khudozhestvennaia zhizn' Moskvy i Petrograda v 1917 godu*, Moscow, 1983).

remained. Most of the nation turned out for May Day, but it was not the hoped-for show of unity.[14] Professional artists helped with the posters and decorations (see Figure 1), but judging from the few pictures that remain, they used only simple color (red), slogans (of all variety), and allegorical figures (usually in classical dress and pose).[15] The center of the Petrograd celebration was the Field of Mars, whose most recent use had been for the imperial review of troops marching off to the front. A reviewing stand was raised and garlanded, and soldiers and workers—some armed—filed past members of the government. Who organized the event is not clear: some claim the Bolsheviks did much of the work,[16] but the municipal soviet (not Bolshevik at the time), the Provisional Government, and Gorky's commission also contributed.

The All-Arts Union likely did not take part in the celebration, even if some members did as individuals. On May 25, however, the union made its contribution to the national welfare by arranging Liberty Bond Day (Den' zaima svobody), the first mass festival in revolutionary Russia to make full use of artists' talents. The event, which included a parade, speeches, and theatrical performances, was organized by Fedor Sologub, the symbolist poet and head of the union's Curia of Verbal Art, and by two members of the Theater Curia: its director,

Figure 2. E. Kruglikova, poster, Liberty Bond Campaign, May 1917 (V. P. Lapshin, *Khudozhestvennaia zhizn' Moskvy i Petrograda v 1917 godu*, Moscow, 1983).

Pavel Gaideburov, and Aleksandr Mgebrov. State war coffers were seriously depleted, so the union organized a parade through town to sell bonds and collect money. Members ranging from imperial actors to futurist artists contributed to what was to be the union's sole concerted action. (Figure 2 shows a poster designed for the event.) Each group, school, or theater within the union was responsible for the adornment of a car. As cars traveled the parade route, speeches were improvised, and music, usually the *Marseillaise*, was played. The holiday was a rousing success, judging from accounts in the newspapers *Rech'* (*Speech*) and *Russkaia volia* (*The Russian Will*). (The Bolsheviks had nothing to do with the war effort, and *Pravda* refused comment.) Copies of a one-day newspaper, *Vo imia svobody* (*In the Name of Freedom*), featuring such unlikely comrades as Leonid Andreev, the poets Igor Severianin and Sergei Esenin, and the radical socialist Georgy Plekhanov, were snapped up in an instant.[17] The parade had a reception that bordered on hysteria:[18] spectators threw money and even jewelry to the Boy Scouts assigned to each car, who passed it on to bankers in booths set up along the route.[19]

Of greatest import for the future of revolutionary theater was a performance of Rachilde's *Le vendeur de soleil* by Gaideburov's Mobile-

Popular Theater, which set an example later followed by the Bolsheviks.[20] It was the first theater performed in the streets. The script hardly conformed to our modern notion of street theater, and the actors, who had no relevant experience, had to find a new style almost spontaneously. They spoke of a temptation to improvise, to address the audience directly, to adapt a monumental style: broad, economic gestures, omission of details, and highlighting of essentials—all of which would have seemed artificial indoors. An anecdote that must have been striking at the time was prophetic for the future: "After the show, played directly on the pavement in the middle of a crowd of soldiers, one of them, deeply moved, approached an actor and asked: 'OK, but who should we vote for?' "

In Moscow, too, artists organized themselves into a union, the Soviet of Moscow Art Organizations, but the center of action was another group, which chose to cooperate with the government: the Arts-Educational Commission (Khudozhestvenno-prosvetitel'naia kommissiia) of the Moscow Soviet of Workers' Deputies. The commission, formed in April 1917, cut across aesthetic and political lines.[21] The other Moscow soviet, the Soviet of Soldiers' Deputies, established a parallel administration, the arts department of which included the artists Kasimir Malevich, Georgy Iakulov, and Pavel Kuznetsov. This group was not as well-funded as the commission, and, to raise money for a program of popular lectures and presentations,[22] it orchestrated a Holiday of the Revolution on July 12 at the racetrack. Sculptors and painters framed the track with posters and panels of revolutionary events; the restaurants and buffets were decorated; and artists of the theater, opera, ballet, and circus gave performances. The holiday raised the necessary funds, but to do so tickets were sold at exorbitant prices, and it can be assumed that a proletarian or even broad public did not attend.[23] None of the celebrations arranged by artists between the two Revolutions of 1917 could or would claim to speak for a large part of the nation.

The October Revolution and the Arts

The October Revolution provoked a realignment of artists and government. Under the Provisional Government, the state and the Revolution had not been identified with any one party. Artists were free to identify their work with the Revolution without subordinating themselves to a party or platform. This was a right that the Petrograd union defended, and a principle upheld by the Moscow commission. Not so after October. The state and the Revolution had become—despite their inherent antagonism—a single body and, furthermore, one under the aegis of a single party.

Bolshevik policy on the arts had not been clearly articulated when power was seized. Left socialist thinkers such as Plekhanov and Lunacharsky, head of the new Commissariat of Education (Narkompros), had speculated on the art of the socialist future, but their ideas did not constitute an official Bolshevik policy. The native tradition closest to materialist socialists was that of Nikolai Chernyshevsky and Dmitry Pisarev, utilitarian radicals who had subordinated art to "reality," which in practice meant negating art's autonomous value. But the newborn revolutionary state made little attempt to regulate artistic activity. Its foremost concern was to gather the instruments of power; art was of secondary importance for the moment. Lunacharsky's policy was twofold: to gain the cooperation, if not the sympathy, of leading artists and, at the same time, to assert administrative control.

For the moment little attempt was made to formulate the relationship between the state and art. No state had ever been socialist, so there was no precedent to rely on. Bolshevik leaders presented the state publicly as an intermediate stage on the way to a stateless society. Speculation was directed not toward the ephemeral present but toward the future. For this speculation there was a rich tradition; but, like so much of socialist thought, it concealed an antagonism latent until power was taken.

Tradition, a cosmopolitan mix of history and utopian philosophy, exerted a decisive influence on the Russians until they could mold their own experience. The most obvious model was the French Revolution. The parallel was welcomed by the Bolsheviks, who saw the glorious festivals of the French as a model for their own. One of the first theater books to come off Soviet presses was Julien Tiersot's *Les fêtes et les chants de la révolution française*,[24] and even in 1920 Lunacharsky regretted that Soviet fêtes had "turned out to have less creative genius in terms of organization and appeal to the masses than the late eighteenth-century French [fêtes] had."[25]

One could disagree with Lunacharsky, however commendable his modesty. French festivals had followed the inclination to allegory of their era. In November 1793, a Festival of Reason was celebrated at the

Cathedral of Notre Dame in Paris; June 1794 saw a magnificent Festival of the Supreme Being. The latter festival, instigated by Robespierre, fired the imagination of future revolutionaries more than any other fête; it was both a sharp attack on the church and a display of civic virtues. Open skies and lush meadows embraced the common people as they filed onto the Champs-de-Mars; encomiums were sung to divine harmony; children were offered to the heavens, not in a pagan blood sacrifice but as a baptism into life. An altarlike mountain erected in the middle of the field inspired most (but not all) of society, which was united by a single emotion at a single place and time. That Robespierre would be purged within a month and the French Revolution would descend into fratricide made this moment all the more precious for future generations. Lunacharsky and other Bolsheviks knew the French festivals from respected peers: Rolland had described them in his *Le théâtre du peuple,* and the anarchist Prince Kropotkin dwelled on them at length in his *History of the French Revolution.*

The French Revolution was a beacon for the Russians, but in Marxist terms it was bourgeois, and Bolsheviks venerated it from a distance. The prerevolutionary writings of those Bolsheviks concerned with art, such as Lunacharsky and Friche, express enthusiasm for mass theater without mentioning the French.[26] Cultural politics made the French Revolution seem particularly less attractive, because its heritage was claimed after the February Revolution by the Provisional Government. That body had, for instance, used the *Marseillaise* as its anthem, and its fêtes were inspired by the French. There was a proposal to celebrate the burning of the Lithuanian Castle, a political prison, in a holiday like Bastille Day.[27] A more ambitious plan, announced in August 1917, proposed a "grandiose carnival-spectacle honoring the epoch of the French Revolution to be organized in the Summer Garden to aid Russian prisoners-of-war. . . . A prop city will be built depicting the Paris of that time. Actors will portray the artistic and theatrical bohemia of the late eighteenth century."[28] The projected director was Evreinov and the designer Iury Annenkov, who would create the grandest of the Bolshevik festivals in 1920.

Based on the French example, mass festivals were thought to be democratic, an assumption not unique to socialists. The theatrical world also saw open-air mass theater as a salvation. Theater had become exclusive; it had fled from the popular arena to intimate chambers accessible only to the wealthy and had succumbed to financial pressures to ignore questions disturbing their relaxation. The Berlin director and impresa-

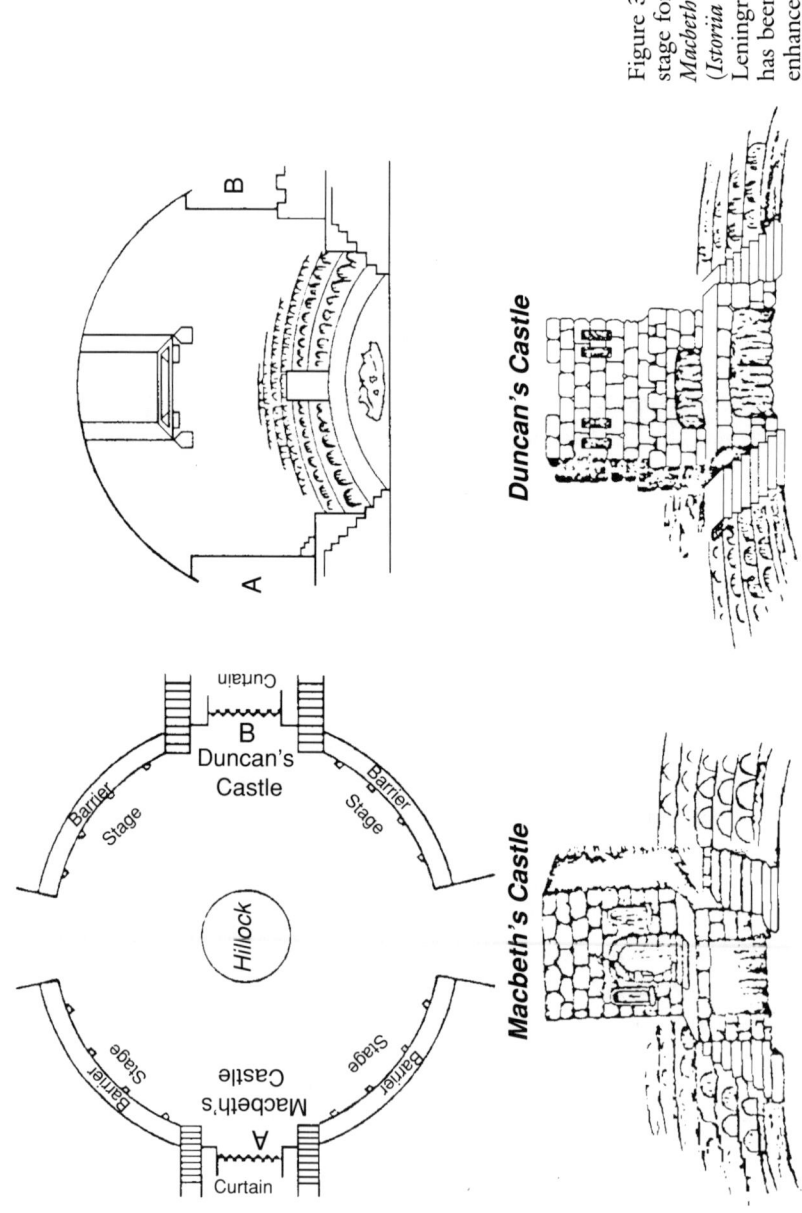

Figure 3. Circus arena-stage for a production of *Macbeth* in Petrograd, 1918 (*Istoriia sovetskogo teatra*, Leningrad, 1933; image has been computer-enhanced).

rio Max Reinhardt tried to revive the open stage early in this century. He looked for inspiration to Greek tragedy and the medieval mystery play, where actors had addressed a broad audience and spoken directly to its heart. Reinhardt eschewed the subdued tones of bourgeois theater for a monumental theater of primitive but strong emotions. He was renowned for productions like Hugo von Hofmannsthal's *Everyman* (1911), a contemporary mystery play that he produced in a cathedral, and *Oedipus Rex,* which was performed in a circus arena. His *Oedipus* was brought to Petersburg's Cinizelli Circus in 1911, with the fabled Sandro Moissi in the starring role.

Reinhardt's revolution was aesthetic, not political. Still, Russians in 1918 found monumental theater apt for their own revolution. The poet Mikhail Kuzmin noted that "many types of drama have fallen to the wayside: psychological drama, the theater of half-moods [i.e., Chekhovian], plays written for a particular social stratum, or comedies of mores and the salon. . . . Our time clearly calls for the tragic theater."[29] The circus arena served better as the center of theatrical life: "More than anywhere else, the changes in the make-up of the audience are noticeable in the circus. . . . The corridors, buffet and auditorium of the circus are closest of all to the camp of revolution."[30]

In March 1918 Iury Iurev, lead actor of the Aleksandrinsky Theater, began negotiations with the Cinizellis to restage Reinhardt's *Oedipus*. The original sets remained intact in Petrograd; and Aleksei Granovsky, a Reinhardt disciple just back from Berlin and familiar with his master's production, was hired as director.[31] Negotiations were difficult: the arena was already let to Arthur Lurich, a popular wrestler, who wanted a part; but in the end the lease was surrendered without conditions. Iurev took the role of Oedipus; Mgebrov was hired to play Tiresias; Granovsky set the all-important choruses and mass scenes. Iurev was a tragic actor of the neoclassical school, and his delivery filled the arena expanses. The play was a huge success, selling out its week-long run to an audience of all social classes.

Gorky and Fedor Chaliapin, the great opera singer, enlisted in Iurev's next project: Shakespeare's *Macbeth*. Again Granovsky was to produce the tragedy in the Cinizelli Circus (a diagram of the stage is shown in Figure 3); Maria Andreeva was cast in the role of Lady Macbeth. Andreeva's assistance was essential: once a leading player in Stanislavsky's Moscow Art Theater, wife of Gorky, and now head of Petrograd theaters, she possessed the talent to play a difficult role and the political muscle (she was close to Lenin and Lunacharsky) to ensure the play would run. Its success rivaled that of *Oedipus,* and Iurev, Andreeva, Gorky, and Chaliapin decided to found a "tragic theater," to be housed in a new building designed specially for monumental productions. It would feature the classic repertory so apt for revolutionary élan: Aeschylus, Sophocles, Shakespeare, Schiller, and Byron. The collaborators (who had played *Macbeth* as a clash of good and evil) saw in these playwrights a clarity of moral vision lacking in the prerevolutionary theater. The Revolution was a time of great passion and striving, and only a monumental theater—a truly mass theater—could meet its needs. Although they did not build their theater (there were no funds during the Civil War), they did found the Bolshoi Dramatic Theater, which made the classic repertory one of the most popular of the time.

The Theater of the People

The mass-theater debate touched on ambiguities of great consequence after the Revolution. The belief that spectacles embodied the spirit of socialist revolution was common, but its roots were tangled. Some, following Wagner, felt that mass drama would, like the Greek drama, express the nation's unified will; others considered it an instrument of political struggle. When the October Revolution placed a party claiming to represent the working class in power, the leaders faced a dilemma: Should mass theater represent the workers in power or the people struggling for expression? Lunacharsky, representing the state, assumed optimistically that both interests could be served.[32] Rolland, whose *Le théâtre du peuple* had influenced his friend Lunacharsky, saw people's theater as an educator.[33] Its task in a bourgeois society was to agitate against the status quo; under socialism, it would introduce workers to progressive culture. Rolland considered people's theater inherently progressive: popular fêtes had furthered the French Revolution; the popular theaters of Maurice Pottecher and Louis Lumet were tools of democratic mobilization; the Swiss popular theater instilled democratic virtues. It would be equally progressive under socialism.

Though innocent sounding, such assumptions raised two issues central to Bolshevism: relations between activist intellectuals and the laboring classes they claimed to serve; and the primacy of politics over culture in party activity. Items of hot debate after the failed revolution of 1905, they had split the party and would always lurk behind the mass-theater discussion. Lenin and his followers, who formed the core of the party, did not entirely trust the popular classes to act in their own interests. Lenin molded the party as a vanguard and considered its first task revolution. Socialist culture was a dream of the future, a task of secondary import during the initial phase of political struggle. Lenin's opponent in the debate was Bogdanov, a fellow exile whose faction felt that socialist society was unthinkable without socialist culture. Bogdanov stressed the vanguard's duty to nurture a socialist consciousness in the working class, which would allow it to realize its own power and form a new worker state. Bogdanov did not deny the utility of political organization, nor did he neglect the role of educated activists; his merit was in balancing this side of the revolutionary equation with popular initiative and cultural consciousness.

In early October 1917, the Provisional Government's dying days, Bogdanov and other culturalists (including Lunacharsky) founded Proletkult, an organization devoted to working-class culture. Born under a bourgeois government, Proletkult kept its autonomy from the state after the Bolshevik coup.[34] The Proletkult board pursued the dogma that socialist culture would be proletarian and collective. Theater, an inherently collective art, was at the cutting edge of its work, and Proletkult clubs throughout Russia searched for a mass theater to express the needs of the working class. Its most ardent adherent was Platon Kerzhentsev. A Bolshevik from 1904 and leader of the Proletkult Theater Section, he had studied mass theater in English-speaking countries and Europe in his years of exile.

Though collective proletarian spectacles were unknown, mass spectacles had been popular in the West before the First World War, and Kerzhentsev was familiar with them. There were two traditions in Europe and the United States. The first was a revival of Greek outdoor drama, part of a general neoclassicism.[35] In California, for instance, Isadora Duncan was reviving Hellenic dance; the Bohemian Club was founded in the woods near San Francisco; and Pasadena instituted the Rose Festival, which back then featured not football but chariot races. The movement placed faith in the tonic of the open air. Outdoor theater was healthier physically and socially; its audience could commune with art and nature, undivided by the architecture of aristocratic and bourgeois theater. Russians carried the faith in open air into their revolution and held to it despite a climate less benevolent than that of Athens or San Francisco.[36]

The eastern seaboard of the United States was the site of mass spectacles more directly presaging those of the Russians. The tradition exemplified by Percy MacKaye (author of *The Civic Theatre*) was of a more rationalist bent than that of the West Coast, which satisfied the Russians' didactic urge. As the title of MacKaye's book suggests, it was a civic theater, based on the reintegration of art into the life of the democratic community.[37] Before the war, MacKaye and his associates organized a number of "civic masques," or historical re-creations: in 1914, for instance, the 150th anniversary of the founding of St. Louis was marked by a pageant in which much of the city participated. The participation of the people, who normally avoided theater and acting, was essential, for the goal of civic theater was "the conscious awakening of a people to self-government in the activities of its leisure."[38] Such participation was an expression of democracy, and though MacKaye's bourgeois democracy was alien to the Russians, both considered mass spectacles an antidote to capitalism.[39]

Kerzhentsev was an eclectic, borrowing from Wagner and Bogdanov, but he was close to MacKaye's practicality. In a series of works published in 1918, Kerzhentsev established the theoretical and practical foundations for much of Proletkult's theater work.[40] (Figure 4 shows the cover for his most famous book.) Like other Proletkult theoreticians, Kerzhentsev treated art from the viewpoint of performance and insisted that people's theater be not a theater for the people but a " 'theater of the people,' i.e. based on the creative work of the lower classes."[41] It would "start from a desire to facilitate the full artistic expression of the proletariat's 'I' in harmonious collective theatrical creativity."[42] Naturally, creativity would not be matched by virtuosity, but, as Kerzhentsev pointed out, "the task of the proletarian theater is not to produce good professional actors who will successfully perform the plays of a socialist repertory, but to give an outlet to the creative artistic instinct of the broad masses."[43] The instinct grew from a broader creative urge called *samodeiatel'nost'* (MacKaye's *self-government*).[44] Mass spectacles fit the twin demands for self-government and collectivity, and offered an aesthetic equivalent to the revolution in politics.

Many Bolsheviks, Lenin in particular, were distressed by Proletkult's flair for independence. Organizers of official celebrations did their utmost to keep Proletkult away. Yet in the early years of the Revolution, there was often no alternative. On May Day 1918 most theaters could not respond to the holiday appropriately. Private theaters were not yet under state control; public theaters—that is, the former imperial theaters—had only reluctantly acquiesced to new administrations. The

Figure 4. Cover of Kerzhentsev's *Creative Theater* (P. Kerzhentsev, *Tvorcheskii teatr*, Moscow, 1923).

only theater in Petrograd with both a stage and an enthusiasm for the Revolution belonged to Proletkult. In the spring of 1918, state expropriation had brought the columned Assembly of Nobles into Proletkult hands, and a ceremonial opening of the oxymoronic Proletkult Palace was scheduled for May Day.

The evening was graced by the work of the new theater studio, 200 students of both sexes led by Pavel Bessalko, Mgebrov, and Victoria Chekan. Bessalko was a "proletarian poet," a writer of verse on the proletariat and its revolution. He was a graduate of the Paris exile, where he had met the other future founders of Proletkult: Bogdanov, Lunacharsky, Pavel Lebedev-Poliansky, and Fedor Kalinin. Mgebrov and Chekan came to Proletkult from different backgrounds. Mgebrov, a graduate of the tsarist Military Cadet School, was a talented and nomadic actor. Early in the century, he wandered from the Moscow Art Theater to the Theater of Vera Komissarzhevskaia and then, in 1911, to Evreinov's Ancient Theater, where he met Chekan. A cycle of seventeenth-century Spanish dramas was produced that year, and Chekan played Laurencia in Lope de Vega's *Fuente ovejuna*. She played the peasant girl with a remarkable vitality—her trademark—and years later Mgebrov would remember her "possessing a rare, completely Spanish temperament.... Some nights she tossed people about the stage like balls, so they fell into the orchestra pit and broke the musicians' instruments. And yet she was a frail woman."[45] Like Chekan, Mgebrov favored a romantic idealism that flourished during the Revolution. A beloved role was the hero of Pedro Calderón's *The Purgatory of St. Patrick*. His gaunt features and pathetic declamation lent themselves to the role of prophet (like Tiresias) or martyr; the die-hard typecasters Meyerhold and Eisenstein found him ideal for the roles of the Prophet in Emile Verhaeren's *Les aubes* (Meyerhold's 1920 reworking) and Archbishop Pimen in Eisenstein's *Aleksandr Nevsky*.

Mgebrov and Chekan left professional theater in the spring of 1917 to direct an after-hours theater in Petrograd's Baltic Factory. They were designated delegates by their club when Proletkult was organized in October, and when the Petrograd branch opened in March 1918, they became theater instructors at Lunacharsky's insistence.[46] Mgebrov's enthusiasm for the February Revolution—he had organized the Liberty Bond Festival—was not held against him, and he transferred his faith to the new revolution. Mgebrov, like Wagner, saw revolution less as a political than as a spiritual movement and felt the "rise of creative powers hidden in man's collective consciousness from ancient times."[47] With many Proletkult leaders, he shared a style: cosmic and ecstatic.

Although most of the students shared his enthusiasm, none had stage experience; given a month to mount a program, Mgebrov wisely started with the basics. He rejected the standard repertory because few authors spoke sympathetically of workers' lives. As Kerzhentsev said: "The repertory situation is abominable. European literature has in essence no repertory for the proletarian theater. The number of authors and works that reflect the aspirations and spiritual needs of the proletariat is extraordinarily thin. Socialist plays can be counted not by the tens, but by the ones. And the majority of those are not on a high artistic level."[48]

Even they were beyond the range of Mgebrov's students, who were amateurs and more amateur than most. Rather than a script they used something called *instsenirovka,* a calque of the German *inszenierung:* an adaptation of nondramatic material, usually prose, to the stage. The trick was not new; the Moscow Art Theater had used it in the 1910s, when Chekhov was no longer around, and two of its adaptations, Dickens's *The Cricket on the Hearth* and Dostoevsky's *The Possessed,* were great successes. When scripts are not available, adaptation becomes a useful approach. The technique would help later festival directors transform the Revolution itself into theater. Proletkult chose the verse of Aleksei Gastev, a leading proletarian poet, for dramatic material. Gastev's recently published *Poetry of the Workers' Hammer* was enjoying great popularity. Although the poetry in many respects was original, the influence of Walt Whitman was evident in the powerful rhythm, propelling lines across the page, and in the imagery of cosmic harmony. In fact, Mgebrov's next project was Whitman. Both poets profited from declamation.

None of the young students was trained to read verse, which prompted a decision that the reading be collective.[49] The motive was purely practical, but the result was lauded by Proletkult theorists. Collective declamation was just reaching the apex of popularity; a Professor Serezhnikov would soon found the Proletarian Studio of Declamation.[50] Collective declamation was simple; it allowed many students to participate and gave them a first taste of art, an experience that, judging by the proliferation of studios in the next five years, did not go to waste.

The May Day 1918 production of Gastev's *We Grow Out of Iron* provides an illustration of the Proletkult method. The *mise en scène* bore a striking resemblance to the new Proletkult emblem unveiled for that morning's procession. As the curtain rose, "wheels, gears and flywheels began to spin, and from this primeval chaos rose the symbolic figure of a worker representing the full significance of the collective and the power based on overcoming the elements through the will to freedom. The bared muscles of arms, an intent pose, a sickle, a hammer and anvil, a hammer stroke frozen in mid-air . . . all this at the same time animated by a truly fiery inspiration and, most important, love and faith."[51]

Mgebrov sought harmony; he chose Gastev's poem to "confirm the full, absolutely harmonic mastery of life by the human collective, and see the possibility of such mastery in continuity of motion."[52] Rhythm provided the unifying impulse. Lines were broken up into phrases, words, and syllables, then distributed among the chorus. As the reading progressed, individual recitations were united into a single ecstatic chorus. In Mgebrov's words:

Suddenly the whistles began . . . At first separate figures of girls and workers rose to its summons as if against a background of dawn and the rising sun. They began with a joyous exchange of shouts that merged with the call of the factory whistles. Then voices, source unknown, responded to a singing and ringing summons drawing nearer and nearer. The summons swelled and hundreds of voices merged into it. With each addition they became more intoxicated. In the end, united, they were no longer distinct from each other and merged into a song created by a single impulse.[53]

The audience received the reading enthusiastically. Some reviewers and all of Proletkult's future critics measured it against the pretension of Proletkult's leaders (Bessalko among them) that they were creating a new culture. By that standard it was a failure. But there is no reason to burden the students with the pretensions of others; they were amateurs, and applying professional standards to them would be unfair. In professional theater only the show, the finished product presented to an audience of strangers, is important; for amateurs, who usually perform for an audience of like people, production is important as a process of participation and education. Something similar should be kept in mind with festivals, which are created for both the spectator and the participant, who are not wholly differentiated. The Proletkult performance belonged more to festivity than to the theater; it was a ritual celebration—stylized, measured, a canvas of ideas and not details. It was a proletarian show for a worker audience. Its peculiar stylistics were absorbed by future festival spectacles.

Festivals of a One-Minded People

The European progressive tradition inspired two approaches to mass drama that differed sharply in defining the "people" of people's theater. The trend followed by Kerzhentsev saw people as the oppressed masses struggling against the bourgeoisie. People's theater thrived in a divided society. The second viewpoint understood the people to be a homogeneous and essentially unchanging mass. Both traditions could be traced to the intoxicating summer of 1848, progenitor of Marx, but also of Wagner and his *Art and Revolution* and *Art-Work of the Future*.[54] The young Wagner shared his generation's infatuation with revolution; but Wagner's vision of revolution was uniquely aesthetic. Revolution was not an inspiration for art, it was an equivalent; both expressed the popular will, both harnessed its chaotic powers. Wagner's democratic art demanded a merging of the artist's will with the people; the historical necessity they embodied would become manifest through the artist's obedient hand. Wagner's ideas were an eternal temptation to Bolshevik materialists; Lunacharsky, for instance, saw mass drama as a "moment of orgiastic exultation,"[55] a recovery of humanity's primeval oneness.

Greek tragedy, the unity of unities, was the precedent for Wagner's drama, motivated by an odd analogy drawn first by the Reverend Johann von Herder: the Hellenes and the people (*Volk*). Both represented the organic ideal, societies that Wagner, following Ludwig Feuerbach, claimed live in "necessity," where "life is a true mirror of nature."[56] Vital harmony was the alleged virtue of both, and "intellect with all its arrogant divorce from life,"[57] the culprit of decline. Wagner also blamed capitalism for the decay of modern society and theater. His aesthetic revolution aimed to reunite both society and the arts. The tragic theater would combine the arts of the poet, the musician, and the dancer, and the tragic poet would find "the noblest part of his own nature united with the noblest characteristics of the whole nation."[58]

The older Wagner's conservatism was evident even in the young radical. He believed that Greek art was concordant not only with society but with the state; it "was conservative, because it was a worthy and adequate expression of the public conscience." But in Wagner's time, which lacked Hellenic harmony, "true art is revolutionary, because its very existence is opposed to the ruling spirit of the community."[59] With the coming of the new society it would be, in Wagner's paradoxical phrase, "conservative anew."⁶⁰

Wagner opened a rich vein for socialism; he established a line of thought that grafted German ideas onto a predominantly French, English, and rationalistic tradition. Wagner's artwork of the future belonged to a complex of ideas that preached revolution but was strongly retrospective. His sense of history was cyclical; revolution culminated a process that shattered an original unity only to reinstate it in finer form.

The mixture of radicalism and conservatism, looking forward and looking backward, was not new; the French revolutionaries had claimed Rousseau as a forefather. Rousseau's ideal was rural and retrograde, but its sanction of democracy had great appeal in 1789. Rousseau was the first modern enthusiast of mass spectacles. His belief that they were vehicles of national unification was accepted by French revolutionaries and then socialists, and given egalitarian overtones. In the *Letter to M. D'Alembert on the Spectacles* (1758) and *Consideration of the Government of Poland and Its Reform* (1772), Rousseau saw spectacles as the people's welfare and as bringing about their unity. They were a model—a microcosm—of harmonious democracy: "Plant a stake crowned with flowers in the middle of the square; gather the people together there, and you will have a festival. Do better yet; let the spectators become an entertainment to themselves; make them actors themselves; do it so that each sees and loves himself in the others so that all will be united."⁶¹ Rousseau inspired the French revolutionaries; Robespierre developed a particular enthusiasm for fêtes. But the revolutionaries translated Rousseau's ideas into their own terms. It is difficult to imagine him approving of the Festival of Reason.

There were differences between Wagner and Rousseau. Wagner provided a historical basis for the ideal; and his modern vocabulary was more digestible than Rousseau's for the socialists. But in one respect Rousseau exerted more influence. Although Wagner's artwork was "collective," it was also Apollonian. Translated into social terms, this meant that "art's life force" is provided by the people, but it is expressed by a single poet. Rousseau's fêtes were an art of and by the people. Both thinkers were influential in Russia, but there is more Rousseau than Wagner in Friche's article: "In socialist society the stage will once again merge with the audience, and theatrical spectacles with their division of spectator and actor will yield to collective fêtes, ceremonial processions, mass choruses."⁶²

The ideology of socialism was systematic, but its broader cultural tradition was a muddle. The confusion was greatest where Wagner entered the picture. Wagner of the socialist tradition was not the historical Wagner, who preferred social integration to dialectical struggle. His *Art-Work of the Future* was an inspiring vision of socialist mass theater, but his conservatism was unpalatable to revolutionaries, so its aesthetic ideal was grafted onto another socialist tradition. The recipient of the graft was Friedrich Engels. In *Origin of the Family, Private Property and the State,* Engels argues that primeval society was based on the *gens,* a family-centered system he thought bore the seeds of communism: a lack of private property and class division, an equal distribution of labor and its fruits, and the communal ownership of the means of labor. Engels looked back for his vision of the future. "Democracy in government, brotherhood in society, equality in rights and privileges, and universal education, foreshadow the next higher plane of society to which experience, intelligence and knowledge are steadily tending. *It will be a revival, in a higher form, of the liberty, equality and fraternity of the ancient gentes.*"[63]

Engels's work, a reiteration of principles in *The German Ideology,* his 1846 collaboration with Marx, legitimized the harmonic ideal for socialists. Ideals travel through a tradition in clusters; as the harmonic ideal passed from Engels to the Russians, the Wagnerian artwork of the future traveled with it and surfaced in unexpected places. Chernyshevsky speculated that the final stage of socialism would be close to primitive socialism, as did Bogdanov.[64] Bogdanov's vision of communism, as expressed in the utopian novel *Red Star,* foresaw that labor would no longer be split by specialization; people would not be divided by class; government would not separate the ruler from the ruled; and philosophy would not differentiate the material from the ideal. Art would be characterized by "extreme simplicity and thematic unity." The art of transitional epochs was discordant; but socialism's final stage would feature a monumental art inspired by the return to harmony.[65] Bogdanov never cited Wagner, but Lunacharsky, who shared his ideals, saw Wagner as gatekeeper for the theater of the future before the Revolution and throughout his stewardship of Narkompros.[66]

The Russians' admiration for Greek drama and their willful misconceptions about the society that engendered it placed them squarely in the tradition of Winckelmann, Herder, Hölderlin, Schiller, and Hegel—a tradition continued by Wagner and the young Marx. Each of these thinkers considered the Hellenes a model for the future, a society free of modern life's great schisms: work and play, theater and church, government and governed, religion and philosophy. Nadezhda Krupskaia could in all seriousness call Soviet Russia "the new Athens" because prebourgeois wholeness was a model for postbourgeois socialism.[67]

The latest and most compelling version of Hellenic culture available to turn-of-the-century intellectuals was Nietzsche's *Birth of Tragedy*. Wagner's theater was a temple where art forms and social classes could be reunited; Nietzschean tragedy was a synthesis of two poles of existence, the Dionysian and the Apollonian, with no middle ground. Dionysus was the elemental, undifferentiated experience powering tragedy; Apollo, the artistic consciousness that rises above chaos and crystalizes it in a serene artistic dream. Associating Nietzsche with socialism was a feat of imaginative reading; nevertheless, grafted to the modified Wagnerian tradition, Nietzsche became more amenable to socialists. Wagnerian drama was the product of a society in repose; Nietzschean tragedy arose from chaotic popular emotions. Its home was not Pericles's marble city, as Wagner seems to have thought, but the muddied byways of lower Athens: a place that bred upheaval. A creative socialist armed with excerpts from the *Birth of Tragedy* could trace an analogy between the tragic artist and the revolutionary: both were imbued with the demotic spirit, yet possessed a clarity of vision beyond that of the common crowd. The artist and the revolutionary stood on the threshold of two worlds: the elite and the demos, the past and the future. They could also see, as many did in 1917–20, an analogy between festivals—tragic or otherwise—and revolution.

If Lunacharsky was profoundly (and selectively) moved by Nietzsche, the transmission of Wagner and Nietzsche to the Revolution was most clearly the work of the symbolist Viacheslav Ivanov.[68] Ecstatic rites of the demotic cult of Dionysus gave birth to tragedy; Ivanov saw theater's only hope in returning to this "democratism." He wanted to take tragedy directly back to its Dionysian roots—without the socialists' historicism. Dionysian rites were the answer to contemporary social problems, for they united the entire people in ecstatic worship, where frenzy obscured class distinctions. Ivanov found a kindred spirit in Aleksandr Scriabin, composer of *Divine Poem* (1903), *The Poem of Ecstasy* (1908), and *Prometheus: The Poem of Fire* (1910). Scriabin saw art as a holiday, the antithesis of everyday life, in which art and life merge into one.[69] His final, uncompleted project was the ambitious *Mystery*, a fusion of sacrament and art. *Mystery* was to be a massive performance without spectators, only participants. Music, dance, poetry, a light show, and even perfumes were incorporated into the score. Its opening chords were to be struck in the Tibetan Himalayas, continue way over to England, and culminate in a moment of mystic union on the banks of the Ganges.[70] *Mystery* would be an expression of a single, universal truth, a synthesis of music, poetry, dance, and light.

Ivanov's retrospective ideal could be given radical political implications; drama was, like revolution, a threshold state. It merged life and art, actor and audience, stage and theater, and overcame Marx's despised differentiation. Critically speaking, it also confused dramatic art and ritual, both covered by the catchall term *deistvo*. Ivanov's retrospective program led him to suggest "reforms" strikingly similar to *The Theater of the Future* (*Die Schaubühne der Zukunft*, 1906) of Munich director Georg Fuchs. In ancient rituals worshipped and worshipper, priest and sacrifice became one: "The spectator must become a do-er, a participant in the drama. The crowd of spectators must merge into a choral body, like the mystic commune of the ancient 'orgies' and 'mysteries.'"[71] If the actors and spectators were to merge, the theater would have to be rebuilt; the footlights and proscenium arch segregating participants of the rite would have to disappear.

Theater's social force was predicated on its communality. The main actor in Ivanov's *deistvo*, as in later Reinhardt and Proletkult productions, was the chorus. It played two roles: "the minor chorus, tied directly to the action . . . and a chorus symbolizing the entire community (*obshchina*), which can be increased at will by new participants—a chorus, hence, that is manifold and inserts itself into the action only at moments of the highest ascent and full liberation of Dionysian energies."[72] Insertion into the action was a curious notion that later Soviet critics and directors would adopt. It implied a bond between stage and auditorium that could transform a theatrical event into a social event. This was Ivanov's "mystery," "drama transformed into a *real* event,"[73] which identified the choral chant (created by the dramatic poet) with the vox populi.

Communal drama was possible only in an "organic age," when art was pannational (*vsenarodnyi*).[74] Here was the source of an unfortunate corollary: art flourishes best under unanimity. Organic art and society spring from a single source, a single body of myth. Embodied by the tragic chorus and expressed in its song, myth is "the perceptible signaling of communal [*sobornyi*—a religious term] one-mindedness and unity of spirit, a manifest testament to the real tie binding differentiated consciousness into a living whole."[75] Myth speaks for the people; artists, engaged in Platonic mythopoeia (*mifotvorchestvo*), embody the myth in their creations. Artists are assigned a tremendous role in social renaissance: apprehending the myths inherent in God's universe and communicating them to the people, they provide a medium for national unification. Poets are, in a phrase that would echo terribly in Stalin's mouth, responsible for "the organization of the national soul."[76]

Ivanov's ideas shared certain profound contradictions with those of socialists. He encouraged self-creativity in the demos, yet channeled it in prescribed ways. There was no provision for a divergence from the leader's guiding vision. If Ivanov's phrase was perverted by Stalin, it reached him through other socialists: Bogdanov, Lunacharsky, and Gorky. Ivanov spoke of mythopoeia in its Platonic sense, as recollection; socialists used the calque, an equivalent of the English "mythmaking," in another sense, as a dynamic and creative principle. They literally wanted to make myths to spur the working class to action.[77] Lunacharsky said (following Georges Sorel), "The leading class of an economically flourishing society is the carrier of the most vital, strong and bright ideal."[78] The "God-builders" (Gorky's phrase) saw consciousness as the molder of reality. Ideology was a motor of consciousness; and mythology, which translated ideology into art (art was presumably a transparent medium), became a tool of social change. Though symbolists and Bolsheviks would seem to have had little in common, they met every Wednesday evening at Ivanov's "Tower" apartment; Lunacharsky contributed an article to the symbolist anthology *Teatr: Kniga o novom teatre* (*Theater: A Book about the New Theater*) (1908); and when the symbolists organized *Torches* (*Fakely*) in 1905 to pursue dreams of a mythmaking theater, one of the group's enthusiasts was Gorky.[79]

The prerevolutionary Bolsheviks' experience with public manifestations was limited to street demonstrations, particularly May Day marches that were often suppressed. The October Revolution brought them power, and power in the Russian tradition was expressed through elaborate rituals and celebrations. The Bolsheviks had few models to fall back on, but there was available a tangled tradition of state pomp, theatrical art, and socialist philosophy that party leaders could selectively exploit for their own festivals. Bolsheviks concerned with the arts, particularly Lunacharsky, were subject to diverse and often contradictory influences. Each influence helped shape the festivals, but this often indiscriminate assimilation led to deep tension. Mass drama was considered an expression of popular will; but many revolutionaries also believed that the popular will should be unanimous and correspond to the will of the Revolution (and its leaders). It was an ambiguity inherent to festivity itself, regardless of its social applications, and one that would play itself out over the next several years.

TWO

Revolution and Festivity

> *All human affairs have two opposite aspects; so that what at first glance seems to be death, on closer inspection is seen to be life, and life on the contrary is seen to be death. The same is true of what is apparently beautiful and ugly, rich and poor, shameful and glorious, learned and ignorant, noble and base, joyous and sad, friendly and inimical, healthful and harmful. In short, you find all things suddenly reversed.*
>
> Erasmus, *In Praise of Folly*

Tsarist celebrations were traditionally composed of two elements: a dynastic observance—a coronation or anniversary—and popular entertainment, with fairground shows, rides, and plenty of food and drink. Solemnity and merriment stood side by side. Bolshevik festivals evolved into a similar pattern by late 1918. Holiday mornings were marked by long demonstrations, eulogies, and speeches. Evenings, if funding was forthcoming from war-pressed budgets, featured fireworks, carnival games, sometimes even burnt effigies. For citizens born before the Great War, celebrations seemed incomplete without both elements.

Voronezh celebrated the first anniversary of the Revolution on November 7, 1918, with a day-long affair. It began with a "Eulogy of the Revolution":

The stage showed a craggy locale. As the curtain rose there was complete darkness on stage. Suddenly the sacrificial altar located on a platform center-stage was illuminated. A chorus dressed in Greek tunics was distributed along the base of the platform. The show opened with a musical introduction. Then the chorus began to sing, explaining in song the hard life of the oppressed people. Then the leader appeared near the altar, and between him and the chorus a dialogue on the power and oppressiveness of Capital began. All this was accompanied by music and ballet numbers. The dialogue ended. A tremole [sic] in the orchestra, fanfares thunder. The altar burned brighter and Destiny [female in Russian] appeared, approving the people. A fugue in the orchestra. Three elders appeared, illuminated by violet reflectors, and three old women. The old women were terrified by the possibility of revolution, and tried to convince the people not to think of it. In reply, the chorus sang of growing rebellion and the necessity of punishing capitalists—perpetrators of the war and the people's hardship. Evil Fate [male in Russian] appeared with his companions to turbulent and triumphant music, rejoicing at the evil he brings people. Destiny supported the people's spirit, which was conveyed by appropriate music. Seven old women appeared, warning the people of their mistake. A conversation was struck up between the chorus and Destiny. The mood of the people kept rising. Unexpectedly Revolution [female] appeared with her companions. The dance of the victory of Revolution was danced. Evil Fate and the old women disappeared. The chorus sang of its readiness to build the future and glorified the Revolution. Children entered, singing joyful songs and promising to follow in their fathers' footsteps. Total ecstasy.[1]

The revolution's bloodier side was celebrated the same night in Voronezh with *The Burning of the Hydra of Counterrevolution,* inspired by a French revolutionary holiday described by Tiersot.[2] A certain Faccioli, visiting town with the Cinizelli Circus, took upon himself construction of the hydra, an art learned in the carnivals of his native Italy. A wire carcass was covered with bast and painted green, and a tail of springy wire was attached. The tail bobbed up and down in unison with the creature's three heads, which featured glistening green eyes and were topped with speaking platforms. The entire effigy was sixty meters long, and it was accompanied through the streets by a mounted guard of forty. An orator atop the hydra's head summoned people to the central square; his call clashed with the laments of 200 "counterrevolutionaries" towed alongside in cages. The procession was greeted in the square by a panel of judges that pronounced a death sentence on the unfortunate monster. Chopped into four sections and doused with kerosene, it was burned; the burning was celebrated with readings from the verse of proletarian poets and Whitman, and it was followed by dancing and fireworks.

Clearly, Bolshevik festivals had many forms. The ideology that inspired the Revolution was often a distant echo; when it was featured, it was sometimes distorted. There are a number of explanations. Local officials were often uninformed about the policies and writings of central party leaders; experts hired to design the festivals were rarely Bolsheviks; and dry ideology could seem tedious to the populace. A more subtle and fundamental cause was the origin and shape of festivity itself. Festivity has an ancient pedigree as both a public forum and an artistic medium. Though festivals seemed democratic to many revolutionaries, the tradition of celebration inherited from Russian culture and from the West was highly ambiguous. When the Bolsheviks celebrated their new holidays, they entered a dialogue with that tradition.

Examining the role of public celebration in the Russian Revolution begs the question of how festivals projected the party's program. In the previous chapter, the Russian and Western traditions were examined. Now the medium itself will be studied. What is festivity and what are its attributes; what is its structure and how does it mold what is celebrated? What parts of the Revolution were most suited to celebration; what parts were not; how was history reenacted?

Of parallel import is the kinship between festivity and revolution, which was perceived then and has been again many times since. Lenin himself claimed that "revolutions are festivals of the oppressed and the exploited. At no other time are the people in a position to come forward so actively as creators of a new social order as at a time of revolution. At such times the people are capable of performing miracles."[3] He expressed the giddy and transient exultation felt at moments of abrupt change, when a new world seems possible, and the old has yet to resurface. There was a another metaphor beneath the phrase, which became evident during the Revolution. Festivity thrives on extremes; it polarizes the world socially, morally, and aesthetically. The experience of revolution has much in common with festivity; both divide the world into clear and discrete camps, and both merge personal and collective experience. Festive expression, in fact, can give the revolutionary experience a clarity it might otherwise lack.

A final point that bears consideration and should shed light on the above questions is the Russian theater world's enthusiasm for revolutionary celebrations. Bolshevik festivals were not the creation of party workers, who were often inattentive sponsors; they were directed and decorated by artists, many of whom were exploring festive culture fifteen years before the Revolution. Turn-of-the-century artistic currents had a profound impact on Bolshevik celebration because of the formative influence of directors such as Meyerhold and Evreinov, who either directed the festivals or mentored the directors. Some artists saw theater as a powerful tool of revolution, but others apathetic to the Revolution saw it as an opportunity to realize their artistic ambitions. Their work, and particularly the collaboration of Meyerhold and Vladimir Mayakovsky on *Mystery-Bouffe*, exemplified the festivalization of culture that first foreshadowed and then distinguished Bolshevik festivals.

The Forms of Festivity

Celebration has performed a unique function in human culture. Societies have traditionally reserved special places and times for the celebration of their fundamental beliefs. Prehistoric man retreated into caves to worship the gods; the priestly caste in Pharaonic Egypt segregated itself in temples, holy ground inaccessible to the laity; medieval monks walled themselves off from the squalid cities of Europe. Guardianship of space and time was an ecclesiastical prerogative: Egyptian priests scanned the heavens for signs of the celestial order; monks created the first daily schedules to chart the pattern of their prayers.

As Mona Ozouf notes in regard to the French Revolution, civic festivals were used to manipulate the value of space and time in modern times.[4] Revolutionaries inherited the Old Regime's civic spaces, which reflected its hierarchy of values: central squares housed monuments to the upholders of autocracy; the nobility lived behind walls along the finest avenues. Festivals reshuffled the urban hierarchy by selecting new routes to be taken through the city, new places to be honored, and new spaces to be declared sacred. Space itself acquired new meaning. Revolutionaries spurned dusty urban squares for sprawling parks whose openness modeled egalitarian society and where fête participants were not divided by class or enclosed in the walls of authority. Time was reset inside the festive circle to show the revolution, and those moments in it that organizers chose to emphasize, as a new beginning to history.

Several aspects of festivals recommended them to revolutionaries. Time and space could be disintegrated in a festival and then reintegrated. A festival is a recollection, a temporary transcendence of time and space that links past and future. Ideally, it refers back to an experience common to all participants and evokes a time of unity. Participants can leave the conflicts of the present behind and return to a common origin in the past. The past is selected and organized to meet the needs of the present; and during the celebration the mythicized past becomes real. Society experiences moments of harmony and order that allow it to function as an entity under the revolutionary party's aegis once the holiday has lapsed.

Robespierre was inspired most by the power of festivals to sway minds, as were the Bolsheviks and many other future revolutionaries. The enthusiasm was founded on a perceived correspondence between festivity and society that proved unfounded. The error has been shared by thinkers ancient and modern, from the left and right of the political spectrum, and it informs influential contemporary theories. In festive space and time, Ozouf sees a model of open society; Mircea Eliade, a hierarchy of sacred space and time; and Mikhail Bakhtin, a temporary utopia of demotic power.[5] Yet function does not always follow form. Autocracies have sponsored carnivals; democracies and revolutions have promoted hierarchical rituals. The forms of celebration exist apart from the purposes they serve and the meanings society attributes to them. A festival is festive not because of the ideas or events it celebrates, not because of its social function or the rank of its celebrants, but because it is a special, separate time and place. To be festive is to stand apart from the quotidian; the festival aesthetic is festive only if it is distinct from the everyday.

The sponsors of revolutionary celebrations assumed that revolution would transform festivity and that any celebration of revolution would be necessarily revolutionary. In practice, however, the effect was reversed: when the October Revolution was celebrated, it was festivalized. A static historical event was re-created, and during the process it assumed the forms of celebration. The misconception was compounded by the sponsors' assumption that festive art was a realistic— that is, transparent—depicter of ideas. When the Bolsheviks hired artists to arrange festivals, they assumed that the medium would match the message. This was an unwise assumption, regardless of the artists' intent. Each age, each school of art has its own principles of selection and reassembly independent of the subject matter: the French Revolution in its bloodiest days projected an epic calm from the neoclassical canvases of David. Politicians could sponsor a festival; ideologists could determine what should be said; but artists were the medium of transmission.

This chapter will examine the revolutionary festivals as a medium. In their missionary zeal, the Bolsheviks intended them as a school of socialist ideas. Yet the messages invested and those transmitted were not always the same. Festivity has a shape all its own that is common to the celebrations of revolutions and autocracies and must be considered as part of the festival's social impact. Along with festive form, Bolshevik celebrations were shaped by the prerevolutionary artistic currents that predisposed artists to collaborate on festivals. Many people of the theater worked in styles eminently suited to festive celebration. Prerevolutionary society offered few opportunities to exploit that potential, but when the October Revolution made festivals a medium of public importance, the artists were ready, and they imported their aesthetic programs into the Bolsheviks' festivals. They helped make revolutionary festivals brilliant expressions of their time and shaped the Revolution as they celebrated it.

Festive Time and Space as Continuity

Public festivities help a political party claim legitimacy by occupying the city center (the seat of political power), decorating it with partisan symbols, and filling it with supporters. The uses of celebration were evident in prerevolutionary Russia. The political opposition used demonstrations to claim a voice in national affairs, and the autocracy defended its monopoly on power by banning them. Bolsheviks participated in illegal May Day marches, and their newspaper *Pravda* encouraged workers to do likewise. The holiday, which commemorated the slaughter of Chicago workers in the 1886 Haymarket Riot, had great symbolic power, but its primary purpose was to show the strength of semilegal and illegal political organizations and spotlight the regime's crumbling foundations.

Festivity can project another type of legitimacy that, though absent from earlier demonstrations, gained importance after the Bolsheviks had taken power. This is a monumental legitimacy—noting the roots of "monument" in memory—that links a party to the past. Festivals, the monuments, commemorate the past in ways that exalt it and emphasize the proper connections to the present.

Eliade describes a cosmic sense of history in which actions are judged legitimate, and thus real, only inasmuch as they repeat "eternal" mythic patterns.[6] Time and space seem to be an undifferentiated, unoriented mass punctuated by "hierophanies," points of legitimate, sacred activity fundamental to the social order. Cosmic time recognizes real moments, when myth is repeated, and nonreal, insignificant moments when it is absent. A festival suspends the everyday experience of time and space and joins distant events across the historic abyss. The immediate and tangible are defied, physical and temporal juxtaposition is declared coincidental. Participants are transformed into their historical ancestors and reenact moments that laid the foundations of the present. The past is retold to reflect the future it created, and the present is legitimized by animating the past within it.

Legitimacy claimed through an eternal past would seem alien to revolutionaries, whose foremost goal is to break history's repetitive cycle. Yet revolution itself was not new with the Bolsheviks, and Lenin and his comrades felt a kinship to all who had once rejected the status quo. They understood their historical mission through a mythic frame in which their movement was a lone island in an ocean of the bourgeoisie, linked with similar islands by symbolic bridges across time and space. When they narrated history in the mythic frame, the Bolsheviks did not follow the tsars or the Provisional Government, they merely occupied the time after; they followed the French Revolution, the Paris Commune, and other great rebellions.

There was abundant cause for the Bolsheviks to retell revolutionary history in 1918. Though the party held the organs of power, it had never established its legitimacy with much of the population, nor could it claim exclusive rights to the revolutionary tradition. Other leftist parties had strong followings, and their ideologies and histories in the underground qualified them no less than the Bolsheviks for leadership of a popular uprising. It was eminently possible in 1918 to consider the Bolshevik coup a historical anomaly, a stroke of chance, whereas to claim legitimacy the party needed to demonstrate the inevitability of the Revolution and the sole right to be its initiators.

Monuments could forward this claim. They are marked by an extended sense of time and space, which is suggested by a stability and durability of form. Such a style was demanded by a reviewer in the provincial city of Saratov in 1918 who asked for revolutionary art distinguished by "harmony of form, the connected equilibrium of separate parts that defines true art"—and that also lends cultural values the veneer of eternal truths.[7] Monuments express a search for the universal in the parochial, the permanent in the temporary. They depict those moments when ideals become manifest in human affairs: the October Revolution could be seen as a hammer and sickle descending from the heavens over Smolny, as in V. Fidman's poster (Figure 5).[8] Monumental

Figure 5. V. Fidman, *Smolny*, engraving (A. A. Sidorov, *Russkaia grafika za gody revoliutsii*, Moscow, 1923).

art idealizes by simplification and amplification. Contour becomes line, shading color: the visible parts of a greater whole. Malevich noted during the Revolution: "Monuments represent systems of perfect stamps recommended for life. In fact the representation of a man in a monument is not the representation of a portrait as it is usually understood. It is rather the presentation of a system or plan which is represented by the individuality in itself."[9] A similar impulse was manifest in the revolutionary theater as well as in statuary. Certainly it explains the otherwise anomalous popularity of medieval mystery plays.

The medieval spirit represented by mystery plays was never entirely alien to socialists; one need only remember the chivalric romances of William Morris, the utopian socialist. It appealed to other artists as well. Wagner used medieval legends for his operatic cycles; Reinhardt considered the *Everyman* mystery exemplary monumentalism; Ivanov saw mystery as the summit of theater. Even Nikolai Punin, a futurist critic, praised the artist's position in medieval society.[10] Medieval theater—as it was understood by modernists—was mythic. It spoke of ideas and issues fundamental to its culture and drew an audience representing the whole of society.

This virtue was compounded by the access mystery plays had to monumental time. Time was sealed off from everyday time and corresponded not to a natural but to a spiritual cycle. These plays represented spiritual states as time: the time before salvation; the time after salvation; and the present, in which good and evil do battle. These times were eternal, in a sense coeval, and could be entered and exited at will. Byron wrote in his mystery play *Cain:*

> With us acts are exempt from time, and we
> Can crowd eternity into an hour
> Or stretch an hour into eternity,
> We breathe not by a mortal measurement,
> But that's a mystery.[11]

Space operated according to similar principles; in fact, as they corresponded to the same spiritual states, time and space were fused. A single movement on the stage, an ascent or descent through a trapdoor, was a step across centuries or into salvation. Up was Heaven, down Hell, and in between was the life of man.

The creator of a revolutionary mystery could move freely and easily between past, present, and future, using them all to legitimize the October Revolution. The form allowed for high solemnity and vulgar jest, abstract philosophy and topical politicking, monumental pageants and mobile skits. It was quickly absorbed into the revolutionary idiom, injected there by artists who had experimented with the form in prerevolutionary years.

Reform in the Prerevolutionary Theater

Turn-of-the-century theater left many observers dissatisfied. Chekhov's plays featured lost souls groping for a meaning that life did not seem to offer; Tolstoy and Gorky, two other leading playwrights, depicted the hopeless struggles of the disadvantaged. Modern theater could not conjure up life's transcendent, intangible truths, truths once found in religion.

The medieval mystery, which had evolved from religious rites, offered a forum in which cosmic themes could be addressed with metaphysical assurance. Modernists had a particular understanding of the genre that excluded the coarseness and humor of the original. Mystery was to them the presence of the divine in the theater; it was a miracle play. In Maurice Maeterlinck's *Sister Beatrice,* the heroine is graced by immaculate conception; in Björnstjerne Björnson's *Beyond Human Might* (Gaideburov's biggest draw) life is preserved by the miracle of faith—which is signaled by an avalanche. A miracle is a moment when the laws of everyday life are transcended, revoked by a higher power; it is an intrusion of the sacred into the profane. The presence of the holy is marked by a suspension of normal laws of time and space.

In a 1902 article, "Unnecessary Truth," the symbolist poet Valery Briusov suggested that there was a limit to the Stanislavsky method then at the height of its success: it was incapable of conveying the new, "miraculous" content.[12] Briusov made a point valid for most symbolists: truth is something spiritual, internal, and intangible, and the reproduction of life—should such a thing be possible—can only hide truth in a profusion of detail. Life and art are not the same. Briusov saw a truth of essences to be apprehended by art, which in its purity was something greater than life. The task of art was not to reproduce details but to distill the truth from them. It required a different, nonrealistic style of play, which Briusov called "conventional" (*uslovnyi*).[13]

The theater of convention established its own rules and language; given only the barest indications, spectators were asked to imagine the rest of the stage. Conventionalism allowed symbolists to discuss eternal questions without superfluous detail. Only essentials, things with symbolic value, were allowed on stage. Malevich later echoed the selective principle as described here by Briusov: "The ultimate aim of art is to apprehend the universe by a special artistic intuition. To this end it strives to single out one aspect of reality, isolating it, making it possible to fix our attention on it. Out of the infinitely multitudinous world of colors, sounds, actions, and emotions surrounding us, each art selects a single element, as if inviting us to bestow contemplation on it alone, to seek in it a reflection of the whole."[14] Symbolist drama sought the universal in the particular. Things appeared on stage in two aspects: as part of the stage's assumed reality and as part of a greater whole. Locality disappeared under a flood of universalized settings that, like most utopias, were not only nowhere but everywhere. They were points of existence in an ocean of nonexistence.

Maeterlinck's plays were frequently performed in prerevolutionary Russia, most notably in the Komissarzhevskaia Theater under the direction of Meyerhold, a former Stanislavsky actor who had forsaken his mentor. Under Meyerhold's direction Mgebrov learned the style he would apply at Proletkult. Meyerhold's first attempt at Maeterlinck was a 1906 production of *The Death of Tintageles*. In the play, as in monumental art, space and time were not specified. Although the castle suggested a medieval setting, the play had broader symbolic meaning extending to the present. As Meyerhold said, "The significance of the play's symbol reaches tremendous heights. It's not Death but he who brings death that arouses indignation. And then the Island on which the action takes place is our life."[15] The island exemplified symbolist dramatic space—a hermetically sealed space into which nothing could intrude but that nevertheless represented all space. In a later production of Maeterlinck's *Sister Beatrice* at the Komissarzhevskaia, Meyerhold used a "bas-relief" setting; the stage was spread out like the flat surface of an icon. Slow, rhythmic speech and choreographed movement mimicked the cadences of a ritual. Lines were chanted, not spoken; actors were distributed about the stage in static, monumental groupings; and, as Mgebrov noted, the performers did not so much act as conduct a religious service.[16]

Space and time in the symbolist theater were marked as in a religious celebration. Meyerhold experimented with *mises en scène* for his new style, and his first attempt bore a striking resemblance to a church. Russian Orthodox ritual is conducted in a shallow space in relief against a vertical iconostasis. Movement is rhythmic, regulated by choral chants, and the iconostasis is flat, depthless. The artistic simplification suited to eternal principles is often accompanied by a loss of the third dimension: essentials are thrown into stark relief against a flat background. Flattened and idealized against the backdrop, action takes on new significance. Meyerhold said:

> New devices of conventional depiction are intentionally worked out in the *mise en scène* and actors' play. Theatrical art is informed with a premeditated condensing—nothing on stage should be accidental. In certain situations the actors are placed as close as possible to the spectator. This frees the actor from the accidental lifelike details of the ever-preponderant stage apparatus. This gives the actor's movement the freedom for more refined expressivity. This helps the actor's voice give more subtle shading, heightens the spectators' receptivity, and destroys the line separating them from the actors.[17]

Theatrical conventions condition spectator response. They frame social interactions and thus serve as social models.[18] Symbolists looked back to the mystery play as a means to reform their audience and the society it represented. Spectators trained by Stanislavsky were unaccustomed to active viewing: they were held captive by the darkness of an unlit auditorium and forbidden to applaud until the performance ended. Because Stanislavsky depicted reality complete onstage, the spectator was allowed little interpretive freedom. Meyerhold realized that for the conventional theater to work, the spectator would have to "employ his imagination creatively in order to fill in those details suggested by the stage action."[19] Spectators were to be a creative element in the theater, actively perceiving the intangible reality behind the action. The director's business was to create a space in which everything would be interpreted symbolically. Moreover, the director would have to signal the viewer that the stage action was not to be perceived and understood as real life: "there must be a pattern of movement on the stage to transform the spectator into a vigilant observer."[20]

The Moscow Art Theater was identified with its building, the famous work of the architect Fedor Shekhtel: it was a theater of one place. Ivanov and Meyerhold dreamt of a theater that could travel to the people and their open spaces: a marketplace, city square, or open field. For the Russians, like the French revolutionaries, open outdoor space was egalitarian. Stanislavsky's theater segregated space (as did most turn-of-the-century theaters); the play was onstage, the audience was isolated in the dark, and the two spaces were separated by a proscenium. Symbolists sought to rupture the proscenium arch; it was to be the threshold over which art crossed into life and life into art. Painting offers a useful parallel: in eras when mimesis is important, pictures are framed; when artists aspire to create reality (as would the later constructivists), the frame is dropped.

Time at the Moscow Art Theater, like space, was "bourgeois": the show schedule conformed to the life of the industrial city. The Industrial Revolution introduced precise scheduling to city life; it regularized time, making it independent of nature. Theatrical performances were repeated daily at the same time. Mystery plays, however, were creatures of feast days, most of which fell in times of slack. Performances were, like the natural clock, irregular; they began when they began. This irregularity created a different audience; because the performance was given only once, all people gathered, undifferentiated, at one place, one time.

The symbolists were assuming that function follows form, that a mystery play would create its own audience, and that the audience would emerge from the theater and change society. The assumption would later appeal to the cosmic aspirations of revolutionary times. Yet symbolists might also have noted that mysteries could be used by more than a single ideology, class, or institution. Probably the most popular mystery play of 1917–20 was *King of the Jews,* written by Grand Duke Konstantin, uncle of the reigning tsar.[21]

The odd history of this play begins with its prewar banishment from the stage by the Church: no figure from the Bible could be represented on stage, regardless of how piously. If the Romanovs would not disobey a church they themselves headed, they could bend the rules a bit. Because no public performance of the play was permitted, in 1913 a production was mounted in the Hermitage Hall of the Winter Palace for a "select" audience of friends—about three thousand people for ten performances. Each of the ten performances was designated a dress rehearsal; an eleventh rehearsal was added for review by the press. The play was a great success with the public and a critical success with the press; even *Teatr i iskusstvo,* published by Aleksandr Kugel, no friend of the Romanovs, had a good deal of praise for it. But the Church, unmoved, still forbade public performance. The ban was finally lifted after the February Revolution, and by November a full production was ready. Its premiere on November 6, 1917 (November 19, new style) was ironically one of the first under the Bolsheviks, whose embarrassment was aggravated when the play repeated its success of 1913.[22]

Though subsequent Soviet critics dismissed it as a mere curiosity,[23] the mystery represented a genre of great relevance during the Revolution. It was an account of the Passion and Resurrection of Christ through the eyes of an average person, written in blank verse. For a member of the ruling family the author expressed some liberal opinions: he claimed, for instance, that the right to rule was based on the mandate of both God and the people—betrayal of either would invite downfall. There was also an attack on capitalism—more from an aristocrat's than a communist's point of view, to be sure. That the play was sometimes anti-Semitic did nothing to impede its popularity.[24] The production at the Nezlobin Theater mobilized some of Russia's best talent. Nikolai Arbatov of the Petrograd Maly Theater directed it; the dances were choreographed by Michel Fokine; and the music was written by Aleksandr Glazunov (Glazunov's student Dimitri Tiomkin claimed it was his best work).[25] In short, it provided a ready example of how mystery plays could have public impact and appeal to a broad audience, both of which had eluded the symbolists.[26]

Time and Space as Discontinuity

Sacred time, when divine order was manifest in human affairs, was the setting of a mystery play. The genre traced humanity's progress from sin to piety, from damnation to salvation. During the Revolution, the notions of the sacred and the historical were often conflated; mystery plays reimagined history to legitimize revolutionary movement. Time was divided into history, when popular movements urged civilization toward its progressive destination in October 1917, and nonhistory, when reaction set in and progress ceased.

The mystery format offered Bolsheviks a unique public forum and lent the party's ideology a mythic dimension. Yet it did not correspond fully to the nature of the October Revolution, which was a violent seizure of power that had split the country and would plunge it into civil war. Families, neighborhoods, and communities were broken, and a nation on the brink of ruin slid toward catastrophe. Revolutionaries could offer a vision of universal equality and justice, popular enfranchisement and progress, but spectators noticed a disparity between this vision and the revolutionaries' violence and frequent disregard for human life. To enlist popular support, the Bolsheviks needed a format that could accommodate both their movement's lofty aims and its visceral politics, that could stake its claim to the legacy of human history while making a radical break with the immediate past. The urgency and impetuosity of revolution were better fit by a carnival, the complementary half of the festive tradition.

Mystery and carnival were integrated elements of the festive tradition; they mirrored and depended on each other. The medieval mystery was performed during a festival; it preceded a riotous carnival, which was followed by a solemn mass and fast. Each aspect drew on a unique understanding of time and space. In the solemn mystery, time and space were continuous. The mystery selected those elements that corresponded to its rules and ignored the rest. Carnival was discontinuous; it overturned and shattered time and space, and was nonselective. The experience was brief, bracketed by the term of the feast; it was a compression of time, a temporary state to be exploited intensively. Carnival was dynamic because it was fleeting.

Any discussion of carnival must contend with the work of Bakhtin, a scholar active in postrevolutionary Russia whose work on Rabelais and carnival culture has been fundamental in defining that culture's aesthetic and social dimensions. Bakhtin's sojourn in GIII in the 1920s likely brought him into contact with thinkers like Piotrovsky and Aleksei Gvozdev, who shaped the Soviet debate on festivity.[27] Although Bakhtin rejected his contemporaries' Marxist slant, he often shared their assumptions and probably profited from their critiques of other thinkers.

Bakhtin, like his colleagues, recognized qualities of celebration alien to the symbolists: it was riotous, excessive, and full of coarse humor. Nothing could be further from the piety of Ivanov and Scriabin than the medieval carnivals that fascinated Bakhtin. The carnival was a rite of reversal in which the underclass enacted (temporarily) its ascendance to the ruling heights of society and subverted the ecclesiastical and social hierarchy. Claiming that carnival was an activity of the church subdeacons (the ecclesiastical underclass) and citing the oft-quoted disapproval of select members of the upper clergy, he claimed that carnival undermined authority. In the Feast of Fools, the strict hierarchy of the mass was inverted: subdeacons and choirboys donned the mantle of ecclesiastical authority and presided over a mockery of sacred rites and symbols.[28] Priestly accoutrements were placed in profane hands; liturgy was recited as gibberish; the commemorative feast became a riotous banquet. Vestments were turned inside out and hymnals upside down. Most of all, the strict discipline of religious law was dissolved in general license.

Bakhtin shared with his colleagues two assumptions concerning carnival's social dynamic that, when applied to contemporary Soviet society, could lead to misconceptions. One is that the mystery and carnival embodied innately incompatible spirits; the other is that carnival represented the popular viewpoint and challenged the ruling order by encouraging role reversal. Bakhtin ignored the interdependence of carnival and mystery (captured vividly by Victor Hugo in the first chapter of *Notre-Dame de Paris*). Each celebrated (in its own way) the same religious holidays. Mystery embodied the higher secrets of the church; carnival turned them upside down. Carnival was dependent on the higher mysteries; like any parody, it needed a subject to distort. Nietzsche understood the two spirits' independence, and in the *Birth of Tragedy* he defined them as the Dionysian and the Apollonian, the essential components of tragic vision. The Greek tragic festivals grew out of an ecstatic popular celebration, and the tragic cycle was not complete without a satyr play.

Bakhtin's second assumption, that carnival expressed the "common folk's" (*narodnaia*) culture, in opposition to that of the elite (like Wagner and Ivanov, he posited a hermetic isolation) was even more misleading. It led to a frequent equation of festival with revolution.[29] The assertion, contestable even in Western cultures, simply did not apply to Russia. Doubtless, there was an old Russian tradition of popular urban carnivals: indeed, seventeenth-century travelers described masked "Pharisees" roaming Moscow and lighting the beards of unwary passersby. Yet the tradition that inspired Bolshevik festivals was more likely autocratic carnivals. Antirites were a feature of court life under Ivan the Terrible (the *oprichina*) and Peter the Great (Most Drunken Council of Fools and Jesters).[30] Masques and rites of reversal were celebrated under Anna Ioannovna (the marriage of dwarf jesters) and Elizaveta Petrovna (masques of gender reversal). Carnival processions were a favorite pastime of Peter; and carnivals were part of coronation festivities from the age of Catherine to that of the final Romanov, Nicholas II (the Khodynka disaster).

To associate the poles of festive activity, carnival and mystery, with specific themes or social groupings leads to contradictions and narrows our understanding of festivity. Festivity is a highly conventionalized discourse appropriate to a wide range of occasions, cultures, and classes; it can be used by mystics and materialists, royalists and revolutionaries. Festive conventions serve not a specific idea or class but rather to isolate festive experience from everyday behavior and discourse. During a celebration, a society focuses on the past and relives memories germane to the present. Foundation events are selected from the past and strung together in a sequence that simulates historical progression. The conventions provide patterns of selection and, once a selection has been made, help string the events into a new whole.

The reason the Bolsheviks, like other revolutionaries before them, turned to festivals in a time of upheaval was that they were a way to grapple with history. Mystery and carnival, the poles of festive expression, could embody the contradictions of the Bolsheviks' historical situation—grand visions of the future and tumult in the present—and their conventions provided the structure of a historical myth.

History is not simply what has happened in the past but a remembrance of the past within a progressive time frame. History is time subdivided; it recognizes both the unity of time and its division by moments of change. Both senses of time are as old as history itself and can be found at the advent of historical consciousness in Western culture. The Egyptian religion was ahistorical and did not segregate time; the myth of the creation was the myth of beginning. This was true of the primitive Greek religion, but as the Hellenes developed a historical sense, new generations of gods conquered the gods of creation; time was subdivided by new myths. The Hebrews, who had a piercing sense of history, had both a creation myth and a separate beginning to religious history—the Covenant.

The relevance of historical myth to Bolshevik Russia and its festivals is demonstrated by a festival spectacle planned for November 1918 (but never realized). Evgeny Vakhtangov, a student of Stanislavsky's who was gradually abandoning his master's strict realism, contemplated staging the Book of Exodus. The Covenant had a particular appeal; it was easily translated from religious terms into the historical terms of social struggle.

1. Moses (tongue-tied). His wife. Aaron. Perhaps he saw an Egyptian beating a Jew. He killed him. That night, aroused, he tells him about it in his tent. At night God speaks with him. God commands him to go to the Pharaoh and as a sign gives him the ability to work miracles (the Rod). Moses, suffering for his people, burning with the thought of liberating his people, prepares to go to the Pharaoh the next morning.
2. Moses before the people. A speech.
3. At the Pharaoh's.
4. In the desert.
5. Moses before the people with the tablets.
6. The ages pass.
7. Dispersed.
8. Night. Far beyond the boundaries of tangible space, a fire. In the night the song of a thousand breasts filled with hope is heard. The people go, go to build their freedom. Curtain.[31]

The Covenant was a moment when the cosmic history described by Eliade, with its repetitions and returns to the moments of creation, was subdivided in the historical present.

Another Stanislavsky student, Valentin Smyshliaev, directed a stage adaptation of Verhaeren's short poem "La Révolte" for the November 6, 1918, opening of Moscow's Proletkult Theater Studio. The play began with a creation scene harkening back to Genesis and to the Gospel according to John. Revolution emerged from the primeval, undifferentiated chaos of prehistory.

The entire auditorium is sunk in darkness, from which the formless, fleeting sounds of music are born, which slowly grow into an ecstatic hymn. The curtain slowly parts, and the spectator cannot make out anything onstage. Streams of golden sparks shatter the darkness and merge with the stars. The howl of a formless, perturbed crowd, the trampling of running feet. Slowly the red reflections of fires disperse the dark. The spectator begins to make out some lines reminiscent of the angles of houses, a window, a door; but these are not sharp lines, rather quivering, smashed, rebelling. He sees a seething, stirred-up crowd. Out of this chaos rise the words.[32]

Revolution was the great beginning.

The Second Symbolist Influence

Integrating these two festive conventions into a single artistic production was a challenge faced by younger symbolists in the decade preceding the Revolution. Although motives and circumstances differed from 1918, the solutions were relevant to revolutionary times and laid the groundwork for Bolshevik festivals.

The mystery plays favored by Briusov and Ivanov offered some advantages, including cosmic reach, but they also locked theaters in a stasis exemplified by Maeterlinck's dramas.[33] The dilemma was more pressing in matters of audience interaction: modernist mysteries proved unable to accommodate an active and diverse public. Overcoming these deficiencies was essential to the poets Aleksandr Blok and Andrei Bely, who saw them as obstacles to their philosophical and social aims. Their ventures in the theater attracted the attention of Meyerhold, whose collaborations with older symbolists were becoming increasingly fruitless. His subsequent work on Blok's dramas suggested new venues, such as fairgrounds and cabaret theaters, that would eventually prove of great benefit to the producers of revolutionary festivals.

Meyerhold encountered frustration in two productions of Calderón's *Adoration of the Cross*, the first in 1910 at the "Tower Theater" (Ivanov's living room), the second, starring Mgebrov and Chekan, on an outdoor summer stage in the Finnish resort of Terijoki in 1912. The productions were attempts to revive medieval theater: its mystery, broad popular audience, and intimacy with the audience. The first performance of Calderón's *auto* (perhaps the best translation of *deistvo*), on Easter Sunday, was radically simplified. The stage was a cubicle marked off by draperies. Candles provided the lighting; the curtains were parted by stage attendants; and there were no set changes, indeed hardly any set at all. The acting was unaffected, almost motionless and in direct contact with the audience.[34] The production realized all but one of Meyerhold's goals: intimacy was achieved by limiting the audience to friends and colleagues.

The 1912 performance was to be larger and attract all classes. The play was presented "at night, in the light of blazing torches, with a tremendous crowd of the local population."[35] It was mounted in a white tent, bare of decorations; footlights were eliminated, and lanterns were set above the stage. The acting space itself was clearly established; "the white curtain had a border of painted blue crosses and represented the symbolic boundary between the setting of the religious drama and the hostile outside world."[36] The last comment suggests a fatal contradiction. Meyerhold had returned theater to the open air, where the people could gather as one and become part of the presentation. Yet he still assumed that life and art were opposed, and that art was superior to life. His open-air public theater broke down the architecture of the bourgeois theater but retained its hermetic stage space.[37]

In a fragmented society, there could be no universally accepted language of truth because there was no universal truth. Theater was without a full public language. Bely pointed this lack out sarcastically: "Picture yourself, reader, in this role for just a moment. Is that us spinning around the sacrificial altar—an *art nouveau* lady, a stockbroker, a workingman and a member of the Privy Council? I am sure that our prayers will not tally. The *art nouveau* lady will pray to some poet in the image and likeness of Dionysos, the workingman will pray for a shorter workday, while the state councillor—to what star does his gaze aspire?"[38] He added presciently, "So long as the class struggle goes on, appeals to aesthetic democracy are grotesque,"[39] a conclusion reached by Wagner before him.

Blok, Meyerhold, and their contemporaries noted the aesthetic and social limits of Ivanov's vision of festivity. It deprived the theater of the coarseness and suddenness of carnival, and kept the popular audience outside its walls. Change was difficult to enact onstage. Action progressed on a principle of continuity; change, when it occurred, was from one substance or level of being to a higher power. Drama was supposed to be a threshold, a point of transition; yet when everything is of a single quality, there can be no change. Blok, after the unrest of 1905, could only ask, "But where is life with its contradictions and its acute and profound struggles?"[40]

Blok himself provided an answer in 1906 when, in his *Balaganchik* (*Fairground Puppet Booth*), Harlequin stood center-stage and announced:

Hello World! You're back with me again.
Your heart has long been close to me!
I'm going to breathe your spring-freshness
Through your golden window.[41]

Blok turned to a form of popular carnival theater, the commedia dell'arte, to remedy the shortcomings of symbolist drama. The commedia offered a rich tradition—layered like the strata of an archeological dig—and Blok and Meyerhold, who directed *Balaganchik* several times from 1908 to 1914, drew on them all: the original Italian players, roaming the country with a mixed bag of scenarios; the stationary commedia dell'arte of seventeenth-century France; the Venetian commedias of Carlo Gozzi and Carlo Goldoni. The commedia dell'arte had a history in Russia too. It was imported from Germany during the reign of Anna Ioannovna (1730–40) in its courtly French variety.[42] Pierrot and Harlequin were stock figures in Russian vaudeville from 1830–40; and the commedia provided a pictorial language for modernists, like Picasso in the West and Benois and Konstantin Somov of Russia's World of Art movement. The title of Blok's play suggests another important source: the Italian characters were Russified and thrived until the late nineteenth century in theaters and puppet booths set up on fairgrounds for market days and holidays. These were the *balagany* of Blok's play.

In *Balaganchik,* Blok tackled two problems whose solutions would reappear in revolutionary festivals. First, his use of the commedia broke down the division between popular and elite art forms. Born as a theater of the city square, the commedia was embraced by the Parisian court; from there it moved to Russia, into the court and back to the popular fairground theater, and was assimilated by modernists from there. With each transfer, standard devices and features took on new functions and meanings, and both levels of Russian culture were enriched.

Blok's second concern was to reintegrate the two aspects of festive expression into a single artistic work. To achieve this unification he exploited the traditional device of the commedia, the unmotivated and sudden jump from farce to mystery.[43] Blok structured *Balaganchik* so that its farcical elements parodied the serious. In this new context, the jumps were no longer formal and meaningless, as they had been in the puppet booth; they became a sharp commentary on the dogma of mystery. Blok mocked symbolism in its more solemn, monolithic variety, turning against his own former dreams with what he called "transcendent," renewing irony.[44] The play opens with a solemn quorum of "mystics" seated at a central table; Harlequin then impishly crawls out from under the table. In the course of the play, characters ask one another whether they understood it; they do not. A clown loses his head and spouts cranberry juice. And Pierrot, poor Pierrot, the hapless puppet who represents the poet in Blok's world, leaps through a window to his death, only to discover the window is a stage prop painted on paper.

Balaganchik was a powerful influence on prerevolutionary theater; it made new demands on the audience and offered new freedom to directors. Spectators were confronted with abrupt shifts from high solemnity to low farce, from refined aestheticism to coarse mockery; directors were forced to develop *mises en scène* accommodating extreme and rapid transformations. The need for structural mobility led them away from the large dramatic genres preferred by their elders to small forms like the skit. New intimate sites, cabarets foremost among them, were opened to house the new genres.

Cabaret had its various masters and locales in those years: the Bat, the Stray Dog, the Comedians' Haven.[45] Even Meyerhold, director of the imperial theater, moonlighted as Doctor Dapertutto (from an E. T. A. Hoffmann story), cultivator of the ironic. Cabaret programs were usually an assembly of short pieces tied together by a *conferancé*, or emcee, who roamed the stage apron and bantered with the audience. Cabaret brought a new spirit and flexibility to the Russian theater: light, intimate, and ironic. Oddly enough, it was also a training ground for directing revolutionary mass spectacles.

Meyerhold established a small studio in Petersburg devoted to the lost craft of commedia dell'arte. Meyerhold and his main assistants, Sergei Radlov and Vladimir Soloviev (no relation to the philosopher), future directors of mass spectacles in revolutionary Petrograd, initiated a program of studio exercises and a theoretical journal, *Love for Three Oranges*. They sought a nonliterary theater; recent literature had denervated the stage, filling it with pessimism and stasis, and they looked to popular traditions to breathe new life into it.

Meyerhold's rival in the world of Petersburg cabarets was Evreinov, another master of the small theater, who in 1920 would direct *The Storming of the Winter Palace*, the grandest of all the mass spectacles. Evreinov had a lightness of touch and a carefree spirit alien to symbolism or, for that matter, to any other creed. Evreinov worked on the Spanish drama, medieval mysteries, and commedia dell'arte simultaneously with Meyerhold and the symbolists, but his motives were different, as he concentrated on their mixture of the solemn and comic, and on theatrical transformation.[46]

Like the symbolists, Evreinov tied the theater and religion into one bundle; but he understood their common mission differently. The instinct for theater was, to Evreinov, prereligious; religion was born of the theater, not the theater of religion: "In order to believe in gods man had first to acquire the gift of conceiving these gods, of personifying them as a dramatist personifies ideas, feelings and passions. Were it not for the gift of transfiguration, of imaginative creation of things and beings that cannot be seen on this earth, man would have no religion."[47]

He asked the same questions as the symbolists, used the same models, and spoke the same language, but somehow Evreinov's answers were unique. He considered the theatrical instinct to be part of a greater instinct for transformation, a need to assume a finer, more beautiful mask. Evreinov shared the symbolist passion for masked drama but with a difference: he was concerned less with the result of the transformation than with the process. The purpose of theater was to find a new identity or inhabit a different personality. The question of truth was irrelevant: theater was not ritual but a game.

The 1907–8 season at Evreinov's Ancient Theater was devoted to medieval *moralités* and mysteries, the 1911–12 season to Spanish Golden Age theater; a commedia dell'arte cycle was planned for the 1914–15 season. His treatment of the repertory differed from his predecessors'. Meyerhold interpreted the Spanish drama in the spirit of a holy day; Evreinov captured the full spirit of the medieval holiday, including its coarse buffoonery. His "holiday theater" went beyond Meyerhold's vision; it re-created the entire holiday spectacle, both the art and its spectators. The life on stage was the life of the medieval city.

The Ancient Theater's premiere production, *Three Magi* (1907), an eleventh-century miracle play, included an eleventh-century audience on stage. The miracle was performed unseen in the depths of a church, while the "audience" center-stage displayed a gamut of emotions: the piety of early comers waiting for the prologue, the fanaticism of flagellants, the outraged reaction to Herod's order to slaughter the innocents. A stage-upon-the-stage was also used in a production of *Fuente ovejuna* (1911). It was a rough wooden platform on barrels surrounded by an outer set designed to look like a sixteenth-century Spanish town square.

Evreinov repaired Meyerhold's neglect; the audience of sixteenth-century Spaniards on stage provided the second audience of twentieth-century Russians with a model of festive behavior.

Theater and Revolution

Even before the Bolsheviks took power, there was a strongly perceived analogy between theater and revolution; theater lives in a similar emotional atmosphere and draws its energy from the polarities that drive revolution. Many, like Aleksandr Tairov, director of Moscow's Chamber Theater, understood revolution in theatrical terms: "Motor vehicles, troops, and guns swept past us. Powerful waves of workers rolled by, flooding the snowy streets—and we stood on the sidewalks, behind the cordon, the audience at an incomprehensible mystery play that was taking place before our eyes."[48]

Others, like Ivanov and Lunacharsky, often interpreted social phenomena in the light of Nietzsche's duad, the Apollonian and the Dionysian.[49] Revolution, in this scheme, was a struggle of popular Dionysian forces for Apollonian expression—a new social order. Festival performance (*deistvo*), which embodied a similar duality, was thus a ready medium for enacting the revolutionary myth. The disposition was manifest in a plan that Lunacharsky submitted to the Moscow Soviet for the 1918 anniversary festival. He proposed "repeating the emotional experience of the October Revolution." The festival would be "split into three parts: struggle, victory, the intoxication of victory. . . . Initially the mood culminates, then attains its high point and ends in general gaiety. . . . Festivals should not only be official, as May Day [was], but should have deep internal sense. The masses should relive the revolutionary impulse."[50]

The foundations of the theater of revolution were present in the work of Meyerhold, Evreinov, and their contemporaries long before the Revolution itself. In mystery plays they mastered the continuous time of cosmic history; from the carnival theater, they learned the art of discontinuity.

Yet without a great event their theaters were empty shells without an appropriate subject or audience; revolutionary Russia could not be, as the Middle Ages had been, created onstage. Meyerhold said at the outset of the First World War: "Working for the sake of joy, in the name of a rebellion or a manifestation, in which can be found so much of theatricality's charms, . . . the contemporary theater's playwright will surely find a point of contact with the country's emotion. . . . The most intensive merging of the auditorium with the stage occurs precisely at the moment when the people are strongly shaken or strongly aroused."[51] Revolution was the only context in which festivity could attain its full significance. There could be no dualism without a demarcation; revolution, the threshold, provided the line. As a critic would soon note, it filled the formal conventions of theater with historical content: "Only in revolutionary eras do all the voices heard from the stage, . . . all the laughter and sobbing, sound like a mighty symphony of the terrible prologue-road that must lead society to its true life. Only in these eras do we catch the trumpeting of revolutionary horns in the harmless tinkling of Harlequin's bells and the call to action on Pierrot's white face."[52]

Several mass spectacles were produced in the five years preceding the 1917 Revolution. In August 1912, for instance, Evreinov staged a "mass production," *1812,* in Luna Park for the centennial of the Battle of Borodino. The scenario, written by his friend Iury Beliaev, consisted of seven acts with a total of thirty-three scenes.[53] At the outbreak of hostilities in 1913, Meyerhold and two assistants, Soloviev and Iury Bondi, set to work on *Fire,* a mass open-air play about the war.[54] Artillery fire, battles swung by betrayal, and a burst dam were all part of the show, the entire thing to be concluded by an apotheosis. Interpreted as political gestures, these productions were unsuccessful. It would be more accurate, however, to call them misfires, plays in search of an audience.

The October Revolution gave Meyerhold the audience he needed; the proper script was provided by Mayakovsky, the futurist poet who would be Meyerhold's comrade-in-arms for the next decade. Meyerhold directed Mayakovsky's *Mystery-Bouffe* in Petrograd's Musical Drama Theater for the 1918 first-anniversary celebration.[55] *Mystery-Bouffe* reworked the Biblical story of the flood into a revue of revolutionary politics: the mystery of the title referred to the proletariat's progress toward the gates of paradise; the bouffe came at the expense of the declining bourgeoisie. It was very much a festival play, written for a special celebration and combining both aspects of the festival aesthetic.

Mystery-Bouffe, as one of the first revolutionary plays, guided subsequent dramatic re-creations of revolutionary history. It was a puzzling mixture of apocalypse, modernism, and folk theater: a concoction that established a pattern for Civil War propaganda. The play was filled with the spirit of revolution: its prologue claimed "we glorify / the days / of uprisings, / rebellions / and revolutions"—but it was conceived before the October Revolution and did not mention the Bolsheviks.[56] *Mystery-Bouffe* was a play of revolution, but of revolution in general: the overthrow of the tsar, the petty bourgeoisie, and the old theaters (p. 170):

> Today
> above the dust of theaters
> our motto's ablaze:
> "Everything new!"
> Stand up and take notice!
> Curtain!
>
> [*The actors separate. They shred the curtain, painted with the relics of the old theater.*]

Old world and old theater, new world and new theater were not notions that the poet and the director differentiated.

Led by the booming voice of Mayakovsky, futurists—during the Revolution, the term covered much of the avant-garde—claimed an exclusive ability to speak for the new society. Their claim was based on an aesthetic program that had evolved before the Revolution rather than on the Bolsheviks' approval. To futurists, the October coup was just a beginning, and futurism an engine to drive revolution along. They cultivated the art of upheaval and displacement, which they credited with the ability to shake society out of its bourgeois torpor. The movement had an ability to express violent change without the symbolists' overwrought eschatology. Punin phrased the relationship between futurism and revolution well when he called futurism "a moment that deepens and widens the cultural base of communism by introducing a new element: a dynamic sense of time."[57] It was the art of displacement and discord: what the Revolution was to society, futurism was to the depicted figure—the great displacement.

The futurists, like Blok and Bely, were shaped by their critique of symbolism. Mayakovsky excelled in depicting the life of the modern city so noticeably absent in Ivanov's work. The twentieth-century city was not like the Greek polis or the walled city of the Middle Ages; it was tense, compact, and dynamic. Conflict and not harmony, discontinuity not continuity were the rule. It was a city that bred revolution, not marble temples. Here the influence of the Italian futurists—the poet-performer Emilio Marinetti, the artist Umberto Boccioni—and their fascination with the modern city. Their art favored dynamism and displacement, confrontation and discord: fragmented paintings tracing frenzied motion; noise machines replacing music with urban cacophony; manifestoes provoking the audience.

The Italian futurists sought to shatter the architectural barrier between the stage and audience; they refused to let the bourgeoisie sit passively in their seats. Ivanov had dreamt of uniting the audience (and the nation) by the magnificence of tragic art; the Italians—like Bely—realized that social conditions made such unity impossible. They chose smaller forms based on popular theaters—the puppet booth or cabaret—and broke down the stage barrier by insulting the audience and instigating its angry reaction.

Futurists both Italian and Russian toured the provinces with variety shows, reading mocking manifestoes and verse. Their antagonism toward the audience was demonstrated in the 1896 production of Alfred Jarry's *Ubu roi*, later considered the first futurist performance, in the Théâtre de l'Oeuvre in Paris. The play had a thematic reach later rivaled by *Mystery-Bouffe:* it was set "in Poland, that is to say: nowhere," but the stage was painted to represent "indoors and out of doors, even the torrid, temperate and arctic zones at once." The first word spoken by a performer was *merde,* and as the play progressed, members of the audience clapped and whistled (depending on their preferences), and fistfights broke out in the orchestra pit.[58] The drama had become, as Ivanov hoped, a real event, but only through conflict, not harmony. Theater controls audience reaction according to its vision of society: prewar futurists exacerbated conflict, just as *Mystery-Bouffe,* a play of revolution, would unfailingly split its audience.[59]

Unique to the Russian variant of futurism was a utopian strain. The Italians, as the poet Vadim Shershenevich noted, preferred destroying the city to re-creating it, while the Russians had a vision for the future.[60] The utopian element that rounded out *Mystery-Bouffe* first found expression in Malevich's abstract paintings and the retrospective Slavism of Velimir Khlebnikov's poems, and it found its first dramatic voice in two 1913 performances: Mayakovsky's *Vladimir Mayakovsky: A Tragedy* and *Victory over the Sun*, an opera by Aleksei Kruchenykh and Mikhail Matiushin.[61]

Mayakovsky's tragedy opens in Hell-City, his vision of modern life. The first act features a "holiday of beggars," a frenzied harbinger of revolution spiced with Nietzsche's Dionysian rites and Bakhtin's Feast of Fools. Overwrought monologues about urban alienation culminate in revolt, when things "shed the rags of worn-out names." The next act takes place in a utopian city, where the poet-protagonist, like Christ the Saviour, accepts the suffering of humanity. *Victory over the Sun*, for the few spectators (including Blok and Mgebrov) who understood it, involves mankind's struggle against the power of the sun. The battle ends with the stabbing and capture of the sun, a triumph that in the final act leads to a utopian Tenth Lands of the future, where the residents attempt to adapt to their new life. Many of these features would find a prominent place in *Mystery-Bouffe*.

Mystery-Bouffe: Apocalypse and Utopia

Mystery-Bouffe, which was begotten by years of experimentation and ferment, festivalized revolution. This version of the Revolution featured seven pairs of the "clean" (the bourgeoisie) and seven pairs of the "unclean" (the proletariat), oppressed and ready for rebellion. They gather on a Noah-less ark to survive the deluge and create a new world afterward. The bourgeoisie, including assorted Europeans and an Abyssinian negus, quickly reassert the old regime onboard. They institute a "democratic republic," banish workers to the hold, hoard foodstuffs, and perform no labor themselves. The unclean suffer but soon recognize the state of affairs. Realizing their own strength, they enact a revolution. With the sudden appearance of A Simple Man (played by Mayakovsky) the revolution has its leader, who guides the unclean through Hell, Heaven, and beyond to the Promised Land.

Mystery-Bouffe drew on the unique abilities of Meyerhold and Mayakovsky. Their prewar experiments shaped a new vision of revolution that gained increasing currency during the Civil War. Mayakovsky's revolution was, like the story of an earlier revolution, a tale of two cities: the revolutionary city of earlier acts and the utopian city of the finale. What these cities were and how their revolution took place were envisioned through festival theater styles, ranging from the commedia dell'arte to the mystery play. They provided the structure of space and time, their resolution as apocalypse and utopia, and the creation and interaction of characters.

Festival theater was, in effect, a model of society. In *Mystery-Bouffe* it was a concentration of hostile extremes. (Figure 6 is a poster for the 1918 production.) There was no passage between the two cities, only an abrupt threshold, an apocalypse. This viewpoint, which many contemporaries shared and associated with Mayakovsky's name, was inspired less by revolution than by artistic change. Its elements existed long before 1917, in the productions of Meyerhold and the futurists.

КОММУНАЛЬНЫЙ ТЕАТР МУЗЫКАЛЬНОЙ ДРАМЫ

7,8 НОЯБРЯ н/с.

МЫ ПОЭТЫ, ХУДОЖНИКИ, РЕЖИССЕРЫ и АКТЕРЫ
ПРАЗДНУЕМ ДЕНЬ ГОДОВЩИНЫ

ОКТЯБРЬСКОЙ РЕВОЛЮЦИИ

Революционным спектаклем.
нами будет дана:

БЕЛЫЕ и ЧЕРНЫЕ БЕГУТ ОТ КРАСНОГО ПОТОПА.

II КАРТ. КОВЧЕГ. ЧИСТЫЕ ПОДСОВЫВАЮТ НЕЧИСТЫМ ЦАРЯ и РЕСПУБЛИКУ. САМИ УВИДИТЕ ЧТО ИЗ ЭТОГО ПОЛУЧАЕТСЯ.

III КАРТ. АД В КОТОРОМ РАБОЧИЕ САМОГО ВЕЛЬЗЕВУЛА К ЧЕРТЯМ ПОСЛАЛИ

IV КАРТ. РАЙ. КРУПНЫЙ РАЗГОВОР БАТРАКА С МАФУСАИЛОМ.

V КАРТИНА. КОММУНА! СОЛНЕЧНЫЙ ПРАЗДНИК ВЕЩЕЙ и РАБОЧИХ.

РАСКРАШЕНО МАЛЕВИЧЕМ
ПОСТАВЛЕНО МЕЙЕРХОЛЬДОМ и МАЯКОВСКИМ
РАЗЫГРАНО ВОЛЬНЫМИ АКТЕРАМИ

„!МИСТЕРИЯ БУФФ!"

ГЕРОИЧЕСКОЕ, ЭПИЧЕСКОЕ и САТИРИЧЕСКОЕ
ИЗОБРАЖЕНИЕ НАШЕЙ ЭПОХИ

Figure 6. Poster for Meyerhold's production of *Mystery-Bouffe*, 1918 (Mikhail German, ed., *Serdtsem slushaia revoliutsiiu. Iskusstvo pervykh let oktiabria*, Leningrad, 1980).

The world of *Mystery-Bouffe* was remarkable for its incapacity for compromise: the very idea had strongly negative connotations for the poet and his contemporaries. On the stage, no meeting of worlds was possible. The revolutionary city was divided into two camps, workers and nonworkers, locked in a territorial struggle. Conflict—the revolution—was a meeting of opposites that could not end in a truce. Mayakovsky did not complicate the struggle by depicting more than a single interest in each camp. To subjugate the proletariat, the bourgeoisie elects itself a tsar; the tsar then declares his sole right to all food. But when the bourgeoisie finds itself hungry, it adopts democratic principles and declares a republic. This makes no difference to the workers; the republic is "the same old tsar, just with a hundred mouths" (p. 204).

When it is festivalized, revolution shuns gradual change for apocalyptic suddenness. Apocalyptic thought flourishes when the gap between two worlds seems unbreachable. Apocalypse is a radical solution, a one-time threshold that closes a gap by eliminating one side of it. It is time compressed to fusion: "the beginning and the end" of the Book of Revelation. Such revolutions are terrible to live through, but they can be aesthetically satisfying, which might explain the attraction felt by artists as diverse as Blok, Bely, Meyerhold, and Mayakovsky.[62]

The model's second attraction was its strongly utopian element. Apocalypse and utopia, like carnival and mystery, work best together. Apocalypse precedes utopia. The clash of worlds leads to the elimination of one, followed by the harmonic reign of utopia. An apocalypse is the "no time" that precedes "all time"; utopia is the "no-where" that is everywhere. *Mystery-Bouffe*'s Promised Land is the final sum of the apocalyptic equation; it is Mayakovsky's image of the city of socialism.

The characters of *Mystery-Bouffe*—the citizens of the two cities—were imported from festival theater, with a strong dose of the fairground. Popular theater—for example, the Petrushka puppet theater or the *Tsar Maximilian* play—incorporated little character development; the introductory epigram determined a character's actions through the entire play. In *Mystery-Bouffe* the clean are portrayed in the mocking tones of carnival, with a particular flair for exaggerated detail: the nose ring of the Abyssinian negus or the top-hat of the Frenchman (see Figure 7).[63] Entrances of the clean are marked by Petrushka-like self-introductions, and national conflicts are reduced to slapstick brawls.[64] Performance style was developed from the prewar work of Meyerhold and Evreinov, with new additions taken directly from the popular theater and the circus. In the future, Meyerhold would even invite a clown, Vitaly Lazarenko, to play a demon in the inferno scene. The unclean were depicted in the monumental tones of the mystery play.[65] They performed collectively, as a chorus, much of the time, and their lines were read with a "firm, strong principle, heroic pathos, and plastic monumentality."[66] Costumes for the unclean repeated a pattern found in "Apotheosis of the Worker," V. V. Lebedev's street decoration for the holiday, and in Vladimir Kozlinsky's drawings to Mayakovsky's verse in a holiday pamphlet: simple lines, uniformity.[67]

Figure 7. Costume sketches by Mayakovsky for the "clean" and the "unclean," *Mystery-Bouffe*, 1918 (Mikhail German, ed., *Serdtsem slushaia revoliutsiiu. Iskusstvo pervykh let oktiabria*, Leningrad, 1980). Photos courtesy of Aurora Publishers.

The revolutionary city of Mayakovsky's play featured endless movement. It was an eternal threshold, and it required a stage space accommodating sudden, unexplained transitions. Unfortunately, Malevich's flat, static decor did not fit the bill.[68] Mayakovsky's own background sketches were a more apt illustration. They depicted the city as a hub; factories, railroads, apartments revolved around the fissionable center.[69] It was the modern city found in his prewar poetry—compact, dynamic, and discordant. Trams put the slums within a few minutes of the palace; neon lights shone on dreary streets.

Once again, festival theater provided the most appropriate model for *Mystery-Bouffe*, this time in the definition of space. The entrance to the Promised Land was depicted as simply as in a medieval mystery, by opening the gates and having the players step in; and Mayakovsky's entrance as A Simple Man used a circus trick: he flew onto the deck along a guy wire.[70] An ark-stage represented the revolutionary city. Boats have an ancient tradition as the symbolic vessels of threshold states. Noah's ark is an obvious model, but there were also Ulysses's ship in the *Odyssey,* Charon's ferry across the Styx, and the medieval Ship of Fools.

The ark-stage provided a graphical representation of revolution as threshold. It was divided into the deck, occupied by the clean, and the hold, where the unclean were banished. The two levels were connected by a trapdoor. When in the third act another set was introduced, the same spatial division was applied: on top was Heaven, below Hell, and in between a trapdoor. This trapdoor, fully motivated by the use of a ship's deck as the stage, traced its genealogy to mystery stages. Its forbears were the English pageant cart, used both as a stage and as a transport for mystery cycles, and the Russian *vertep* (crèche), an itinerant puppet booth featuring the Christmas story on a two-level stage: the Slaughter of the Innocents on top followed by comic interludes below. The trapdoor was suggested by Alekseev-Iakovlev, who showed Mayakovsky the model of a *balagan* hell-mouth when he was first planning *Mystery-Bouffe*.[71]

Drawing on futurism and carnival theater, Mayakovsky provided a rousing version of the old regime's fall; but to satisfy the duality of festivity, and to offer a compelling vision of the future, he had to speak of what lay beyond the threshold. The apocalyptic equation, like the Revolution itself, begged for a utopian solution. Here too, Mayakovsky profited from Blok's experimentation. Blok's response to the Revolution, *The Twelve* (1918), was a poem of chaos: figures emerge from a

Petersburg blizzard and are swallowed again as the violence of revolution plays itself out. Blok looked to the carnival theater—the puppet booth—for his central character, Petrukha (Petka), and his misadventures resembled those in a *balagan* melodrama.[72] At the poem's conclusion a sudden clearing in the whirl of snow gives a glimpse of the potential future: Christ, clad in white with a crown of red roses standing out against the blizzard, leads the twelve.

The final act of *Mystery-Bouffe* was set in the Promised Land—beyond Hell, beyond even Heaven—a utopia in which the curses of modern life, differentiation and alienation, were absent. Like Blok, Mayakovsky looked to Christianity, particularly the poetic Christianity of Ivanov, for his image of utopia. If the city was socialist, it was only because it lacked individuality. The social order's greatest virtue was a lack of conflict between things and people. Mayakovsky looked back for his embodiment of the future: the Simple Man, the savior come to lead the final revolution, was none other than a new Christ, complete with a "new Sermon on the Mount":

> In my paradise, halls are packed with furniture,
> the rooms fashionable with electrical services.
> There the sun plays such tricks
> that each step sinks in a sea of sunlight.
> Here the age pores over the gardener's experience—
> flooring of glass, manure embankment,
> and from roots of dill
> pineapples grow six times yearly.[73]

Mayakovsky's progress from revolution to socialism reversed the course of symbolist history; a layered grotesque gave way to a world of oneness. His festival drama, one of the first in revolutionary Russia, ended aptly with a festival of the new city; yet it was celebrated as Ivanov (and Rousseau before him) might have wished, with a hymn and a choral dance. Festivity and its many forms had given Mayakovsky a model for his play of revolution; his collaboration with Meyerhold familiarized him with the experiments of his symbolist predecessors. The combination made for a convincing story of revolution that would last many years in Soviet culture.

THREE

The Politics of Meaning and Style

> *When any one of these pantomimic gentlemen, who are so clever that they can imitate anything, comes to us, and makes a proposal to exhibit himself and his art, we will fall down and worship him as a sweet and holy and wonderful being; but we will also inform him that in our State such as he are not permitted to exist; the law will not allow them. And so when we have anointed him with myrrh, and set a garland of wool upon his head, we will send him away to another city.*
>
> Plato, *The Republic*

Rejecting the politics of the past was easier than rejecting its culture. Many older Bolsheviks, like Lenin and Lunacharsky, saw the cultural legacy as a resource and advocated saving whatever could serve the new order. Progressive culture could be salvaged and reactionary culture discarded. The more radical Proletkultists and futurists, on the contrary, saw the past as dead weight. They considered little worth saving; and even the bits of ore in the dross needed reworking. Neither side of the debate seemed to understand the dilemma fully. Lenin saw the foolishness of radical rhetoric, yet believed naively that the past could be exploited selectively. His wish to preserve the Bolshoi Theater and Tchaikovsky's operas rested on the assumption that a socialist environment would dissolve their old-regime associations. Radicals perceived the sticky web of associations that could entangle a socialist culture built on tradition, but they could not create culture in a vacuum.

THE POLITICS OF MEANING AND STYLE 73

Even developing partisan symbols was enormously complex. The Bolsheviks came to power with few symbols of their own. They were not the only revolutionaries in Russia (though they were perhaps the most ardent), and they shared prominent symbols with other parties. The songs, colors, and heroes now associated with the October Revolution were not always exclusively Bolshevik. Though the creation of the hammer and sickle emblem in early 1918 signaled a start, the inadequacy of Bolshevik iconography caused complications in the two major festivals of 1918, May Day and the November 7 anniversary celebration.

Festivals test a symbol more rigorously than other environments do. An emblem sewn on a shirt or decorating a pamphlet lies in a congenial context that supports and complements its message. Symbols displayed in a public festival must compete for attention, and they must drive home their message through a stew of competing symbols and hostile interpretations. The cultural heritage was particularly formidable during festivals, when it was embodied by the city itself. The language and medium of a festival is the city, its people, streets, and buildings. In other instances when the cultural past proved recalcitrant, the revolutionaries dealt with it summarily: paintings were put in the basement, musical scores in the archives, books on the back shelves of the library; but streets and buildings could not be hidden.

The desire of festival planners to celebrate the Revolution in harmonious style was often frustrated by the cities themselves, particularly by Petrograd, the former imperial capital. Petrograd's ceremonial center was dominated by the neoclassicism of later Romanov buildings. In an attempt to overcome the vestiges of autocracy, statues of the tsar, some of which were already slated for removal, were covered with strips of red material.[1] The center of Uprising Square (previously Znamenskaia Square) was occupied by Pavel Trubetskoi's fine equestrian monument to Alexander III. But any tsarist monument was considered an embarrassment, no matter how artistic; so a massive triumphal arch of planks was put over it for the November 7 celebration. On another occasion a tribune resembling a medieval keep was built.

Autocracy's symbols could be concealed or excised, but neoclassicism was a more lasting influence. Faced with a cutback of funds, organizers of the May Day 1918 demonstration in Petrograd settled for a single centerpiece, a float "modeled on a Roman float with a statue of the goddess Freedom in a white tunic, a torch in her upraised hand, standing against a background of the slogan 'Having proudly made it through the centuries of oppression, we celebrate the worldwide May holiday.' "² On a smaller float, labor was depicted allegorically by "the figure of a woman dressed in a Greek tunic with a torch in her right hand.... Sometimes [in later years] the figure of Lady Liberty [*zhenshchina svoboda*] was somewhat altered in the new spirit, receiving the dress of a female peasant or worker."³ Neoclassicism also impinged on the emblems of revolution: in a contest for the Russian Republic's new monetary seal, Sergei Konenkov depicted a satyr and bacchante. The trend continued up to the November anniversary. There were "a depiction of a worker leaping onto a winged horse (the classical Pegasus), angels blowing their trumpets, classical heroes wreathed in laurel, or warriors in helmets and with swords, . . . triumphal arches with columns, sacrificial altars and towers, . . . coats of arms with complete heraldic detail—crests, mantles, and so forth."⁴ Tsarist iconography also was apparent: the Legend of St. George was used to depict the Revolution as a "handsome young folk hero with broken chains and a red banner in his hand, liberating a naked woman (Russia), at whose feet a dragon with a crown on its head (tsarism) was coiled."⁵

Although these were festivals of revolution, expressing themes of conflict or disorder led to a certain difficulty: here again the cities were not inclined to cooperate. Few seemed to notice the incongruity; Saratov artists blithely draped the triumphal arches and obelisks erected by the old regime in garlands and bedecked them with emblems of labor.⁶ In Petrograd, a city of rigid order and imperial grandeur, the combination jarred some observers. Because decorations harmonized with the city's architecture, the anniversary of the Revolution was not terribly revolutionary. For November 7 Dobuzhinsky decorated the Petrograd Admiralty and surrounding square, which were adjacent to the Winter Palace in the center of town. The square had been the site of popular carnivals in the late nineteenth century, but Dobuzhinsky preferred the building's neoclassical architecture for inspiration. Staying within the facade's stylistic limits, he draped the cornices with red flags and garlands. Naval code was used as a motif, including a ship decorated with sea horses and an emblem of the Russian Republic. Obelisks and spheres were placed on the Admiralty and decorated with a ribbon bearing the signs of the zodiac.⁷ Dobuzhinsky's work was a stylization of eighteenth-century ceremonial art. Punin observed:

The October festivities differed little from what the worldwide bourgeoisie did in its own time. The same streets decorated with material, wooden arches, garlands, electric and even just colored lanterns, somehow dully reminiscent of the notorious "days of the tsars," with their gaslit designs and stars. . . . This happened only because the organizers themselves did not think much about the idea of "celebration" and performed their assignment offhandedly, "with whatever fits." For the foundation of their plan they took the alien and dead idea of "decoration." They found it necessary to decorate the old city and old, primarily "bourgeois" streets.[8]

Yet there were possibilities. Moscow was a city of many architectural styles, which offered artists a wealth of options. The Moscow decorations for May Day, under the direction of the Moscow Commission, matched the city's style without succumbing to its spirit.[9] The Vesnin brothers' work on Red Square and the area surrounding the Kremlin created an appropriate ceremonial center, both solemn and brash. The focus was the Red Square reviewing stand, "a monumental three-tiered tribunal with an enormous wreath of fir branches. . . . Bright purple banners and panels clashed with black ribbons of mourning."[10]

The Conversion of Symbols

Festivals were a recollection of the past; but to avoid ensnaring the new culture in the old, the past had to be remembered selectively. Such was the radicals' compromise: the artistic heritage could be exploited, but only on the terms of the present. The issue was not just theoretical, at least not in the theater, where a dearth of new plays brought proletarian culture to a halt. Blok proposed searching the censors' archives for quality plays suppressed by the tsarist bureaucracy; but he found to his dismay that there were none.[11] Kerzhentsev proposed tackling two problems at once by rewriting the classics to fit contemporary needs.

The present day increasingly forces us to realize that we still have no new repertory, that the creation of plays, if only by reworking and adjusting them, is essential.[12]

Some fine plays have become absolutely unacceptable, for instance, because of their reactionary (by today's standards) tendencies. Why not change the authors' intentions and give the plays meanings that will find resonance with the contemporary audience?[13]

The problem of the new culture could be solved for the time being by the old, by taking the classics and resetting them in a revolutionary context.

Proletkult was a leader in bringing these remakes, or *peredelki,* to the stage. Ivan Krylov's fable *The Quartet* was remade by the Moscow Proletkult into *A Conference of the Entente* on May Day 1919; "the monkey . . . [became] a Frenchman; the goat was an American; the bear an Englishman; and the ass, an Italian. Instead of Krylov's sparrow [the *raissoneur*] there was a worker with a hammer who dispersed the foul musicians whose 'scraping and strumming' had made the whole world sick. Another Krylov fable, *The Slaughter of the Beasts,* was restaged as a satire about priests, capitalists, policemen, 'high-society' ladies, and their associates."[14] *Peredelki* could be quite topical. Mikhail Glinka's *Ivan Susanin (A Life for the Tsar)* was reset from the Time of Troubles to the 1920 Polish-Russian War, with its original patriotic sentiments unaltered.[15] And five years later, on May Day 1925, the Maly Opera would perform Giacomo Puccini's *La Tosca* as *The Struggle for the Commune*.[16]

Clearly, remakes could be overdone, but the method also brought positive results. Meyerhold's third-anniversary (November 7, 1920) production of Verhaeren's *Les aubes,* in which fraternizing at the front leads to a revolution (the revolution was Meyerhold's addition), was striking and original. On May Day 1919 in Kiev, Konstantin Mardzhanov, one of prewar Petrograd's leading directors, produced Lope de Vega's *Fuente ovejuna* as a revolutionary spectacle.[17] Scenes of the royal court (which were abbreviated) and the peasant village were placed on opposite sides of the stage and contrasted by acting style and lighting. As Evreinov had done in the Ancient Theater, Mardzhanov stressed the theme of popular struggle against oppression. The king and queen were, in the revolutionary version, identified as the oppressors. The restaged ending of the drama included a rebellion and victory; and soldiers present at the premiere marched straight from the theater to the front.

Nor was music neglected by the new order. On November 7, 1918, at the Workers' Soviet Opera (the former Zimin Theater), Theodore Komissarzhevsky transferred the setting of Beethoven's *Lenore*[18] from Spain to revolutionary France; cuts were made, revolutionary speeches added, and the whole thing was renamed *Liberation*.[19] A piece of music could be given new meaning simply by changing its context. Scriabin, although he had died in 1915 and was never associated with the Bolsheviks, was enjoying great popularity in 1918. His symphonic poem *Prometheus* (a figure dear to revolutionaries) was performed in the Bolshoi, with a curtain by the artist Aristarkh Lentulov that provided a visual complement to the music.[20] The Bolshoi, which had not welcomed Bolshevik management, was trying to catch up on some of the new themes invading Russian theaters that year. The Scriabin performance was only part of an evening "unified by the theme of rebellion, of the people rising up in the name of reason, light, and liberty."[21] It was followed by the Veche (Popular Assembly) scene of Nikolai Rimsky-Korsakov's *The Maid of Pskov*, and the last piece of the evening was Aleksandr Gorsky's ballet *Stenka Razin*.

For artists searching the past for a myth of popular rebellion to supplement the precursors of the Revolution, the seventeenth-century Cossack and peasant revolt led by Razin seemed suitable. It had several advantages. Razin's biography was known sketchily by most Russians. There were songs, dramatic games, poems, and tales about the robber; in fact, the first Russian movie production (1908) was about Razin. Certain symbols were universally familiar: the long boat and the Volga river, which represented the brigand community and its freedom-loving ways, and the captive princess who captured Razin's heart and almost lured him from his comrades.

This brigand already had a history as a revolutionary icon. Socialists had tried to adopt him, but his spirit was probably closer to anarchism. Mikhail Bakunin (Marx's rival in the First International) had seen Razin's uprising as a prototype of his own rebellion: unfettered, rising from the depths of the people, destructive, perhaps also aimless.[22] The anarchistic sailors of Kronstadt even used a song from the popular Razin lore, with new words, as their battle cry in 1917:

From the island-fortress Kronstadt,
To the expanses of the Neva,
A fleet of vessels sails outward—
The Bolsheviks sit at their prow.[23]

Bolsheviks had further reasons for using the Razin legend. Marxist tradition held the peasantry in low regard, but the Bolsheviks found themselves ruling a predominantly peasant nation and maintaining an uncomfortable alliance with the countryside. An attempt was made to absorb the Cossack rebellions that had shaken the old order into the genealogy of the Bolsheviks (who had, after all, done the same). Lenin made the connection nicely on May Day 1919, speaking from Lobnoe Mesto—the site of Razin's execution—at the dedication of his monument: "This monument represents one of the representatives of the rebellious peasantry. Here he laid his head down in the struggle for freedom. Russian revolutionaries made many such sacrifices in the struggle with capital. The best of the proletariat and peasantry perished, fighters for freedom, but not the sort of freedom proposed by capital, a freedom with banks, with private factories, with speculation."[24]

Razin was prominent in the November 7, 1918, celebration even though the lore, which embodied the peculiarly Russian notion of freedom (*volia*) that cherished unfettered will, was scarcely the stuff of Bolshevism. Nevertheless, party propagandists and sympathizers used Razin to represent the revolution's utopian aims: freedom, equality, brotherly love.

Not all versions of the Razin legend were necessarily like Lenin's: artists had their own interpretations. Kuznetsov did a large panel for the Maly Theater in Moscow under the curious title *Stepan Razin on the River Beats Back the Advance of Counterrevolution*.[25] Kuzma Petrov-Vodkin's panel on Petrograd's Theater Square, *Stepan Razin*, showed a benign soul, tall and erect—less a Cossack than a peasant Christ with his disciples.[26]

Perhaps the most curious and compelling Razin—one antithetical to Lenin's—was found in a verse play by the futurist poet Vasily Kamensky, *Stenka Razin—Heart of the People*.[27] Kamensky's image of Razin, which he had created long before the Revolution,[28] was the truncated Razin who would remain popular throughout the war: an elemental force dedicated to the good of the people; a "revolutionary before the proper time" to quote Lunacharsky's paraphrase of Hegel. Razin was naturally destructive, but destructive in a good way, breaking down social obstructions that should not have been there in the first place. It was an optimistic image patched together from a range of sources. Folk songs were a strong influence; futurism, in the rural variety peculiar to Russia, was felt in the "transrational" exclamations; the martial camaraderie celebrated by Denis Davydov returned to Russian poetry after a century's absence; and also present was an ideal of social harmony that appealed to socialists and symbolists alike:

> There'll come the day—and the gates will open
> Each—for free guests
> So that in life any trouble
> Will be equal for every venture.
> There'll come the day—and forever friends
> Will spin roundabout in a choral circle
> The poor man—and merchants—and princes.[29]

This was Razin as Rousseau might have liked him, a utopian Razin. There was in fact a strong utopian element to the folk legends of brigandry: after the nobility were burned out of their manor houses, a more just popular order would reign in the countryside.

Russian popular culture had in general a rich vein of utopianism,[30] yet with notable exceptions, the utopian visions present in 1918 festivals were drawn from other sources. Foremost was Christianity, which Blok and Mayakovsky used so effectively: the Revolution in Russia was analogous to the advent of Christ. Lunacharsky had given this imagery a broad sanction. In his *Religion and Socialism*,[31] he reiterated the by-then traditional claim of socialism to the spiritual heritage of Athens and early Christianity. Revolutionary culture took over Christianity's language of exaltation and spiritual ascent. Old symbols were placed in a new cultural context (revolution) that gave them new meaning. In 1918 a decorative panel on the Moscow headquarters of Narkompros depicted a worker and peasant in a style familiar from icons of Cyril and Methodius, the Byzantine missionaries to Slavdom; Petrov-Vodkin's *1918 in Petrograd* (1920) depicted a simple Russian girl standing against the background of Petrograd with her child in her arms as a Madonna and Child.[32]

Christianity was not the only source of a utopian vision. In Vladimir Kirillov's "May Day Hymn" (1918)—the first occasional verse for a Soviet holiday—the language of popular liberation merged with the May celebration's pagan roots (perhaps Rousseau would have been pleased).

> Glorify May Day in all of its greatness,
> The holiday of Labor and the dropping of chains.
> Glorify May Day in all of its greatness.
> The holiday of freedom, and flowers and spring.
> Sisters get into your wedding dresses,
> Cover the pathways with garlands of rose,
> Brothers, open your arms to another's embraces.
> The years of our suffering and tears are all gone.[33]

It sometimes seemed that symbols and the traditions attached to them exerted a stronger influence on the festival than the festival exerted on the symbols. May Day had always competed with the Orthodox Easter, which fell on April 28 in 1918. Another poem written for the holiday suggests how strong the crossover could be:

> Arise, O mighty Russia!
> Come down, Crucified, from the cross!
> The element of liberty is upon us,
> Our chains are smashed forever more![34]

In fact, even the banners (*khorugvi*) that bore images of Marx, Engels, and Lenin in the May Day demonstration were a direct borrowing from traditional Easter processions.[35]

Proletkultists most frequently resorted to the utopian symbols of religion. Their Christianity was not always borrowed directly but obliquely through Wagner and the symbolists. Part of the cultural redefinition provoked by the Revolution was that responsibilities that had traditionally belonged to high culture were assumed by new poets and playwrights, of whom the Proletkultists were representative. These responsibilities included speaking to and for the conscience of the nation, giving the epoch historical definition, setting a social agenda—all very abstract tasks, but ones that could not be accomplished fully by popular traditions. The last artists to accept and perform these duties had been symbolists; and when proletarians assumed the responsibility, they leaned on symbolists for experience and an idiom. The Russian artist who wishes to speak for the nation assumes a certain tone of voice and a certain style. In symbolist times the tone was often apocalyptic.

On May Day 1919, the Petrograd Proletkult Studio presented *The Legend of the Communard*, which eventually ran for over 200 shows. The play was written by Petr Kozlov, a peasant soldier who presented himself as a *samouchka*, or self-taught artist. Before the Revolution, Kozlov had written a decadent-symbolist mystery entitled *Above Life*.[36] Clearly, Kozlov's self-education had included some Wagner; in a scornful review, Viktor Shklovsky called *Legend* "Wagner without the music" ("*Vagner, vospriniatyi po libretto*").[37]

In the first scene the Communard, whose coming has been prophesied by a Wise Man (arrayed in astrological emblems), is created; his birth occurs in a dark Wagnerian forest.[38] Bent over a fire, the Son of the Sun and the Son of the Earth (the latter is dressed, like Tarzan, in a leopard skin) forge the Communard's heart, which springs to life at sunrise. Meanwhile various evil things, including a Vampire, lurk in the shadows and gnash their teeth. The Communard reflects a familiar ideal: he is "a strong, handsome young man. In him are combined all the elements of the earth: wisdom, happiness, thought, earth, and sun. Long, curly black hair. His face reflects energy and will power, combining kindness and goodness. He is almost naked; only a belt with a symbolic hammer and sickle encircles his waist."[39] Sundry prophesies accompany the Communard's birth; and as he ventures into the world, the Wise Man presents him with a symbolic ring. In an abrupt and inexplicable shift, the second scene opens on a factory floor, where the proletariat is suffering and exploited. Manifold complaints, however, have not led to any rebellion; that initiative is left to the Communard, who appears to the workers in an upper window. Curiously, in this near-naked youth with the flowing black hair, the workers recognize someone "dressed just like us."[40]

The Revolution had brought *egalité* and *fraternité;* naturally leaders and followers would resemble one another. But "the Marxist's communism is not at all the same as the communism of a hick straight from the farm," as Mgebrov noted.[41] If a Russian worker could see himself reflected in long curly hair and a leopard skin, the mirror was less Bolshevik ideology than popular culture. There was, as one critic put it, a "petty bourgeois–peasant [!] element" in the culture, which expected revolution to arrive with a Savior: someone extraordinary, above the common crowd.[42] Religion offered a paradigm for such a historical event.

If the heroic and utopian traditions were Christian, symbols of struggle could also be drawn from the Covenant and Exodus. The fourth and final scene (there is no third scene) takes place in "a gloomy ravine. All around—rocks and the outcroppings of cliffs."[43] The resemblance to the Sinai was not accidental. The people have been liberated from the factory floor and led into the desert toward the Land of Freedom, but the hardships of the trek have disheartened them. A rebellion challenges the workers' leaders; they are accused, like Moses, of leading the people from well-fed slavery to the sure death of freedom. As the rebellion reaches a climax, the Communard again appears to the people and convinces them to continue their journey. They take only a few more steps when their new city—the socialist utopia—appears on the horizon. The play ends (like *Mystery-Bouffe*) with a Dance of Labor, performed in harmonic plastic movements: reaping grain, mowing hay, striking an anvil.

Meaning as Power

Artists could find icons of the Revolution in the past. Razin could become a Bolshevik, Christ a socialist. Borrowing and revamping old symbols were essential for establishing a new culture. The process has been given considerable and illuminating attention by historians of the French Revolution, who have gauged popular attitudes by the changing face of political icons such as Marianne, the female embodiment of France, and Hercules, the popular battler.[44] One aspect of the process has, I believe, been neglected: symbols are an instrument as well as a reflector of struggle. At any moment a symbol has a number of potential meanings; and which meaning a symbol gets is often a matter of political struggle. Symbols do not simply acquire meaning; meaning is given. It is not enough to assert that a political power expresses and defines itself with the historical figures it honors.[45] More emphasis should be put on how history is honored; power expresses itself not in how it defines itself by history but in how it redefines history according to itself. Memory is active and selective; it emphasizes what serves its purposes, rejects what does not. A sign and prerogative of political power is the cooptation of history; and an essential exercise in power is to establish oneself as a focus or center, a set of standards and symbols around which history must be arranged.

Early in 1918 the Bolsheviks, insecure in their power, attempted to create and disseminate their own version of the past with a government-sponsored "competition to produce designs of monuments intended to signalize the great days of the Russian Socialist Revolution."[46] Since only six months had passed since those "great days," such an attitude was hardly appropriate, and the plan might have been dismissed outright had it not originated at the top: Lenin had suggested it to Lunacharsky, who in his own words was "stunned and dazzled by the proposition. It was extraordinarily to my liking, and we set to its realization immediately."[47] Included were three undertakings: the removal of monuments raised to the tsars and their "servants"; the renaming of streets and squares; the creation of monuments to the forerunners and heroes of socialism. These three tasks suggested a strategy for creating a new culture. Tearing down the monuments of the old regime would remove its symbols from the Soviet city. Still, all of the national past could not be forgotten or jettisoned. Before a new culture could be created, the remaining elements of the old had to be redefined. In 1918 the monument plan was, for the most part, an effort to grapple with the past: new names were given to old symbols; monuments and symbols that could not be renamed were placed in a new context.

Quick progress was made on the first undertaking: work begun under the Provisional Government on the removal of tsarist emblems from public buildings was continued, and a monument to General Mikhail Skobelev was pulled down as part of the May Day festivities in Moscow. That autumn, monuments to Alexander II and Alexander III were also removed.[48] The constructive side of the project was not so quickly commenced. By August 1918 a long list of monuments had been drawn up,[49] and a most interesting list it was; not only were socialists such as Robert Owen, Jérôme Blanqui,[50] Marx, and Engels included, but historical "revolutionaries" such as Brutus, Razin, and another Cossack rebel, Ivan Bolotnikov, were honored. Most intriguing was the list of "cultural figures," an eclectic group: writers of socialist sympathies such as Verhaeren found themselves side by side with the likes of Fedor Tiutchev and Rimsky-Korsakov—unlikely champions of socialism.[51] The monument plan reached its apogee on the November 7 holiday with the unveiling of monuments in the center and outlying districts of Moscow and Petrograd. A representative of the party—in some cases Lenin himself—gave a speech at each unveiling, which then developed into a political rally.[52] As the original list presaged, the choice of subjects was eclectic: Marx, Engels, and Robespierre were honored, but so were such nonsocialist cultural figures as the poets Aleksei Koltsov and Ivan Nikitin.[53] Even Dostoevsky was honored, which might have surprised him had he lived to see the Revolution.

Symbols acquire meaning not only through their given properties but through their context. The very fact that a monument had been erected by the revolutionary regime and the subject commemorated suggested a new interpretation: the subject belonged to revolutionary history. For a Brutus or Razin this interpretation was feasible, but when the Bolsheviks claimed the Russian heritage (by honoring Tiutchev, for instance), it was not. To ensure that the desired aspect of each subject was memorialized, the unveiling speech set the tone, and an inscription, chosen from the subject's more progressive statements, was chiseled onto the pedestal. The Chernyshevsky monument, for instance, was graced with the quote: "Create the future, strive for it, work for it, and carry as much of it as you can into the present." The proper interpretation was thus engraved in stone for each viewer.

The monuments, born of symbolic confusion, were often ungainly, and popular understanding resisted the sponsors' interpretations.[54] Some, like the monuments to Robespierre and Volodarsky, were blown up by vandals. Marx himself seems to have suffered most, and that at the hands of his own admirers. One Moscow Marx was, for some reason, gilded; a Moscow statue of Marx and Engels was nicknamed both "Cyril and Methodius" and "the bearded bathers"; a Petrograd Marx, placed before Smolny Institute, was described as "a horrible statue, . . . thick and heavy, standing on a stout pedestal and holding an enormous top hat like the muzzle of an eighteen-inch gun behind him"; there was even a plan for a "Karl Marx, standing on four elephants."55 His plight drew embarrassing attention:

> Karl Marx has fled the town of Penza.
> Actually, it wasn't Marx but his recently erected monument.
> Contradictory rumors about the causes of his mysterious disappearance are circulating about the city.
> Some say that his horse was seized during the recent mobilization, and Marx refused to continue on foot.
> Others . . . claim he went looking for a more appropriate site than Penza. He's decided to tour the cities of the Russian Republic, knowing that every city would be flattered to have such a monument but not every city could afford such a luxury. Marx—the monument—will arrive in some city, stand on the square for several days, and then leave for the next city.56

The Lenin plan confronted the old dilemma of how a revolution should celebrate itself by straddling the fence between the permanent and the revolutionary. The two involve contradictory senses of time: the permanent, a sense of eternity in which concrete moments disappear; the revolutionary, a momentary, dynamic present. Lenin seems to have sensed the conflict and suggested naming the plan "monumental propaganda," satisfying both eternal values and the demands of the moment. If this term was not sufficiently unclear, he added, "For the time being I'm not thinking about eternity or even duration."57 The weather sensed his ambivalence; most of the monuments, cast in gypsum, melted away in the first rain.

Lenin was not alone in his confusion; it represented utopian longings that were strongest when the struggle was fiercest. The idea had a precedent in the revolutionary tradition: Lenin himself mentioned Campanella and his plan to cover the walls of the City of the Sun with edifying frescoes.58 The plan would also have been familiar to the residents of Utopia, who "put up statues in the market-place of people who've distinguished themselves by outstanding services to the community, partly to commemorate their achievements, and partly to spur on future generations to greater efforts, by reminding them of the glory of their ancestors."59 A more tangible influence was the efforts of French artists like David (*Oath of the Tennis Court*) to memorialize their revolution.60

The oddities of the Lenin plan should not eclipse an important point: the Bolsheviks saw festivals as a source of legitimacy. They could rewrite the past to project their presence back onto it, to include themselves in Eliade's cosmic history. Monuments have great power to alter the structure of time, a task dear to revolutionaries from Robespierre to Lenin. Revolutionaries, in fact, have often used their newfound power to legislate time. One of the Bolsheviks' first legislative acts, passed on January 23 (February 5), 1918, was to switch from the Julian calendar of the Russian Orthodox church to the Gregorian calendar used in the West. Celebrations of the Romanov dynasty were annulled, but as a concession to the religious feelings of the populace ecclesiastical holidays were retained. There were clear political consequences to the calendar changes—church rites no longer had legal authority[61]—yet it is also true that the calendar change was long overdue.

A May 12 decree published in *Izvestiia* introducing a new schedule of holidays was close to the radical legislation of revolutionary France. In the brief life of the French Revolution, profound changes were made in the measurement of space, as were equally profound, albeit temporary, changes in the measurement of time. The first and most controversial change was the conversion to metric measurement; its success is shown by the fact that nobody today remembers that it was first legalized by the Convention. Even fewer remember that this wise decision was followed by the legislation of time in an equally logical manner. The year was divided into twelve months of thirty days each, and the seven-day week of Christianity was replaced by a metric ten days. A new era was declared, its advent being the establishment of the Republic.[62] Bolsheviks, fortunately, were less radical and more generous. The year 1917 remained 1917, and where French workers had exchanged one day off in seven for one in ten, the Russians gained a few holidays: January 1 (New Year's Day), January 22 (Bloody Sunday), March 12 (Overthrow of the Autocracy), March 18 (Paris Commune Day), May 1, and November 7 (the anniversary of the Bolshevik takeover in the new style).[63]

The Bolsheviks also attempted to claim urban space as their own; streets and squares were renamed during the anniversary celebration. Most of the new names were appropriate in a city that had just overthrown the tsar: Palace Square was renamed Uritsky Square after the recently slain Chekist; Nevsky Prospect became the Prospect of October 25; Palace Bridge became Republican Bridge. Not only central points were changed: Big and Little Gentry Streets became the First and Second Streets of the Rural Poor; and Guardian Street became Self-Governing Street.[64] The plan could be bold and aggressive, as when the Iberian Chapel, one of Russia's most sacred shrines, had a plaque reading "Religion is the opium of the people" attached to it for the November 1918 celebration.[65]

Although the Iberian Chapel plaque was a strong measure, it would be an overstatement to say that the Bolsheviks, having seized political control, could manipulate symbols at will. Symbols do not always succumb to redefinition; nor can the redefiner assume that the new definition will be accepted. Pilgrims continued to stream into the Iberian Chapel until Stalin leveled it in the 1930s; and unpredictable symbols upset festivals from the very start.

Symbols sometimes gave notice that they were real things, not to be manipulated freely. Airplanes were considered an outstanding emblem of modern science, which Bolsheviks liked to think was on their side. Moscow artists, including Vladimir Tatlin and Kuznetsov, proposed decorating fifteen airplanes, which would perform aerial stunts over Khodynka Field.[66] The intractability of the symbol, however, was discovered in Petrograd, where a plane hired to fly over the celebration crashed in the center of town, killing the pilot and embarrassing the government.[67] Monuments were also unreliable. The dangers of appropriating national or folk heroes into the revolutionary pantheon were made plain at the monument to Taras Shevchenko (see Figure 8), the Ukrainian poet who "with his peasant instinct understood the idea of the Internationale long before its dissemination," when a delegation from the Ukrainian consulate offered a wreath in the name of Hetman Pavel Skoropadsky, head of the nationalist and anti-Bolshevik government.[68]

Perhaps most dangerous in the symbolic game was the outright negation or desecration of an opposing symbol. The Kremlin, which had become the center of Bolshevik power, also had a long history as the symbolic center of the Russian autocracy and Orthodox Church. Iakov Sverdlov ordered the Kremlin commandant to decorate its walls with Soviet symbols and gave him an unlimited budget for the task. On the Troitsky Tower an icon, one of the more sacred of Orthodoxy, was covered by a large panel of a hero in red, flying over the earth.[69] An overwhelmingly religious crowd was offended, and when the panel was blown down by the wind, revealing the icon, rumors of a divine portent spread through Red Square. In the end, the Latvian Riflemen were called in to quell a riot.[70]

May Day 1918: The Struggle for Meaning

The sponsors of most Bolshevik festivals in 1918 saw them as educational events, which would instill in the people the new

Figure 8. Monument to Taras Shevchenko, Moscow, built as part of Lenin's monument plan (Mikhail German, ed., *Serdtsem slushaia revoliutsiiu. Iskusstvo pervykh let oktiabria,* Leningrad, 1980).

ideology and unite them in the revolutionary cause. In this sense, the Bolsheviks agreed with many modern commentators, who have seen festivals as a prime instrument of socialization into the Soviet system of values.[71] One must beware, however: intention is not execution. Artists commissioned to create festivals often thought differently from their sponsors; symbols, which have histories of their own, were sometimes interpreted differently from the way the makers intended. And, finally, sponsors were not of one mind; as we have seen, there were different opinions and traditions as to how a revolution should be celebrated.

The festive tradition itself was ambiguous, and preparations for the May Day celebration of 1918 sparked conflicts between incompatible notions and hostile factions. To Bolsheviks forged by a decade of political struggle, May Day was a weapon. In prerevolutionary times it was a rare occasion for street gatherings; the demonstrations were actually revolutions in miniature. But another tradition, begun by Wagner, saw festivity as an analog of socialism, a temporary utopia. This abstruse theoretical dispute—what function should a workers' demonstration have when workers control the state—became an acute dilemma with the establishment of a workers' state.

In a pamphlet released for the 1917 observance, Bogdanov wrote, "The May Day holiday is organized to demonstrate . . . that the proletariat is an army of labor in constant battle with capital."[72] Although this goal remained, May Day 1918, coming after the October Revolution, also gave the Russian proletariat reason to celebrate. May Day had been a holiday of struggle against the existing order; and now that workers were the existing order, something would have to change. The holiday could either celebrate what was or continue the struggle for what would be.

Lunacharsky tried to bypass the problem entirely by asking, "But isn't the very idea intoxicating that the state, up 'til now our worst enemy, is now ours and celebrates May Day as its own greatest holiday?"[73] Yet many would have answered with a flat no because the holiday was also a show of power. Before the Revolution, the May Day demonstration had represented the underclass; now it stood for the state, not only as a symbol of power but as power itself. It was a test of the ability to organize the people. Resurgent opposition groups like the Mensheviks, the Special Assembly of Petrograd Factory and Plant Representatives, the Church, and even the anarchists called for a boycott of May Day.[74]

Grigory Zinoviev threatened to "crush the boycott in the most decisive manner,"[75] yet for a celebration with so much at stake, organization was sloppy—a mistake the Bolsheviks would not repeat in the future. By spring 1918, the Revolution was in crisis, and it was only in mid-April, two weeks before the event, that the Petrograd party committee headed by Zinoviev decreed that the holiday should be celebrated at all and that the Petrograd Soviet should assume responsibility for the arrangements. The soviet assigned direction of the festival to several groups with little in common. Scholars to this day are not sure who did the actual organizing—and nobody seems to have known in 1918. Reports indicate several possibilities: that the organizers were local labor unions and the Petrograd section of Narkompros; that the soviet took sole responsibility, its efforts directed by a special committee under the leadership of Andreeva; and that celebrations were directed by the Central Organizing Committee, chaired by a certain Antselovich, and the Commission for Decorating the City, both created jointly by the municipal soviet and IZO (the national arts section of Narkompros).[76] The report on this combined effort also states that the groups met in the Smolny Institute and Winter Palace, respectively, which would have made coordination difficult: the two headquarters were located on different sides of a city where communications were notoriously unreliable. Even Proletkult tried to infiltrate and take over the Central Organizing Committee.[77] It is clear enough, though, that organizational lines were not explicit; in fact, the director of the festival's Arts Section, Iakhmanov, ultimately refused all responsibility.[78] Nevertheless, disorganization, a flaw by political standards, allowed for a broad array of styles that makes the festival rich and interesting to our time.

The central newspapers, *Pravda* and *Izvestiia* in Moscow and *Severnaia Kommuna* (*Northern Commune*) in Petrograd, were charged with publicity for the event, which they produced in a format that became the subsequent standard. Several days beforehand, official May Day slogans, approved by the municipal party committee, were published, as were march routes, which went through every city district. Pages were filled with recollections of bygone days, when May Day was not celebrated openly. The official papers failed to mention the decorations, as if such efforts were alien to a solemn affair. Should the solemn air, however, have concealed the day's triumphant essence, the April 30 headline of *Pravda* declared May Day "a workers' holiday, the holiday of the victory of socialism." If it is true that a party in opposition is concerned with the downfall of the old and that a party in confident power is concerned with the construction of the new, then surely triumph was reflected in the slogans of the day: of eighteen total, fifteen were of the "Long live . . ." variety, while a paltry three proclaimed "Down with. . . ." Obviously, no mention was made of the boycott.

Stylistic multiplicity, political rivalry, poor organization, and Bolshevik ambivalence complicated May Day 1918. The diverse meanings acquired by a single symbol in a single festival—like the panel erected on the Kremlin tower—showed a lack of consensus. Symbols acquire meaning within a context, an interpretative framework: the events they are associated with, the system of ideas they are placed in, the habits of observation that bring some facets into focus and shut others out. The ways that a culture can give meaning to latent signs—at all times dynamic and complex—become terribly tangled in times of revolution. Language itself drifts from its mooring even in a stable culture, and words take on many meanings. Interpretation becomes problematic; one can never be sure that a statement is interpreted according to its design. The act of making a statement assumes that speaker and interpreter can find among many strands of culture a common interpretive framework—and that they wish to.

A competition of contexts can enrich a language and make it flexible in times of change, but if there are too many meanings available, the commonality necessary for communication is lost. The alternative is to assign meaning arbitrarily, by fiat. This is meaning created not by the framework but by the center. For this process to take place, however, there must be a commonly accepted, defining center. On May Day 1918, the Bolsheviks could not even create a unified organization or style, and to speak of a defining center would be premature. They did not yet occupy the central position that permits the creation of meaning: they did not have the power or legitimacy.

To speak of a single meaning in 1918 would be simplistic. It is wiser to find the festival's potential meanings and watch the outcome. The contest for meaning demonstrated how interpretation can be an exercise in power. The Bolsheviks and their opponents, who still controlled party newspapers, had considerable interpretative latitude.[79] Each reporter tried to place the festival in an advantageous context. May Day was, as it had been originally, a day of struggle: to the Bolsheviks, it was a struggle for the new society; to the opposition, against the existing regime. The Bolsheviks called for a demonstration, while opposition leaders called for a counter-demonstration: to the naive observer, both look like a march through the city streets. But when rank-and-file members of opposition parties voted to skip the march altogether, the Bolsheviks claimed they were rejecting the counter-demonstration, while the opposition claimed they were avoiding the demonstration. Now, both sides of the debate were faced not with a city of full streets waiting for interpretation, but with empty streets; and at this time the opposition strategically called for a boycott.

The May Day demonstration drew moderate gatherings: although the streets were decorated gaily and filled with marchers, the crowds predicted by the Bolsheviks failed to materialize. Most embarrassing was the absence of workers from the Obukhov and Putilov factories, strongholds of Bolshevik support.[80] Though sheer weariness was a likely cause, people had good reason to honor the boycott. Support for the Bolsheviks was lagging because of failures in the agricultural and industrial economies, the introduction of radical socialist policies, and the Brest Litovsk peace, among other reasons. Nevertheless, there was interpretative latitude. True, the workers did not march in large numbers; and the city was not entirely red. Yet city walls were covered with red banners and posters, and the streets abandoned by workers were filled—mostly by soldiers and by clerks dependent on the Bolsheviks for their jobs.

Given a festival to interpret, the newspapers could provide an acceptable meaning. *Izvestiia* boasted of the fine weather and defended the workers' right to celebrate—neither of which anyone contested. *Pravda* admitted some disappointment but drowned the admission in a sea of enthusiasm. *Krasnaia gazeta* (*Red Journal*) took the easy route, adding a zero to some attendance figures.[81] The Bolshevik press called the festival a success; the opposition pointed out that the marchers were soldiers and claimed the Bolsheviks had received no support from the workers. The Bolsheviks said the soldiers were the workers . . . and so on.

Published pictures illustrate—graphically—how a proper framework could create the proper meaning. Photographers on the Field of Mars, the central congregation point, framed their pictures to show tightly packed crowds around a speaker; but in some pictures a slightly larger frame showed that much of the field was empty.[82] (See Figure 9.) May Day 1918 was the last holiday covered by an independent press; for the anniversary celebration in November, regulations made independent photography virtually impossible.[83]

Although the tradition that recommended mass festivals to the Bolsheviks had a strongly pluralistic element, the dominant characteristic of its underlying cultural model was unanimity. If the Soviet festivals were

Figure 9. Grigory Zinoviev (top photo, standing in car) addressing the May Day 1918 parade on the Field of Mars, Petrograd. The lower photograph shows the same celebration from a more revealing angle (*Plamia*, 12 May 1918, pp. 8, 9).

to attain the results imagined by their sponsors, conflicting voices would have to be silenced. In this sense, the holiday was a success with those inclined toward the Bolsheviks; they were given an experience of unity and a taste of the culture of the future, while the boycotting opposition gained nothing. The Bolsheviks succeeded in making May Day their own. Herein lies the only possible explanation of Lunacharsky's rather odd—considering the reality of the holiday—recollection eight years hence:

As to the holiday's solemn, unusually piercing and joyful mood, and the beauty of form in which the first May Day after the October Revolution was cast, it was the most successful. I've lived through many a May Day since with the proletariat of Leningrad and Moscow. Each was significant, each was well attended, each was what a proletarian holiday should be, but they were also business, days of accounting, days of self-organization, days of inspection. But not a one so impressed me with its many wonderful pictures, hundreds of thousands of people united by unblighted joy, and the efforts of artists who met the masses with open hearts.[84]

He was remembering either May Day 1918 as others were supposed to or May Day 1917 as it was.

November 1918: The Struggle over Style

The variety of interpretation found in 1918 was also caused by a diversity of styles. The administrators controlling festivals after 1918 were not ambiguous about how the new order should celebrate itself. Friche, who took over in Moscow, preferred displays of harmony and unity along the lines of Rousseau's choral circles; Andreeva, who dominated Petrograd festivals, liked the theme of magnificent endeavor. Neither had a taste for futurism. When Mayakovsky and Meyerhold proposed their anniversary production of *Mystery-Bouffe* to the Petrograd Theater Section (PTO) headed by Andreeva, she did her best to prevent it.[85]

All parties to the debate over style agreed that artists should devote themselves to the Revolution. The real disagreement was over the nature of the duty and how it should be met. Russian lacks the articles *the* and *a* (*an*); rarely has grammar made as much difference as it did in November 1918. All concurred with the slogan "*Da zdravstvuet revoliutsiia*," but in Russian the phrase can mean two entirely different things: "Long live revolution" or "Long live *the* [Bolshevik] Revolution." November 1918, the first anniversary of Soviet power, was celebrated under this slogan, and it turned out to be a struggle between the artists' iconoclastic exuberance and the organizers' wish to tame that exuberance.

In Moscow the festival was directed by the Organizing Committee for the October Festivities, established in early October by the municipal soviet. Its work was overseen by a troika of Vadim Podbelsky, Afonin, and Lev Kamenev, who was head of the soviet.[86] Most of the artwork eventually became the responsibility of the municipal Arts Department,[87] and theaters were administered by Olga Kameneva—head of the Narkompros Theater Section (TEO), wife of Kamenev, and sister of Leon Trotsky.[88]

Although a Narkompros committee consisting of Petrograd's most talented artists, including Blok and Meyerhold, had been meeting since August to plan that city's celebration,[89] a mid-September decree of the municipal soviet placed Andreeva in charge of its Central Organizing Bureau for the October Triumphs. The bureau was given sweeping powers for "the requisition and confiscation of all necessary materials and technical means."[90] Should this seem an idle decree or the festival a trivial matter, it might be noted that the bureau was able to requisition all construction workers from the Petrograd region and, when they did not suffice, additional workers from the Pskov, Novgorod, and Vologda regions.[91] The Central Organizing Bureau returned the favor to those who had granted them such power with a gesture that set an unfortunate precedent: it commissioned hundreds of busts and portraits of Lenin, Zinoviev, Lunacharsky, and other Bolshevik leaders.[92] Because Andreeva had already been appointed head of the Theater and Spectacle Section of the Northern Commune's regional Narkompros,[93] she was given effective control over the entire celebration and did her best to prevent futurist participation.

The Civil War was in full swing by November. The Bolsheviks were engaged in a struggle for life, and the holiday was seen by officials much as May Day had been before the Revolution, as a day of solidarity and struggle. The official mood was best expressed in one of the slogans of the day.

> Both crying and singing are useless to dead men:
> Pay tribute to them differently.
> Step over their corpses without any fear,
> And bearing their standard march on.[94]

Andreeva, whose preference for stately celebration was evident in May, spurned the word *festival* for the more official *triumphal celebration,* and in a September 25 speech to the Petrograd Soviet called for a solemn affair: "The anniversary celebration will generate the proletariat's confidence in the final triumph of its cause. But while celebrating the anniversary we must not forget that the struggle continues and that our holiday will be of an austere character."[95] And a decree issued by the Moscow Soviet backed official taste with a warning: "In the great days of the anniversary of the proletarian revolution, an exemplary proletarian order must reign in the Red Capital. Only the strict comradely discipline and self-restraint of the working masses will create such order."[96]

Despite the organizers' austere intentions, the holiday mood was celebratory. On November 7, the second day of the long weekend, Moscow awoke early to the sounds of singing in the streets. Although some might have preferred to sleep late, the sacrifice was rewarded by bolstered rations: two pounds of bread, a half-pound of candy or fruit preserves, two pounds of fresh fish, and a half-pound of creamery butter per person, which were indescribable luxuries in a country on the brink of starvation.[97] Cafés and restaurants were kept open, and food was served without charge; a free dinner was given to the children of Moscow. Similar privileges were extended to the citizens of Petrograd and Saratov,[98] and perhaps other cities.

Lenin's monument plan was in full swing by the November anniversary celebration. Interpretations and reactions to the work attested to the ongoing stylistic debate. Punin's warning against stylistic passivity went unheeded when Dobuzhinsky's treatment of the Petrograd Admiralty met with official approval—despite his recent antipathy to the Bolsheviks. Punin was not alone in objecting to revolutionary monumentalism. Another critic, for instance, feared that "the new revolutionary monuments will be made in the same 'official-domestic' style as the statues to 'the tsars and their servants.' "[99] The alarm was justified. On November 7 an *Obelisk to International Revolutionaries* was unveiled in Moscow's Aleksandrovsky Garden; the obelisk—a traditional symbol of autocracy—had been erected in 1913 as part of the Romanov dynasty's 300th anniversary celebration, but the two-headed eagle was removed and the names of revolutionaries were carved over those of the tsars.[100]

Avant-gardists insisted that any style that harmonized with the old cities could not be revolutionary. They disdained the coward's evasion—covering statues with red banners—and attacked monuments head on. Often the weapon was humor. In Moscow Annenkov, assigned the distribution of slogans, told how "among the slogans chosen by the Party Central Committee was Marx's well-known, ancient quotation: 'Revolution is the locomotive of history.' In convulsions of laughter, we assigned the slogan to railroad workers and distributed enormous banners, on which a locomotive was drawn with a bearded portrait of Marx on its 'breast' over the cowcatcher."[101]

Theater Square, spread out before the Imperial Bolshoi Theater, was transformed into a field of color; trees were spray-painted in lilac, and bushes were covered with muslin of the same color. The grass was given a coat of paint through a fire hose.[102] Hunters' Row, an outdoor produce and meat market, was also given a face-lift. Its booths, famous for abundance and variety before the Revolution (and for private trading after), were never known for beauty. A brother-and-sister team, the Alekseevs, covered the booths with bold geometric designs in bright reds, blues, oranges, and purples.[103] A garland of flags stretched over the row between two masts—a traditional decoration for Russian fairgrounds. In the Belorussian town of Vitebsk, house painters scandalized citizens by covering their buildings with the designs of Chagall.[104]

An even more aggressive attack on the old city, and the biggest scandal of all, was raised by Altman's work in Petrograd. Legend claims that futurists used discord inside the Petrograd Central Organizing Bureau to slip their work into the festival.[105] Considering that Altman's work was placed in the city center, that similar work had been hung on Palace Square for May Day, and that it was made of 20,000 arshins (12,000 yards) of bright material,[106] the possibility that it was slipped past anyone is doubtful. More likely, Andreeva, who disliked modern painting, refused to let futurists participate in the festival, and they had their plans approved elsewhere.

Altman's rendering of Palace Square was a mixture of the moderate and the radical; he intended to make its enclosed area suitable for popular festivals.[107] To begin, the autocratic associations had to be removed, which he did by creating a carnival atmosphere. Carnival refutes old meanings by mocking the framework or surroundings that create that meaning. Buildings lining the square were connected with geometrical banners of red, green, and blue. A row of trees on the open side of the square facing the Admiralty was covered with green shields; each carried a few letters that in series spelled "Proletariat of the world—unite!"

Meaning was also attacked and exploded from the center. The center of autocratic Russia was Palace Square, and its center was the most monumental of monuments, the Alexander Column, erected in honor of the European victories of Alexander I. Altman took the ponderous column and translated it into the terms of the surrounding festival; he did a futurist parody. The heavy, three-dimensional masses of the column and its base were fragmented into odd geometrical figures, which came out of the process flat. These figures were arranged in a swirl of fire around the column, which provided an axis that they seemed to spin around. Altman took the muted reds and yellows of the Palace and

General Headquarters and intensified them; the new square was ablaze in orange and red. What had a year and a half previously been the center of an empire became a bright and splashy carnival.

The Reaction

The holiday was enjoyed by many celebrants. The futurist work and its carnival gaiety garnered most of the praise, from various semiofficial papers and from the official organs *Pravda* and *Izvestiia*. The official solemnities received little notice; the less official a paper was, the less space it devoted to the "triumphs." As a young member of the Proletkult Literary Studio noted:

> What was remarkable was that the "triumphs'" official side—the passing of marching columns, the unveiling of memorial plaques and statues—paled before the universal exultation and immediate feeling of joy. It was majestic, but the majestic took a back seat to carefreeness, solemnity to gaiety. . . . It was not the celebration of an anniversary, the memory of sacrifices, or the ecstasy of a future victory and creative spirit, but the joyful greeting of [the] revolution, the childlike merriment of the great masses' laughter that made the day of [the] Overturn great. . . . The anniversary of the October Revolution became the first day of a new era.[108]

The mood of the day and its peculiar sense of time are captured admirably here.

Articles of the time were in unanimous praise of the festival.[109] Hostile reviews did appear—these are the articles that scholars now quote most often—but they were written long after the fact, in 1919, when criticism of the futurists had gained official backing and was somewhat fashionable.[110] Still, to call the exultation universal was an exaggeration; those antagonistic to the Revolution—a sizeable part of the population—did not share in the celebration and seem to have been rather frightened by the whole affair. As Tamara Karsavina, prima ballerina of the imperial stage, commented, "One was safer indoors."[111]

Oddly enough—and unfortunately since it was a formative event in Soviet artistic policy—many Bolshevik officials agreed with Karsavina. In Petrograd, Andreeva expressed strong disapproval of futurism and claimed the support of the Petrograd proletariat. At a rally of the "working intelligentsia," Andreeva took the podium and read what she claimed were excerpts from the letters of workers incensed by the futurist decorations.¹¹² Initially, the Petrograd Soviet confirmed its support of the futurists, and the brouhaha quieted down for a few months.

Meanwhile, the battle flared up in Moscow. Modernists were situated in the Moscow branch of IZO Narkompros, a national organization; the aesthetic conservatives (who were often political radicals) were in local soviets. In early February 1919, Lunacharsky decreed that local branches of IZO would be in charge of decorating cities for May Day.¹¹³ Friche, by now director of the Moscow Soviet's Department of People's Festivals, whose control was threatened by Lunacharsky's decree, initiated a long series of antifuturist polemics in the soviet's *Vechernie izvestiia* (*Evening News*), for which he was arts editor. He set a mean-spirited tone in an initial editorial,¹¹⁴ which was followed by articles by other authors, all under Friche's editorship. The articles, incidentally, inveighed mostly against IZO futurists; Moscow futurists, many of whom worked with the Moscow Soviet's Arts Department, do not seem to have bothered the authors. Kameneva, a vocal advocate of futurists before November 1918, when they worked under her in TEO Narkompros,¹¹⁵ joined the antifuturist campaign in February, when she was organizing a festival for the Moscow Soviet,¹¹⁶ and Andreeva initiated antifuturist polemics in Petrograd through her editorship of *Zhizn' iskusstva* (*The Life of Art*).

Friche and Andreeva soon found official support. Friche turned to the soviet, which, after the IZO commission had published its May Day plans, met and decreed that the festivities should be conducted under "the direct control of the Moscow proletariat"—that is, Friche's department. The department vowed to pursue a policy of "neutrality" in matters of artistic taste, at the same time stating that "foolish, tasteless, and antirevolutionary artistic manifestations should not be sanctioned by soviet authority or waste the people's money."¹¹⁷ In other words, anything but futurism was acceptable. At the same time Andreeva, who stayed in close touch with Lenin, discovered that he was equally displeased: he thought the monuments "outright mockery and distortion" and was particularly miffed when the paint did not come off the trees on Theater Square.¹¹⁸ Andreeva sent Lenin what amounted to a denunciation of the futurists and, for good measure, blamed her rivals in TEO, Kameneva and Olga Menzhinskaia, who could hardly have been at fault.¹¹⁹

By late February, antifuturist sentiment was running strong. When Petrograd painters when to Moscow on the 23rd to help with decorations for the Day of Red Gifts (to front-line soldiers), they were criticized for being alien to the workers; Kameneva's letter was the strongest but not the only condemnation. Andreeva transported the charge to Petrograd and in an unsigned article described the Petrograd painters in a way that stuck in Soviet criticism: "The driving forces of the Revolution were accumulated by degrees, in the depths of the same way of life that the futurists turned their backs on with disdain.... To create a work of art answering the demands of the Revolution, to [make] a revolutionary work of art, can be done only by someone in a position to artistically interpret the Revolution. An absolutely necessary condition for that is a close connection with the authentic life and psychology of the people."[120] This was the same argument anti-Bolshevik commentators had forwarded on May Day 1918;[121] and it smelled strongly of prerevolutionary conservatism.

Andreeva's previous complaint to the Petrograd Soviet had met with no sympathy (she was carrying on a notorious feud with Zinoviev's wife, Lilina).[122] But now that administrative control was at stake, the antagonists rallied together; two months after the Narkompros decree was promulgated, the Petrograd Soviet decreed that "in no circumstances shall the organization of the May Day festival be given into IZO futurist hands" and assigned organization to Andreeva, Antselovich, and Nikolai Tolmachev.[123] The Moscow Soviet soon put Friche and Kameneva in charge of its May Day celebration. Because soviets controlled the only available funds, IZO was shut out of the celebration.[124]

IZO made extensive—and ultimately useless—plans for the May Day 1919 celebration. A commission headed by Altman met on March 7 and decided that the holiday would celebrate international proletariat solidarity, a theme to be emphasized by the decoration of important gathering points in harmony with the surrounding architecture.[125] The futurists forsook the brashness and discord of November 1918. Projects were drawn up for "obelisks, architectural barricades, and arches to be erected in squares, streets, and parks. The themes of these decorations will be: the arch of factory labor, the obelisk of farm work, arches and obelisks for the trade unions, science, art, literature, and arches dedicated to revolutionaries."[126]

These projects were far from the modernist "degeneracy" that had so offended Friche, but too much ink had been spilled for polemics to clear. In an article kicking off the February antifuturist campaign, Friche had blamed the failure of previous festivals on the fact that most were organized in a mere week's time.[127] The bureaucratic scramble preceding the May Day 1919 festival, alas, had the same result: plans were not completed until a week before the holiday.

Discussion of the social role of festivals in the Bolshevik Revolution would be helped by information on mass reception. Unfortunately the masses did not write newspaper articles, and the only accounts we have are of suspect impartiality. The Russian intelligentsia's timeworn tradition of using the people as a rhetorical fig leaf for partisan opinion was continued after the Revolution. Officials steeped in the nineteenth-century academic tradition and speaking in the name of an imaginary people subsequently became the bane of innovative Soviet artists, so it would behoove us to examine Andreeva's charges closely.

The legend that futurism was rejected by the masses—a charge repeated by Russian scholars (often understandable for political reasons) and by their Western colleagues (less understandable)—is unsubstantiated. It was certainly possible that the masses did not like futurist work (though I have seen group portraits from November 7, 1918, taken in front of Altman's column). Andreeva's distaste was not feigned, and it probably represented some portion of popular taste. In Saratov (one of the few well-documented provincial cities), officials were mortified by a tribune decorated, after Henri Matisse, with unclothed female figures painted an unrestrained red.

Nevertheless, we cannot simply declare that popular audiences disliked modernism, whether or not we sympathize. Common Russians, after all, did not share the intelligentsia's prejudice—that art must depict something. Folk art itself was often nondepictive (for example, the applied arts); the simplified and stylized futurism most common on November 7 was familiar to the people from *lubki* (woodcut illustrations); and abstract work like that of the Alekseevs fit in with popular traditions of carnival decoration. Most of the Russian intelligentsia in 1918 was unfamiliar with modernism, so that the popular audience was in many ways better prepared to receive futurist work—even if they did not understand it as painters intended.

Few if any of the numerous press accounts of the time are reliable indicators of public reception, and speculation on our part is unwarranted. Nevertheless, there is much to be learned from the stylistic debate of 1919. Although we cannot distill a single meaning from the revolutionary festivals, we can discern many potential interpretations. The dynamics of revolutionary culture are manifest in the ways that potential meanings were rejected by and others accepted into Bolshevik mythology. Perhaps most important, we can watch the Bolsheviks reacting to a society that did not always act as expected. Revolutionary Russia was filled with diverse nations, classes, and factions whose divisions did not always mirror the formulas of Marxist ideology. Commentators of most every stripe agreed on one thing: each felt free to describe the voice of the people as if there could be only one. That notion, shared by Wagner and Ivanov as well as the Bolsheviks, was just one of the authoritarian seeds latent in revolutionary festivals that would bear fruit within a decade.

Official reaction shows how difficult it was for Bolsheviks (and not the Bolsheviks alone) to deal with dissenting views. They saw subversion in stylistic unorthodoxy and division in diversity. Their trepidation was fully manifest in the banishment of futurists, whose unorthodox art actually expressed revolutionary fervor. In his *Ode to Revolution*, written for the 1918 anniversary, Mayakovsky asked:

How else will you turn out, you of two faces?
A well-balanced building,
Or a heap of rubble?

Judging by their reaction, the Bolsheviks were not sure which he preferred. Their anger at futurists resembled the fulminations of clerics ancient and modern against the license of carnival: both saw beliefs and rules they cherished mocked and defied, and both meant to put an end to it.

Perhaps disapproving officials saw in the futurist decorations an unwelcome hint of anarchy. The year 1918 had seen acute conflicts between the anarchists and the state apparatus; by November they were over but not forgotten. What to the futurists was displacement was to disapproving Bolsheviks anarchy. Alexei Tolstoy, a novelist who never hesitated to inform his readers of the mood in official circles, made the identification of futurism and anarchism explicit in his *Road to Calvary:*

Moscow under the black [anarchist] flag! We are going to celebrate our victory—do you know how? We'll announce a universal carnival, set up winebooths in the streets and let military bands play in the squares. A million and a half men and women all masked. There's not the least doubt that half of them will come stark naked.... We will put up hoardings to the full height of the houses along the streets and paint them with architectural subjects of a new style never seen before. We are going to repaint the trees—we consider natural foliage impermissible.[128]

Yet revolution was the message in 1918, and futurism told it well. This, at least, was the impression that German prisoners of war quartered in Moscow got from the celebration. On Sunday, the final day of the festival, they stormed their own embassy and raised the red flag on its roof. Revolution had broken out in Germany.

FOUR

New Uses for Popular Culture

*The highest note comes oft from basest mind,
As shallow brookes do yeeld the greatest sound.*
Sir Philip Sidney, *The Lady of May*

The restrictions on professional participation that resulted from bureaucratic antimodernism and war-tightened purse strings encouraged popular participation in mass festivals during 1919. The pressing matter of survival diverted officials' attention from holidays, and the initiative sometimes made it to other hands. The popular spirit that had inspired Rousseau, Rolland, Lunacharsky, Kerzhentsev—even Wagner—finally infiltrated revolutionary festivals.

People's theater (*narodnyi teatr*) had been a beacon for nineteenth-century liberalizers; no mere artistic phenomenon, it was a rhetorical icon for the creative energies that common people would manifest once liberated from tsarist oppression. The passion of the advocacy often obscured the phrase's muddled meanings. It could mean folk theater, specific to peasant culture; theater where peasant amateurs performed the classics; theater taken directly to the lower classes with the didactic strain typical of playwrights like Leo Tolstoy; popular theater of the urban masses; state-run theaters like the prerevolutionary People's Houses (sponsored by the imperial family or temperance groups), with a special "people's" repertory—fairy plays and operetta; classics on the order of Sophocles, Shakespeare, or Molière, which some fancied to represent the spirit of an entire people; or even pan-national theater, as envisioned by Ivanov. Proletkultists were joining a hoary debate, and their contribution was not the already-old notion of popular participation but an emphasis on its class nature and a rejection of precedent.

Intellectuals rarely acknowledged the existence of a truly popular theater: the *balagany* and puppet booths of the holiday fairground. Russian popular culture seemed too vulgar and too familiar to most Russian intellectuals, and they ignored its distinct features in their sincere quest for a people's culture. The prejudice eluded political pigeonholing. Most older Bolsheviks considered high culture good, popular culture pernicious. Lenin wanted to replace the popular block prints (*lubki*) he despised with cheap reproductions of art classics.[1] Lunacharsky, who saw a continuing role for fairground culture, preferred to co-opt its antiauthoritarian streak:

Long live the jesters of his Majesty the Proletariat! Although jesters once told tsars the truth, . . . they were still slaves. The jesters of the proletariat will be its brothers, . . . keen and eloquent advisers.

Why shouldn't Petrushka or another herald of popular opinion appear on the fairgrounds, urban squares, or at our rallies as a beloved character who could exploit the inexhaustible resources of popular humor? . . . Surely [that humor] will be permeated with the caustic humor that animates the revolution's destructive side.[2]

Even Blok, Meyerhold and Evreinov, who welcomed popular culture, looked mostly to Western variants: the puppet booth of *Balaganchik* was inhabited by an alienated Pierrot rather than the bawdy Petrushka of the Russian fairground.

Disdain for popular culture had several roots; the deepest root, perhaps, was an imprecise image of the "people" for whom so many struggles were waged. The Bolsheviks often neglected popular culture because they confused it with the folk (peasant) culture they despised so thoroughly. Here they burlesqued the attitudes of *narodnik* populists who had distrusted popular culture because it seemed like an impure version of the folk. The outcome was a failure to recognize that popular culture had strong and legitimate artistic traditions that could appeal to the very people the Soviet state represented.

Nevertheless, the vigorous process of assimilation proceeded. Although some forms of popular culture faded, others found new homes. Cultural forms are mobile; they move into new contexts within a culture and assume different meanings. A particularly fruitful source for festivals proved to be fairground culture. *Gulianiia* (carnivals or fairs;

from *guliat'*, "to stroll") were distasteful to many Bolsheviks because of the sponsors: the Romanov family, with a more recent influx of entrepreneurial help. Yet the fact that carnivals were state run and state sponsored made the tradition exploitable. The opinion eventually prevailed that fairground culture should not be disavowed; rather it should be harnessed to the task of political education. Carnival culture was slowly transformed from raucous entertainment to pious proselytizer.

From the Fairground

Urban carnival culture in Russia thrived from the early eighteenth to the late nineteenth century.[3] Associated with Yuletide and Shrovetide, carnivals were bursts of color and celebration that bracketed the long Russian winter. Carnivals were confined to particular—but varying—spots within the city: in Moscow, Novinskoe Field, Maiden's (Devichee) Field, and Khodynka; in Petersburg, Admiralty Square (next to the Palace), later the Field of Mars. The Shrovetide and Yuletide holidays occupied a special time in the popular culture; as one saying had it:

> Shrovetide comes only once a year;
> I drinks a bit, don't spare the change
> For holiday cheer.[4]

Shrovetide was the only time of year that the Finnish sleighs came to Petersburg; dancing bears would sometimes even appear in the city.

Carnivals were the only time and place in Imperial Russia where all classes could meet and mix. Early in his reign Nicholas I was known to visit with the people on Admiralty Square; and a foreign visitor noted that during a fête, commoners and courtiers met as equals.[5] Decades later, merchants and officers still found the holidays a fashionable time to promenade. Even the sheltered wards of the Smolny Institute for Noble Girls were known to circulate around the edges of the crowd in their carriages (or so they were represented in popular lithographs). By mid-century, however, the fashion had faded, and by the end of the century mixing was uncommon.[6]

Up until the 1880s, when the socialist International claimed May Day as its own, that holiday was also celebrated with a carnival: for Petersburgers, it took place in Ekaterinhof, a park outside the city.

106 NEW USES FOR POPULAR CULTURE

Although the Ekaterinhof carnival was revived for May Day 1919, it lacked the splendor of former years.[7] Carnival thrives on excess; in 1919, Russia was starving and in the middle of the Civil War. Alcohol was forbidden as it had been during the war years; and the rich *bliny*, thin pancakes dripping with butter, were also a distant memory. Gone were the huge wooden swings of the traditional *gulianie;* gone were the ten-yard-high slides, coated with ice in the winter, on which a young boy could slide half the length of the Admiralty.

Bolshevik celebrations never provided the license of a true carnival; but this was due no more to a censorious Red soul than to the inroads of modernity. By the late nineteenth century traditional carnival amusements were being challenged by the products of the industrial age, the carousel and the roller coaster—which most of Europe called "Russian mountains," but which Russians called "American mountains." The vivid entertainments of the penny theaters were threatened, if not tamed, by the edifying shows sponsored by the People's Houses. Even when the old *balagan* master Lentovsky directed the 1903 May Day spectacles in the Nicholas II People's House, the show lacked the splash of yesteryear.

As holiday culture changed, the location it occupied within the city also shifted. From the early to mid-nineteenth century, the site of Petersburg *gulianiia* was Admiralty Square, next to the Palace. In the 1870s the fair was moved from city center to the Field of Mars, and the end of the century saw the Shrovetide carnival moving farther and farther toward the outskirts, coming to rest in the filthy Semenov Place. Carnivals of a sort were established in the once-elegant Mikhailovsky Manège near the center of town, where they resided until the First World War. The sponsor there was, at first, the Guardians of the People's Temperance; later, private enterprise was the organizer. The Guardians—representing a Victorianism alien to the carnival spirit—saw the fairs as an opportunity to attract the people away from the harmful influence of liquor.[8]

By the twentieth century, carnival culture had been redefined by the industrial city. Industrial culture, with its standardized sense of time, was opposed to the erratic, intensified time of carnival. No time or space was allotted for carnival in industrial society. The essential change brought about by capitalism was the disassociation of carnivals from holidays; this link had made them central to earlier cultures. The time frame of carnival was rendered obsolete by the advent of entrepreneurial financing; profits were highest when the carnival ran every day.

Carnivals, which had once occupied a central position in an alternative, holiday, culture, were now consigned to a peripheral role in a single culture—one without alternatives. Removed from the center of social life, the carnivals were removed from the center of the city. The Mikhailovsky affairs were designed strictly for simple folk; no self-respecting officer or merchant would be found there. The broad, open spaces of the central squares were replaced by an enclosure, a roofed indoor space. The program had also changed considerably since the advent of the *gulianiia*. Entertainment, confined to a variety stage, combined *balagan*-type skits, vaudeville, and circus. Indoors there could be no ice mountains, no fireworks; no longer did hawkers roam the crowd selling hot *bliny*. Drinking, obviously, was banned.

The Russian carnival should in no way be associated with a rebellious vein in the culture; as a matter of fact, the Baron N. N. Wrangel (brother of the future White general) had led the prewar fight to revive carnivals on the Field of Mars.[9] In a great city, arranging and sponsoring a carnival is a complex process that can be accomplished by only the most powerful institutions, such as the autocracy. Yet the system that marked a carnival a holiday could be translated into an aesthetic of upheaval.

This transformation was what *Mystery-Bouffe* accomplished and what Meyerhold planned for November 7, 1918 (the first day of *Mystery-Bouffe*), when he tried to revive the Manège carnival as a celebration of the Revolution. Meyerhold collected a remarkable organizing commission of artists who had used popular art forms in their work: Blok, Evreinov, Konstantin Miklashevsky (assistant to Meyerhold and Evreinov, expert on the commedia dell'arte), Lentulov, Sergei Prokofiev, Khlebnikov, Mayakovsky, and the choreographer Fedor Lopukhov. Also included were the finest performers of vaudeville and circus.[10] The program did not differ radically from earlier Manège carnivals: vaudeville, dance numbers, musical and circus skits, puppet theaters. The Manège itself was different; the huge statue of Nicholas II standing before it had been taken down for the holiday, and its bronze was given for reuse in the Lenin monument plan.[11] Yet the essential difference was Meyerhold's aim to return carnival to its former place at the center of the culture and restore the association with a holiday. The vitality, splash, and color dimmed by the Guardians and entrepreneurs would be restored. The commission planned for carousels, swings, and even extravaganza/melodramas—a *balagan* specialty. Alekseev-Iakovlev was hired to produce *Song of the Merchant Kalashnikov* (a repeat from the turn of the century), based on a Mikhail Lermontov poem; and when the commission discovered that the amphitheater where *The Taking of Azov* once played was still standing, it voted to organize a new spectacle there. The planned revival was not entirely faithful: alcohol, an essential ingredient of the old carnival, was still banned, as were lotteries, a huge draw in prewar days. Strict censorship was to be enforced; but that too was part of the Russian carnival tradition.

Failure to realize the plan tells us more about the official side of Soviet culture in 1918 than about the popular side. The work of the commission, pursued over two months of meetings, fell victim to the bureaucratic skirmishes preceding the first anniversary. TEO, sponsor of the commission, moved its headquarters to Moscow in mid-summer; PTO, which took over operation of Petrograd theaters and spectacles, was run by Andreeva. She simply refused to recognize the commission and its plan; when funding disappeared, the commission dissolved.

Redefining Popular Culture

Popular culture was a ready conduit of images to the mind of the demos, and the Bolsheviks, who relied on their ability to disseminate ideas, never completely neglected it. Although older leaders such as Lenin and Krupskaia sometimes disdained its baser tastes, others, like Lunacharsky, saw considerable value and potential in it. Performance in the circus and *balagany* was of an extraordinarily high level of skill, and technique was frequently superior to that in the theater of high culture. There was a great tradition to be preserved, and great enthusiasm. Much of it belonged to younger, often anonymous workers in the political-education apparatus. Confronted by a vast, mobile, and often unschooled audience, local workers used familiar formats to transmit unfamiliar knowledge. By the early 1920s, thousands of local propagandists had developed a broad array of agitational and propaganda techniques, many of which relied on the legacy of fairground culture.[12]

Underlying the enthusiasm was a frequent disregard for the vagaries of communication. The assumption was that old popular forms could carry new ideas without extra burden and that their symbols and rhetoric would suffice for the job. Yet popular culture exerted an influence on the message it carried; it had rules and traditions of its own, many of which resisted new ideas. Conventions and types, for instance, which were the essence of *balagan* theater, were often imperfect expressions of Bolshevism and, as in the case of *The Legend of the Communard,* could thwart the intentions of sincerely revolutionary work.

Perhaps even more treacherous was the play element in popular entertainment. Plans for Moscow's May Day 1919 celebration, in which traditional May Day games such as tug of war and sack racing were to be used for propaganda, demonstrated the strain that political messages could put on games. A Soviet version of the Maypole dance was entitled the *Carousel of Craft-Guilds:* the title itself suggests how choreographed the dance—a traditional show of spring-inspired freedom—was to be. The Maypole was topped by a female figure symbolizing Soviet power, and the dancers were arrayed in their occupational costumes, one of which appeared to be Phrygian caps.[13] The traditional climbing of a greased pole was also changed by placing on the pole not a pig but an effigy of the White admiral Aleksandr Kolchak, which the winning contestant "overthrew."[14] Assimilation was clearly not an easy process. The fun of a game like pole climbing is in the effort and suspense, yet uncertain outcomes make propaganda an unreliable tool. Imagine the message conveyed if contestants did not scale the greased pole, and Kolchak rested atop it unassailed.

One type of popular game that adapted well to propaganda was the dramatic game (*igrishche*). Dramatic games partook of both play and theater; the rules of dramatic progression, which regulate free variation, helped dramatic games carry political messages. Dramatized trials were a particularly useful game; though popular in origin, they were familiar to the intelligentsia as a prerevolutionary debate forum. The law, criminals, courts, and detectives were always a fertile topic for popular culture. They offered clear-cut situations and intriguing characters, sharply drawn divisions, and action that generated endless variations. Courtroom disputation fueled the plots of literature as diverse as Pinkerton (detective) stories and Dostoevsky's *Brothers Karamazov,* and it was also an integral element of traditional peasant weddings.

A common game in Cossack country was the *Trial of Ataman Buria,* which survived up to the First World War.[15] Buria, a figure from popular Ermak lore, sat in judgment over merchants, innkeepers, and landowners—the people's traditional foes. The trial was improvised but only in the sense that the commedia dell'arte had been—improvised from an inventory of ready speeches and situations. The conduct of the trial eschewed legal precedent and substituted the conventions of popular and folk theater: accusers came forward from the audience, and the accused, when given a chance to speak, tended to incriminate themselves no less than their accusers had. These self-incriminations were a variant of traditional comic self-introductions.

Political-education workers of the Southern Army made a dramatic trial into an effective agitational skit, *The Trial of Wrangel,* performed in the autumn of 1919 before ten thousand spectators.[16] The performance took place in Crimea Village, Kuban region—Cossack country. The plot was simple.

> The court session is declared open, and the secretary reads the allegations, in which Baron Wrangel is accused of violating and murdering workers and peasants, of associating with foreign capitalism, of signing secret pacts with foreign powers delivering Russia into slavery, of aiding White Poland, etc. Then the interrogation of the witnesses begins. A turncoat from the Volunteer Army tells of Baron Wrangel's career in Crimea. A worker from Novorossiisk describes the Volunteer Army's "work"; then a Red soldier who fought in the Crimea speaks, then a port worker from Sebastopol; then a worker from Batum tells of hydro-aeroplanes transported on steamships with Russian prisoners. A wealthy merchant tells of the charms Wrangel holds for the bourgeoisie. . . . Each witness represents a type, a particular social class, and gives a live picture of recent events. Finally, following the concluding arguments of the prosecution and the defense, and Wrangel's final speech, the sentence is announced: Wrangel will be destroyed, a sentence to be fulfilled immediately by the workers of Soviet Russia.[17]

The dramatic-game skeleton accommodated topical political material easily; and as the agit-trial (as the form came to be known) gained popularity, criminals as diverse as deserters and lice were put into the dock. Constant use brought changes to the play format. Though organizers claimed that the original agit-trial was improvised from a bare scenario, the scenario published was closer to a full text. The play element had to be disciplined if it was to become a reliable vehicle for propaganda; in fact, the question of how spontaneous an agit-trial should be became a hot item of debate among political-education workers in the 1920s.

Dramatic forms of popular culture offered ready vehicles for a political message, and melodrama was perhaps most apt. Like courtroom drama, it offered a simple skeleton that could bear unaccustomed loads. Melodrama first appeared in Paris in the wake of the French Revolution and was originally a musical drama. Soon however the term came to connote the unsophisticated dramatic convention by which good and bad are always unalloyed, terror and pity are liberally elicited, and the outcome is always happy (at least for the hero or heroine). This was the version that reached Russian *balagany* in the late nineteenth century and ultimately became a mainstay of the cinema.

Lunacharsky and Gorky were conscious of the genre's power even before the Revolution. It involved constant action, a key to popular drama. When action was preserved as a primary feature, secondary characteristics of the melodrama, which determined propaganda value, could be put to use. Following Rolland, they believed that melodrama sustained in its audience the optimism needed for social renewal;[18] and its broadly drawn emotions and actions were essential for mythmaking. Melodrama was the seed of communist tragedy.[19] The analogy motivated a PTO commission chaired by Gorky to sponsor a melodrama contest in 1919, in which the style was defined as "psychological primitivism" and authors were asked to "clearly underline [their] sympathies and antipathies."[20]

The enthusiasm was not unadulterated. The melodrama had originally been a revolutionary form, that chose middle-class heroes in contrast to tragedy's aristocrats. But its evolution made it the preferred style of the Nicholas II People's House, no revolutionary institution. So when Lunacharsky and Andreeva gained control of the People's House through the Petrograd Municipal soviet in summer 1917, they replaced melodrama with the socially conscious plays of Gorky, Tolstoy, and Aleksei Pisemsky. This high-minded decision attracted everyone but an audience, which preferred entertainment.

Message is a notion to be applied to popular culture with only the greatest caution. Popular culture can, of course, be interpreted, as can anything given the proper observer at the proper distance. But often popular culture that seems from the outside like art, an ordered system of signs subject to interpretation, seen from within becomes play, an open-ended series of actions requiring no interpretation. Russian artists recognized that quality of popular culture and bent it to their own goals; in dramas like Andreev's *He Who Gets Slapped* and Blok's *Balaganchik*, it was a metaphor for meaninglessness.

These distinctions are of import to propagandists as well as to artists. The distinctions determine how ideas can be passed along and how they can outlast the moment of performance. A message is conveyed by an artist through controlled selection; game playing is impossible without randomness and risk. The controlling artistic consciousness, and the reader or viewer, must to some degree stand outside the work of art, aware of the conventionality of its rules; participants and viewers must temporarily immerse themselves in a game, forgetting that the rules are conventional and arbitrary. Play is as ephemeral as holiday culture; it occupies a special place and special time and generates its own conventions. Once the game is over, and its rules are again suspended, it loses its significance.

Play's greatest taboo is to step outside its boundary during its progress. In revolutionary Russia the use of popular culture as propaganda was precisely such a step, yet it had ample precedent. Popular entertainments like the carnival and circus were traditionally associated in time and place with holidays and fairgrounds. But by 1917 they had long ceased to be associated with holiday culture; they had settled in permanent buildings and consisted of patriotic pantomimes all through the Great War. Bolshevik propaganda violated popular culture's boundary, but it was a boundary already rubbed thin.

In addition, popular culture had particular rules of linkage that conditioned any attempt to convey a message. The circus, like vaudeville and other popular entertainments, was a string of short performances that, except for belonging to a single stage, had little structural connection. Animal trainer followed tightrope walker. Segmentation lent an emphasis to the parts, not the whole, in popular culture. Characterization, for instance, came from a single feature representing the whole, as in *Mystery-Bouffe;* episodes were the dominant building block of prose, as in the picaresque novel or serial tale. Selection and ordering of parts were quite often tenuous, determined more by tradition than by meaning. Circus and vaudeville acts were strung together in free order; pictures in the fairground peep show (*raek*) were connected only by the barker's commentary. In a *lubok,* diverse segments were placed side to side in timeless simultaneity, while "in the popular theater, episodes were merely juxtaposed, laid next to one another without reference to the movement of historical time."[21]

Time in popular culture, as expressed by the progression of segments, is loose, accommodating, and disjointed; yet within episodes driven by action it is continuous and concrete. Constant action keeps it from drifting into the timelessness of monumentalism. This dual time system was at the foundation of early attempts at mass spectacles. The November 1918 festival was to feature "the staging of [seventeen] *lubki* depicting scenes from the revolutionary past."[22] For the same celebration, PTO's Repertory Bureau suggested a plan for an *instsenirovka* of six episodes: Spartacus, Vasily Nemirovich-Danchenko's poem about the troubadour who threw down the gauntlet before the king, the German peasant uprising, the uprising under William of Orange, Garibaldi, and both French revolutions.[23] This selection of episodes seems somewhat abitrary, but it was not alien to popular culture.

Revolution was not the only subject to be treated in this way. In innovative Voronezh, the Free Theater began its life with *Rus'*, a synthetic spectacle directed by Nikolai Forreger that summarized Russia's cultural history. The first play of the cycle consisted of five acts: "A Pagan Ritual," featuring priests, priestesses, and witches; "Anna Yaroslavna's Departure for France"; "Market Day in Kudrino," with boyars, Tatars, and jesters; "Theater under Aleksei I," in which a medieval *débat* was performed; and a folkloric performance of "Dances of Peasant Women."[24]

Such a simple collection of episodes was an effective instrument of propaganda; the selection of episodes alone dictated a particular concept of history and its movement. Episodes had been linked thus in the medieval mystery cycles, as they were in *lubki*. In the second year of the Revolution this method, which originated in popular culture, proved handy to established artists. In this time of great cultural shifts, popular culture was a ready source of new models.

The most ambitious project was Gorky's planned *History of World Culture*. Conceived as an educational series, *History* employed some of Russia's finest writers to illustrate key stages of world development.[25] The monumental theater Gorky had formed with Iurev, Chaliapin, and Andreeva was devoted to great manifestations of the human will; and *History* selected (somewhat randomly) moments when civilization had made great leaps forward, revolutions of the human spirit. It was a concrete conception of history, if one not entirely consonant with Marxist theory. Blok wrote or planned episodes on Ramses (surely the worst thing he ever wrote), Tristram, and even the building of the first boat; Gorky planned one on the Norman Conquest; and in a patent allusion to the present Zamiatin wrote *The Fires of St. Dominic,* about the Spanish Inquisition. Plays were written in prose dialogue, in folk (*bylinnyi*) verse, and in fourteenth-century language; the only requirement was that subject matter be part of the humanity's logical progress in time. Professionals such as Mardzhanov were invited to direct the episodes—both for film and for mass festivals.

The Circus

Partisans of popular culture could follow two paths: remain faithful to tradition and develop a theater in which message yielded to action, the whole to the part; or tie the disparate segments of popular entertainment into a unified artistic whole. The ways that the new authorities used the circus provide illustrations of both paths.

When the Soviet circus became a focus of artistic attention in 1919, it was a reservoir of untapped performance skills. The TEO Circus Department was staffed by talented artists: Kamensky, Ilya Ehrenburg, Ivan Rukavishnikov, the avant-garde artist Boris Erdman, Kuznetsov, and Konenkov, and the choreographer Kasian Goleizovsky.[26] Artists fascinated by the circus were not entirely new; the circus had been fashionable with the prerevolutionary artistic intelligentsia.

The Sovietization of the circus could not be effected with the entire repertory. Some elements did not undergo transformation easily. Shklovsky suggested that only clown acts and pantomimes could be performed as art; acrobatics and other skill-based performances, in which plot, rhythm, and meaning-bearing structures were marginal, could not.[27] The more risk or chance in an act, the less suitable it was for the new circus. Randomness resists a message or ideology. The early Soviet circus shied away from the risk factor, from trapeze artists and tightrope walkers, preferring the verbal performance of clowns and the dramatic art of pantomime.[28]

The clown in the Russian circus was traditionally verbal; Lazarenko and the Durov brothers, supporters of the new regime, read verse they had written themselves as part of their routines. Lazarenko even performed a series of anti-White couplets written by his old friend Mayakovsky, entitled *The Soviet ABCs*. Clowns could function as spokesmen for the Bolsheviks without violating the traditions of their craft. Pantomimes, which had been popular during the First World War, could be assimilated, as the Cinizelli Circus in Voronezh in 1918 had shown. New figures could be grafted onto old plots: the Turks and Germans of World War I could be replaced by French and English interventionists; the cops and robbers by Reds and Whites. The same traditions, however, made clowns a double-edged sword. The most popular entertainment in Civil War Moscow was the clown duo of Bim and Bom. Their popularity, alas, rested not only on their wit but on its target, the Bolsheviks. Bim and Bom desisted from mocking the Bolsheviks only when their couplets so offended Latvian Riflemen in the audience that they shot up the circus and threatened to do the same to the clowns.[29]

For some popular spectacles to carry the new political ideas, they first had to undergo radical revision. Wrestling, a major circus attraction in the early twentieth century, could be exploited only at the expense of its sporting qualities. Skill and strength determined the outcome of the sport, but propaganda demanded a fixed conclusion. Lazarenko performed a skit written by Mayakovsky entitled *World Wrestling Championship,* in which David Lloyd George, Woodrow Wilson, Wrangel, and József Pilsudski squared off unsuccessfully against the Russian champion, Revolution (the Russian words for *wrestling* and [class] *struggle* are the same).[30] Combats of skill, which might have culminated in a bourgeois victory, became instead a symbolic battle in which Revolution inevitably triumphed.

Circus spectators were unpracticed in the interpretation of wrestling. A wrestling match with a plot—a controlled sequence with an established ending—was unaccustomed entertainment; wrestling as a political language was unfamiliar; and most alien of all was the notion that wrestling could be language. If the message was to find its target, the audience needed to be warned that new cultural functions were active. Propagandists had not only to create the message but to highlight it and even supply the proper interpretation—much as they had for May Day 1918.

Popular culture provided a ready vehicle for this function, the intermediary. Intermediaries were essential to circus, vaudeville, and fairground-theater performances, which were filled with gaps as they passed from one skit or episode to the next. Because dead air was the greatest sin imaginable, gaps were filled by the appearance of an intermediary. The role allowed for great freedom of movement; it breached the time gap between skits, and the space gap between performers and audience. The role was filled by, among others, both the clown and ringmaster of the circus, vaudeville's master of ceremonies, and the *compère* of the artistic cabaret. Intermediaries performed an invaluable function when popular entertainment moved to a lecture hall: continuing to provide a structural bridge, they also explained the action to the audience and guaranteed that the proper message was received. The intermediary was a carrier and enabler of meaning. In *Championship,* the role was filled by the ringmaster, who combined the duties of referee and announcer, and helped spectators along by providing narration and exegesis.

All these functions were featured in one of the most influential shows of War Communism, Annenkov's August 1919 production of Leo Tolstoy's *First Distiller.* Performed in, of all places, the Heraldic Hall of the Winter Palace, the *First Distiller* used Tolstoy's antiliquor tract as the scenario for a concoction of circus, vaudeville, and *balagan.*[31] Tolstoy's original intent, and much of the text, disappeared in Annenkov's remake. The fable involved a demon sent to earth to tempt a peasant with liquor. It was a "modernized *lubok,*"[32] and Annenkov used popular culture's loose time structure to insert clown acts, risqué folk ditties (*chastushki*), and other tidbits into the action. Although some of the insertions were justified by the text, many were not: "Ditties were incorporated as the songs of peasants drunk on the 'devil's brew.' Accordions and choral dances were also inserted into the drunken scene. Acrobats appeared as demons; a circus was the model for Hell. And, lastly, an eccentric clown in red wig and broad 'formal' trousers appeared without the slightest motivation. He simply showed up in Hell and strolled around as though it was a nightclub."[33]

Assuming that the skeleton taken from Tolstoy was still present (some critics claimed it was lost entirely), the insertions were essentially full stops, moments when the progress of Tolstoy's play was suspended. Most were performed by the clown Georg Delvary, whose role was specially created by Annenkov. The clown had no place in the plot as such; rather he fulfilled an intermediary role traditional for clowns, standing on the forestage and commenting on the action occurring behind him. Annenkov claimed that his insertions could effectively carry the message: "A five-minute number can with a few phrases or gestures offer a joyful and convincing solution to any problem and convert an unexpected zigzag in the action into a weapon of propaganda, stronger than a public speech. . . . It screams, knocks, and burns a thought into the spectator's head—instantly, unimpeded by thought, at full swing."[34] But the claim was doubtful. The devil's antics, similar to commedia dell'arte *lazzi,* were entertaining, but carried no message. Not only did the antics not correspond to the play's specific message, they did not always assign the desired positive or negative value, which is a cardinal duty of propaganda.

Directors of the popular school faced a considerable quandary in propaganda productions like *Mystery-Bouffe* and *First Distiller*. Negative, anti-Soviet characters were depicted comically; positive characters were depicted monumentally. But in popular culture (for example, the Petrushka puppet play) comic characters were often more praiseworthy (more entertaining if less ethical) than the straight characters, usually pompous boors. The bad guys were more fun than the good. Interpretation was further complicated by the lack of signals about what in the play was significant (demanding interpretation) and what was not: insertions interrupted the intent of the play; halting the progress halted the transmission of the message. Ultimately, *First Distiller* was well done and well liked; only the claims to a message were unjustified.

Meyerhold, who had started the circus fashion in theatrical circles, warned against its going too far. "The circus must not restructure itself at someone else's bidding," he said. "Reform must unfold within the circus, initiated by the circus itself. There cannot and must not be a theater circus; each is and must be a thing in itself, [although] the work of masters of the circus and the theater can draw close to one another."[35] The distinction went unheeded by the TEO Circus Department. Its artists fancied circus the art form of the future and were interested in it less as a popular entertainment than as a series of disconnected acts to be formed into a unified drama. One of the first reforms the department set about introducing was the "elimination of separate circus numbers and the reduction of circus performance to a single, unified action [*deistvo*]."[36]

This approach was not entirely contrary to circus traditions; there were wartime precedents. At the Manège, for instance, popular attractions had been allegorical processions and *tableaux vivants* celebrating tsar and country, and pantomimes starring trick riders and special effects, such as *Russian Heroes in the Carpathians* and *The Inundation of Belgium*.[37] Lazarenko, who would produce many such spectacles for the Bolsheviks, gained experience during the First World War. On December 16, 1914, before assembled diplomats of the allied nations, his circus had presented *The Triumph of the [Allied] Powers,* a play in two acts, five scenes, written by A. V. Bobrishchev-Pushkin (who in 1919 would denounce Meyerhold to White forces in the South). The characters were Russia, France, England, Belgium, Serbia, Montenegro, Japan (played by Lazarenko), Breslau, Alladin, Sultan-Bey, two dancing girls, and a dervish.[38]

Still, giving the circus new Soviet functions entailed some redefinition. Wartime pantomimes afforded spectacular action, but the Soviet pantomimes praised more abstract qualities. The circus was robbed of its dynamism; and the resulting spectacles, but for the fact that they took place in the circus arena, were indistinguishable from allegories like that performed in the Voronezh Opera House in 1918 or even baroque court spectacles. In fact, one TEO proposal, which was rehearsed for almost a year in the Second State Circus, was a revival of Sumarokov and Volkov's *Minerva Triumphant,* first performed at the coronation of Catherine the Great.[39]

It seems that the greatest obstacle to imbuing circus with a message was its essence, action. Circus action is simply unreliable. Perhaps for this reason artists turned to *tableaux vivants,* an older, less eccentric form. Tableaux are allegorical and static, and can be counted on to make their point. The sculptor Konenkov, who had just completed a group of wooden figures from the Razin lore for Lobnoe Mesto, was hired to direct a performance at the Second State Circus for the November 1919 anniversary. His choice of a theme, *Samson and Delilah*, was unfortunate (although he claimed it was a "song of the struggle for freedom"). The performance was a series of static tableaux, like a comic strip, portraying the stages of the Samson legend: the slaying of the Philistines with the jawbone of an ass; the seduction by Delilah; Samson's imprisonment; the final test of strength.[40] Konenkov employed wrestlers as the material of his sculpture; he made wigs and costumes, and carved wooden figures to encircle the tableaux. As the papers reported, "A long series of rehearsals was needed to create muscular memory in the performers and to force them to portray the sculptures with super-balletic exactitude."[41] The wrestlers, naturally enough, wanted nothing to do with it.

Another allegorical tableau presented that day in Moscow, *Standing Guard for the World Commune*, almost completely ignored the principles of the circus. It was based on the pyramid, a tumbling formation that had obvious social implications in revolutionary times.[42] The skit could have been played anywhere: "In the center of the arena a red stage rises up into a rainbow-shaped tower. There, on a platform, is the symbolic figure of a woman, Freedom, around which are grouped a peasant, a worker, a sailor, a soldier, and an intellectual. . . . Below on the steps are the corpses of Bavaria and Hungary, crushed by the imperialists. The figure reads poetry, expressing . . . confidence in the impending arrival of world revolution."[43] During the reading, statues of Marx and Engels flanking the tower came to life.[44]

Oddest of all circus presentations on November 7, 1919, was *Political Carousel*. Written by Rukavishnikov, whose wife ran the Second State Circus, where it was shown, *Political Carousel* was directed by Forreger, who by now was the director of the Moscow Balagan.[45] Forreger should have known better. This mass drama was performed on a three-tiered stage designed by Kuznetsov.

> On the top level is a monster depicting imperialistic capitalism; near it are the Russian tsar, his court, family, and ministers. On the second level are bureaucrats. . . . On the third tier a prison is shown in which workers are imprisoned, guarded by soldiers and cannons. . . . The war with Germany is symbolically depicted, with the participation of all the imperialistic countries. The pantomime closes again with a symbolic representation of the Russian Revolution: the people drag the monster out of the tower onto the street, burn the monster, then dance and make merry.[46]

One could only agree with Shershenevich when he accused Rukavishnikov and the Circus Department of destroying the circus.[47]

The Mobile-Popular Theater

Perhaps prerevolutionary Russia's finest example of popular theater was Gaideburov's Mobile-Popular Theater, located on the outskirts of Petrograd. The Mobile-Popular Theater was the first to perform on the streets of revolutionary Russia, in May 1917; and it was there, not in Proletkult, not in Narkompros, not in the heart of Ivanov's imaginary demos that the first and strongest impulse for mass spectacles arose in Soviet Russia.[48]

Founded in 1903 as the Popular Theater by Gaideburov and his wife, Nadezhda Skarskaia, a daughter of the great Komissarzhevsky acting family, it was located in the Ligovsky People's House, funded by a wealthy Social Revolutionary, the Countess Sofia Panina. Its mission was to supplement the thin cultural fare offered Petrograd workers. People's Houses sponsored by the Guardians of the People's Temperance typically featured melodramas, patriotic plays, and "extravaganzas"; others offered a "special" repertory designed for the simple folk.[49] To Gaideburov, the *gulianiia* and other "people's entertainments" were the "greatest enemy of the rebirth of popular theater."[50] He demanded more from his audiences; the first production of 1903 was Ostrovsky's *Storm,* and the repertory continued with a variety of Russian and foreign classics.[51]

Gaideburov was one of the rare members of the prewar intelligentsia who could bridge the abyss between educated and untutored Russia. He respected the potential of the people and demanded respect in return. Initially, the audience needed some training; at the conclusion of an early performance, instead of the traditional roses an enthusiast threw a bottle of vodka onto the stage.[52] But soon the theater had educated a generation of viewers who appreciated drama. By 1907 the Popular Theater had merged entirely with its alter ego, the Mobile Theater, which, staffed by the same actors, spent summer months touring the provinces with a modern repertory aimed at the local intelligentsia (Figure 10).

Symbolist theater was gaining an audience in those years, as were the symbolists' rather mystical notions of how to close the gap between the people and the intelligentsia. Although not always evident in his practice,

Figure 10. Emblem of the Mobile-Popular Theater, Petrograd (P. P. Gaideburov, *Literaturnoe nasledie,* Moscow, 1977).

Gaideburov felt the influence of Ivanov. He believed that true theater, like all true art, brought the spectator into contact with the universal. It was classless, uniting all classes and nations through a common heritage.[53] Art was a door from everyday reality into a world of ideals; the spectator, momentarily aware of the divine, left the theater stronger, ready to live creatively.[54] If theater occupied a special, ideal position in culture, it also occupied a special time; it was "a holiday in the life of man. After all, it is special precisely because it is different from the everyday."[55] Theater was a festival.

Although Gaideburov shared some of Ivanov's basic tenets, there were essential differences: Gaideburov saw symbolism as Lunacharsky or Gorky did, as an art of dynamic change. He avoided static plays like the *Death of Tintageles;* the mainstay of his repertory was Björnson's *Beyond Human Might,* which ran for over 200 shows. In Gaideburov's interpretation, the drama was a paean to the power of faith to change human life.

When the theater's ambitions outgrew the bounds of spectacle, traditional forms became a constraint; Gaideburov, like his contemporaries, found his faith limited by stage conventions. The theater was to be like a church; and the drama, a *deistvo,* a service in which "the people will be led to a pan-national creative illumination of life, in conditions of pan-human brotherhood and love. Life itself will be the object of creativity, and life will become a perfect work of art."[56] The contemporary drama, with long denouements, short climaxes, characters trapped hopelessly in the material world, and a passive audience, would not suffice.

Like his contemporaries, Gaideburov sought a theater on the threshold between ritual and drama. Early in 1918 he developed a hybrid theatrical form which he called "Masses" (*mèssa,* as in ritual). These occasions bore some resemblance to the poetic "requiems" hosted by the liberal Literary Fund at the turn of the century.[57] The first Mass of 1918, the Turgenev Evening, a memorial to the great novelist and poet, was as much about its maker as its subject. The Mobile-Popular Theater's Turgenev was deeply mystical; the Evening, like a church ritual, was an ascension to communion with his spirit.

The first segment opened on a stage decorated with only a bas-relief of Turgenev carved on an obelisk. The figure was draped in black, as was the entire set. The stage design was borrowed from Meyerhold's symbolist period at the Komissarzhevskaia Theater; and the ritual style of acting most probably had the same source. Figures came onstage chanting "the Great Pan is dead"; then figures entered the stage chanting an antistrophe, "the Great Pan lives."[58] The performers settled themselves about the stage and shared personal recollections of Turgenev's verse with the audience. The second section of the Evening was an oration illustrated by dramatic fragments, followed by the final section, a staging of scenes from Turgenev's works. The selection was mystically slanted: from *Klara Milich, Spirits, A Strange Story,* and the death of Bazarov from *Fathers and Sons.*[59] Like patriotic variety shows of the Great War, the Mass concluded with an apotheosis, a reading of the poem "The Russian Language."

The Mobile-Popular Theater's trip to the front in autumn 1917, immediately preceding the Bolshevik takeover, was a first attempt at "extramural" theater; and the Liberty Bond Day street production of *Le vendeur de soleil* showed how well it could be received by the people. But what Gaideburov really wanted, and what he advocated in a series of articles in 1918–19, was "theatrical, popular festivals. . . . Let it be the celebration of a national holiday, into which go speeches, processions, and songs. . . . Let it renew long-lost habits: Lenten celebrations, spring celebrations, celebrations of driving the cattle to pasture, of the arrival of a new car—

all this is theater that has been taken into the thick of the people, the theatricalization of life, artistic phenomena of a different artistic order, but still emanating from the nature of theatrical action."[60]

Clearly, he wished, like Ivanov, to take the theater out of the theater and to the people; and the Masses were a synthesis of theater and religion. But in his calls for national festivals, Gaideburov remembered a third element of festival performance, play, that Ivanov neglected. Here he was closer to Evreinov: "We must use the theatrical instinct, characteristic of everyone, which once helped create the forms of national life: games [play], holidays, rituals. Today, too, it can create a new ritual of national life, new forms of holiday interaction."[61]

Gaideburov pursued this idea less in the Mobile-Popular Theater, where the classics were still dominant, than in classes he and his actors conducted for the Adult Education Department (Otdel vneshkol'nogo obrazovaniia) of Narkompros. The courses were based on a philosophy different from that which had inspired the intelligentsia to organize theaters for the people before the Revolution: "We must depart from the previous educational view of theater, which saw the rationality of theatrical art in its literary side. . . . Play, specifically popular and specifically theatrical play, the activity of the people themselves, rich in artistic mysteries, will bring enlightenment."[62]

Acting, or play, was not to be taught; it was to be released from the people, where it had rested latent for centuries. The process involved a notion alien to Ivanov's ritual theater, improvisation. The Adult Education Department used the Skarskaia method, step-by-step instruction that introduced neophytes to the essentials of theater. The Skarskaia method stressed instinct over rational consciousness, inspiration and emotion over technique; the method was one of revealing, not inculcating, as "creativity is more or less inherent in everyone."[63]

Courses in improvisation were taught by Nikolai Vinogradov-Mamont and Dmitry Shcheglov, members of the theater who would soon produce the first mass spectacles in Red Petrograd. Other instructors were Elena Golovinskaia, N. V. Lebedev, Viktor Shimanovsky, and Vsevolod Vsevolodsky-Gerngross;[64] these teachers, along with Grigory Avlov, another member of the theater, and Piotrovsky, who joined the group in late 1919, would be (along with Meyerhold's students Radlov and Soloviev) the most prolific producers of mass spectacles and directors of amateur theater in Petrograd until 1927.[65]

Gaideburov himself never took part in Bolshevik festivals. In 1918–19, relations between the Mobile-Popular Theater and the new regime were acrimonious. In the difficult decade up to 1917, the Ligovsky People's House had offered shelter to many Bolsheviks, including Lenin. The party conducted meetings and lectures, and the nucleus of what would become Proletkult opened its first circle there.[66] But after the Bolsheviks took power, relations soured. The Countess Panina, who served the Provisional Government as deputy minister of public education, was jailed by the Bolsheviks for refusing to hand teachers' pension funds over to the usurpers.[67] Needless to say, Gaideburov and Skarskaia, who had the highest respect for the countess, did not approve of the action.

Differences ran even deeper, to basic philosophy. Gaideburov abhorred civic violence, particularly when it pitted class against class. His art had always strived to transcend class differences. In a letter published in the Mobile-Popular Theater's newsletter, Gaideburov defended his vision and roundly condemned the notion of a distinct proletarian art.[68] In 1919, those were fighting words. Rejection of class conflict meant rejection of the Revolution. The first of Gaideburov's disciples to object to the letter and to leave the theater was Vinogradov-Mamont.

The second half of Vinogradov's surname (which means "mammoth") was actually a nickname coined by the famous operatic bass Chaliapin to honor Vinogradov's infatuation with monumental theater.[69] Like Gaideburov and Ivanov, Vinogradov believed the theater to be a universal art; and he modestly formulated his ideas in the following "Seven Points":

1. The theater is a temple.
2. Universality.
3. Monumentality.
4. Creativity of the masses.
5. An orchestra of the arts [synthetic art].
6. The joy of labor.

Naturally, the last point of his plan was

7. Transfiguration of the world.[70]

Vinogradov worked with advanced students at the Adult Education Department on this new type of theater and planned a production of Aleksandr Pushkin's *Boris Godunov* as an open-air choral tragedy.[71] After seceding from Gaideburov's theater, he took his plans to the Political Administration of the Petrograd Military District (PUR), which was sufficiently impressed to entrust him with 100 soldiers and the task of creating a new art. For the next two years, PUR was sponsor of Petrograd's most ambitious mass spectacles.

The Red Army Studio

The Theatrical-Dramaturgical Studio of the Red Army, or Red Army Studio, as the PUR group was called, was awarded the status of a special military unit.[72] Though just about all the soldier-pupils were amateurs—such was the selection by design—the instructors were professionals. From the Mobile-Popular Theater came Golovinskaia, Lebedev, Shimanovsky, and I. M. Charov; Shklovsky would later join the staff; Meyerhold, Vinogradov's old teacher at Kurmatsep (Master Courses in Scenic Productions), was prevailed on to help; Meyerhold's disciples Nikolai Shcherbakov, Soloviev, and Radlov joined in; N. N. Bakhtin, Meyerhold's collaborator at the Instructor's Courses for Children's Theater and Festivals, also assisted.

Long before the Revolution, even before the intelligentsia interested itself in the popular theater in the 1880s, the army had served to acquaint simple Russians with theater. Soldiers had their own special repertory: melodramas and the like, such as *Kedril the Glutton* and *Filatka and Miroshka's Rivalry,* which Dostoevsky noticed before anyone even suspected that Russian popular theater existed.[73] Most popular with the soldiers were dramatic games (*igrishcha*), particularly *Boat* (*Lodka*).[74] As opposed to the ritual dramas common in folk culture, *Boat,* which survived in cities up to the Revolution, was a bare skeleton onto which action was attached and improvised. The game was given a dramatic framework by "Down the Mother Volga" ("Vniz po matushke po Volge"—the song adapted by Kronstadt sailors as they sailed into revolutionary Petrograd), which was sung as accompaniment and narration.

Festival theater was born on the borders of drama, ritual, and play. If Gaideburov's own Masses mated drama and ritual, Vinogradov followed another example, that of his other mentor, Meyerhold, and trod the border of drama and play. *Boat* was an excellent model, with its origins in mimetic play; there was no stage, no props, and few costumes. Performance began with players arranging themselves as if in a boat, one player taking a position at the helm and singing "Down the Mother Volga," the others clapping hands in a rowing rhythm. It ended the same way. The song provided a frame onto which episodes from the lore of the great Russian brigands—Ermak, Razin, and brethren—were attached.

Boat was less a drama than a cycle of episodes joined by a common theme and characters. Its time was the time of popular culture, a loose structure of stops and starts, which can expand and contract to accommodate new episodes. Like commedia dell'arte, *Boat* was improvised from a pool of traditional spoken lines and actions; and even more than in the commedia, connections between episodes could be loose. Yet *Boat* shared the ability of popular culture to take these disparate elements and unify them. Action within episodes was continuous. Perhaps most important to their new function within Soviet culture, dramatic games traditionally alternated tragic and comic scenes.[75]

The Red Army Studio's first production, performed March 12, 1919, was an *igrishche* on the topic of the February Revolution, *The Overthrow of the Autocracy*.[76] The first mass spectacle of Bolshevik Petrograd thus celebrated the February Revolution the Bolsheviks had overturned. The performance was a game in all senses of the word; it was play at revolution, a make-believe revolt by soldiers who had participated in the real one.[77] The performance, which would eventually be repeated 250 times,[78] was based on the Skarskaia method of improvisation. Most of the actors had taken part in some of the events and needed little directorial prompting. This, however, is not to suggest that improvisation engendered a deep, "elemental" understanding of historical events; nor should it suggest that the acting was necessarily spontaneous, direct, natural. Game playing has its conventions: the actors split off into two teams and, like little boys playing at war, depicted the historical conflict through a series of skirmishes and battles. Yet the play was about a bloodless revolution!

Vinogradov claimed that the oppressed masses of *The Overthrow of the Autocracy* were equivalent to the chorus of ancient tragedy and, because the ideals of the Russian Revolution were superior to those of slave-owning Athens, that the production was superior to the dramas of Aeschylus.[79] This analysis was perhaps overstated; but it would be unwise to ignore the production's artistic ambitions. Vinogradov's claim suggests a dilemma running through the Red Army Studio's history: Was it to be a popular undertaking, as the military theater traditionally had been, or was it to fulfill the great artistic ambitions suggested by symbolist theory?

The play did provide solutions to problems first pointed out by modernists. The division between stage and spectator, so porous in popular performance, was breached by the studio; this had also been an aim of symbolists. Popular culture's free combination of episodes was subjected to dramatic discipline; yet the structuring elements of the performance were taken from popular culture. Perhaps the similarities to simplified symbolist realism were apparent and desirable to Vinogradov; but the simplicity came from the exigencies of working with soldiers.

Whatever the cause, benefits were forthcoming. No decorations were used for the performance; real space was freely redefined by the action. As in melodrama, characters were divided into rebels and oppressors, good guys and bad guys. The stage itself was broken up into two platforms, each at one end of the Steel Hall of the People's House, where the play was performed. Linking the two stages was a broad aisle that passed through the audience.[80] The game principle, which split the characters into two "teams," had accordingly split the stage into two platforms; individual scenes were performed on the platforms; battles were conducted in the aisle. The aura of authenticity that brought spectators so close to the stage was intensified by the placement of actors in the audience. There were no costumes; dressed in army greatcoats, they were indistinguishable from the audience, and when they stood to deliver their lines, it seemed to spectators that one of their own was sharing a spontaneous reaction. Nevertheless, it was not the popular audience but the great artist Meyerhold who recognized what his pupil Vinogradov was looking for; when a young soldier, killed on the barricades, was borne down the aisle to "You Fell Victim," a song of revolutionary mourning, Meyerhold took the soldier's rifle from the ground and leapt to join the procession.[81] This was a *sliianie*, the merging of stage and audience the symbolist avant-garde had awaited.

The Overthrow of the Autocracy resembled a popular game, but it was supervised by professional directors. Their influence was visible in the formation of a unified play from discrete segments of improvisation. Episodes were not chosen at random, and neither was their order. The play comprised eight episodes chosen from the downfall of the Romanov dynasty: a prologue about the riots of 1905 was followed by the arrest of underground students, a revolt in a military prison, the seizure of the arsenal by workers, the sacking of Police Headquarters, the erection of barricades on the streets, the revolution at the front, and the tsar's renunciation of the throne (later observers would find the absence of the Bolsheviks unfortunate). The episodes were strung together in chronological order, with the dual platform providing a spatial model for temporal progression. One stage accommodated the primary action, with mass scenes of the proletarian struggle for freedom; on the other was the counteraction, the reaction of the conservative camp. Later observers were correct in asserting that the split stage, free definition of space, and other features of *Overthrow*, which arose naturally from its game-playing nature, laid the foundation for future mass dramas.[82]

After several performances, young studio members found themselves praised to the stars by Gorky, Chaliapin, Iurev, and others. This was heady inspiration, and for May Day another spectacle, *The Third International*, was developed.[83] Like *Overthrow*, *Third International* was an improvised *igrishche*. The stage was the same, except for a symbolic globe placed center-stage—a prop borrowed from *Mystery-Bouffe*. One thing was new about *Third International;* it was played outdoors, in front of the People's House. The mobile stage used in both the studio's works made outdoor performance fairly easy; any place could be made to fit the play.

As in *Overthrow*, improvisation in *Third International* tended to degenerate into simple fighting, to the point that the play was not dissimilar from its predecessor. In fact, most revolutions depicted in subsequent mass spectacles would look similar, which had unanticipated political consequences. In the case of *Third International*, the conventions inherited from *Overthrow* distorted the historical picture. Fighting, which made up the bulk of action, had little to do with the Third International, founded only two months before in a conference hall; and the production's thousand participants far outnumbered the International's roster. Art predicts life, as Vinogradov might have answered.

Play-based *Overthrow* worked with a historical reality familiar to players and spectators alike. The basic episodes were taken from this reality; and if improvisation departed from historical facts, its creative license revived the emotional experience of revolution more vividly than an accurate re-creation could have. *Third International* did not satisfy itself with mimetic play based on a simple, concrete experience; it aimed toward symbolic, universal truths, as the globe in the middle of the stage signaled to spectators. The stage was not just a stage but the world beyond; people were not just people but allegorical types. Mayakovsky had done the same to wrestling in his *World Championship*.

The Red Army Studio, despite Meyerhold's tutelage, was just not up to these additional requirements. There had been no characters in *Overthrow*, just masses. Characterization demanded greater continuity between scenes, a stronger focus on montage and its meaning, and, alas, greater acting skills. It demanded, in general, more art, less play. When studio actors began to portray characters and work from a text in *International*, it quickly became apparent that they were poor actors. The sharp division of characters into comic and heroic, pioneered by Meyerhold in *Mystery-Bouffe*, did not work for the studio; there was no one skilled in comic acting, which was much more difficult than Mgebrov-style heroic declamation. A need for professionals was becoming apparent.

The Red Army players had run up against what was becoming a familiar problem: play-based culture bore the burden of meaning poorly. Meaning-bearing structures were often a hindrance to play. When their ambitions shifted, those who devised the simple but fresh performances praised by critics began to fancy themselves the creators of a "new proletarian art," and their work evolved toward allegoric ritualism. It happened in the circus; it would happen in Proletkults all over the country; and it happened in the studio.

The next development was a tragedy—perhaps more a baroque allegory—written by Vinogradov and intended for performance by the studio, *The Russian Prometheus* (1919).[84] Picking a common theme (both Scriabin and Ivanov had written *deistva* of that name), Vinogradov wrote on the conflict between Peter the Great and Crown Prince Aleksei. The central figures (along with Peter and Aleksei) were two choruses: a tragic chorus of *raskol'niki* (members of religious sects) and the comic chorus of Peter's Most Drunken Council of Fools and Jesters, led by the jester Balakirev. Tragedy, according to Vinogradov, was the conflict and synthesis of equal and opposing principles.[85] The conflict led to the deaths of both Aleksei and Peter and, in the finale, Peter's ascent to heaven on a bank of clouds (perhaps Alekseev-Iakovlev could have provided the special effects).

The play was never performed,[86] and it would not merit attention but for the strong praise of some very talented contemporaries: Aleksei Remizov and Blok.[87] Lunacharsky took a more sober view: he noted that, yes, it did in many respects correspond to the theater of the future, but he also noted the strong and perhaps unintentional influence of decadent symbolism.[88] Lunacharsky's subtle criticism did nothing to discourage Vinogradov, who next wrote a *deistvo* entitled *The Creation of the World*.[89]

Graduates of Vinogradov's studio were sent to all parts of the country by PUR, and reports of similar performances began cropping up in the press. *The Overthrow of the Autocracy* was performed in Arkhangelsk;[90] *Third International* found its way to Perm.[91] Students sent to Cossack country organized topical political games, *The Taking of Rostov and Novocherkassk* and *The Smashing of Kolchak,* using the same dual stage and the same acting methods.[92]

One of Vinogradov's assistants, Shcheglov, left the Red Army Studio for a studio of his own at the Petrograd Proletkult. Shcheglov, who had directed the Red Army Studio on a trip to the front, lost no time in applying the lessons of Gaideburov and Vinogradov. On May Day 1919, in the Porokhovye factory district on the outskirts of town, he produced the first (and only) of Proletkult's mass spectacles, *From the Power of Darkness to the Sunlight.* As the title indicates, Shcheglov too was guilty of allegorical excesses. The production, an "outdoor agitational show," was assigned to the Proletkult studio by the Petrograd party leadership, which kept a close eye on its creation.[93] Shcheglov knew from his Red Army experience that uncontrolled improvisation could not be allowed; he took the writing upon himself. But because there was little dialogue, which would have been lost in the open air, most of the performance, including the gist of the plot, was conveyed by pantomime. Speech was mostly slogans, delivered either by a worker chorus or by individuals with megaphones.

In popular culture, a bad script can always be saved by a good spectacle; *From the Power of Darkness* was rescued by Alekseev-Iakovlev, in whose hands heavy-handed allegories became wondrous sights:

On a special platform, emaciated people smeared with soot spun flywheels and spoke sad words . . . taken from the proletarian poet Tarasov. . . . Occasionally a colossal figure in black with a whip in its hand would rise above the group, precisely in those moments when murmuring began and voices of protest were heard. The figure's first appearance was so unexpected, and its dimensions so huge, that the public oohed and aahed. Alekseev was truly a master of his trade. . . .

But then a red figure ran directly through the surprised crowd of spectators. . . . It stopped, raised its hand, and a red Roman Candle flared up above its head. Red "specters of communism" immediately appeared from all sides. Their appearance halted the wheels' movement: they were followed by exhausted people, but the "specters" ran past and underneath a broad old tree, in the branches of which appeared an "agitator." He read Tarasov's poem, and the workers answered from the stage: "We are here, we are ready! Battle approaches, and smoke spreads through the valley."

Hands raised hammers high to break the cursed chains; a woman with a child on her breast raced toward the "red tree" [mahogany]. But suddenly something hissed and exploded in her path, and clouds of smoke began to spread. However, this barrier could not impede the laboring masses. Raising high their hands bound in chains, the workers left the tribune for a place that augured freedom. But suddenly from all around there appeared the "shades of evil," huge figures in black. They cracked their whips, and the orchestra began to play music from a long forgotten adaptation of Gogol's *Terrible Vengeance* that Alekseev had once staged in the People's House.

Bowed and tamed, the workers retreated without casting away their age-old chains. And again the wheel began to turn with its sickening screech. The woman with the child returned to the action. Climbing the steps she read:

> They laid there in the corner,
> In the dirt of the stinking police station,
> The blood thick like paint,
> A puddle congealed on the floor.
> My friends! The enemy won't yield,
> He will buy the sacred rights of an uplifted nation
> At the price of new victims, a cruel price.

Having finished her reading, the woman ripped the black shawl from her head. Underneath was a bright red one. Others began to repeat her words, and the gray-black light on the platform where the wheel spun quickly turned red. The workers again set to breaking the chains, but, the moment the last chains were to be cast from a girl in a white dress and broad red ribbon, the forces of darkness reappeared. To the pounding of kettledrums a symbolic battle began.... Figures in tunics tumbled down to the enthusiastic cries of surprised spectators, and the performers themselves in their excitement forgot that the "evil forces" were only young men from the factory, standing on each others' shoulders and holding up yard-tall poles with capes and heads in top hats and "stupendous" yellow teeth bared for effect. Boys from the crowd threw themselves with exalted howls and whistles into the "battle with evil"—that is, they went to knock the giants over. The spectators applauded, ... but suddenly everything fell quiet. One of the "forces of the past" that had managed to save itself stole up to the girl on stage who had not yet managed to free herself entirely from her chains. A duel between the girl and the enormous figure began: the girl waved a red cape; the black figure cracked its whip, all the while getting smaller and smaller. The liberated workers approached them from behind and, crushing the last "knight of darkness," took his remains to another platform, where they hoisted the head and cape and set them on fire. First there were hissing clouds of smoke—"the stench of the past"—the head caught fire and burned long and bright, throwing out multicolored sparks. From all the trees where the "red specters" had clustered bengal lights burned, and the workers again stepped onto their old platform, where the machine wheel turned out to be decorated with ribbons and flowers. The whole thing ended with a collective reading of *Glory to Labor*.[94]

From the Power of Darkness pleased the authorities, and in November Shcheglov was invited to produce another spectacle, *From Darkness to Light,* in the city center. The second spectacle could scarcely be distinguished from the first.

Late in 1919 leadership changes in the Red Army Studio sparked changes in the plot of *Overthrow*. A young poet, scholar, and playwright, Piotrovsky, an enthusiast of the Revolution and follower of Ivanov, took charge.[95] Piotrovsky quickly spotted a major deficiency: although the play concerned historical change, little sense of history was conveyed. Perhaps more damning was that the play, which celebrated the Revolution, failed to include the Bolsheviks. If dramatic games like *Overthrow*, which featured continuous action and uniform episodes, were to portray the sweep of history and the Bolsheviks' sense of historical mission, changes were necessary, but not along the lines of Vinogradov's later plays. Recognizing that the Bolsheviks' mission was manifest not in events but in the progression of events, Piotrovsky portrayed the Revolution as a process beginning in February and culminating in October. He added two episodes: a comic interlude about the Provisional Government and a heroic finale about the October Revolution. The whole thing was renamed *Red Year*.

The introduction of discontinuous episodes brought up the question of how they could be assembled into a whole. Piotrovsky took structures characteristic of popular drama and assigned them new functions, for which *Mystery-Bouffe* offered a ready model. The alternation of tragic and comic, which Mayakovsky had used for characterization, was used to stitch together episodes in *Red Year*. Space operated on a similar principle; in the final two scenes, Kerensky and Lenin face each other from the two stages, and the final conflict occurs in the corridor between. This principle of simple oppositions, spatial, temporal, political, and moral, would be a rule for most future mass spectacles.

Piotrovsky also introduced changes in the performance. The full-length *Red Year* was held together by concrete historical figures and fictional characters, who replaced the faceless masses of *Overthrow*. Such characterization required disciplined acting and costumes to make figures like Lenin and Kerensky identifiable, but it also changed an essential principle of *Overthrow:* actors were now separated from the audience. Improvisation also gave way to a scripted text, which fixed the proper message but suppressed the playlike character of *Overthrow*. Improvisation had been intended to release the soldiers' creative instincts, but true improvisation, like true play, is a risk. Improvisation had been to a large extent desirable in *Overthrow*, which was an emotional experience of the tension and uncertainty of revolutionary days, when the future was unknown. From a strictly Bolshevik point of view, though, history was not uncertain. The October Revolution was an inevitable conclusion to the events of 1917 and, for that matter, to a century of history. This was in fact the Bolsheviks' greatest claim to legitimacy, particularly in opposition to the claims of other leftist parties.

The changes were regrettable but perhaps inevitable if the play was to fulfill the edifying function that its sponsors intended. Much the same was happening at Proletkult. Shcheglov, like Piotrovsky, attempted to discipline improvisation in his next production, *Popular Movements in Russia*.[96] Although improvisation was not entirely discouraged, the creative process was subordinated to the director's will. For the first time, soldiers were portraying events unfamiliar to them; they had to study events, not relive them emotionally.[97] Themes were chosen by the director. Improvisation continued unhindered in rehearsal until it deviated from the plan, when it was halted and corrected. The final result of all rehearsals was then treated as a fixed text.[98]

The episodes, selected and assembled during rehearsals, presented a new concept of revolutionary history that would much later gain broad currency in Soviet Russia: the October Revolution as the culmination of national history, ignoring Western influence. *Popular Movements* was something of a misnomer: it tied together the Bolotnikov, Razin, and Pugachev peasant uprisings, the rebellion of the aristocratic Decembrists, the revolt of the tiny village of Bezdna (Bottomless Pit) in 1861, the 1905 revolution, and the Bolshevik seizure of Moscow in December 1917. As the last episode of a series, the Bolshevik takeover was the assumed heir of a great historical progression.

The limits of the popular style were reached by the Red Army Studio in February 1920, when *The Sword of Peace* was produced for the army's second anniversary.[99] The play was called a "variation" on *The Overthrow of the Autocracy*, but the resemblance was distant. To emphasize ties to the popular theater, it was performed in the Cinizelli Circus, yet Piotrovsky's text was written in the blank verse of high tragedy. Radlov directed the play and employed the dual-platform stage of *Overthrow*, but of course, with a text in blank verse, there could be no improvisation. The plot was built from the basic stages of the Red Army's history. The play opens with a soldier in a greatcoat and helmet, spotlighted center-stage, portraying Trotsky at Brest-Litovsk. Unrolling a long scroll (the treaty) he declaims:

> Comrades! the workers and the peasants
> Are neither murderers nor thieves! We don't need
> A predatory war. We need peace. . . .
> Red soldiers, you are the hope of peace!

> You are the sword of peace. The future of the Commune
> Is on your banners. In bloody splendor
> The Red Star ascends above the world.
> In truth, a new world has been born.[100]

To Berlioz's *Symphonie fantastique* a shower of red stars rains down from the big top, and the Red Army rushes into battle. Battle scenes, like those in Vinogradov's productions, ensued; but an interlude, in which Three Wise Men crossed the stage in search of the Red Star rising in the East, separated the battles into episodes.

The Revolution prompted shifts in the cultural hierarchy. Popular forms once consigned to the periphery of Russian culture moved to the center and were given new responsibilities. These responsibilities could be met only at the price of structural changes. The play element that had been the essence of popular culture could not always bear the messages thrust on it by the Revolution.

When popular theater began to serve official purposes, changes could be observed: the subordination of improvisation to directorial design; a shift of emphasis from episodes (most early amateur depictions of the Revolution were one-act plays) to the way in which episodes were strung together; and the loading of symbolic interpretations onto play-based actions. Individuals replaced mass characters and choruses; costumes were introduced to identify the new characters; acting became increasingly complex. These changes were an early example of a trend in Soviet Russia: popular performance, an autonomous branch of culture with values and a style of its own, was replaced by amateur performance, a secondary reflection of high culture.

Mass spectacles had caught the attention of Bolshevik leaders and had shown the potential to project a compelling view of the Revolution. Yet to realize their significance within the new culture, they would have to expand beyond the local audience. Greater organizational skills were needed; and if an audience unfamiliar with the actors and their locality was to be attracted, the full resources of the theatrical heritage would have to be exploited. There was only one option. Professionals would have to take control.

Plate 1. Holiday fireworks display, Moscow, 1744 (A. F. Nekrylova, *Russkie narodnye gorodskie prazdniki, uveseleniia i zrelishcha: Konets XVIII–nachalo XIX veka*, Leningrad, 1984).

Plate 2. *Opposite, top of page*: Lithograph of the carnival on St. Petersburg's Field of Mars, 1825 (A. F. Nekrylova, *Russkie narodnye gorodskie prazdniki, uveseleniia i zrelishcha: Konets XVIII–nachalo XIX veka*, Leningrad, 1984).

Plate 3. *Opposite*: Mariinsky Palace, Petrograd, November 7, 1918 (I. M. Bibikova and N. I. Levchenko, comps., *Agitatsionno-massovoe iskusstvo: Oformlenie prazdnestv*, Moscow, 1984).

Plate 4. *Above*: Demonstration in Red Square, November 7, 1918 (I. M. Bibikova and N. I. Levchenko, comps., *Agitatsionno-massovoe iskusstvo: Oformlenie prazdnestv*, Moscow, 1984).

Plate 5. *Opposite*: Decoration of Hunters' Row, Moscow, November 1918 (I. M. Bibikova and N. I. Levchenko, comps., *Agitatsionno-massovoe iskusstvo: Oformlenie prazdnestv*, Moscow, 1984).

Plate 6. *Above*: Tribune covering Pavel Trubetskoi's equestrian statue, Uprising Square, Petrograd, May Day 1919 (I. M. Bibikova and N. I. Levchenko, comps., *Agitatsionno-massovoe iskusstvo: Oformlenie prazdnestv*, Moscow, 1984).

Plate 7. *Opposite*: Boris Kustodiev, *Celebration for the Second Congress of the Third International,* Petrograd, July 1920 (Mikhail German, ed., *Serdtsem slushaia revoliutsiiu. Iskusstvo pervykh let oktiabria,* Leningrad, 1980).

Plate 8. *Above*: *Toward a World Commune,* mass spectacle, Stock Exchange, Petrograd, July 1920 (Mikhail German, ed., *Serdtsem slushaia revoliutsiiu. Iskusstvo pervykh let oktiabria,* Leningrad, 1980).

Plate 9. *Above*: Vladimir Tatlin, *Monument to the Third International*, Petrograd, 1920 (Camilla Gray-Prokofieva, *The Russian Experiment in Art, 1863–1922*, London, 1971).

Plate 10. *Opposite, top of page*: The Red stage, *Storming of the Winter Palace*, mass spectacle, Petrograd, November 1920 (I. M. Bibikova and N. I. Levchenko, comps., *Agitatsionno-massovoe iskusstvo: Oformlenie prazdnestv*, Moscow, 1984).

Plate 11. *Opposite*: Liubov Popov and Alexander Vesnin, design for a theatricalized mass maneuver in honor of the Third International, Moscow, 1921 (Angelica Rudenstine, ed., *Russian Avant-Garde Art: The George Costakis Collection*, New York, 1981).

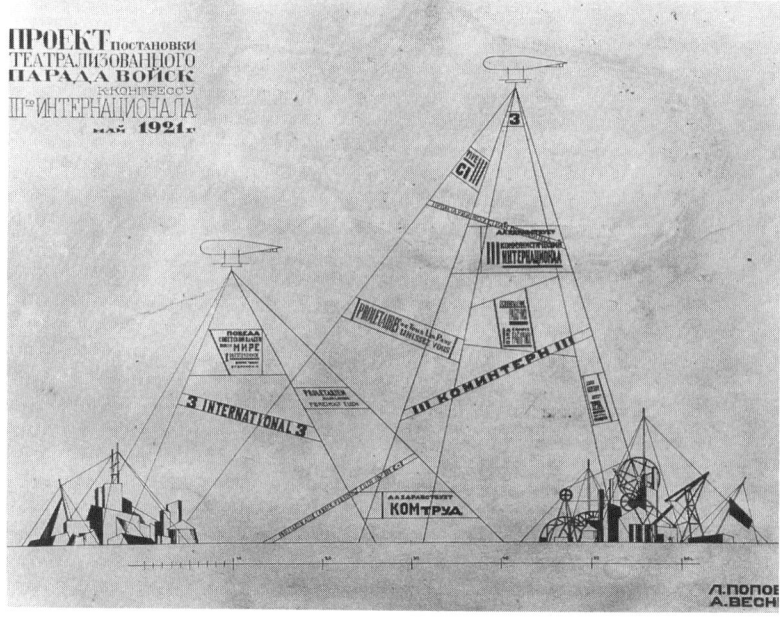

FIVE

Transformation by Festival

Mass Festivals as Performance

> *Our revels now are ended. These our actors,*
> *As I foretold you, were all spirits, and*
> *Are melted into air, into thin air,*
> *And, like the baseless fabric of this vision,*
> *The cloud-capped towers, the gorgeous palaces,*
> *The solemn temples, the great globe itself—*
> *Yea, all which it inherit—shall dissolve*
> *And, like this insubstantial pageant faded,*
> *Leave not a rack behind.*
>
> Shakespeare, *The Tempest*

Holidays, festivals, and spectacles rapidly acquired overriding substance in Russian political culture. In 1919 crises and landmarks were manifold: the White general Iudenich's approach to the outskirts of Petrograd; the Allied blockade; the founding of the Third International. When *Petrograd Pravda* printed a New Year 1920 chronicle of the past year, accompanied by a full page of photographs, events that had placed the Soviet republic's fate in jeopardy were strangely muted. Instead, leading items were the November 7 anniversary celebration; Soviet Propaganda Day; the May Day burning of a dragon (of counterrevolution) in effigy. Readers might have surmised some of the year's axial moments, but the moments themselves went unmentioned. Accounts of pivotal battles were supplanted by victory speeches; legislative bodies were noted not for the laws they passed but for their convocations. The only reference to the winter's dire heating crisis was the following paragraph:

Battling the fuel crisis: On November 15 the Petrograd Soviet met to discuss the question of the struggle against the fuel crisis.[1]

Ivanov's dictum was being realized: the show was becoming the event.

The "show become real," Ivanov's notion of *deistvo,* seemed increasingly prescient during the Revolution. Ivanov, like the socialists Sorel, Lunacharsky, and Gorky, understood myth as a contemporary, living phenomenon; and he saw it not as a remote narrative but as flesh-and-blood dramatic action. He surpassed his contemporaries in grasping the mechanics of myth. *Deistvo* amalgamated several elements,—drama, ritual, and myth—into a single festive performance. Ivanov anticipated modern anthropologists, such as Victor Turner, in seeing celebration as a dynamic symbolic field transforming the past it commemorates.

Mass Drama and the Professionals

Deistvo was at the heart of the debate over amateur and professional participation in festivals. Remuneration was not ultimately the issue: "amateurs" were often paid to perform, while "professional" participation was often voluntary. The issue was rather the relationship of the artist to art, and the relationship of both to the audience. The optimistic assumption underlying some early festivals was that if the working class sponsored a festival and if participants were from the working class, then the working class would identify with the festival. *Deistvo* theory suggested alternatives to such overly direct formulations.

In early 1920, a few professionals expressed the heretical thought that the director's skill, not class origin, was most critical to a mass spectacle. According to Tairov (who also began his career with Gaideburov), much of the rhetoric surrounding mass festivals was utter nonsense. "We are going through a period of amateurism, when everyone fancies that he can create new forms of theater." Only skilled professionals created new forms; only they could elevate mass festivals to the artwork of the future. Tairov addressed a root paradox: "Popular festivals, as such, are not theater, but when they have been created by directors and producers, they lose their popular character and become nothing more than an expanded application of the directorial art of 'mass scenes.'"² The gist of the paradox was that revolutionary festivals could be popular or they could be the grand artwork of the future envisioned by Wagner, but they could not be both.

Tairov was attacking a premise cherished in one way or another by Ivanov, by Lunacharsky, even by many Proletkultists. The controversy aroused by his jibes gave proof to the rule that any exchange concerning festivals, in particular the question of popular participation, pertained also to the politics of revolution. Let the reader substitute—as did many contemporaries—uprising for festival, country for theater, politician for director, working masses for audience, and Tairov had provided a critique of Leninism. Bolsheviks declared soviet power in the name of the people, and their ultimate goal was a society arising from the people; but they did not trust the people to choose their own route. The contradiction underlay the notion of *samodeiatel'nost'*, which inspired mystic reverence in many revolutionaries and meant something different to each of them. It inspired Lenin's understanding of the revolutionary party, which represented the working class and guided it—even against its own immediate inclinations. As might be expected, Lunacharsky, faced with the same paradox as Tairov, suggested a more Bolshevik solution: "Many think that collective creation denotes a spontaneous, independent manifestation of the masses' will. But . . . until social life attunes the masses to an instinctive observation of a higher order and rhythm, it is impossible to expect anything but merry noise and the multicolored flux of holiday clothes from the masses."³

Similar motives instigated the subordination of popular theater and festivals to bureaucratic control in 1919. The people's culture could not be trusted to the people. The TEO Subsection for Worker-Peasant Theater was created, and it convened at the end of 1919 to establish policy guidelines.⁴ Though theater professionals were banned from the conference, administrators, professionals from other arts, and professional critics were not.⁵ In fact, amateur participation was minimal, and no nonprofessional opinion was recorded in the conference minutes.

Ivanov delivered the keynote address. Although he had adopted some of the new political vocabulary, his ideas had changed little in fifteen years. His message, that revolution could beget the pan-national art of mass festivals, was received warmly by delegates.⁶ Vsevolodsky-Gerngross made a similar appeal. The old stage structure had rendered spectators passive. A new drama, in which people were active participants, would bridge the abyss between actor and spectator. Russian holiday games and rituals had once provided such a drama, and Vsevolodsky claimed that "the people must create a theater from its cultic rituals. . . . The foundation of the theater of the future will be the drama of the choral dance."[7] V. V. Tikhonovich, who presided at the congress, claimed that theater's highest purpose was to "aestheticize life"; artistic discipline would help participants transform their everyday existence.[8]

Two tendencies were evident: debaters ignored urban popular traditions, and they viewed the theater as anything but theater. Their ideal was a merging of ritual and drama that expressed and instigated national unanimity. Kerzhentsev, who came to the congress as a Proletkult delegate, gave a speech, "On Festivals of the People," in which he defined their purpose. Mass festivals were to be:

1. a means of political education, a rallying point for the slogans of the day, . . . and a means to introduce the masses to all manifestations of art
2. creative *samodeiatel'nost'*
3. a theater school for the laboring masses . . .
4. collective creative activity preparing the way for socialist theater, where actor and spectator are not separated, where drama (*deistvo*) will be improvised by the laboring masses
5. a means to combat religion in the countryside. . . . The influence of the church has been strong to a significant degree because it offers sumptuous theatrical spectacles, often with the participation of the believers themselves
6. . . . closer to forms of drama, which give them connected dramatic unity, . . . and aim for the direct participation of those gathered in a holiday ritual.[9]

The congress mandated a national body for mass-festival organization. Oddly, Ivanov, Kerzhentsev, Vsevolodsky-Gerngross and Tikhonovich were not included on its staff. Meyerhold and Evreinov, trapped in the South by fighting, and other professional directors were also absent.

Plans for the TEO Section for Mass Presentations and Spectacles predated the congress. It was formed in October 1919 from representatives of the Association of Worker-Peasant and Red Army Theater, the subsection of the same name, and the TEO Subsection on Repertory; it was mandated to be a theoretical group concerned more with planning than with practice.[10] Members were chosen from the various arts, in line with the belief that festivals were a synthetic art form: Smyshliaev from the theater, P. S. Kogan (a literary scholar soon to be director of the Academy of Artistic Sciences) from literature, Sofia Kogan from music, and M. V. Libakov from the plastic arts. Aleksei Gan, a former colleague of Malevich, so radical that he considered Proletkult conservative and Lunacharsky counterrevolutionary, and N. I. Lvov were also added.[11] The section did not meet until December; by that time, according to Gan, it was controlled by its radical Communist faction.[12]

In the section's "Appeal" for members, festivals were described as "an organic need lying deep in the popular consciousness," to be "created only by the masses themselves in the process of collective creation."[13] This description, of course, made the section superfluous. Despite the rhetoric, plans (never realized) were made for May Day 1920.[14] Kogan provided a balanced formula for the contributions of artist and people: the people were to supply raw energy and enthusiasm, which artists would guide into the finished forms of art. Mass festivals were, following Nietzsche's Hellenic tragedy, a product of the dialectic of Dionysian people and Apollonian artist:

> We must invite on the one hand proletarian collectives . . . and on the other hand individual artists . . . whose ideology inclines toward the proletariat, who can merge [with the proletariat] in a single creative impulse.
> These people of art are the masses' artistic leaders, who arouse the creative urge [*samotvorchestvo*] of the masses and find the appropriate forms to express their enthusiasm.
> On their part the proletarian collectives contribute to the festival their internal content—i.e., the revolutionary pathos, their intoxication, orgiasm—without which a mass theatrical drama cannot be created.[15]

Kogan's formulation, which found common ground roots in Nietzsche with the ideas of Ivanov and Lunacharsky, showed the tangled legacy of the popular-participation issue and, moreover, its kinship with the pairing of ritual and drama.

Ritual, Drama, and Myth

The desire to merge ritual and drama into a single notion, *deistvo*, reflected the theater world's confusion about the Revolution. Even artists and intellectuals who embraced the people's seizure of power and welcomed their participation in social governance were not always prepared for the tumult that resulted. The intelligentsia had often imagined the people to be a homogeneous mass waiting to receive its directions. Such was the audience of the imaginary *deistvo*.

There are, however, essential distinctions to be made between ritual and drama that concern the relationship between the stage (and, by analogy, intellectuals) and the audience. Ritual and drama use symbols in different ways, mostly because they address different audiences. They also narrate their stories differently. Ritual, which speaks to a united community, can assume the audience comes acquainted with its conventions, while drama can create and define its own. Yet drama, because it makes its own language, can address a large and diverse community, and help it identify with unfamiliar ideas. As the Russians increasingly understood the nature of their divided audience and felt the need to reach beyond a narrow partisan group, they came to recognize the merits of drama in festival performance. It would enable them to create a new myth of revolution that could unite large segments of society.

These questions, and the solutions we are about to see the Russians try, are being probed now by modern anthropologists, foremost of which is Turner, who have described the discursive features of festival performance.[16] Correcting a functionalist inclination that narrowed celebration to a socializing agency, the anthropologists have discerned complex mechanisms of conflict resolution. Festivity's power to mediate tension is predicated on its separation from everyday social intercourse. It is defined not by the attitudes or beliefs expressed but as a discursive environment, which is symbolically isolated and must be entered across a threshold.

The festival threshold takes many forms: in time, it can be a special moment in the natural or cosmic cycle, or the anniversary of a moment in the past; in space, it can be a sacred place, a cave deep in the womb of mother earth or a consecrated house of worship. Participants in a rite must prepare themselves for crossing into the environment: they paint their faces, perform ablutions, enter the dream state of the shaman. Within the environment, their behavior is highly conventionalized; each movement, if it is to have symbolic significance, must accord with a preestablished and sanctified pattern. The language of festival performance is compact, symbolic, and mysterious. It segregates the environment from its surroundings and is meaningless outside the celebration, which enables societies to enact their fundamental myths and contradictions safely.

The language, symbols, and environment of a festival preselect and govern its audience. A highly conventionalized environment implicitly relegates outsiders—those unfamiliar with the language—to the role of spectator. Members of the community, who are familiar with the language and perceive its significance (which they cannot always express in everyday language), are not split into spectators and performers. Society—or the members admitted to a ritual—participates as a whole and finds its wholeness in the performance.

Societies confronting periods of rapid change use myths of tradition for internal consolidation and structuring.[17] The reassuring presence of the past can help a society move into the future with confidence, while the selective presence of the past can be manipulated for political advantage. Revolutionary festivals in Russia were, as they had been in France, a way of choosing which future to pursue. Each past that was celebrated in the festivals—and there were many to choose from—suggested a different path forward.

It would be wise at this point to investigate precisely how myths are made and why some find more popular resonance than others. The assumption that the content of myths determines their fate is perhaps unwarranted. Myths are not created intuitively; like dramas, they follow formal conventions. Turner's work is valuable in that it provides tools for examining these formal aspects. It also shows a particular affinity to Russian ideas. When Turner conflates ritual with drama and claims that they are "making, not faking," he is very close to Ivanov.

Turner ascribes to festival performance the same features that tantalized Ivanov, Meyerhold, and their peers. For them, the *deistvo* was drama restored to its ritual origins. *Deistvo* drama occupied a special environment, the temple stage; performers prepared themselves with masks in order to inhabit a new personality. Dramatic language was conventionalized and deeply symbolic, and could thus address universal truths that transcended ordinary language. Drama participants (actors and spectators were not differentiated) were initiates sharing a language, setting, and beliefs. The *deistvo* brought them together and provided a common experience through which they merged into a united whole.

That Russians, whose society was rent by internal division, should feel the need for healing rituals is no surprise; the belief in merging (*sliianie* is the Russian term) was begotten by wishful thinking and historical habits. Bolshevik mass festival advocates, including feisty class partisans like Kerzhentsev and Friche, dreamed of the fraternal masses dancing and singing on city streets bathed in communal togetherness. They would in coming years occasionally fancy they had seen such a thing. They had not. Russia was torn by internecine war. The Bolsheviks, in fact, were largely responsible for the fighting, and class struggle was a foundation of their program.

The illusion was spawned by a refusal to discriminate between drama and ritual. Ideally, festival dramas would commemorate revolutionary history, generate socialist myths and a new socialist culture, and unite the people under socialist ideology. Each potential was, in theory, latent in festivity. However, the three could not be realized together. There were, as became evident, differences between drama and ritual that had been ignored by Ivanov, were ignored by Bolshevik commentators—and are often ignored by modern anthropologists.[18] The differences were of broad consequence and should not be dismissed as marginal. Blurring the boundaries of ritual and drama obscured the contours of the historical events depicted and negated political distinctions essential to Bolshevik ideology, including some that had justified the October Revolution. Ultimately, the confusion revealed an underlying uncertainty about the nature of the Revolution and ambivalence about the creative contribution of the masses.

Drama and ritual should be viewed as poles of a single phenomenon, the symbolic activity of festivity. The differences lie in how ritual and drama create symbols and how the symbols condition audience composition and response. Symbols are more cohesive in drama than in ritual, where the kinship can be more conventionalized. The symbols of drama are created within the narrative structure and are interpreted according to its framework of meanings. Drama can yield many meanings to many interpreters, who can belong to many cultural communities. Rituals are celebrated by a community of shared discourse, usually of shared belief. Symbols can be imported into the ritual environment and do not need to harmonize with the ritual scenario or surrounding symbols. Participants are already aware of the proper interpretation and need not postulate new ones. Few people object, for instance, when the president of the United States swears on the Holy Bible to uphold the Constitution; nor did Communists object when the visage of Karl Marx was borne on a gonfalon of ecclesiastic origin or, more jarringly, when a "Red star" rose over a "tree of freedom" seen through "golden gates."

The symbols of a festival shape audience composition. Symbolic language stipulates a greater or lesser degree of foreknowledge, and the performance solicits or deters audience participation. Ritual dramas, which spoke a hieratic language, often made poor propaganda. The sponsors were preaching to the converted, for nobody else could understand the symbols. A more common strategy, as is already evident, was to assign new values to the prerevolutionary lexicon of ritual. Audiences were conscious enough of ritual conventions to sense the air of solemnity summoned by the symbols; and with timely prompting they read new messages into them.

The May Day 1920 celebration in Samara illustrated both the adaptability and the incoherence of ritual symbols. The holiday was observed with a demonstration, speeches by various dignitaries, and the unveiling of monuments. The demonstration was the main event. An assembly of people of different ages, professions, and classes presented the audience with an image of social solidarity and was meant to reflect the audience itself. At the center of Samara's main square, through which the demonstration passed, was a huge globe, emblazoned with the slogan "Long Live Labor."

> At its base along the sides stood two trucks: one held children with flowers, the other, boys with garlands. To the side stood various workers with the attributes of their industries: machine tools, hammers, etc., and a group of peasants with agricultural emblems: plows, harrows, seed drills, etc. Before the globe in the middle of the square . . . was the Altar of the Proletariat, an anvil and hammer garlanded by flowers. Here stood representatives of Soviet power and the municipal administration. They symbolized the mature years of the children surrounding them. A procession of thousands of people was routed past the group. The marchers were divided by category; a representative of each pronounced a greeting and presented an emblem of labor as they approached the altar. The children would then decorate the emblem with flowers, the boys with their garlands. The emblem was returned with a reciprocal greeting, and the group continued on to music. Amongst the groups were representatives of aviation, of the typesetters that had printed the slogans of the day and tossed them to the crowd along the parade route, firemen, metalworkers (with a flaming forge), and the band of Stepan Razin.[19]

If the Altar of the Proletariat was not sufficiently ambiguous, the demonstration was followed by the *Coronation of the Revolution*.[20]

Russians of the Civil War period were quite aware of the kinship of drama and ritual.[21] Ritual and drama both arrange symbolic events in time with dramatic plot serving a function analogous to the ceremony of ritual. Rituals, like drama, mark transitions: a change in season, a change in status, a key moment in history. Ritual consists of three distinct phases: the before-stage, the middle time of transition (the threshold, or limen); and the aftermath; drama evolved from the threshold phase. The Russians, like their anthropologist descendants, preferred to observe the similarities and ignore the differences. The key distinction lay in the dynamic middle phase. Ritual focuses on the initial and final phases, which represent concrete stages in the life of a person, society, or nature. Transitions between phases can be abrupt and discontinuous. The middle phase is a symbolic, often brief, acknowledgment of transition. Drama, however, is born of the middle phase, the dynamic and often arduous passing between two phases of life.

This rather abstract discrimination had implications for mass drama; it determined how revolutionary events were depicted and how spectators perceived them. The phases of festive performance corresponded to three distinct historical periods; the before and after phases represented prerevolutionary oppression and postrevolutionary salvation, while the transition phase in the middle represented the October Revolution. The outcome was that revolutionary rituals, which highlighted the before and after, never actually depicted revolution. They were static representations similar to the basic performances Kerzhentsev recommended for beginning actors: "[Show] a proletarian children's colony housed in a former lords' manor house. Show what sort of people used to live there, the savage scenes of violence that were played out.... Such contrasts... can be drawn in all fields. Before, the 'gentlemen' drank and partied; now they sell newspapers and haul lumber. Before military discipline was based on slavery; now it's built on a feeling of comradeship."[22]

For Ivanov, Lunacharsky, and many contemporaries, drama and ritual were inseparable from myth. All three were subsumed by *deistvo:* the representation of a crucial transformation in the life of an individual that spoke for the whole of society through its symbolic essence. The terminology was foggy, as nineteenth-century idealism could be, and it was more likely to synthesize than to analyze, yet it harbored a truth of practical significance to poets and propagandists alike. Myths are dramatic; Greek drama evolved from ritual as the enactment of a mythic past. The ultimate ambition of many festival planners was to create a myth of the October Revolution. If they were to succeed, they would have to dramatize it.

Myth shared two features of drama that were likely to appeal to a mass audience. The first was its symbolic language; mythic symbols, like the dramatic, must be cohesive. Symbols carry a continuous meaning throughout a drama or myth, and they share a common source with other symbols in the narrative. Any transformation or conversion undergone by a symbol must be explained by the narrative. Dramatic symbols can be viewed by a diverse audience, not only initiates, because they are less conventionalized and are construed by the course of the drama.

Ritual is celebrated by a community, in which participants and spectators share beliefs; drama is performed by a specialist for any spectator.

Of equal import to a mass audience was the second shared feature of myth and drama, the process of identification. This process was not the same in ritual. Myth and ritual might celebrate similar experiences; but myth assigns specific identities to person, place, and time. Ritual place and time are indeterminate—as Meyerhold noted in his Maeterlinck productions. They assume a broad applicability: rituals can be used by many people to observe birth, marriage, or death. The indeterminacy of ritual allows all eligible members of a social group to celebrate. The identity of the participant is irrelevant to the ceremony; the role and the performer are one. In myth, space is identified, and time moves by the rules of narrative progression. The leading role is assumed by a single figure, the protagonist, and cannot be transferred to another person. Action, linked by a single figure, is assembled into dramatic plot.

The paradox of dramatic identification, which runs against basic instincts operative during the Revolution, is that the collective identifies with the individual. The audience of a ritual consists mostly, often exclusively, of those who have performed or will pass through the ritual. They are initiates. Yet most rituals begin with celebrants separating themselves from the community by a symbolic act of cleansing or distancing. The transition phase is passed alone, after which the celebrant can reenter the community. In drama, the actor and audience stand apart from the role of the protagonist. Yet both identify intensely with the protagonist's experience, which generates drama's emotional impact.

There were complexities to myth that had not been foreseen. Many Bolsheviks had a grasp of its social implications, but a tendency to equate myth and ideology blinded them to its mechanics. Smyshliaev developed a plan for May Day 1920 that was a patent attempt to create a myth of revolution. Smyshliaev proposed using the myth of Prometheus, which had traveled a long road through Russian social thought. Marx was the most frequent holder of the Promethean title, while Ivanov and Scriabin had seen it as a myth of Western civilization. Vinogradov was attracted by the myth; and sovietization was consummated in the *Golden King,* a synthetic production about the battle of labor and capital, performed to Scriabin's *Prometheus* theme.[23] In Smyshliaev's socialist version, Prometheus symbolizes the "proletariat, bound to the rock of capitalism," and the Red Army effects a revolution by freeing him from his chains.

At sunrise heralds . . . spread out through the sleeping city and with a loud fanfare summon citizens to previously announced squares and streets. . . .

The square is surrounded by smoking torches, near which stand people with strange, night-black posters, black masks, holding rods of gold; these are pompous, bombastic figures, cretinous. . . . They let the citizens file by [and] assemble in the center of the square by the black figure of a deity, monstrous and oppressively large. . . . The citizens see that a man in a blue workers' shirt [Prometheus] is bound to the idol with a steel chain. . . .

Dawn arrives and the people with the rods of gold turn restless; they try to block the sun from the crowd with their black shields. But from the thick of the crowd emerges a Red Army detachment, which makes its way to the pedestal of the idol, unchains the man in the blue shirt, and topples the idol. The liberated man raises a red banner, at which time a tremendous choir, dispersed among the crowd itself, begins to sing *Prometheus,* a hymn written specially for the occasion.[24]

The plan concludes with a call for the obligatory merging of audience and actors.

Both drama and ritual make assumptions about the audience that determine their symbolic language and its interpretation, and ultimately condition their ability to create myths. Soviet festival planners, and not Smyshliaev alone, failed to imagine their audience fully. They made an eminently Bolshevik miscalculation; they assumed that, confronted with a properly proletarian myth, the proletariat would adopt it as their own. Lunacharsky's prerevolutionary writings left little doubt as to his unabashed wish to give the masses a myth of revolution. But ideology alone does not create myths. As we have seen, myths must be structured like myths, their symbols must be mythic, and they must account for the audience and its culture. Smyshliaev, for instance, failed to note that his audience was unfamiliar with the Prometheus myth. If the Russians wished to create a myth of revolution, they would have to feature the Revolution itself, an experience shared by all Soviet Russia—and interpreted differently by its various constituents.

As Emile Durkheim suggested in *The Elementary Forms of Religious Life,* ritual needs—and is meant to create—an atmosphere of unanimity. Spectator-participants cooperate with their community. The tendency of festival planners to assume unanimity and to fabricate myths for the whole nation was inspired ultimately by a disregard for spectator autonomy.[25] They blithely foresaw revolutionary fervor and symbolic identification. That this assumption did not correspond to the popular mood was noted by young members of Moscow Proletkult who were asked to judge Smyshliaev's proposal. They first pointed out the obvious: it was much too expensive for wartime. More telling was the criticism that if the masses were to participate, they needed to have the same intentions as the planners: "Drawing the masses into the action is technically impossible: how can thousands of participants be inspired [to the same purpose]? How can the desire be aroused in them to take part in the drama? And, finally, how can the masses' movement be led or guided if they do not go as the initiating groups intend them to?"[26] Bely, by now an instructor at the Moscow Proletkult, had made the same objection fifteen years before in reference to Ivanov's theories.

Like the antagonists in the antimodernist campaign of 1918–19, festival planners had trouble acknowledging spontaneous mass reaction. Herein lay the paradox of *samodeiatel'nost'*. Participation by the untrained masses was welcome, but their creativity had to be controlled, even instigated. Several strangely contrived solutions showed the depth of the organizers' discomfort. Smyshliaev suggested putting barriers in the path of the demonstrators; the effort to overcome them would force the marchers to manifest self-activity.[27] Another suggestion, which in a few years would become general Soviet practice, was to distribute among the crowd "cells of fomenters" (*iacheiki zazhigatelei*), whose premeditated enthusiasm would inspire spontaneous emotion.[28]

Play and Imagination

Overlooked has been the third element of the performative triad: play. The Hellenic Olympics consisted of rituals to honor the gods of Olympus, dramas for the tragic competition, and athletic contests to glorify national heroes. A similar interweaving of ritual, drama, and play is fundamental to festivals and performative theory.

Play takes many forms: there are competitions of skill, like sport; mimicry, the habitation of a new personality; and games of risk and vertigo.[29] The first two are most relevant here. Play exhibits features of festive behavior found in ritual and drama: a special environment, whether the playing field of games or the attitude of mimicry (the shaman's or oracle's possession); behavior distinguished from everyday conduct by conventions—the rules of the game or the "what-if" of make-believe. In game playing, these conventional, even artificial, traits free behavior from social constraints and allow creative latitude.

Mass spectacles developed from the tension of all three performance types, in which play offered a potential for spontaneous participation and creativity. *The Overthrow of the Autocracy* was an *igrishche*, a game; it was a replaying of the Revolution. Play acting stimulated a feeling of revolution that was otherwise missing. Yet *Overthrow*, which was performed for army units, played to a limited audience associated with the players; either they were directly acquainted, or they were, like Vinogradov's students, soldiers. The barrier between stage and audience was breached, which Russian theorists had—perhaps mistakenly—assumed was the essence of a mass *deistvo*; but it was breached because of previously shared experiences, the Revolution and Civil War, that lay outside the performance. If the performance was to be a unifying medium— that is, if mass spectacles were to unite a divided society—it would have to fabricate a common experience that carried symbolic moment beyond the performative environment.

Play is not essentially symbolic, although it can be symbolic because it can be interpreted. Most anthropologists would in fact take strong exception to the idea that play is nonsymbolic, and the "meaning" of play is described in great detail in John MacAloon's work on the modern Olympics. The contradiction though is not so great. Play as such is not meaningful; but it certainly can be a carrier of meaning. Placed in a proper context, like the Olympics, play can become highly symbolic. But in another context, the same game will have entirely different connotations or none at all. Significantly, the same cultural system that reads political meaning into the Olympic Games also senses that politics detract from sportsmanship—a notion that elevates game playing to noble stature. Vinogradov seems to have sensed the limits of *Overthrow*. The dramatic game provided a dynamic principle for depicting the Revolution, yet lacked a generalized, symbolic setting to transport the soldiers beyond immediate experience. Thus, in the next spectacle, *Deistvo of the Third International*, the overtly symbolic globe was placed center-stage.

Play could make several contributions to revolutionary fêtes. Dramatic games like *Overthrow* were capable of depicting revolution dynamically, a welcome contrast to the ostentatious rituals sweeping Soviet Russia. Of greater import was a quality that had been neglected, even by Vinogradov: make-believe. Although the materialist Bolsheviks, who were often guilty of excess sobriety, left no room for play in their cultural theories, there was a role for it in an evolving socialist culture. Make-believe asks participants to imagine themselves in new surroundings and to create behavior appropriate to that environment. The setting and rules of behavior can be strictly defined, as in a board game, or freely generated, as in child's play. Make-believe shares essential features with drama and ritual: conventionality and the assumption of new identities by participants. It lent revolutionary festivals a lightness that was distinctly lacking; moreover, it encouraged participants to act as they might under communism and to create new types of behavior.

The role of play in festivity is perhaps the best explanation of why Evreinov, so unmaterialist, so unserious, and, finally, so un-Bolshevik, should have directed the most powerful and most mythic of the revolutionary festivals. In opposition to the symbolists, who returned theater to its ritual origins, Evreinov took theater along the axis of play. For Evreinov, theatricality was the essence of theater. Theatricality, theater for theater's sake, meant to him the element of play, of make-believe, a preaesthetic instinct in all life. Play was the principle of eternal creation. Children make a theater from their five fingers; dogs chase their own tails; adults ceaselessly don and doff social masks: life is a series of transformations. Play is a release from everyday exigency, a time when the imagination can transform and beautify life.[30]

Evreinov saw great therapeutic value in inhabiting new personalities. His idea was best illustrated by *The Main Thing*, a comedy written by him and directed by Nikolai Petrov at the Free Comedy Theater in 1921.[31] It was a simple play of changing masks. Paraclete, the protagonist, is an amalgam of goodwill, deceit, and boundless fantasy. He convinces a troupe of talentless provincial actors to deceive a group of unfortunates. The troupe's romantic lead feigns love for a fading spinster; the dancer convinces a disheartened student of her infatuation. Despite set-backs, the illusion serves its purpose; the objects of the deception are given reason to live, the actors learn the value of charity. The lives of all are transformed through art and artifice.

Evreinov believed that play was carefree; but its imaginative capabilities could have more practical uses. Play posits a conventionalized situation in which participants assume new identities and behave according to new rules. The environment imagined by play can be entirely artificial, as in sport, but it can also parallel real-life situations. Participants can perform duties they will later have to perform in a real environment; play is a form of practice in which mistakes are not followed by dire consequences.

The benefits of play were evident in attempts in 1920 to experiment with and even create socialist forms of culture in festivals. After three years of socialism, the most attractive models for socialist culture still came mostly from utopian novels and tiny, short-lived communes. There was however a tremendous enthusiasm waiting to be harnessed, and some intriguing ideas. They were tried out by various organizations, with varying success, in mass festivals.

The army, which had already sponsored Vinogradov's studio, sponsored play as well in 1920. The military has frequently used play to prepare soldiers for war: they can learn tactics and maneuvers without the immediate dangers of the battlefield. Not only was Waterloo won, as Wellington claimed, on the playing fields of Eton; Indian warriors trained for battle by playing lacrosse, and modern armies train with war games. The military parade, like its cousin the demonstration, trains a military body to be perfectly organized. It is not just a spectacle— though a stirring spectacle it can be—it is a form of discipline without immediate utility. An army that marches well fights well; or so the theory runs. As leaders of the nascent Red Army knew, the birth of the first great Russian army had been in the spectacular war games, the *instsenirovki*, of young Peter the Great. In one instance a mock fortress of huge proportions, Pressburg, was built on the river Yauza; Peter's soldier-playmates bombarded it with cardboard bombs and stormed the walls with play guns in their hands. The weapons might have been fake, but the wounds received in battle were often real. Furthermore, from these games Peter acquired a very real knowledge of military technology, and from his boy-soldiers emerged a generation of competent commanders and disciplined soldiers.

Red Army leaders went further; they conducted exercises as dramatic performances. On August 26, 1919, the reserve army delivered two thousand young recruits to Piotrovsky for theatricalized maneuvers.[32] The aim of the production was to give the recruits, who were preparing to enter the war with the Poles, "an emotional conception in images of the fundamental stages of the revolutionary movement and the goals of the Civil War."[33]

The Krasnoe selo camp where the tsar and his retinue had often retreated for military maneuvers during the First World War housed a natural amphitheater: a slope opening onto a large patch of flat ground. On a small stage set in the middle of that patch, actors enacted the basic plot. The maneuvers were based on the scenario of a mass spectacle performed July 19 for delegates of the Third International. It included the struggles of the First International, scenes from the First World War, and the struggle of the Red Army against its internal and external enemies. The enactment culminated in the triumph of the socialist republic.

At its most ambitious, play could propose models for life under socialism. Here, Soviet festival organizers struggled with an unfortunate property of play; it is impermanent. Gan's plan for May Day 1920 was to create within Moscow a temporary socialist city: an environment, like a festival, in which the socialist culture of the future could be fashioned. Gan had grand ambitions for his festival city; it was to be a real thing, a form of activity that could transform the course of life. Gan was of the *deistvo* school that wanted to provoke permanent change. As he remonstrated, "Play has no place in the theater."[34] His stern-faced, "materialist" vision of revolutionary drama did not allow for make-believe; yet he too expected its magic to conjure the future: "Our everyday is a day of great struggle, and at this time there is nothing more important than intense revolutionary labor directed toward communism.... [We must] infuse performative [*deistvennyi*] content for the unfolding of new social relations, a new discipline for social labor, a new world-historical structure for the entire national and then the international economy."[35]

Constructivism, which Gan claimed first developed in 1920 among the ideologues of mass drama,[36] was art designed to have a specified effect on the social and cultural consciousness of its consumers.[37] It was a belief that proper environment makes for proper culture; constructivists engaged in devising things for socialism. In its emphasis on total environment, constructivism was related to mass festivals, but constructivism intended to create permanent environments. Festivals prefer the temporary to the permanent, the illusory to the real, a choice that Gan would not make.[38] He insisted that no props be used in his city; everything must be a real thing. Communal rest and eating were theatricalized; a socialist society, both make-believe and real, was created.

All the squares where action occurs are to be named for the arts and sciences.... Geography Square [on Agitation St.] [is to have] an enormous globe, the land sections of which will be colored red for the smoldering world revolution....

Outside the city (perhaps Khodynka Field) a Field of the International will be set up with a wireless station and an aerodrome. On this field the main drama of the festival unfolds.

In the early morning prologue ... a powerful siren calls from the Sparrow Hills and is answered by the whistles of all of Moscow's factories.

On that signal cavalry detachments, motorcycles, and cars ride from the seventeen city gates to local squares, summoning citizens into the streets along the way. On neighborhood squares, groups [of agitators] await them ... to involve them in the active *deistvo* of the holiday. Here the drama of the First International unfolds.

When this is over the masses move to the city center, . . . where the Second International is celebrated.

Finally citizens move on to the Field of the International where the fall of the Second International and the rise of the Third unfolds, as well as the transition to a socialist society.[39]

Play, in the end, requires a light touch, like Evreinov's; it tends to be irresponsible. It does not obligate its participants and makes no claim to permanence. Ironically, for all his rhetorical practicality, Gan did not take into account Moscow's dilapidated public transport. Any Muscovite wishing to watch the drama, much less participate, would have walked across the city twice that day.

In the end, Gan never had the chance to confront these problems. As had been the fate of earlier Narkompros projects, plans formulated by the Section for Mass Presentations and Spectacles were never realized. May Day 1920 was instead given over to a nationwide *subbotnik*, a day of voluntary community labor. In this festival, work—the foundation of socialism—was transformed into play by the special rules of holiday.

Labor Transformed

Revolution introduced socialism to the state before it did to the workplace. Socialist labor was a term as vague as it was common. To radicals, it meant worker control of factories, which the Bolsheviks tried briefly and disastrously. To Bogdanov, it meant voluntary work of the utmost efficiency and variety. To Gastev, it meant rhythmic labor movements that seemed poetic to him—and robotic to others.

The Civil War did not leave much room for experiment. Capital assets were destroyed, and resources that might have gone to repair the destruction were reallocated. Industrial labor was absorbed into the new Red Army; displacements in the work force and the aging of the industrial plant led to a sharp drop in productivity. The emergency led to a command economy in which labor conditions were not so different from those of capitalism: workers were compelled to work long hours for low pay. There was no real opportunity to try out new principles. Mass festivals offered a chance, albeit temporary and nonbinding, to establish an ideal setting and let participants act as if the socialist economy were a reality.

Revolution can blur the distinction between holiday and everyday, but even before the October Revolution there was a strong tradition that labor would become one with leisure: it was one of many differentiations to wither away. In *News from Nowhere,* Morris depicted labor as its own reward and relaxation; Gastev thought of socialist work as a festival, an experience of beauty, joy, and unity. Lunacharsky went even further: he saw festivals as an organized environment in which normally "unorganized masses . . . merge into the organized."[40] This was the converse of Morris's inversion. The hope was that festivals would serve as "shock-moments [*udar-momenty*] that will compel a more serious attitude [toward labor], greater discipline, and that gradually these 'abnormal' methods will become normal, everyday."[41]

Industrialization introduced a new concept of time to culture: standardized and regulated, without the irregular bursts of the natural, agricultural clock. Industrialization was impossible without standardized time; but in 1920 standard time was not enough. A superhuman effort was needed, what Lenin called "revolutionary-style" work (*rabota po-revoliutsionnomu*). Work was subject to compressed, intensified holiday time. If work conditions could not be changed, the space/time environment around it could.

Work was introduced to festive culture by measures such as honoring outstanding laborers with the title of "shock worker" (*udarnik truda*) and by the introduction of *subbotniki* and *voskresniki* (Saturday and Sunday workdays). "Shock work," a concept forgotten during NEP and revived by the Cultural Revolution, was in fact proposed for May Day 1920 by Kogan, chairman of the national Bureau of Mass Festivals.[42] He suggested that productivity could be spurred if labor was performed in bursts. There were corresponding proposals to bring labor into ceremonial culture: on May Day, outstanding workers were honored throughout the country. The ritual recognition of labor quickly spread; workers were thrilled that "their everyday life had become an object of ceremonial recognition."[43] The movement culminated at the December 1920 Congress of Soviets, which created a medal for outstanding labor: the Order of the Red Banner of Labor.

The most radical manipulation of labor time attempted in Soviet Russia was the *subbotnik*. *Subbotniki* were begun on the initiative of railroad workers of the Moscow-Kazan line on May 10, 1919, and a week later the initiative was taken up by Communists and "sympathizers" of the Aleksandrovsky railroad. Because transport was damaged horribly by the war, the workers contributed five hours of free labor toward restoring rail lines. This was not just overtime; it was a "special" time for special effort, and productivity for those five hours was two to three times the norm. One of the first legislative actions of the Soviet government in 1918 had been to establish the eight-hour workday; and *subbotniki* could be seen as a reasonable attempt to correct that well-intentioned but impractical act. In the months following the first *subbotnik,* Communists and sympathizers sporadically arranged their own, each chronicled with great praise on the pages of *Pravda* and *Izvestiia.*[44]

The first *subbotniki* seem to have been both local and voluntary; and the participants viewed them as economic contributions. But the attention of central party organs was quickly attracted; and *subbotniki* acquired symbolic value to complement the economic. A signal moment was the publication of Lenin's article "A Great Beginning."[45] Lenin paid little attention to the economic aspects of *subbotniki;* for him they represented "a cell of the new, socialist society," where workers accept voluntary discipline and labor for their own benefit. Festivals act as temporary environments in which new social structures can be created; and Lenin charged the *subbotniki* with "the creation of new economic relations, of a new society." *Subbotniki* were not additional time spent on everyday labor; they were moments of "exemplary communist work" that created a model for every day.

As party attention focused on the *subbotniki* in early 1920, the voluntary nature of participation became more dubious. Nonparty workers were encouraged to enlist;[46] and, judging from announcements published regularly in the central papers, many railroad workers of the Moscow region were so consistently working *subbotnik* hours that the pre-1918 workweek was restored. The Moscow Party Committee even formed a Department of Subbotniki; in September of 1920, the department claimed that attendance at *subbotniki* was good, but it also noted that Communists were taking part with great reluctance.[47]

The rhetoric generated by *subbotniki* became thicker as the snow of winter 1920 grew deeper on the streets. A front-page article in *Pravda* proposed transplanting *subbotniki* to the Soviet village;[48] but the very concept of *subbotnik* was unthinkable without urban industrial time. Saturday work was even proposed as an educational tool for children.[49] Holiday *subbotniki* were becoming the norm, a reversal of the socialist promise that "labor will become a holiday." The pages of the Moscow press would announce a series of *subbotniki* every day; and in Odessa, for example, March through June witnessed thirteen straight *subbotniki*.[50] When the Central Executive Committee of the Russian Republic decreed May Day a *subbotnik*, it came as no surprise.

There were merits to introducing work into holiday culture as a production incentive, but there was also a disadvantage. In March through early May 1920, Soviet Russia was swamped with holidays. There were Lent and Easter; and the Soviet anniversaries of the Overthrow of the Autocracy, Paris Commune Day, International Women's Day, and May Day. The latter three were observed with *subbotniki*, and in March and April, special week-long (!) *subbotniki* were held for the newly christened Cleanliness Week, Transport Week, Labor Week, and Labor-Front Week. There was even a *subbotnik* to celebrate the anniversary of the first *subbotnik*. This work, incidentally, supplemented the compulsory, unremunerated work done by most citizens in shoveling snow off the streets. Even if workers were given no better hours than they had before the Revolution, the mental division of those hours was different. Eight hours a day was obligatory, everyday work, which no name could transform; but the rest of those hours were free, holiday labor to be performed voluntarily. As tenuous as this claim might seem, and however exaggerated the rhetoric in the central press was, productivity was much higher on those days, and work was performed more willingly during *subbotnik* hours.[51]

The leaders of Petrograd went to tremendous lengths to ensure that the May Day *subbotnik* was conducted in a holiday environment. Its mood, which contrasted with the grimness of the previous two years of war, resembled more the atmosphere and intent of Parisians' splendid Champs-de-Mars cleanup for the 1790 Fête of Federation.[52] Petrograd's Summer Garden, situated between the two work sites (Field of Mars, Palace Square) offered an ideal festival site; it was first plotted in the mid-eighteenth century, when festive culture was at its apogee. Distributed around the gardens in 1920 were classical orchestras, puppet theaters, folk musicians; a phonograph played revolutionary speeches; mandolin music filled the central canals from passing gondolas; and Euripides's *Hippolytus* was performed on the steep staircase of the Engineers' Castle.[53]

Previous *subbotniki* had been dictated by economic need and were focused on the transport crisis. Some critics, particularly the Mensheviks, felt that by grafting the May Day and *subbotnik* traditions together, the Bolsheviks "made a holiday into everyday." But the Bolshevik leadership countered by placing the *subbotniki* within the "intensified, compressed time of holiday: before the Revolution May Day had been a time of intensified effort [struggle] and now too May Day was a period of intensified effort [productivity]."[54]

This was more than a rhetorical flourish. The labor assigned on May Day was overwhelmingly symbolic.[55] Palace Square and the Field of Mars were the last places in Petrograd that needed repairs. The *subbotnik* was designed not to rehabilitate the city's economy but to renovate its primary ceremonial spaces. Being a national festival, it could not enlist just a segment of the population, only the whole: a great effort was made to get the entire city out, and huge attendance was claimed.[56] News coverage was thorough, and the central press ensured that ordinary folk knew even Lenin had done his share, by clearing the Kremlin courtyard of loose timber.[57]

The symbolism of this May Day, whether or not it was acceptable to the populace, went deep; like the Easter that would soon follow, it symbolized a "new beginning," a resetting of time for a fresh start.[58] Much of the day's work went into symbolic groundbreakings for office buildings, factories, even new cities; in Orel, two-story apartment buildings were reportedly built in the course of a holiday spectacle.[59] The dirt of the past was to be washed away, forgotten: as an official slogan proclaimed, "The garbage you are picking up was left by capital[ism]." With the dirt, the unnatural, doglike attitude toward work that the tsarist regime had inculcated in Russians would also be swept away.[60] Khlebnikov, of all people, gave the clearest idea of what the holiday should be in his poem "Labor Holiday":

> Scarlet afloat, scarlet
> Held up by the lances of the crowd.
> That's labor passing by, scampering
> A flick of the heel in stride.
> Workweek! Workweek!
> The skin of shirt fronts glistens.
> And a song flows on
> Of yesterday's slaves,
> Of workers, not slaves.[61]

Work in Petrograd was directed at cleaning the vestiges of tsardom from the symbolic centers of Palace Square and the Field of Mars, cornerstones of the baroque city. The *subbotnik*, which the newspapers dubbed "the destruction of the old world,"[62] was designed to break down the symbolic separation of the palace from the city whose center it occupied: a graphic illustration of festivals' ability to cross impermeable thresholds. That morning, as a cannon roared and a military band played, tens of thousands of citizens charged the fence enclosing the square and began to tear it down.[63] The Field of Mars had hosted displays of military might under the tsars; but after years of war and revolution, it had been pounded into a huge dust bowl. The architect I. A. Fomin was commissioned to convert the square into a park;[64] a miraculous transformation from desert to garden, as in ancient tales, was to occur in the course of the holiday.

There was little spontaneity to the *subbotnik* and little of the play that might have sparked a creative attitude to work. Organizers viewed the work more as a ritual. Gan saw the *subbotnik* as the forerunner of his ideal *deistvo*.[65] It was "real" work; but it was also symbolic work, a work performance breeding new social attitudes. Movement, inspired by orchestral music, was theatricalized and ritualized: marching to the square and planting in time with the music.[66] Piotrovsky called the holiday the "birthday of labor," in which art and work became one;[67] and the May Day headline of *Pravda* proclaimed it the "great new ritual of the Red holiday."

Subbotnik labor was absorbed into holiday culture. A holiday is a discrete unit of time set off from the everyday, yet revolutionary festivals frequently featured attempts to fuse holiday and everyday, to have cake and eat it too. Introduced into holiday culture, labor was subject to holiday time: bursts of intense effort, followed by times of slack when that effort is forgotten. Such was the fate of the work of May Day. The fence was successfully removed from Palace Square, but not enough time remained to clean up the debris. The twisted fence and massive stones supporting it were left on the Palace Embankment, where they could be seen for years. The fate of the Field of Mars was even sadder; the holiday had not allowed time for careful planting of the trees, and afterward nobody came to tend them. All sixty thousand trees and bushes had died by mid-summer.[68]

History as Mystery

By the spring of 1920, the Bolsheviks were more confident of their power than ever. May Day, as is already evident, was celebrated with great pomp and pageantry. One of the central activities in Moscow was the unveiling of a monument to Liberated Labor (on a pedestal formerly occupied by a statue of Alexander III). The exultation of participants was captured, perhaps even embellished, by the Proletkult poet Mikhail Gerasimov:

> By the temple of Christ, on the bloody granite,
> When the cannons' salute had fallen silent,
> And the sun had halted at its zenith,
> Lenin unveiled the monument to Liberated Labor.[69]

In Petrograd the theme of liberated labor was observed even more grandly with the first of the great mass spectacles, *The Mystery of Liberated Labor*. This spectacle was performed by some two thousand people, mostly army conscripts, organized by PUR in the person of Tiomkin. Tiomkin, who some forty years later would be the proud holder of four Oscars for film scores (including the score for *Old Man and the Sea*), was in 1920 a young pianist just graduated from the Petrograd Conservatory.[70] He solicited the services of some of Petrograd's finest directors: Annenkov, Kugel (owner and director of the Crooked Mirror cabaret), and S. D. Maslovskaia (director of a school for opera extras); Annenkov, Dobuzhinsky, and Vladimir Shchuko—a famous architect working as a designer for the Bolshoi Dramatic Theater (BDT)—were put in charge of the set. The scenario, in keeping with the nature of "collective creation," was written by a "collective author," which included Annenkov, Shchuko, Dobuzhinsky, A. A. Radakov (BDT), Hugo Varlikh (conductor, until 1917 director of the court orchestra), Kugel, Granovsky (a Max Reinhardt student), L. N. Urvantsov (playwright), Lopukhov, and N. I. Misheev.[71] This was a mostly non-Bolshevik but very competent crew.

The former stock exchange was chosen as the site of the performance. It was a highly theatrical building; the classical portico, framed into a natural stage by white columns, made the tip of Vasilievsky Island, at the confluence of the Great and Little Neva rivers, its gallery. The square before the exchange would soon be renamed Peoples' Festival Square. The building and the square could be used two different ways: as real space or as conventional, theatrical space. The square was a part of revolutionary Petrograd; but the stock exchange, with its capitalist function and imperial architecture, was not, and the directors chose to create a purely conventional space. Canvas backdrops were painted, effectively turning a three-dimensional real space into two-dimensional conventional space; and the area surrounding the building was cordoned off.

The play did not transform the space; rather, the architecture of the exchange became a guiding metaphor for the depiction of revolutionary events.[72] The stock exchange was something of an anomaly; a neoclassical building used in the northern capital of an autocracy for capitalist commerce. It was never fully integrated into the city or its culture: not really part of Vasilievsky Island nor of the imperial center nor of the Petrograd River bank, which flanked it, the exchange was one of the few parts of Petersburg that never made its way into national literature or mythology. It was perhaps the most artificial point in that unnatural city; and it did not have the strong associations that an established space, such as Palace Square or the Field of Mars, had. That it should be used as a conventional rather than a real space is no surprise. The columned, open porch, with its sweeping staircase and the cobbled "pit" at its base, created a natural stage for mystery plays. The three-leveled space, as described in the scenario, was populated at its lowest rung by the "oppressed peoples" of history; the porch was the "paradise" of the powerful; and the staircase was the field of their battle.

ACT I

Scene i. *Workers' Labor.* Scene ii. *Dominion of the Oppressors.* Scene iii. *The Slaves Are Restless.*

From behind a blank wall come strains of enchanting music and a nimbus of bright, festive light. The wall hides the wondrous world of the new life. There liberty, brotherhood, and equality reign. But the approach to the magical castle of freedom is guarded by threatening cannons.

Slaves on the steps are weighed down by incessant hard labor. Moans, curses, sad songs, the scrape of chains, screams, and the laughter of overseers is heard. Occasionally the burdened grief of the prisoners' song quiets down, and the slaves stop their work to catch strains of captivating music. But the overseers return them to reality.

A procession of oppressive rulers comes into view surrounded by a brilliant suite of their underlings. The rulers climb the steps to the banquet hall. Here oppressors of all times, all peoples, and all forms of exploitation have gathered. The central figure[s] . . . [are] an eastern monarch in sumptuous dress, covered in gold and jewels, a Chinese mandarin, an obese king of the stock market, . . . and a typical Russian merchant. . . . The finest fruits of the earth grace their table. Music plays. Male and female dancers amuse the rulers, who have no interest in the wonderful, free life hidden by the gates of the magical castle. They have given themselves over completely to the drunken orgy, drowning the moans of the slaves with their shouts.

But the enchanting music has its own power. Its bewitchment makes the slaves feel the first glimmerings of the natural urge for freedom, and their moans gradually become mutters. The banquet is seized by alarm. The music of the bacchanalia and the music of the kingdom of freedom clash. Finally there is a deafening thunderclap. The revelers jump up from their seats, terrified by their impending demise. The ecstatic slaves stretch their praying hands toward the golden gates.

ACT II

Scene i. *The Battle of Slaves and Oppressors*. Scene ii. *The Slaves Defeat the Oppressors*.

The carefree, happy mood of the banquet is spoiled. . . . The slaves are abandoning their labor; . . . the isolated flames of rebellion are flaring and gradually merging into a great red bonfire. The slaves try to storm the banquet table, but their first attack is easily repelled.

Spectators are shown individual scenes from the long history of the proletariat's struggle. Roman slaves led by Spartacus race under a canopy of red banners; they are spelled by mobs of peasants led by Stepan Razin, raising the red flag of rebellion. Threatening and grand sound the strains of the *Marseillaise* and the carmagnole. The forest of red banners grows thicker and thicker. The sovereigns are seized by terror; their underlings flee in panic. Drums beat victory. A huge red banner, held aloft by the crowd of rebellious slaves, approaches the sovereigns. The potentates flee, dropping their crowns. Yet this is still not the final triumph of the slaves: again the bronze throats of cannon roar, and again a spirit of despondency seizes the workers. But the star of the Red Army rises in the eastern sky. With rapt attention the crowd follows its ascent. The din of drums and Red Army songs combine into triumphal music. The ranks of the Red Army grow, and the crowd is exultant. Revolutionary music reaches a crescendo. One more effort, . . . and the gates of the magical castle crash down.

ACT III
The Kingdom of Peace, Freedom, and Joyful Labor

The final act is an apotheosis of the free, joyful life that begins for the new humanity. A choral dance of all nations forms around the symbolic "tree of freedom." The powerful stanzas of the *Internationale* are heard. The Red Army lays down its weapons for the tools of peaceful labor. The spectacle ends with a fireworks display that pours joyful, festive light on the scene as the new life begins.[73]

The traditionalism of holidays was evident in the socialist paradise. It was introduced by the leitmotif of Wagner's *Lohengrin* and symbolized by the tree of freedom, borrowed from the French Revolution and going back to the pagan "tree of life." The socialist city was itself described as a festival: a special, magic place.[74]

The greatest innovation of May Day 1920 was to combine drama, ritual, and play into a single, mass festival. Even the French fêtes, which had incorporated contemporary spectacle culture, never featured dramatic art. The fêtes had been oddly ahistorical, preferring allegoric tableaux to the high arts of tragedy and comedy, or the low art of boulevard theater.

Dramatic presentation gave the Bolshevik festivals a new dimension: history. The narrative rules of drama were translated into the laws of history. The mystery play provided the directorial collective with a historical model, as it had Mayakovsky and Meyerhold. The "before" stage was the time before revolution; after came the state of grace; on the threshold humanity struggled for salvation with the dark forces of capitalism. The scenario of *Mystery* was, in fact, one of the earliest Bolshevik creation myths.

Mythic time, like festival time, is remote, a remote past isolated in the festival's remote present. Creation myths rely on both festive time frames: continuity to link the past to the present; discontinuity to subdivide it into history. The monumental or linking principle in *Mystery* was provided by a vast chorus with an identity that shifted but always represented the people. The chorus were unnamed slaves in the first act, then the rebels of Spartacus, and finally revolutionary Russians; their history was subdivided into progressive moments of revolt. In the crucible of the May Day presentation, Bolshevism became, contrary to its own dogma, the last in a series of spontaneous, leaderless revolts against the oppression of capitalist autocracy. The "oppressors" included Napoleon, the pope, a sultan, and a merchant; "struggle" included the rebellions of Spartacus, Razin, the Jacobins, and the Red Army.

The shift from ritual toward drama forced the directors to contemplate the new roles to be assumed by the audience. A ritual is a real thing, meant to mark and instigate changes in the outside world. Rituals make certain assumptions about spectators. They share a cultural and social background with participants and other viewers; they are acquainted with the symbolic language; perhaps they might, at sometime in their lives, become participants. Ritual, in other words, assumes an audience predisposed to understand and even accept its content. Drama, which creates and defines its symbols in the course of performance, can reach a diverse audience, including outsiders. Spectators are linked temporarily by their common viewing of the performance, but they are invited to interpret it according to their own experience. There was a trade-off: drama had a terrific power to depict history and address a broad audience, but it sacrificed ritual's hold on the community of participants.

The sponsors and directors of *The Mystery of Liberated Labor* seemed to court the benefits of both, the potentials of mythmaker and propagandizer. Their ambivalence was confirmed by the impulse to make *Mystery* a "real thing" and by indecision over whether to bring spectators into the performance. Ivanov's claim of reality for a *deistvo* was taken literally: there was real noise from real explosions; real battleships lit the stage with their floodlights; and real troops executed real maneuvers on the square. But clearly the producers, all theater professionals, had no intention of allowing the spectators, all thirty-five thousand of them, to participate; nor were the thousands of actors encouraged to improvise. Spontaneity would have been a license for pandemonium.

A trend away from free participation toward directorial control, discernible in *Third International* and pronounced in *From the Power of Darkness,* became emphatic in *Mystery.* Newspapers announced that "preventive measures will be taken against the accidents normally associated with large crowds"; the militia formed a cordon between stage and audience, while government officials and foreigners in attendance were segregated from the masses.[75] There was nevertheless a desire to see the performance as the long-sought *deistvo;* and Kerzhentsev claimed to have seen a merging of stage and audience.

> The entire spectacle concluded with brilliant fireworks display, which cascaded joyful holiday light on the birth of a new life.... During the finale of the spectacle, an enormous chorus of workers from the entire world sang the *Internationale* against the background of a rising red sun. The electrified masses broke through the cable barrier separating the spectators from the place of action, surged toward the portal of the stock exchange, and joined the common singing. A grandiose choir was formed, with the spectators mingling with the actors.[76]

Kerzhentsev was in Moscow on May Day, so he could be excused for this misrepresentation. Others who saw the merging that never happened, and provided the reports Kerzhentsev relied on, had fallen prey to the old refusal to see the people—which the audience was assumed to represent—as it was, a variegated and idiosyncratic viewer. Spectators themselves seemed to sense the ambivalence of the performance; they burst through the cordon to join the final chorus but stopped dead when they reached the steps of the exchange, the beginning of "theatrical space."[77]

The legendary *deistvo* had a profound synthesizing capacity: it merged different arts, different ideas, different symbols, and different classes and races. Yet the expressive power of *Mystery,* as of all subsequent mass dramas, was in the ability to differentiate. The ability to differentiate was as essential as the ability to unite; both would be part of a myth of revolution.

The need to differentiate and divide elements of a spectacle was increasingly evident when complex historical topics were raised. These changes in content entailed changes in form. Professional directors began tackling the enormous technical difficulties of mass theater. The use of a detailed scenario was a major innovation; it allowed directors to break the performance into separate episodes and thus divide revolutionary history into individual events. Yet the production of this first full-scale mass spectacle revealed more problems than it solved. Comparing early scenarios with the final draft, one can see how much expressive material was lost in the vast expanse of the square.[78] The potentates of the first scenario were characterized by facial expression: one face "reflected haughtiness and a consciousness of its own divinity"; another was "marked by the stamp of debauchery and depravity." This at a distance of 100 yards. A more serious impediment involved the various rebellions and revolutions, which had to be differentiated if historical change was to be portrayed. Early rebellions were the work of a leader: "not everyone in the oppressed crowd of slaves . . . raises his voice; no, only the leaders do." Each revolt was also supposed to appear more organized than the last—as Leninist historicism would have anticipated. Thus, the first occurred when a "disorganized crowd stormed the staircase," while in the final the Red Army "headed for the [golden] gates in an orderly march." These differences were not visible in the performance. Each revolt was a swirling mass of bodies—no leader could stand out in their midst; and each revolt was equally unorganized as it stormed the staircase.[79] The acting mass was not subdivided; movement was choreographed for groups of a few hundred, which made all but the most elementary maneuvers, such as storming the staircase, impossible.

The inability to break elements of the spectacle into small units made the show ungainly and inexpressive, and led to contradictions between the intended message and the actual message. Without recourse to the fundamental expressive means of a mass spectacle, the directors were forced to rely on the spoken word, which was drowned in the outdoor vastness. Space was divided vertically (the lower classes below; the rulers above) but not horizontally (left and right halves of the stage mirrored one another). The episodes of the scenario were selected and assembled on a principle of similarity, with intervening time being eliminated; along with the use of the chorus, this meant that episodes, the basic components of the production, all resembled each other. History seemed to be cyclical.

The Influence of Popular Theater

The leaders of Petrograd were so impressed by the performance that they decreed that "the stock exchange will be used this winter for the production of mystery-type spectacles."[80] An entire series was planned, including: *War against White Poland,* on the steps of the Engineers' Castle; *The Taking of the Bastille,* in the Summer Garden; *The July Days,* at the Narva Gate; and the *Holiday of the Defense of Petrograd,* in front of St. Isaac's Cathedral.[81]

Calmer heads and more critical minds counseled modesty. One person objected entirely to the appropriation of the noble title of *mystery* for the production: "I remember *The Taking of Azov,* a cannonade in three acts with artillery pieces, the navy, and the destruction of fortresses.... The producers of that show called it an extravaganza [*feeriia*]. That, at least, was honest."[82]

But, pretense aside, *Mystery* had been entertaining. Shklovsky, for instance, was impressed by the ability to incorporate "real" things—for example, a military parade.[83] His was a common-sense approach that said the spectacle was wonderful—it just was not art. He proposed another performance in which two sections of Petrograd, the Vyborg and the Petrograd sides, be pitted against each other in mock battle.

Not everyone had Shklovsky's sense of humor. On May 3 Radlov and Soloviev directed an amateur production, *The Fire of Prometheus,* and some rather grandiose claims were made. The play was performed by Red Army dramatic circles, which led some to proclaim the "creation of a proletarian Red Army theater."[84] Piotrovsky was even less restrained. He announced that socialist society would be "theatrocratic." The lifting of financial considerations from theater circles had returned the element of "free play" to their performances.[85] Play would give birth to a new theater; and the theater would give birth to a new society. The theater should not be illusory, but a real thing; and there should be no spectators, just participants. Theatrical performance would lead to the creation of great festivals; and everyday life (*byt*) would be remade there.[86]

Produced in the Bolshoi Opera, *The Fire of Prometheus* matched the pomposity of its locale. Piotrovsky and Radlov had learned little from their earlier collaboration on *The Sword of Peace*. The only extant description comes from an unsympathetic critic: "The first scene features Samson and Delilah; . . . the second features the Spartacus uprising; following this is a high-society ball in a setting that suggests the court of Louis XIV, mixed up with suggestions of other styles, including the . . . foot wrappings of one of the marquises. In the final act, after the heavens have parted, an amateur pair . . . dances a sultry Argentinian death tango.[87]

The Fire of Prometheus was a victim of its own ambitions. Amateur performances could not create both a new society and a new theater (assuming they could create either one). Konstantin Derzhavin, alluding to some of Kerzhentsev's claims, said that however wonderful "collective drama" was, it was not theater. Play is real; art is illusion.[88] Shklovsky conceded the value of play but added "such games [*igrishcha*] have always existed, but nobody has called them theater. Theatricality [artifice] is essential to the theater."[89] Kuznetsov made perhaps the most telling observation on the limits of the form; play was a healthy sign in theater circles, but it could be of interest only to friends of the players. Such a presentation could not go beyond a limited audience.[90]

After the failures of *The Sword of Peace* and *The Fire of Prometheus*, Radlov rethought two theses that had thwarted mass productions: first, that "a spectacle performed for the broad masses must be a 'mass' spectacle in that a tremendous number of performers take part"; and, second, that "historical events instigated by a great quantity of people (such as a revolution) should be depicted in theatrical action by another great quantity of performers."[91]

Like other mass-spectacle directors, Radlov had reached the genre by a circuitous route. His background and education, which he shared with Piotrovsky and Soloviev, was in the ancient theater. Radlov was the son of Ernst Radlov, a renowned classicist and friend of the philosopher Soloviev; Piotrovsky was the son of another great classicist, Tadeusz Zielinski.[92] Radlov and Soloviev also shared years of apprenticeship under Meyerhold, where they studied Zielinski's ideas about ancient Greece. They also studied the renaissance theater with Meyerhold; and in fact, Soloviev co-wrote with Meyerhold the 1913 mass production *Fire* based on commedia dell'arte principles. Radlov spent some time as well with Evreinov, writing prologues for the Ancient Theater's Spanish productions.

Their first postrevolutionary collaboration was at the Petrograd Theater-Studio, organized by Meyerhold; participating were, among others, Radlov, Soloviev, Piotrovsky, and Annenkov. The studio's first production, Nikolai Gumilev's *Magic Tree* (*Derevo prevrashcheniia*), was a children's play. The production introduced what would become staples of agitational theater: stage business involving devils, acrobats, and so forth.[93] The studio directors intended to revive the intimacy of high theater and popular culture, and they preferred writers like Calderón, Shakespeare, Molière, and styles like commedia dell'arte that addressed broad audiences. They sought a theater that, but for its size, was a splendid model for mass spectacles.

Popular mobile theater, . . . like the wandering troupes of old France and England, can serve both city and country [and] is based on genuine showmanship and healthy humor. [The troupes] will be able to give a show at any moment and any place . . . at the asking, meeting all the requirements of artistic theatricality. Easily mounted, with new actors . . . experienced in pantomime and verbal improvisation, . . . freed from an overload of psychologism, with a repertory and acting techniques close to the popular understanding, the new theater will revive collective theatrical creation. . . . We must forget about psychological subtleties and work toward scenic hyperbole and catching the spectator's eye.[94]

The Theater-Studio was soon dissolved, and many of its staff moved on to the new Theater of Popular Comedy directed by Radlov. The Popular Comedy was one of the first Soviet agitational theaters—theaters performing topical skits with a strong political slant. The staff of the Popular Comedy included Miklashevsky and Golovanskaia; leading members of the cast were Delvary and Konstantin Gibschmann, the clown and vaudevillian who worked in Annenkov's *First Distiller*. "Serge" and other clowns filled many other important roles, as did prerevolutionary Meyerhold students.

Radlov, like Blok and Meyerhold, Mayakovsky and Annenkov, believed that the new theater would evolve from forms of popular theater, such as the commedia dell'arte or the circus, that bordered on play. Precedents were the theater of Shakespeare, in which the clown Will Kemp played a leading role, and the comedies of Molière, which were influenced by Italian fairground comedies.[95] Radlov's was not a theater of excessive sobriety, as symbolist dramas had been, nor was it a theater given to psychology. Action, not the word, was the medium of expression. It was a compromise between Evreinov's pure theatricality and Meyerhold's conventional theatricality.

In the People's House that had once featured melodramas and extravaganzas, that had seen melodramas banished by Lunacharsky and Andreeva, that had hosted Vinogradov's *The Overthrow of the Autocracy*, Radlov orchestrated the triumphal return of melodrama and the Pinkerton genre. Radlov gave popular forms a new function appropriate to revolutionary Russia: agitation. Popular Comedy performances were mobile, funny, coarse, and topical. They were based on rough scenarios that could accommodate a variety of outside material and employed a troupe of exceptionally skilled players, who were equipped to handle any contingency. If Lord Curzon made the headlines, he would wind up in the next day's skit.

Festivals, which encouraged give-and-take between actors and spectators, were particularly suited to Radlov's style. On May Day 1920, the troupe broke up into five groups and toured the city on tram platforms, giving short performances at each stop. The scenarios were written by Radlov. His group performed a skit, *The Partition of Russia;* another performed the *Magical Accordion* and *The Good Men of Versailles* (*Capitalist Intrigues*); Soloviev and Piotrovsky directed other groups; and a Popular Comedy troupe under Vladimir Voinov (trained as a scenario writer in the Cinizelli Circus) performed a skit entitled *Blockade*.[96] Also shown that day was *The Monkey-Informer*, based on another Radlov scenario, which adapted the ancient concealed-identity plot to the purposes of anticapitalist propaganda. The traditional commedia figure Pantaloon was replaced by J. P. Morgan, who introduced himself to the audience in the manner expected of fairground buffoons:

> In Vienna, New York, and Rome,
> They esteem my full pocket.
> They esteem my loud name.
> I am the famous Morgan.[97]

The lead player was the monkey Jimmy, whose efforts to foil the capitalists took him over the heads of the audience on a high wire.

Radlov was disingenuous when he claimed that popular conventions had been adapted smoothly to new purposes. Rather, he performed adeptly a task performed ineptly by his predecessors: he integrated the play element of popular spectacles—for example, clowning or acrobatics—into a unified dramatic style. As noted by his colleague Derzhavin, Radlov accomplished this integration in three ways: the acting of actors and circus performers was reduced to a common denominator (a single style); the circus numbers were woven into the action; and a harmonic pattern was created from tricks specific to the circus.[98]

The key was fusing the time structures of play and drama. The Bolshevik notion of history was inherently dramatic. Like drama, it featured an ordered progression of events through time, which fit into a pattern of cause and effect. Dramatic time is continuous; the clock set in the first act winds down to an inevitable conclusion. Action is divided into episodes, and the principle by which they are strung together conveys much of the meaning. A diversion of dramatic action is a breach of its structure.

The depiction of protracted historical developments like revolution stretched fairground theater. There, time was closer to the inconsistent, expandable time of play. Play is action generated not by the inevitability of its resolution, like drama, but by a set of rules. These rules can generate new actions eternally and are not defined in time. Typically, most games need arbitrary limits, either a set amount of points or a timespan. Popular theater, particulary Radlov's beloved commedia dell'arte, used a scenario more often than a text. The scenario was a short series of events: an initial situation, an intrigue to fuel the action, and a resolution. Around these events speech and action (for example, acrobatic escapes from jealous husbands) were improvised. The structure was flexible; its events were only required stopping points along a circuitous and varied route.

Radlov saw flexibility as opportunity; if time in popular theater could be stopped, then current events could be worked in at the juncture. Scenarios were used by the Popular Comedy as a format to introduce current events. The popular audience was already accustomed to dramatic stops and starts, and never rebelled against the introduction of propaganda; and the comic acting of the clowns was ideal for satirizing enemies. Radlov coupled these elements with conventions he uncovered in his experiments with renaissance theater that facilitated "continuous action . . . founded on the subtle use of contrast."[99] These conventions offered great latitude in moving between local and universal, ephemeral and eternal themes.

Radlov's hybrid theater was a powerful vehicle for propaganda, and it was a good show. Its greatest merit was the respect for and consideration of the spectator. *Deistvo,* the model for previous mass spectacles, invited spectators to participate but discouraged their autonomy. There was only one outcome, one meaning, one possible audience. Theater as play had little pretense to meaning, yet it gave spectators the illusion of an active experience. Genres like the detective story allowed several potential resolutions for each performance. Convention dictated a certain outcome—the crook is caught—but this ending was more like the time limit of a game than the death of a tragic hero: it was not an inevitable conclusion giving meaning to the action but a way to draw it to a close. The twisting, not the closure, of a plot was the purpose of popular theater because it created the feeling of suspense. Suspense was not really the result of an unknown conclusion; the outcome was highly conventionalized. Rather suspense was a way for the spectator seated outside the play and aware of its conventions to experience the action as if it were open-ended.

Vacation Island

Radlov believed that his work at the Popular Comedy was similar to directing a mass spectacle; both were forms of popular theater, and both were subject to the same laws of composition. The spectator of a mass production could derive its full benefit watching from a seat; the merging of stage and audience was not at all necessary and would ruin the aesthetic whole.[100]

Success inspired his players to venture outside. On June 17, a group of actors and clowns performed a short play outside the People's House to celebrate the first graduation of students from the new Soviet Literacy School. The directors were Voinov and Annenkov. Although the reviewer was not entirely clear how the performance was tied to the theme of literacy, he knew that the play had been entertaining. The audience was passive in the sense that it took no part in the action, but the text was improvised by jesters planted in the crowd. For the first time in an outdoor spectacle, locale was exploited well: the topography of the building was brought into play. Acrobats escaped up vines growing on the facade, and scenes were played on the balcony.[101]

Three days later, Radlov directed *The Blockade of Russia* on the newly christened Vacation Island (Ostrov otdykha). Formerly called Rock Island (Kamennyi ostrov), this had been the site of the opulent dachas of wealthy Petersburg. The Revolution had driven away many occupants; the rest were evicted. During the Civil War this neighborhood on the outskirts of town was neglected, and by 1920 there were gaping potholes in the road and rusting automobile shells in the thicket. Expropriated by the state in a doctrinaire fit, the properties had been left to rot.

The Petrograd Soviet finally decreed that several mansions be converted to worker spas, with the opening set for May Day, the holiday of Liberated Labor. As of late May nothing had been done, and a troika was appointed by the municipal soviet to speed things up. One of the troika's assistants was Emma Goldman, the American anarchist, who later detailed the corruption and shirking that went on at the work site.[102] Somehow, toward the end of June work was completed, and the rest homes were ready to receive guests.

A decision was made to inaugurate the rest homes with a festival. Festivals celebrate moments of change and transformation; sometimes they even instigate the change. Such had been the May Day *subbotnik,* and such was the July festival on Rock Island; it was to embody "a window into tomorrow, a slice of the new life [*byt*], . . . the new order of transformed things."[103] Vacation Island—a holiday island—was to be a model of the socialist city. Ironically, in a culture where work had been absorbed into the holiday schedule, relaxation merged with work: "As heirs conscious of our lawful right to joy, happiness, and rest, we turn Rock Island into a place of repose for laborers. Here along lilac paths, here by beds of flowers, . . . they will gather the strength for new feats, for new struggles."[104]

Decorations temporarily transformed the decrepit island into a city reminiscent of the "ancient urban democracies."[105] Athens, perhaps, or Florence might have been graced with a neoclassical arch like the one built by Fomin along the central avenue leading onto the island.[106] The avenue ended in a large Square of People's Gatherings, the center of which was dominated by a monumental sculpture intended to continue the tradition of Phidias: Mikhail Blokh's *Metalworker* (Figure 11). Ten meters tall (and temporarily made of gypsum), this figure was supposed to rival Michelangelo's *David.* It surpassed its model in all respects but one, quality. Monumentality had become something of a mania in Petrograd, and the leaders of the soviet who attended the celebration would have been delighted had not *every* single part of the figure been monumental; as it was, the dignitaries insisted that the gypsum proletarian be given a fig leaf and, when that did not suffice, an apron. The apron would fit only after "a couple parts were knocked off"; and the next day Blokh suffered a heart attack.[107]

Blokh was a humorous case of a serious problem—the passion for

Figure 11. Mikhail Blokh, *The Metalworker*, monumental sculpture, Petrograd, July 1920 (Mikhail German, ed., *Serdtsem slushaia revoliutsiiu. Iskusstva pervykh let oktiabria,* Leningrad, 1980). Photo courtesy of Aurora Publishers.

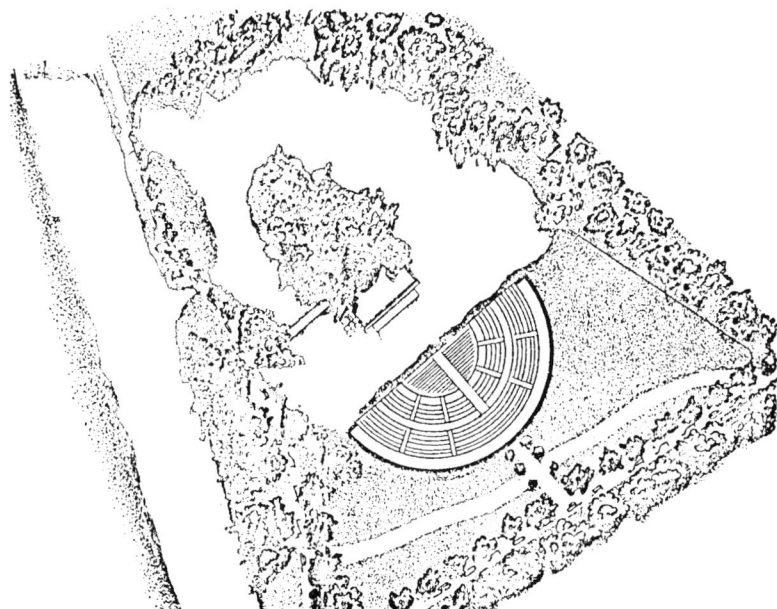

Figure 12. Amphitheater, Rock Island, Petrograd (*Istoriia sovetskogo teatra*, Leningrad, 1933; image is computer-enhanced).

monumentality. Mayakovsky had been sacrificed to that passion the year before; and even Annenkov had succumbed to its lure in *Mystery*. If a purely monumental art was to mark a change for the better, it could only get bigger and bigger.

Radlov chose another route: he divided monumental space and time into manageable units. He broke with the mystery-play paradigm and its constricting conventions of time and space. The stage itself solved many of the difficulties.[108] On Rock Island was a small lake with steep banks; and on the lake was a small island. Radlov, Valentina Khodasevich, and Fomin constructed a special amphitheater there; boards were placed on the island for a stage, and benches were built up the slope of the bank. In this outdoor theater, the orchestra pit was filled with water, creating a proscenium that no spectator would think of crossing. Radlov had chosen a place where real topography defined theatrical space (see Figure 12).[109] Space was divided and given definite, if highly conventional, values. The island represented the Russian republic; the water around it held blockading navies; and a bridge joining the island to the shore was used by various capitalists and capitalist lackeys to infiltrate Russia.

From four thousand to twenty thousand people, depending on whom you believe, saw that night perhaps the finest, certainly the funniest, of the Soviet mass spectacles. The presentation began with a brief tableau of peaceful labor. Its serenity is broken by the appearance of a skiff, decorated with the attributes of a battleship, carrying Lord Curzon, who surveys Russia through a spyglass. (The good Lord Curzon was played by Gibschmann, the clown from the Popular Comedy.) The workers, annoyed by his spying, open fire with roman candles (a trick from *The Taking of Azov*, which had been produced by Alekseev-Iakovlev in a similar amphitheater), and Curzon, after suffering various acrobatic falls and contortions, fails to escape and is plopped into the water by a volley that destroys his vessel.

The simplicity of the scene belied the complexity of its conventions. Characters were treated like the masks of commedia dell'arte: lacking psychology, they were flattened. The reduction of the enemy to a simple label made for effective propaganda; but it was motivated by artistic considerations. A mask can replace a mass character; and where in *Mystery* the potentates were portrayed by an unwieldy mass of gluttons, the enemy in *Blockade* was a dynamic, single figure. Parts requiring a great deal of action were played by an individual, others by groups; the same vessel could be a toy boat and the English navy.

Time too was flexible; it alternated between the monumental time of "peaceful labor" and the episodic comic pacing of clown interludes. Time advanced easily because episodes were clearly divided; the clumsy progression of *The Mystery of Liberated Labor* was replaced by the rapid shifting from island to water and back, each of which corresponded to a change in time. Time was associated with space; a shift in one indicated a shift in the other. Episodes in *Blockade* were also marked clearly in space; segueing was swift and simple. In *Mystery*, where successive episodes occurred in the same space according to the same pattern, these transitions were resisted by the very bulk of the production.

Following Curzon's demise, action shifts back to the island for an interlude of peaceful labor and then to the bridge, where a Polish spy (played by "Serge") is infiltrating the country. A chase begins, with the spy escaping through treetops, branch to branch, and concealing himself in bushes. This was a smooth way to introduce current events into mass spectacles. Certainly, the agit-trials had used current events; and in

Figure 13. Stereotypical Polish nobleman of Civil War posters (Mikhail German, ed., *Serdtsem slushaia revoliutsiiu. Iskusstvo pervykh let oktiabria*, Leningrad, 1980). Photo courtesy of Aurora Publishers.

the small front-line town of Berezovye Rudki, there had even been a mass production of *The Negotiations of Krasin and Lloyd George*. But these were actionless events, based solely on the word. Radlov portrayed current events by action alone. The evil intentions of the British and their instigation of the Polish invasion were conveyed by a simple juxtaposition of episodes; and for spectators who could not identify Curzon by his plumed hat, it was still clear who were the good guys and who the bad.

When "Serge" has safely concealed himself in the bushes, attention shifts back to the bridge, where the Polish invasion is beginning. The battle was portrayed by small troop formations and accompanied by lots of noise and fireworks; but when the battle ends in Polish defeat, the Polish side is once again personified by its general, played by the acrobat Delvary. Delvary was dressed as the quintessential Pole, familiar to any Russian spectator from propaganda posters: arrogant, pompous, in a nobleman's robe and plumed, four-cornered cap (see Figure 13).[110] Defeat is signified by a double flip-flop from the bridge into the water, and the war is continued out on the lake. Two fleets of skiffs, identified by their flags as the Western allies and the Soviet Navy, clash between the island and shore. All of Alekseev's technical mastery from wartime battle plays was employed: boats maneuver between rocket flashes; and the battle is decided when the imperialist warfleet is taken by Russian marines in hand-to-hand-battle. The victors move to the island to view the apotheosis. From behind the island another fleet of ships with bright, decorative sails goes by; these are representatives of the nations of the future, come to recognize and greet the victory of the Russian republic. All are dressed in their national costumes.

Later that summer, the stage was reopened for a performance of the ballet *Swan Lake*.

SIX

Marking the Center

Festivals and Legitimacy

> Since Copernicus man has been rolling from the center toward X. The nihilistic consequences of the ways of thinking in politics and economics, where all "principles" are practically histrionic: the air of mediocrity, wretchedness, dishonesty, etc. Nationalism. Anarchism, etc. Punishment. The redeeming class and human being are lacking—the justifers—
>
> Nietzsche, *The Will to Power*

The Bolsheviks seized power in the name of an ideology that deplored centralism. Yet after the coup an attack on central authority constituted an attack on their own power. Root contradictions that underground existence had left dormant—for example, party discipline and popular initiative, revolutionary iconoclasm and central authority—could no longer be ignored. Revolution and Civil War were not times to wallow in moral vacillation, nor were the Bolsheviks given to public introspection. Yet the question of just what the party represented demanded debate and resolution. In the end principles that had united the prerevolutionary party and inspired the Revolution—for example, egalitarianism and pacifism—were discarded. How could this be the same Bolshevik party? How could it maintain authority when it violated the ideals that first legitimized its power?

The Bolshevik identity was woven of many strands. There was Marxist ideology, which Lenin and his colleagues had digested and adapted to Russian conditions; it proclaimed the proletariat the class of the future. There was the revolutionary underground, where a core of elite revolutionaries had formed and developed a conspiratorial modus operandi. There was the Civil War, when many whose allegiance to Marx and the party seemed temporary had joined. Revolutionary exigency held these strands together, but many alliances formed during the Civil War could not be permanent. In the summer and fall of 1920, when victory seemed closer than it ever had, the Bolshevik leaders began reinstating the tight discipline essential to a stable party identity. They had to choose, by calculation or by reaction to onrushing events, what the Bolsheviks ultimately were: what was incidental to the party and what lay at its center.

Revolution had fragmented Russia's centers of power. The mythic sources of Romanov authority were cast in fatal doubt; the Provisional Government was torn apart by a duality of power. Even the Bolsheviks' first social models separated the political from the cultural centers. Ideology, power, culture, and society stood apart. The center—the source of power—was adrift, waiting to be seized; if the new regime was to stake an uncontested claim to the country's destiny, it would not only have to drive opposing forces from its soil, which it was about to do, it needed to claim the symbols of the center.

Finding the center—the core—of the party's identity was made all the more critical because it was instrumental to maintaining political power. Authority, as Edward Shils notes, is deemed most legitimate, and is most secure, when it radiates from a society's "central value system."[1] It can then claim an inviolable sacredness (or its secular equivalent), which exacts the unconditional subordination of all other values and claims to power. Shils and Clifford Geertz, following Max Weber, find "charisma," the ineluctable impression of "standing in a privileged relationship to the sources of being," the main attribute of the center.[2] Charisma is concentrated in a place, institution, or person that embodies and projects the structure of power.

Several emendations must be made to the notion of center before it can describe the fluidity of revolutionary Russia. According to Shils and Geertz, the center is expressed by rituals and symbols, which embody root "values and beliefs" (Shils formulation). The assumption of consonance among symbol, entity, and values, which is often justified, did not hold during the Russian Civil War. The symbolic center could be the true seat of power, as the Kremlin under Stalin would be, but it could also stand apart from the institutions of political control. The symbolic center was a separate dimension of power that supplemented institutions and ideology. In fact, in Civil War Russia it was often inconsistent with them. A profound ambivalence animated revolutionary symbols and spectacles. Atheism and sacredness, egalitarianism and hierarchy mixed freely; worker holidays were celebrated by marching from the proletarian outskirts to the government center; a regime seated in Moscow projected its mythic origins to the heart of imperial Petersburg.[3] The center was dynamic, mobile, shifting; the Bolsheviks did not so much have to attach themselves to the center as to fix it in one spot.

The elusiveness of the center comes from a paradox of origin: power is conferred by the center; yet the center is created by power. Power generates a logo-center, the illusion of origin, a fixed point that prevents the onset of chaos and allows for meaning and hierarchy. This essential attribute of the center, noted (ironically enough) by Jacques Derrida, creates the right to name, to fix the principles of a society.[4] The Bolsheviks demonstrated some awareness of the problem in 1918, when they expended considerable effort to ensure the proper interpretation of their festivals. They understood what this relatively minor issue represented: the right to speak for the nation and thus to govern it. To rule the country, they had to speak for it; to speak for it, they had to project a common origin.

The Bolsheviks' program did not mandate the absolutism that had become standard practice by 1920. They had come to power as egalitarian democrats who promised to convene the Constituent Assembly and end the war. They consequently dispersed the Constituent Assembly and plunged the country into a civil war that destroyed its economy and killed many of its citizens. The traditional source of party identity, Marxist ideology, did not justify such a program, which actually isolated the party from the masses. Only the growing sense of historical mission that animated the party could serve as justification. It made the most despotic policies seem the instruments of divine ordinance, separated the Bolsheviks from all other parties on Russian and foreign soil, and embraced classes and groups that other sources of identity would have led the party to exclude. The legitimacy of the October Revolution rested most firmly on the myth of historical inevitability.

The great festivals and spectacles of 1920 helped create a foundation myth of the Revolution. Festivals can attack the center—the *sacra* of religion or the monuments of the state—but they can also raise new monuments and create new identities. They arrange time and space around moments of origin and embody its principles in the flesh and blood of myth. A nascent mythology of the October Revolution was discernible in Lenin's monument plan, in the dramatic games of the Red Army Studio, in holiday speeches and presentations, but they were all lacking. The flaw was less in the content of the myths than in their form; they were diffuse and inclusive. Myth is compact and concentrated; it is embodied by individual people, in single places, and in concrete times.

In 1920, directors finally conquered the mass-spectacle form. They faced issues similar to those confronting the Bolsheviks: how to harmonize mass participation with efficient administration; how to include many origin tales without unraveling the thread of narrative. The solution was a strengthening of organizational hierarchy and a reduction of the chaos of revolutionary events to a compact narrative focused on a single time and place. Just as the Bolsheviks sacrificed old principles in the interests of a new identity, directors sacrificed historical veracity in the interests of myth. The results were striking. The mass spectacles of 1920 were dynamic, gripping, moving; through them, the Bolsheviks claimed an inalienable right to direct the fate of their country and the worldwide proletariat.

The Third International

If ever an organization was created by its own pomp and circumstance, it was the Third International. Barely fifty people attended its First Congress in Moscow in March 1919. Of those fifty, only twelve held credentials from any political group; of those twelve, eight were Russian Bolsheviks. Yet the Third International claimed to embody the aspirations of the world proletariat.

Perhaps it was fitting that some of the organization's funds were raised in *subbotniki;* the symbolic work of the holiday financed a symbolic proletariat.[5] The International, and the Russians who constituted the bulk of its Executive Committee, were in 1919 acutely aware of how tenuous their claim to world leadership was; so they complemented their political efforts with a series of symbolic gestures that laid claim to the center. The Red Army Studio's *Third International* was just one example. Most of the gestures were directed toward claiming the retired mantle of the First International; Marx's famous slogan, "Workers of the World Unite," was adopted as a motto. In the next five years the symbolic merging of the Russian state and the international revolution, exemplified by a 1921 poster linking the Paris Commune and the Russian Soviets (Figure 14), would receive prominent attention. In 1924,

Figure 14. The Bolsheviks claimed the heritage of the Paris Commune, as illustrated by this poster, captioned "The martyrs of the Paris Commune were resurrected under the red banner of the Soviets" (1921).

Zinoviev presided over a ritual in which a "holy relic" of the Paris Commune, one of the last banners to fly over its barricades, was presented by French Communists to the Russians and laid on Lenin's tomb.[6] But in 1919 claims were more modest. Moscow was meant to be only a temporary headquarters; a permanent nerve center would be established in Berlin once communist revolution had swept Germany.[7]

The year between the First Congress and the Second in July 1920 brought an unpleasant surprise: world revolution did not break out. Moscow became the permanent center of world revolution by default. The Executive Committee of the International, mandated to direct operations between congresses, was an essentially Russian body, and its control of the movement solidified. The publication of Lenin's polemic *"Left-Wing" Communism: An Infantile Disorder* was a first attempt to impose Russian standards on foreign parties; and the Twenty-One Conditions for admission to the International, promulgated at the close of the Second Congress, established Moscow as model and center.

The magnificent complex of church and palace that is known as the Moscow Kremlin was given its present shape in the fifteenth and sixteenth centuries under the first great Muscovite rulers, Ivan III and Ivan IV (the Terrible). Set atop a hill in the middle of the city, surrounded by massive walls, it is an architectural apotheosis of the medieval Russian autocracy: the center as source of power (state) and ideology (church). The creation of the Kremlin and its symbolic aspect coincided with the birth of the most powerful myth of Russian autocracy: Moscow as the Third Rome. The Russian state claimed through its church the mantle of the early Christians, forfeited first by Rome when it strayed from Orthodoxy and then by Constantinople when it was captured by the infidel Turks.[8] The Second Congress of the Third International, held in 1920, when the Soviets claimed the leadership of the world proletariat, convened in the Kremlin. As one of the delegates commented without irony:

> Its architecture is supposed to symbolise a temple of honour of the sacred dignity of imperial power. A series of gilded columns run down the hall, but these were now swathed with red bunting in honour of the new power. Where once stood the throne now stood the platform for the presidium of the Congress. Over the throne, under the sweep of an arch, the "All-Seeing Eye" looked down. Long rows of desks stretched across the hall and red carpet covered the parquet floor.[9]

For the first time since the Revolution, the imperial eagles atop the Kremlin towers were regilded.[10]

Literature and posters issued for the congress emphasized the theme of Moscow as center. The cover of the publication of the First Congress had depicted a worker beating the chains off a globe;[11] but a poster of the next year, Dmitry Moor's "Long Live the Third International," showed the same worker hailing the Kremlin (see Figure 15). A commemorative plate by Maria Lebedeva pictured the world movement as a series of concentric circles: on the outer ring, the world proletariat; next, the first stanza of the *Internationale;* then the city; and, in the inner circle, a red star radiating the bolt of life from the heavens like Jehovah in the Sistine Chapel (see Figure 16).[12] Vladimir Narbut published a poem for the occasion:

> Mongols, Negroes, and Arabs,
> And you too, West of fiery aspect,
> Use the wisdom of Socrates to create
> The unhewn features
> Of a Proletariat Atlas.
> And may he, tremendous, made-of-steel,
> Tense his muscles, as before
> And take the Heavens on his shoulders,
> Feet planted in Moscow and Resht.[13]

The Congress was first transported to Petrograd for a ceremonial opening in the Tauride Palace (built for Potemkin by Catherine II on her return from the Crimean tour). The Russians used that city's ceremonial center to receive their guests. The British and Italian delegations, who showed signs of cooperating with Bolshevik designs, were fêted with magnificent demonstrations by the army and trade unions through Palace Square; Zinoviev addressed the gathered multitudes from the same balcony once used by the tsar to address his people. (The French, who were intransigent, were given no such greeting.)[14] On the Field of Mars a Red Mass was performed, a requiem at the memorial grave of the "victims of the Revolution"; a brass orchestra and choir performed Wagner's *Götterdämmerung.*[15]

The foreign delegates could not have failed to notice the political irregularity of some of the symbolic gestures. Two monuments were erected in Petrograd: the one devoted to the Paris Commune was appropriate for a group that claimed the mantle of Marx; but the monument to Karl Liebknecht and Rosa Luxemburg, who one year before had objected strenuously to the founding of the Third International, was not.[16] Nor is it clear whether the visitors appreciated the *Trial of the Yellow [Second] International,* an agit-trial produced for the benefit of

Figure 15. Graphic representations of the Third International, 1919 and 1920 (Mikhail German, ed., *Serdtsem slushaia revoliutsiiu. Iskusstvo pervykh let oktiabria*, Leningrad, 1980). Photo (right) courtesy of Aurora Publishers.

Figure 16. Maria Lebedeva's commemorative plate for the Second Congress of the Third International. Photo courtesy Aurora Publishers.

delegates who had yet to break with that organization.[17] But most outrageous was surely the fact that the *Internationale*, Pierre Degeyter's hymn of the workers' movement, was sung to new music; a competition for its composition had been held to which no foreign composer was invited. The jury was headed by Glazunov, ex-director of the Imperial Conservatory of Music.[18]

Any censure was quieted, though, by the magnificent spectacle *Toward a World Commune*, presented at the Stock Exchange from 10 P.M. to 4 A.M. on July 19.[19] Modeled on *The Mystery of Liberated Labor*, this production by four thousand soldiers and theater-circle members enacted the history of the Third International for foreign delegates and the citizens of Petrograd. Presented in the form of a mystery play, it portrayed history as cyclical; and the Russian Revolution, the dramatic climax of the performance, took on an inevitability it might not otherwise have had. The fact that the directors were given only ten days to prepare the performance could explain why they relied on tried-and-true methods.

Andreeva once again was the organizer of the event. She delegated directorial duties to Mardzhanov, just returned from Kiev (where, after his success with *Fuente ovejuna*, he had planned a mass spectacle entitled *King Saul*).[20] Mardzhanov further delegated authority for separate episodes to young assistant directors. Petrov, of BDT and the Crooked Mirror, was assigned the first act; Radlov, the second; and Soloviev and Piotrovsky were given the third. For himself, Mardzhanov reserved the coordinating duties of the main director.

The preliminary scenario projected three acts: mankind's past—his enslavement; the present—struggle and victory; the future—the good life. The Third International was shown to be a by-product of European revolution.[21] Yet if the Russians were to be at its helm, they would have to claim its historical source. At Andreeva's instigation the play was changed to reflect the centrality of the Russian Revolution to the International, and to show that the Third International was the rightful heir of the First. The myth of the International was thus rewritten, and the Russians were at its center.

ACT I

Scene i. *Communist Manifesto*.
The rulers of the world, kings and bankers, erect a monument to their own power with the hands of the workers.... On top, a sumptuous celebration of the bourgeoisie; below, the workers' involuntary labor.

The laboring masses bring forward . . . the founders of the First International. The Communist Manifesto.

Only a small group of French workers answers the call to battle. They fling themselves into an attack on the stronghold of capitalism. The forward ranks, met by shots, fall. The red banner of the commune flies. The bourgeoisie flees. The workers seize its throne and destroy the monument to bourgeois power. The Paris Commune.

Scene ii. *The Paris Commune and the Death of the First International.*

A merry holiday for the Communards. Workers dance . . . the carmagnole. The Paris Commune decrees the foundations of a socialist order. New danger. The bourgeoisie . . . sends the legions of Prussia and Versailles against the First Proletarian Commune. The Communards build barricades, defend themselves bravely, and perish in unequal battle, without having received help from the workers of other nations. . . . The victors shoot the Communards. Workers remove the bodies of their fallen comrades and hide the trampled red banner for future battles. . . .

ACT II
The Second International

The reaction. The triumphal celebration of the victorious bourgeoisie. Below, the involuntary labor of workers reigns. Above, the leaders of the Second International, . . . noses buried in books and newspapers.

Call to war in 1914. The bourgeoisie shouts: "Hurrah for the war. Death to the enemy." The working masses murmur: "We don't want blood." . . . Again the red banner flies. Workers pass the banner from hand to hand and want to present it to the leaders of the Second International.

"You are our leaders. Lead us," shout the masses. The pseudoleaders scatter in confusion. Gendarmes . . . exult and tear apart the hated red banner. The horror and moans of workers.

The graveyard silence is broken by the prophetic words of the people's leader: "As that banner has been rent asunder, so shall the bodies of workers and peasants be torn by war. Down with war!" A traitorous shot strikes the tribune. Triumphant imperialists suggest a vote for war credits. The leaders of the Second International raise their hands after a moment's hesitation, grab their national flags, and split the previously unified mass of the world proletariat. Gerdarmes lead workers away in different directions. The shameful end of the Second International and the beginning of fratricidal world war.

ACT III
The Russian Commune

Scene i. *World War.*

The first battle. . . . The tsarist government herds long rows of bleak greatcoats to war. Wailing women try to hold the departing soldiers back. Workers, exhausted by starvation and excessive labor, join the women's protest. The wounded are brought back from the front. . . .

The workers' patience is through. Revolution begins. Automobiles, bristling with bayonets, charge by with red banners. The crowd, swept by revolutionary wrath, topples the tsar, then stops dead in amazement. Before the crowd are the new lords: the ministers of the Provisional Government of appeasers. They call for a continuation of the war "to a victorious conclusion" and send the workers into attack. A new courageous blow by the workers returning from the front, supported by a stream of unleashed workers, sweeps away the . . . government. Over the victorious proletariat flares the red banner of the Second Commune with the emblems of the Russian Socialist Federated Soviet Republic. . . .

Scene ii. *Defense of the Soviet Republic—the Russian Commune.*

Workers and soldiers, having shed their weapons, want to begin building a new life. But the bourgeoisie does not want to accept the loss of its supremacy and begins an embittered fight with the proletariat. The counterrevolution has temporary successes, . . . and only the greatest surge of heroism by the workers' Red Guard saves the Commune. Foreign imperialists send the Russian White Guard and mercenaries. . . . The danger increases. To the leaders' summons "To arms!" workers reply with the creation of the Red Army. Fugitives from areas razed by the Civil War appear. After them come workers from the smashed Hungarian Soviet Republic. The blood of the Hungarian workers calls for revenge. . . . The Red Army leads the heroic battle for the Hungarian and Russian workers, and for the workers of all the world.

Red labor befits the Red Army: it battles against the dislocations of war. The Communist *subbotnik*. Allegorical female figures of the proletarian victory issue a clarion summons to the workers of the world to the banner of the Third International for the final and decisive battle with world capitalism. The first lines of the workers' hymn.

APOTHEOSIS
The Third International. World Commune

A cannon volley heralds the breaking of the blockade of Soviet Russia and the victory of the world proletariat. The Red Army returns and is reviewed by the leaders of the Revolution in a ceremonial march. Kings' crowns are strewn at their feet. Festively decorated ships carrying the proletariat of the West go by. Workers of all the world, with emblems of labor, hurry to the holiday of the World Commune. In the sky flare greetings to the Congress in various languages: "Long live the Third International," "Workers of the world unite."

A general triumphal celebration to the hymn of the world Commune, the *Internationale*.[22]

As it had in *Mystery*, a holiday acted as the symbol of revolution and political ascendance in *Toward a World Commune*. The scenario as it stood differed little from the scenario of *Mystery;* the abstract scheme of oppression and revolution was the same, with the roles assigned to more contemporary rebels. The apotheosis also differed little. As in previous mass spectacles, the Russian Revolution was the inevitable climax to the human drama.

The Craft of Mass Spectacles

Commune went beyond its predecessors, however, in production methods. Mardzhanov divided and delegated authority to his assistants; the cast was divided into smaller, more manageable groups, and the stage space was divided into sections, each with a distinct spatial value. (See Table 1 for a sample of the organizational chart used for the production.)

Marking the center was dependent on these new production skills. A center is a point alone, marked off from the rest of space and time; from it connections radiate out. It is created by both differentiation and unification. In *Commune* a myth of revolution was made by linking separate moments in historical progression. New production techniques enabled Mardzhanov to depict each moment distinctly and to shift rapidly between them. Mastery of the artifice of theater made the myth compelling and real.

Designs for the stage were done by Altman. Altman planned to do for the Stock Exchange what he had done for Palace Square in November 1918: subdivide the space by the use of color and shape. The outer three columns on each side of the portico were to be wrapped in red, and the middle six, uncovered, were to open up onto the central stage. The contrast between the two sets of columns would create an illusion of recessed space in the center. For this space Altman planned a dynamic composition, a "garden" of green triangles, before which was to be set a fiery red prism. At the back of the stage, on the second facade of the building there was to arise a huge golden sun, the "sun of October."[23] Altman redesigned the space of the Exchange for increased dynamism and flexibility. Andreeva, however, never forgot an old grudge, and she rejected the plan: green, she insisted, was the party color of the Constitutional Democrats.[24] Instead, the front cornice of the Exchange was hung with banners proclaiming "Long Live the Third International," appropriate more for a rally than for a spectacle.

Toward a World Commune was, more emphatically than *Mystery*, a theatrical spectacle. Curiously, when the theatrical, conventional use of a property was most clearly underlined, that object could be used most easily in its "real" state. This was a paradox Radlov had discovered in *The Blockade of Russia* and that the directors of *Mystery* had failed to fathom. In that production, music was limited to providing an inexact thematic consonance: the rise of the proletariat was accompanied by the leitmotif of Wagner's *Lohengrin* and Rimsky-Korsakov's *Sadko*. Music in *Commune* was used as a real part of the everyday culture depicted: the privileged classes dance to Strauss's *Vienna Waltz;* the Paris Cummune sings a carmagnole and buries its dead to Chopin's *Funeral March*. The stage was lit by the floodlights of a minesweeper moored on the Neva.[25] Battles were conducted by real soldiers and sailors firing from real guns and cannons (they fired real blanks, as had the *Aurora* on October 25, 1917). The apotheosis was a parade of the victorious army, represented by troops of the Petrograd garrison, with armored cars and cavalry. Above the parade floated a dirigible trailing a banner that proclaimed, "The Kingdom of Workers Will Last Forever."[26] Of course, none of the forty-five thousand spectators would have noticed the difference had actors and props replaced the real things, and, according to Radlov, the soldiers would scarcely have minded missing the march.[27] "Real," it seems, is a highly conventional notion. Spectators were alerted from the start that the spectacle was theater. They were summoned to the performance by heralds galloping down the city streets; but when they reached the Stock Exchange, they found a cordon of soldiers protecting the building and square (no protection had been provided for *Mystery*).[28]

The differentiation of real and artificial, and the subdivision of the cast and acting space, offered the directors new opportunities and allowed them to gain control over an ungainly performance. In *Mystery,* the masses were led by a director placed in their midst. By the July 19 spectacle, the crowd of actors had become too big to control, and it was broken up into basic units: potentates, rebels, "yellow socialists." These units, defined by character and plot, were then subdivided into units of ten. Each unit elected a leader; thus, a group of ten potentates would have a representative, who took commands from the chief of the potentate group. This numerical pyramid worked its way up to Mardzhanov at the tip. For rehearsals only the representatives were present; they in turn were to instruct the ten members of their cell and be responsible for their movements during the performance. With the moving crowd broken up into smaller units, the creation of patterns and rhythms was feasible. Crowd movements could be contrasted in geometrical patterns; individual movements like the lifting of a hand could trigger a contrasting mass

Table 1. Segment of production chart from Toward a World Commune

No.	Action	Players	Leaders	Costumes	Props	Enter from	Toward	Music group	Music	Light effects
35	Appearance of Hungarians fleeing reactionary horrors.	50 men, 50 women, 25 children	Cherkov, Fedorov, Zueva	100 fugitives, 25 children	Household utensils, a "Hungary" poster	Below, from left corner of Exchange	Extreme right parapet	Fanfares		
36	A new wave of workers appears from behind a column.	300 workers, 100 female workers	Beliavsky, Semenova	300 worker blouses		Below, from right side of Exchange and from behind columns	Central stage	Central orchestra		
37	Leaders appear in the middle. "To arms." The crowd responds, "To arms." A red star flares. Red soldiers enter. Leaders scatter red stars. Soldiers raise their weapons. An oath. They leave the steps with weapons leveled.	500 soldiers, 15 leaders	Pakhomov, Smirnov	500 overcoats, 15 leather jackets	200 red stars, 500 rifles, poster: "The Workers' Defender Is the Red Army"	Leaders and soldiers from the middle	Scatter below to left and right	Fanfares, choir	"Bravely Forward, Communards"	Red star lights up
38	Workers and children remain on the steps. Sirens. Female Victory figures appear on the parapets. "Workers of the world unite" is on the pediment. The arms and eyes of everyone are turned ahead.	10 female figures of Victory	Right—Iazykov. Left—Mamaeva	10 allegorical costumes, 10 wigs	10 gold horns	Behind the columns	5 to the left, 5 to the right parapet	Flanking orchestras, minelayer sirens	A summons and siren sounds	"Workers of the World . . ." written in fire
39	Figures of Victory maidens appear on the rostral columns. Pause.	10 maidens on the columns	Right—Nikolaev Left—Arkhipova	10 allegorical costumes, 10 wigs	10 gold horns	Behind both rostral columns	Tops of left and right rostra	Orchestra by rostra	Summons	Signal fires on rostra, torches

#	Description	Participants	Costumes/Props	Location	Location	Location	Music	Effects
40	Cannon salvo from the Fortress. The square is crossed by an armored car carrying allegorical figures of Victory, scattering crowns and sacks of gold.	15 men, 10 women on the vehicle	Freidin	25 allegorical costumes	Armored car, crowns, and sacks of gold	Around the Exchange corner, from the right	Drive left across square	Central orchestra, salvo from fortress	*Internationale*
41	Parade of the Red Army.	Mil. band, cavalry, artil., cadets, inf.	Garrison commander			The embankment near Exchange Bridge	Across Exchange along University Emb.	Military band, salute from fortress	
42	Smoke screen on the Neva. Disperses. Contours of ships. Skirting the columns from the jetties, representatives of the world's workers appear with emblems of labor and posters.	100 representatives of Europe, 100 from other countries	Decade commanders	100 male, 100 female ethnic costumes	Emblems of labor	Left and right rostral passages	Exchange staircase	Rostral choirs	*Internationale*	Smoke screen on Neva
43	Closing group of everyone on Exchange pediment. Large hammer and anvil in the middle. Small anvil on the parapets.	All			Large hammer and anvil, two small hammers and anvils				
44	Rockets fly from ships on the Neva. Airplanes scatter proclamations. A dirigible unfurls a banner "Long live the III International." Searchlights from the columns and fortress. Fireworks.		Minelayer commander, Fortress commander		Two airplanes, bundles of colored proclamations, dirigible, poster	Group on the Exchange pediment		All orchestras, all choirs	*Internationale*	"The kingdom of workers and peasants is eternal" written in fire, searchlights, fireworks

SOURCE: *Massovye prazdnestva* (Leningrad, 1926).

response, a charge. Sound, which had been drowned in *Mystery,* once again became an expressive component. Choral readings and singing were the main applications of the human voice; but voices could also be used in contrast, as when the thousand-throated groan greeting the declaration of the First World War was followed by a measure of silence, then a single voice: "As this banner is rent asunder...."

To better control the massive spectacle, the directors removed themselves to a platform around one of the rostral columns that loomed across the square from the exchange. The platform was equipped with a bank of telephones and colored lights and flags that relayed signals to the minesweepers and Petro-Pavlovsk Fortress, and to the performers on the stage.[29] When the directors were distanced from the performers and the division between participant and spectator was explicit, there was little room for the creative participation of the masses. The performers, in fact, were mostly army conscripts, tired and hungry like the rest of Russia, and "mobilized by force."[30] Yet the changes did make for clearer expression.

The production's power was in the articulation of time and space. As in *Mystery,* the tripartite stage was used, but this time its conventions only abetted the sponsors' intentions. The Bolsheviks saw the history of the three Internationals as a cycle, with the Russian Revolution its rightful culmination. But this convention did not prevent the artistic categories of time and space from being subdivided. The stage wings were not removed from the action, and opposing sides did not necessarily mirror each other. The bourgeoisie could attack from the right, the workers from the left. Actors did not operate as a mass; they were divided into sections, static choruses, and moving groups.

Stage space was easily broken up and given definite identity. It could come, for instance, from the group occupying that space or from a simple emblem: when the tsar was toppled, the double-headed eagle fell and a banner proclaiming the soviets was raised. In the third section of the scenario the Allied blockade was depicted. At this point battleships on the Neva laid down a thick blanket of fog that enveloped all but the exchange and audience. The square, enclosed by these temporary walls, operated as a theater and was assigned a new value as conventional space. It represented the blockaded, isolated Russian republic. On the river beyond the fog the battleships, representing the Allies, blew their foghorns and fired cannons. The lighting of the huge flames of the rostral columns broke the fog and signaled the lifting of the blockade. The fog defining the theatrical enclosure melted away, and armored trucks came driving through real space, across the bridge from the Petrograd side, to repel the enemy.

Staging historical material was a matter of selecting the proper episodes and assembling them into an artistic whole. In *Commune,* the basic incidents of the play were divided into 170 episodes, each defined by an exit or entrance.[31] Such a fine division was made possible only by the system of cueing and signaling and the separate directorial platform. The Spartacus rebellion and the October Revolution had differed mainly in the uniforms worn by their participants in *Mystery*. Adding episodes to *Commune* allowed for more details so that successive revolutions looked less and less like each other. Historical progress could be detected.

Problems remained. The additional episodes required speedier transitions than could be made, and *Commune* was plagued by dead time—it was six hours long! The episodes also made the spectacle more complex; it is doubtful that most of the forty-five thousand spectators understood what it was about. The hundred or so delegates of the International, who were given pamphlets containing the plot in their native languages, could follow, and the performance, in any case, was directed at them, not at the spectators or the participants. To those people without a scenario in their hands, however, *Toward a World Commune* was "brightly colored, full of variety, majestic, but utterly incomprehensible."[32] Spectators probably saw little anyway; the directors' platform blocked part of the view, and a reviewing stand for foreign delegates was built up in the air, front-row center. Most of the Russians already had the suspicion the performance was not for them anyhow. It was initially scheduled for July 18, and the performers and spectators arrived hours early. At performance time all was ready, but the delegates of the International, still in conference, had not arrived. Rather than do the play without them, Andreeva dismissed the players and asked them to return the next day. Same time, same space.

Finding the Symbolic Center

At the advent of Bolshevik rule, there was a profound ambivalence toward Russia's symbolic centers. The ceremonial centers of Petrograd were inherited from previous regimes and had to be symbolically reoriented, which had been one objective of Lenin's unsuccessful monument plan. Parade routes were another instrument of reorientation. Parades can be linear, with each place and spectator along the route being addressed equally; or they can be centripetal, with a central point being served above others. American towns usually define the town center as a street; the linear Veterans' Day parade marches down Main Street. Russian cities have always defined the city center as a point, and their parades have been centered. Moscow of course offered an ideal central point, Red Square, which had the additional advantage of centralizing celebrations in front of the seat of government. Postrevolutionary Petrograd was a more difficult problem. There were many potential central points: Palace Square, which would have been appropriate but for associations with the old regime and Provisional Government; the Field of Mars, centrally located yet a "neutral" site associated with both revolutions; and Smolny, the source of the Revolution and seat of the party yet located at the edge of town. May Day 1918 was focused on the Field of Mars (as had been May Day 1917); November 7, 1918, was celebrated at Smolny. And for the 1919 anniversary celebration, Uprising Square (formerly Znamenskaia), "where the first revolution began," was chosen.[33]

Parades also signal centers of power by whether they are made to see or to be seen: the first makes the marcher the center, the second the viewer—usually the VIPs on the tribune. On May Day, the marchers were taken all around Petrograd to see the fine decorations put up by artists and to let the marchers be seen by the city.[34] Afterward all gathered on the Field of Mars for some speeches, but this part of the festival was secondary, almost impromptu.[35] The Winter Palace was also deliberately assigned a "democratic" value; it was renamed the Palace of the Arts and was opened to the general public for the first time. Lines were tremendous, and the gesture was the most successful of an otherwise equivocal holiday. On November 7, a centralizing tendency absent on May Day was noticeable. A hierarchy of places and symbols developed, and with this a new centeredness, a hierarchy of participants. All parade routes led to Smolny; maneuvering the marchers past a single point led to the long periods of standing and to the human traffic jams that became a lamentable tradition.[36] Perhaps the most critical innovation was the tribune; leaders were segregated from the people and marked as the primary spectators.[37] The marchers filed through a seventy-five-foot temporary arch decorated with the new Soviet seal and past a smoke-curtained altar. Around the arch were placed obelisks, on which rested busts of Lenin, Trotsky, Zinoviev, Volodarsky, Uritsky, Lunacharsky, Kamenev, and Sverdlov, as well as Marx and other socialist heroes.[38]

Palace Square would have to wait until 1920 for its time. Like Red Square, Palace Square was ideally suited to project an image of strong central authority. Marking the center of the city, occupying and imposing on its most valuable space, Palace Square also offered an opportunity for the central review of a parade. Only those unfortunate associations interfered. If the festival wanted the square for its own purposes, the image of the square would have to be "cleaned up." Renaming it Uritsky Square, after the slain Chekist, was an important change; and Altman's November 1918 decorations had subverted its old values; but symbolic reorientation was most fully effected by the May Day 1920 *subbotnik*. In the early eighteenth century the square before the palace had been a tree-lined park for public use; but it was gradually transformed by the dynasty into a appendage of the palace, a process completed in 1900, when Nicholas II ordered it enclosed by a massive iron fence. The *subbotnik* reopened the space to public circulation and linked it to the surrounding city. Still, though it was suitable for a review of the demonstration for the Third International in July, the square was not yet the mythic Palace Square, "center of the Revolution." That honor belonged to Smolny, as it should.

Agit-Prop, the state propaganda agency, issued a decree for the third anniversary forbidding large expenditures,[39] which essentially removed the outskirts and peripheries from the festival. In Petrograd only the central places, Smolny, Palace Square, and the Field of Mars, plus the graves of fallen revolutionaries in Lesnaia were to be decorated.[40] In that same spirit of frugality, Mayakovsky did a series of Russian Telegraph Agency posters condemning sumptuous celebrations:

> He celebrates [the anniversary] correctly
> who forgets all sort of carnivals,
> and
> tirelessly
> fixes the railroads.[41]

But the message never made it to the Petrograd Soviet and the Northern Army. With victory close at hand, they ordered a magnificent festival, one that—if all plans had been realized—would have restructured the center of Petrograd. Petrograd was a city of long, broad avenues and yawning spaces embodying the values of order and power.

Festivals have often had a hand in determining the growth of a city; ancient Olympia was built entirely to the specifications of a festival, and the modern Olympics usually change the face of their host city. In fact Lazar Kaganovich, leader of Moscow in the 1930s, justified tearing down the jumbled alleys and churches of the capital by saying, "*My aesthetics demands that the demonstration processions from the six districts of Moscow should all pour into Red Square at the same time.*"[42] But in 1920 Petrograd was far from its former imperial splendor; as Osip Mandelstam noted in an image of both degeneration and regeneration, grass was sprouting through the pavement.[43] There would be no major construction in Petrograd for many years; and the festivals, by gestures such as the placement of monuments, could define the city only by reorienting extant symbols.

That is not to say there were no plans for the physical reworking of Petrograd, just no funds. The third anniversary of the Revolution led to the formulation of one of the first postrevolutionary plans for altering the face of Petrograd. A massive spectacle was envisioned as the centerpiece of the festival; and had it been produced, the performance would have required great changes in the city. The performance was to stretch from Semenov Place to the Admiralty—about a mile altogether. Because the space between was not completely open, planners decided to clear several buildings to open a view.[44] On Semenov Place a monument was to be erected (as a model) that would have fixed a new center for both Petrograd and the world revolution: Tatlin's Monument to the Third International.

Tatlin's monument was designed to remedy the obvious deficiencies of the Lenin Plan. His working group was assembled in 1918 to draft plans for a monument that could change with time,[45] which would overcome the basic contradiction noted by Shklovsky: "I'm always surprised . . . by the intention to erect monuments to the Russian Revolution. It seems the Revolution hasn't died yet. It's somehow strange to build a monument to something still alive and developing. . . . The attempt to create this revolutionary art leads to the creation of false works of art."[46]

The Monument to the Third International rested on the tradition begun by Altman's restructuring of Palace Square for the first-anniversary celebration. Tatlin's monument, however, was designed to be permanent. Using the materials and reflecting the dynamics of the new (as yet nonexistent) urban environment, it was to consist of three great glass chambers connected by a system of vertical axes and spirals.

These chambers are arranged vertically above one another, and surrounded by various harmonic structures. By means of special machinery they must be kept in perpetual motion, but at different rates of speed. The lowest chamber is cubiform, and turns on its axis once a year; it is to be used for legislative purposes; in the future, conferences of the International and the meetings of congresses and other bodies will be held in it. The chamber above this is pyramidal in shape, and makes one revolution a month; administrative and other executive bodies will hold their meetings there. Finally, the third and highest part of the building will be used chiefly for information and propaganda, that is, as a bureau of information, for newpapers, and also as the place from where brochures and manifestos will be issued. Telegraphs, radio-apparatus, and lanterns for cinematograph performances will be installed. . . .

The use of spirals for monumental architecture means an enrichment of the composition. Just as the triangle, as an image of general equilibrium, is the best expression of the Renaissance, so the spiral is the most effective symbol of the modern spirit of the age. The countering of gravitation by buttresses is the purest classical form of statics; the classical form of bourgeois society, aiming at possession of the land and soil, was the horizontal; the spiral, which, rising from the earth, detaches itself from all animal, earthly, and oppressing interests, forms the purest expression of humanity set free by the Revolution. . . .

Most of the elements of architecture hitherto in use possessed no practical importance, and remained unorganized. To-day the principle of organization must rule and penetrate all art.[47]

Monuments define the symbolic center of a city; but dynamic constructions—like Altman's—tend to negate symbols and move to the periphery. There was some ambivalence about where the monument should be placed: in Moscow or Petrograd; in the center of the city or in the factory zone on the outskirts.[48] The issue was decided in planning for the third anniversary, when the Petrograd Party Committee decided to build the monument in Petrograd.[49] The model was to be exhibited as the center of the festival, and the space cleared would afford a view of the new center once it was constructed. The model, however, was never exhibited on the square; and the buildings were never knocked down. Petrograd would have to content itself with the old center of town, a center symbolically redefined.

In 1920 the center of Moscow was set firmly in Red Square. Previously, there had been ambivalence. The first-anniversary celebration of November 1918 provoked some controversy as to what the center of revolutionary Moscow was: organizers proposed creating an artificial center, a "Red city," extending from Red Square to the Metropolitan Hotel. The March-Route Committee thought Red Square should be the center, but the Central Organizing Committee preferred Theater

Square. Furthermore, as one delegate noted; "Those who will appreciate the entire majesty of the holiday with their hearts live, after all, on the outskirts. Why should they march to the center to amuse the bourgeosie?"[50] On May Day 1919, the demonstration was routed to Red Square; and it was there that Lenin addressed the masses. Yet even Red Square was not a uniform space; the placement of Lenin's Mausoleum by the Kremlin wall in 1924 would connect it to the center of power, but in 1919 Lenin gave his address from Lobnoe Mesto, located on the opposite side of the square and associated with Razin—a subverter of power.

The International Congress of 1920 helped fix the point. The Russians centered the International in Russia, in Moscow, in the Kremlin; and a huge military demonstration through Red Square marking the conclusion of the Congress on July 29 emphasized the symbolic claim to the center. Judging by their memoirs, the delegates were susceptible to the symbolic assault. Trotsky, the organizer, pulled out all the stops to show off Soviet power. Mayakovsky wrote striking verses that caught the spirit of the demonstration and the rhythm of its march.

> We sally forth
> a revolutionary charge.
> Above the ranks
> the scarlet flag of fire.
> Led by the million-headed
> Third International.
>
> We advance.
> No beginning to the flood of our ranks.
> No end to the Red Army Volgas.
> A belt of red-armies
> to the West
> from the East,
> encircling the Earth
> from the poles.[51]

Trotsky, flanked by delegates atop a tribune, reviewed the demonstration from noon to 5 P.M. The tribune, set by the Kremlin wall for the first time, was a mark of the center, concentrating the symbolic and political center in one. Around it were arrayed trophies seized from the allied intervention forces: cannons and transport, tanks and "other useful inventions of the bourgeois mind."[52] Buildings surrounding the square were hung with slogans stenciled on linen; marchers greeted the delegates with gold-lettered placards that sparkled in the sunshine. Sausage-shaped balloons, trailing red pennants and streamers, were anchored to the crosses of St. Basil's onion domes.

The real show was the people. All of Moscow was turned out to march in the parade, though citizens were not allowed onto the square as spectators.[53] Boy Scouts trooped by and saluted the tribune; Caucasian tribesmen in native dress rode by. Athletes clad only in swim trunks made a particular impression. According to the press this was a perfect example of the potential of festivals to "create the new Soviet man." Exhausted workers had only to pass through the square with the rhythmic columns and they were transformed from "decrepit old men into handsome youths."[54]

Perhaps, but the political message sent to the foreign delegates was surely of greater consequence. Karl Radek's claim that "the demonstration . . . meant more than all the theoretical discussions [of the Congress]" was probably close to the truth. It established the claim of the Russians to be the source of international socialism's strength. A foreign delegate was overheard observing that it was "absolutely clear [!] that nobody could *force* such a mass onto the streets," a comment Radek used to refute Karl Kautsky's claim that the Russian workers' initiative was not manifest in the Revolution. But it was the pounding rhythm of marching feet, the tremendous organization of the demonstration that transmitted its message. The delegates, some of whom had been in Soviet Russia now for months, had not been impressed, to say the least, by the organization they had encountered. The Bolsheviks arranged the festival as a special show of organization, five hours of demonstration to erase months of contrary observations. The event seems to have made the proper impression. When Trotsky turned to a French Syndicalist and asked, "With all this, won't counterrevolution be impossible in Moscow?" the French comrade only silently nodded his head.[55]

The Myth of the Revolution

The Bolshevik claim to the center was best staked by a myth of origin: a myth that distilled the Revolution to a single moment. It was the instant of transition: the moment when history began and from which the future unfolded. Marx and ideology were irrelevant to this center of revolutionary history: it was the storming of the Winter

Palace that became the central theme of the Petrograd celebration after the plans for Semenov Place were jettisoned.

How was it possible to propagate a myth in the very city that had witnessed the event itself only three years before? Myths, contrary to what some symbolists and the "God-builders" thought, are not constructed at will. They are a function of memory: the more remote the memory, the more extreme the mythologization. Perhaps the Revolution was not very old, but already the recollection was slipping away from the facts and surrendering to art. Symbolically, John Reed, who left a distinct record of the events of October 25, 1917, died on October 24, 1920; and Podvoisky (one of the commanders of the palace storming), who was always consulted for productions of this kind, would later admit that he "could not remember how [he] crossed the barricades" (he hadn't!).⁵⁶ The Red Guardsmen remembered even less. Not that anyone forgot altogether; their recollections were if anything more vivid. It was just that some parts of the event were gradually neglected and forgotten, some were magnified, and the whole was rearranged.

History itself provided an outstanding example of such revision: the storming of the Bastille, which 130 years before had been made the center of the French Revolution by the popular imagination. The directness of the influence, and the inspiration it provided the Bolsheviks, was evident in a poster released for the anniversary:

> Three years ago, comrades—do you remember? . . .
> The Winter Palace fell—capitalism's Bastille.
> And now Soviet Russia has become the center
> Of the whole Laboring world—and with us
> The peasants and workers of all countries are raising
> The Red Banner of the Proletariat Revolution.⁵⁷

A festival is not a neutral or "transparent" system; it is an artistic system in and of itself, with its own rules of aesthetic construction that it imposes on the material at hand. In this process remembered events are changed. Such a reformation of recollection was publicly enacted in *The Storming of the Winter Palace,* a mass spectacle presented for the third anniversary celebration of November 7, 1920.⁵⁸ The directors created a dynamic center for the Revolution, the moment of creation essential to any foundation myth.

The performance was sponsored by PUR. Tiomkin was again chosen to produce the festival, and he in turn chose Evreinov as director—an odd choice indeed for the epitome of political theater: a director at best indifferent to the new ideology, who with his producer and designer would soon end up in the Paris emigration. For Evreinov the Revolution served the purposes of the performance, not the performance the Revolution. The facts were given an explicitly artistic organization. *The Storming of the Winter Palace* was a step beyond his "theatricalization of life"; it was a theatricalization of history, history as it should have been: "Historical events, serving as material for the creation of this play, are reduced here to a series of artistically simplified moments and situations. The directors did not consider reproducing exactly a picture of the events that took place three years ago on Palace Square; they could not because theater was never meant to serve as history's stenographer."[59]

But the storming of the Winter Palace, of all events commemorated by mass spectacles, was historically the most concrete. It was a localized event, one that had occurred at the same spot on which it was reenacted. Palace Square was at the same time a stage and a real historical place (see Figure 17). The directors went to great lengths to make the performance seem actual: trucks bristling with bayonets roared across the square, machine guns chattered, and out on the river the cruiser *Aurora*, which three years before had fired the (blank) "shot heard round the world," repeated the signal for the performance. Evreinov enlisted participants of the 1917 takeover as performers. The production staff even rebuilt the wooden barricade that had protected the palace's front gates and manned it with the Women's Death Battalion, which legend claimed defended the gates to the end. The highly theatrical gesture was not dimmed by the fact that the Death Battalion had, in 1917, wisely abandoned its position. Obviously, a distinction must be made, one that in a theater such as Stanislavsky's never received recognition: the distinction between "real"-ness and authenticity.

The mass performance would distill and improve the historical event. According to the directors, participants and spectators would in the course of an hour experience what in 1917 had been experienced in the course of many hours[60]—or, more accurately, it might be said, had never been experienced at all. The event of 1917 had, after all, been something of an anticlimax, occurring a day after the seizure of power. More important to the transfer of power had been attaining a majority in the Petrograd Soviet and the slow process of propagandizing the Petrograd garrison. On the actual day of the Revolution, Palace Square was one of the few peaceful points in the city: the Bolsheviks rightly thought the train stations and post offices of more import, and that was

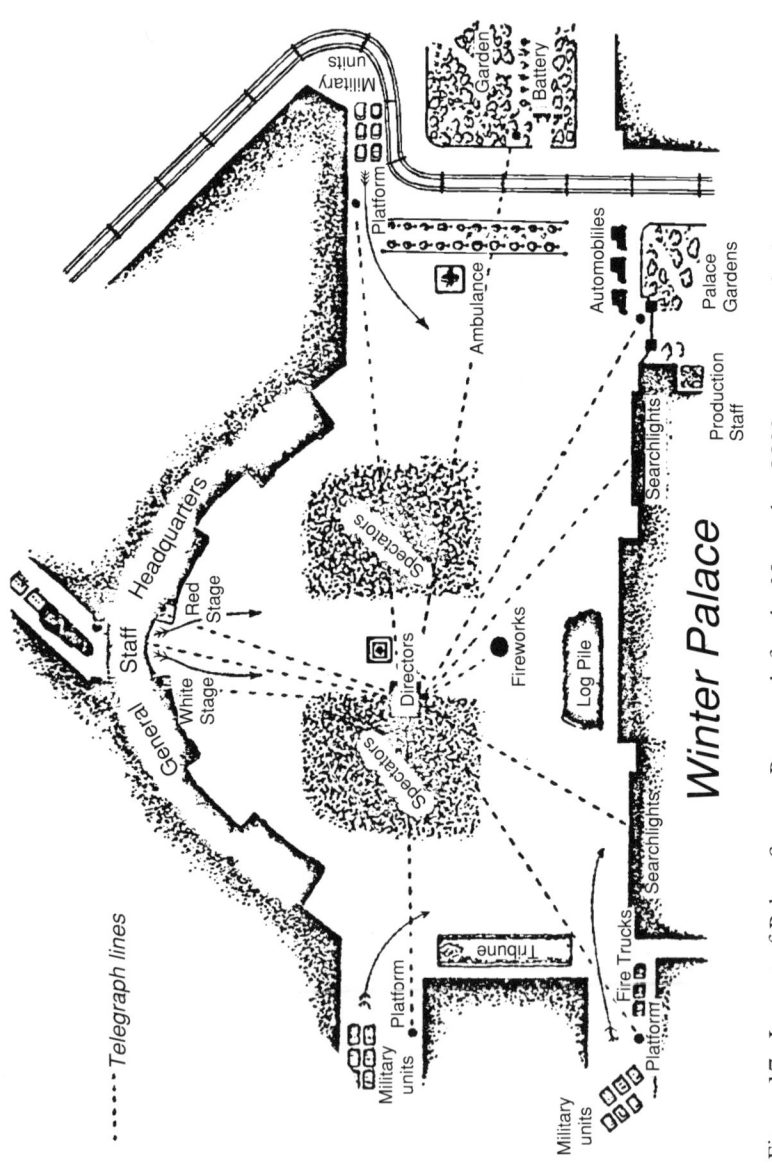

Figure 17. Layout of Palace Square, Petrograd, for the November 1920 mass spectacle; image computer-enhanced (*Istoriia sovetskogo teatra*, Leningrad, 1933).

where conflict, what little there was, occurred. Winter Palace was surrounded, and Lenin desperately wanted it taken, but the commanders were in less of a rush. Vladimir Antonov-Ovseenko, Podvoisky, and Grigory Chudnovsky, directors of the operation (in the production the trio was replaced by the single figure of Lenin), preferred to avoid senseless bloodshed and waited for a surrender. The troops defending the palace surrendered unit by unit over the next day, until finally the numerically superior Red Guard charged the building with scarcely a shot being fired. The eight thousand participants in the 1920 spectacle far outnumbered the attackers of 1917.

Although one hundred fifty thousand spectators were expected that night for the performance, because of dampness, chill rain, and slush, only one hundred thousand showed up—around one-quarter of the entire city. The spectators were well prepared; newspapers warned that the events would all be theatrical and requested that the audience not panic at the gunfire. There would be no reason to move during the performance; the stages were placed so that everyone could see.[61]

Spectators were placed right in the middle of the action (as they had been in Evreinov's Ancient Theater). Built against the facade of the General Staff Headquarters across the square from the palace was a huge stage designed by Annenkov. On the left side he constructed a Red city; dynamic, vertical buildings of red, factories, a large square, and even a memorial obelisk. Action on the Red platform was directed by Petrov. To the right (naturally) was the White platform, directed by Kugel and Derzhavin. Evreinov remained in charge of the entire production. The White platform was a horizontal construction made up of smaller platforms, none of which represented a specific place. On its left side, ladies and gentlemen in evening clothes campaigned for the Liberty Loan—here, Evreinov parodied an earlier mass festival. To the right, ministers of the Provisional Government, wearing top hats and sitting behind a long table, listened to Kerensky give a hysterical speech. Between the two platforms was a gangway, an architectural duplicate of the Headquarters Arch behind it, along which the two worlds met and did battle. The directors were placed on a large platform encircling the Alexander Column, equipped with a complicated network of electric signals. Spectators were cordoned off in large squares on both sides of the column and between the palace and headquarters. A few lucky ones watched from windows of the palace and surrounding buildings.

The Storming of the Winter Palace was conducted with a masterful sense of theatrical timing. At the stroke of ten, Palace Square was plunged into darkness. A cannon shot shattered the silence, and an orchestra of 500, placed under the arch and directed by Varlikh, struck up Henri Litolff's *Robespierre* overture, introducing the White (!) platform. One hundred and fifty searchlights mounted on the roofs of surrounding buildings were switched on at once, illuminating the Whites, who opened the action. The *Marseillaise,* orchestrated as a polonaise, was begun as the ladies and gentlemen of high society awaited Kerensky's arrival. The prime minister, whose appearance caused some stir among the crowd on stage, was parodied brilliantly by an actor dressed in his characteristic khakis. The Whites formed a chorus, with Kerensky in the role of the coryphaeus (the figure who initiates and leads the chorus's response).

Directors of previous mass spectacles had avoided using individual actors, preferring to use masses of bodies to represent mass movements. The directors of *Winter Palace* reasoned correctly that in a large square filled with human bodies it would not be the huge mass that stands out but the single figure, particularly when that figure is spotlighted.[62] The proposal of Annenkov and Kugel to have twenty actors moving in unison play Kerensky was turned down. The advantages were immediately apparent. Kerensky, like the rest of the Whites, was played in the style of the opera-bouffe and the circus. The actor caught his histrionic gestures perfectly as he mimed a speech. The response of the White chorus was performed in the same style: Kerensky was showered with roses and ovations (all this had occurred during his Moscow Liberty Bond tour). Bankers, pushing money bags across the stage, volunteered their services for the Liberty Loan. Bureaucrats, backs bent in humility, vowed fealty to the first minister. And officers in cocked hats, monocled and bedecked with medals, held posters proclaiming "War to a Victorious End!"

Previous mass spectacles suffered most from an inability to transfer action from one episode to the next. This difficulty was similar to that experienced by writers of the medieval annals. The "syntax" of events was a coordinate system: this happened, then that happened. The subordinate syntax of events that underlies historical understanding was not truly available to the directors of the first mass spectacles, just as it had not been available to the annalists. In *Mystery,* the scenario might have specified that action shift at a certain point from the failed Spartacus rebellion at the top of the steps to renewed popular unrest, led by Razin, at the base of the staircase. The spectators, however, would see it differently; several hundred people in togas would still be milling about at the top of the steps, and viewers would have to wonder what Romans were doing in Razin's Russia. The directors, then, had to take time out to clear the stage of the previous scene, as if erasing a blackboard. As a result these early performances took from four to five hours to complete.

Winter Palace, uniquely, was produced simultaneously as a drama and a film.[63] The analogy to film provided a solution to the time problem, which reduced Evreinov's production to only one and a half hours. In film, scenes can shift instantaneously; the time wasted in the theater occurs while the movie camera is turned off. In *Winter Palace,* action was moved not by shifting its location, but by shifting spectators' attention. The 150 searchlights were the solution: after Kerensky had made his speech and held court, and the scene shifted to the Red stage, a director on the column platform simply flicked a switch, plunging Kerensky and retinue into darkness, and another switch, lighting the Reds.

Lighting for the first time allowed for the division of a mass spectacle into distinct episodes and sharp contrasts. The dramas would no longer operate on "uninterrupted, festival" time[64] but on the subdivided time of theater, which yields to the manipulations of a director. In ritual drama (medieval mysteries or early Soviet mass dramas) there is a unity of performance time—the time frame in which the performance is viewed. There are no breaks in performance, no time when the performance is "turned off" and the spectator leaves the performative frame. Depicted time, however, is not unified; sharp, unexplained breaks and shifts—for example, from Spartacus's Rome to Robespierre's Paris—are the rule. Modern theater works on another scheme: performance time is broken, while depicted action is more continuous. *Winter Palace,* which finally solved the technical problems of mass spectacles, was the first in which depicted time was unified. With action concentrated in a single place and time, the festival was able to establish the palace seizure as the center of the Revolution. No historical myth is complete without that center, the moment of absolute change.

Action on the Red stage was in a monumental style; performers wore no make-up.[65] Acting was done in "collectives": characters were groups, not individuals like Kerensky, a device that demonstrated the collective character of the Reds. A few hundred workers come onstage from the factories Annenkov built for his city. While about half the group stand forestage and hold statuesque poses, the other half rhythmically strike anvils with their hammers. More people flood onstage and gather round a large red flag. The ever-increasing crowd falls silent, as if straining to hear something. The *Internationale* becomes faintly audible; then cries of "Lenin, Lenin!" echo from the audience until the word is caught up by the chorus. The Red stage has been changing throughout this scene. Beginning as a gray mass, the workers grow brighter as the searchlights illuminate them ever more intensely. As the masses, which have been pouring onstage chaotically, become increasingly more organized, they gather around the flag and take up the chant. When the *Internationale* breaks out at full volume to end the episode, the gray mass has completed its transformation into the Red Guard.

Now the Reds can attack the Whites, with their troops surging over the connecting arch; this mystery-play device, used in every mass spectacle from *The Overthrow of the Autocracy* on, had its place in *Winter Palace*. Many troops from the White side go over to the Reds; only the Junkers and the Women's Battalion remain to defend the government. Oblivious to the unrest, Kerensky continues his oration, but his ministers, whose bench has begun to rattle and sway to the rhythm of the Red chants, crash to the floor at the clap of the first Red volley. Kerensky nimbly escapes to a car (American flag waving) waiting before the stage and drives away. His ministers follow in another car.

Up to this point, the performance could have taken place on any large stage. Space was conventional, its value assigned by the decor. Time was conventional; the events of a few revolutionary months of 1917 were summarized in an hour's dramatic action. But when Kerensky stepped over the proscenium, he stepped into real space. For Kerzhentsev, Meyerhold, and the symbolist generation, theater would attain its ideal when the audience crossed the same line in the opposite direction. That was the theater as ritual. Evreinov, however, pursued the theatricalization of life, the theater as play; history was replayed according to the rules of art. Ironically, *Winter Palace,* the height of artifice, was the most real of all the mass spectacles. Previous spectacles could have been performed anywhere anytime and have been about anything. By substituting a different set of revolutions *The Mystery of Liberated Labor* could become *Toward a World Commune;* that scenario could be replayed at Krasnoe selo. *Winter Palace* could only be about the October Revolution, it could be played only on Palace Square, and only on November 7. This performance fixed the final, irreducible center of the revolution.

Kerensky and his ministers, having driven madly across the square between the two masses of spectators, are admitted to the palace. Meanwhile, action continues on the stage, where the Red Guard and White soldiers battle for control of the city; this segment is performed like a wartime battle spectacle. Suddenly, the lights inside the palace spring on, and in the brightly illuminated windows silhouettes grapple for control of the palace. A different stage of the struggle is depicted in each window, and the battle unfolds as each is illuminated in progression. The Reds gradually take the upper hand in these duels, and the palace finally falls under their control. The Revolution is accomplished. The searchlights of the *Aurora*, which have backlit the palace in an aura, switch to a point above the palace, where a tremendous red banner is raised, and red lights flash on in the windows. The performance ends with a comic scene from the revolutionary apochrypha; Kerensky flees the palace dressed as a woman. A cannon salute from the *Aurora* and fireworks end the festival and herald the dawning of a new age.

Epilogue
Time Moves On

The Bolshevik program was inspired by Marx's philosophy, and it was shaped by years of underground struggle. Yet neither source truly prepared the Bolsheviks for the frustrations of governance or provided a political lexicon accessible to the general public. These had to be developed in the revolutionary cauldron, by trial and error. The process of adapting their complex program to mass communication compelled revolutionaries to rethink their movement, to emphasize aspects that had been secondary before the Revolution, and to push others into the background.

Mass festivals were one of several venues of communication with the public, one that offered a unique conjunction of elements. They were perhaps the most public of media, which brought representatives of many groups with many opinions into intimate contact. Politicians, artists, and simple citizens were mixed in a single great performance, with the needs and particulars of each group contributing to the final product. In this sense, festival enthusiasts were correct in believing that festivals were models of the greater society surrounding them.

The mixed sources and tangled communications of festivals revealed the uncertainty and intricacy of revolutionary cultural processes. The sponsors' ideology was only one factor determining the final outcome. Bolshevik festivals grew from a political culture that predated the October Revolution. The Romanov dynasty was renowned for the majesty of its pageants and the richness of its rites, and the tradition proved adaptable to socialist ideology. The politics of celebration fascinated leading revolutionaries, who saw several possible uses for festivals. They could be instruments of class struggle, but they could also unite the nation in the joys of socialism. The millennia-old art of festivity fulfilled both needs.

Although the Bolsheviks understood the need to communicate with the population—perhaps better than any political movement before them—they betrayed a profound ambivalence about opening a dialogue of equals. The political opposition, which still existed in 1918, brought contention to that year's festivals; and the artistic avant-garde brought the spirit of mockery. Some Bolsheviks, however, damned the lighter side of festivity, believing that it derided their cherished principles. By 1919 they occupied the upper rungs of festival committees, and they used their power to solemnize celebrations. The condemnation was inspired by more than sobriety. Festivals were a bid for political legitimacy, an attempt to lend the Revolution a sacred aura, and that aim might have been thwarted by dissonant voices.

The sponsors of revolutionary festivals courted popular participation, but the invitation was belied by efforts to limit mass initiative. At the heart of the uncertainty lay the contradictory notion of self-activity (*samodeiatel'nost'*), according to which revolution was spawned by popular volition yet needed the guidance of professional revolutionaries. The Bolsheviks were failed by their imaginations in their dealings with the masses; they did not account for the variety and unpredictability of reactions. When official commentators remarked on popular reactions, they projected their own views onto the people; and when mass participation was integrated into festival plans, it was usually with the intent of constraining it.

When older revolutionaries discussed the historical role of popular celebrations, they usually mentioned fêtes of the French Revolution, Hellenic tragic festivals, medieval mystery plays—anything but their own rich native tradition. The neglect was remedied by 1919, when the artists invited to direct revolutionary spectacles—who were themselves not always so revolutionary—began incorporating popular traditions. The innovation proved beneficial. Popular theater provided a variety of forms ideal for propaganda and made the message highly accessible. Clowns proclaimed revolutionary couplets from the circus arena; Petrushka puppets pummeled the heads of reactionaries; wandering players performed skits about the benefits of Bolshevism and the detriments of dysentery.

People's theater was a common phrase during the Revolution, but it meant many things to many people. It could be a vast ritual bringing together classes and nations; a childlike dance of the liberated masses; troupes wandering the countryside performing propaganda pieces; vast spectacles simulating revolutionary action. These concepts merged in the mass festivals, where—according to planners—the people would unite to spontaneously create revolutionary dramas. But practice showed that the notions of people's theater contradicted each other. Popular theater did not always preach the message of socialism; ritual dramas did not always re-create the tension of revolt; and traditional spectacles discouraged viewer participation and segregated audience and actors. Producing the desired artistic results and prompting the desired audience reaction did not seem compatible.

Professional directors hired for the mass spectacles confronted the contradiction between popular initiative and mass organization already familiar to the Bolsheviks. Mass drama was an unwieldy form that made questions of management paramount. Masses of bodies had to be moved up and down sweeping staircases; scores of searchlights had to be focused on precise spots at precise moments; massive choruses had to sing to a baffling array of cues. Maintaining order in the face of thousands of ecstatically improvising citizens was unthinkable. The directors adopted a stricter dramatic organization that changed the social dynamics of mass festivals but increased their power to dramatize the October Revolution.

Mass festivals and their centerpiece spectacles had a tremendous potential to project legitimizing myths. The Bolsheviks restated their revolution as the culmination of a long historical process rather than as a tenuous partisan uprising and thus demonstrated their legitimate claim to leadership of the Russian and world proletariats. The political advantages of the myth were apparent, yet its genesis could be explained aesthetically as well as politically. The great spectacles of summer and autumn 1920 were more organized, more streamlined, more managed than before; because of their stricter form, the historical narratives enacted became more compelling. A diffuse, unfocused story became centered; history was no longer cyclical, but hierarchical, teleological, closed. The drama made the October Revolution seem inevitable and the Bolsheviks the legitimate rulers of Russia.

Mass drama was an essential feature of Soviet Russia's cultural life, yet the conclusion of the Civil War diminished its importance. The Army had funded the biggest spectacles of the Civil War years and provided conscripts for their mass scenes; when it was demobilized, a needed sponsor was lost. Closer inspection suggests, though, that the end of the war should have freed resources, not eliminated them, and that if the government had wanted to sponsor mass spectacles, it could have.

Although the first months of NEP saw calls for a centralized festival administration, such an organization was not in the spirit of the times—nor within the country's abilities. The scaling down of the armed forces meant that no single organization had the funds to sponsor or control celebrations nationwide. The party did seek influence in the May Day 1921 celebration in Petrograd, but this was a local incident that did not repeat itself.[1] The Moscow festival was organized by the local branch of the political-education arm of Narkompros, Glavpolitprosvet;[2] and while the November 1921 anniversary in Moscow was created by the All-Russian Central Committee for October (Celebrations), this grand rubric concealed a group that operated only in Moscow and disbanded after November 7.[3] Most holidays were actually the work of local cadres provided by unions, factory committees, and workers' clubs.

Civil War festivals often led to clashes between central organizers and artists, which led to a vigorous artistic variety. During NEP, there was less need to present a monolithic face and more desire for popular expression; as the Moscow May Day Commission said in 1923, "We reject the strict centralization of celebrations that was once necessary to demonstrate to the West the strength and power of the Soviet Republic."[4] Despite the slackening of discipline and the absence of central leadership, however, NEP festivals were remarkable for their stylistic uniformity. Decorations and slogans changed little (they were often reused); the festival was significant not for what it said but for the fact that marchers showed up. A temporary committee would usually plot the holiday schedule: where and when marchers should congregate; the marching order through Red Square; a nighttime fireworks display. Street decorations and performances would be assigned to smaller groups, such as a local workers' club or Proletkult. Floats were the focus of the parade. Each factory club was assigned the construction of a float, which combined a theme relevant to the factory with the central political theme of the day. Some contributions were clever: in 1923 Skorokhod, the Petrograd shoe factory, seated effigies of the Entente in a galosh ("to be in a galosh" means to be in a jam). Still, most often they were of a few basic types. Much work was done on a popular level, yet it was guided by club cultural instructors; and in large cities instructors were in close contact with each other.

Newsreels, which regularly brought images of festivals to the entire country, were another source of similarity.

Official indifference did not always discourage artists and directors from hatching grand schemes. Lunacharsky wrote a grandiose scenario for the Moscow Comintern conference of 1921 that was to be produced by Mardzhanov in Red Square—the first time that this ideal space would have been exploited. Its subject was history from caveman times to the present. The first act portrayed prehistoric life:

> Groups of people march in to parade music carrying props that depict cliffs and rocks. . . . Prehistoric people enter; they light fires, dance about, and swing their clubs, perform large choral *corrobore* (mass ceremonial dances of the Australian aborigines); the women dance on the central stage (ballet); horsemen gallop between the cliffs, hunting beasts; life seems free and joyful; however, distinct groups attack each other with a howl and create a wild ruckus. Meanwhile, atop the stage a primitive fetish is constructed: a large boulder, which is gaily decorated. Shamans, wailing and producing noise on primitive instruments, summon the people to bow before it; a human sacrifice is brought. A cannon shot signals the end of the first act.[5]

The next acts featured pharaonic Egypt, feudal Europe, the capitalist West, the triumph of the Third International. In many ways—in the massiveness of the production, the clumsy editing, and the confusion of size with grandeur—Lunacharsky ignored the lessons of 1920. The finale could have come from a Jacobin production:

> A group of workers appears with new props and builds the city of the future. It is a complex of wondrous and fantastic buildings shimmering with the colors of the rainbow (I would recommend using light, inflatable materials) with the names "Free Labor School," "Temple of Science," "Temple of Art," and so forth. The main task is to create a truly captivating picture, which would be a hint of the "Promised City." Children, women, young men, girls, and elders appear. The children frolic and play. The youths march in a proud procession, half-bared; they wrestle and run tag races (use Vsevobuch [Universal Military Training Corps] here). Women's games, their procession and choir . . . Everyone gathers round the elders, who bless the future generation.

The plan was canceled, perhaps wisely, in the face of economic collapse and starvation.

There were also less-immediate causes of the decline of mass spectacles. Grand and often impractical ventures that had seemed exhilarating during the struggle no longer seemed so powerful. The flush of revolution was not something that could last forever; its bright colors faded. In 1918, when David Burliuk hung a futurist painting on Kuznetsky

Bridge, this act was taken as a bold foray of art into life; but when NEP rolled around the painting was still on the wall, sun-faded and rain-splotched, invisible to the eyes of pedestrians who had seen it too many times before.[6]

Conventions, like fashions, begin to seem silly with time, and by late 1920 parodies of mass spectacles began to appear, some in good fun, some malicious. *The Legend of the Communard*—an easy target—was mocked by the same Proletkult students who a year before had played it with all due solemnity. The young people were growing up, acquiring sophistication.[7] A mock agitational skit performed in Astrakhan's Lenin Theater on New Year's Day 1921 attacked another easy target: "An *International Proletarian Political Review,* featuring the "Entente Giving Birth" [standard journalese], was shown. Onstage the pregnant Entente, portrayed by an actor [!], went through birth throes, complaining that it was embarrassing to give birth in public and uttering unprintable vulgarities."[8] The most tempting target was *The Storming of the Winter Palace.* In a children's performance Vladimir Durov, the famous clown and animal trainer, led a phalanx of rabbits in storming the palace: over the captured palace they hoisted the slogan "Rabbits of the world unite!"[9] Russia's greatest master of parody, though, was Evreinov himself, who did not let the opportunity for a jest pass him by. His *World Contest of Wit*[10] mocked the rhythmic military maneuvers of mass spectacles, including his own.[11]

Small theaters specializing in small productions proliferated under NEP, while funding for mass spectacles dwindled. Parody, wit, and lightness, which suit the café more than the city square, fit the mood; and mass drama was not, after all, a profitable venture. Yet it was not financial considerations alone that diminished mass spectacles. Funds were still available for decorating cities, for processions, and for most spectacles with political utility. Rather the unbroken solemnity and zeal needed for mass drama were gone. The intensified, often euphoric days of the Civil War had spawned the genre. Symptomatic would be the remark found in an instruction book printed for the tenth anniversary celebration in 1927: the best subject for a mass drama was still the Civil War.[12]

Early Bolshevik festivals had combined two prerevolutionary traditions: grim May Day worker demonstrations and the magnificent spectacles of the autocracy. During NEP, demonstrations and mass spectacles once again went their separate ways. The change was in many ways salutory: participants in spectacles were no longer involuntary conscripts but young and enthusiastic members of workers' clubs. The great artists who had directed the spectacles of 1920 eventually emigrated or moved on to other things. Though NEP spectacles no longer held the artistic world's imagination, much more popular participation was possible. What happened was not that mass spectacles disappeared but that they moved from the cultural center to the periphery.

With their great victory in the war, new tasks stood before the Bolsheviks. The regime ruled a society that was sometimes hostile to and often ignorant of its plans; simply legitimizing the seizure of power was not enough. Political education, which demands a calmer voice and more detail than festivals, was now imperative; and if mass spectacles were to continue, new conditions had to be acknowledged. During the Civil War, the central aim of any festival was to enlist popular support. A binary choice was posed: Red or White, past or future, for or against. More complex messages, though they might have been present, were extraneous and were not always understood. As party propagandists became more aware of the consciousness gap separating people and party, they looked to more complex media.[13] Organizers began to view spectacles as the Jacobins had, as a school of citizenship.

The military continued to sponsor and exploit mass dramas as training exercises. In fact, theatricalized military maneuvers and militarized theatrical spectacles—the line was blurred at times—were popular during NEP. In May 1925, the Baltic Fleet was handed over to a theater director for a re-creation of Iudenich's 1919 attack on Petrograd. Writers and commanders collaborated on the script, which was performed in the Luga district. Spectators—sailors and local peasants—watched from a hill as the battle unfolded. It involved naval maneuvers and an amphibious landing that came right up to the foot of the hill.[14] The fashion stretched even further in Orenburg in 1927, when during a war scare the entire city was treated to theatricalized battles and participated in civil-defense alarms and simulated evacuations.[15]

Meyerhold was enthusiastic about ties to the military and security organs. He supervised theatricals for three different GPU (later, KGB) clubs;[16] and on Book Day 1925 he produced a thematic skit employing "artillery, the Engineering Corps, the Air Force, and the Chemical Warfare School, which demonstrated a chemical attack."[17] His grandest plan, conceived for the 1921 Comintern conference, would have cost a fortune in military supplies. The site of the spectacle, entitled *Struggle and Victory,* would have been Khodynka Field, and its cast would have included 200 cavalrymen, 2,300 infantry cadets, sixteen artillery guns, five aeroplanes mounted with Zeiss projectors, armored vehicles, and tanks. The show was divided into twelve brief episodes, showing that Meyerhold had absorbed lessons learned by Evreinov.

In the first five action moments, various national groups of the army of the Revolution conduct a unified attack on the bastions of capitalism, surrounding them in a tight circle, blanketing them with a smoke screen, and exploding ten-pound powder mines.

The armored transports release tanks into the smoke of the artificial fire, which cross artificial obstacles and barriers. The smoke screen disperses. Capitalist emblems fall from the bastion, and national flags disappear. The tall, flaming cones of flamethrowers rise high above the bastion. . . .

Moment VI. The troops file by the tribune, where all members of the III International Congress are located. . . .

Moment VII. The projectors create a curtain of light.

Decorated with the emblems of labor, trucks transport Vsevobuch athletes dressed as laborers past the tribune onto the field, where they form ranks in front of the city of the future.

Moment VIII. "The victors do not forget their weapons." They throw the javelin and the discus.

Moment IX. The hammer and sickle. In time with an orchestra, the former soldiers perform the movements of blacksmiths and harvesters.[18]

Podvoisky, a commander of the Palace Square operation on October 25, 1917, then director of Vsevobuch during the war, was an early enthusiast of mass festivals, and he helped promote them through the 1920s. Podvoisky occasionally collaborated with Meyerhold, though he was not involved in Meyerhold productions like *Struggle and Victory* or even *Dithyramb of Electrification*.[19] Podvoisky preferred the pseudo-Hellenic classicism of the prewar years, and he founded a colony on the Sparrow Hills where children wore tunics and frolicked in the lap of nature. Isadora Duncan herself toured the facility, and she was so enraptured that she called Podvoisky "a man like a god." She observed the children's upbringing in freedom and health, their happiness, the great stadium being built on Moscow's outskirts—and, with some disapproval, a game in which the children skipped down the mountain and sang "Death to Speculators."[20]

Podvoisky saw a new social role for Vsevobuch with the introduction of NEP: "In the initial period of conflict, Vsevobuch considered its main task to be the creation of fighters and warriors; at the present time its most important task is to train the bodies and wills of our youth. . . . Physical culture, closeness to nature, and mass theatrical dramas are the [major] factors in the creation of a new, collective humanity."[21] He reorganized the remnants of Vsevobuch into a network of sports clubs that was the military's main civilian training agency, and gave birth to the popular physical culture (*fizkul'tura*) movement. During the mid-1920s, *fizkul'tura* training was often combined with war games—scenario-based games in which thousands of participants acted out failed revolutions, capitalist attacks, and socialist victories. In 1924, the Sparrow Hills, now renamed the Lenin Hills, was the site of a revolutionary war fought by India, Britain, and the "Reds" (led by Trotsky). In 1928, the same site hosted an international conflagration entitled *Worldwide October*.[22] Participants—who were all volunteers—learned the basics of drill discipline and more complex maneuvers, like amphibious attacks. The exercises were discontinued only in 1930, when a game entitled *Stepan Razin* was marred by serious maulings.[23]

The third-anniversary celebration in Petrograd was the advent of the most important trend in NEP-period mass spectacles: amateur theater clubs took over festival performances. Perhaps young club members did not have professional skills, but as players they were far superior to the soldiers conscripted for Civil War–era spectacles. One group, the playwrights' circle of the Karl Marx Club, wrote a script, *Along the Thorny Path to the Stars*, that was performed by the dramatic circles of central Petrograd. The first scene represented the October Revolution: "Cannon fire is heard, and a woman runs by with a child. Soldiers dash by, snapping their rifle chambers shut. Cowardly citizens cluster on the street. A worker with a hammer appears among them and speaks of the workers' coming triumph over the bourgeoisie."[24] The second scene depicted postrevolutionary moments: bureaucratic sabotage, the field after a battle, a *subbotnik*, the return of soldiers from the war. The apotheosis was a *tableau vivant* in which a worker, soldier, peasant, and sailor held a globe aloft. Above them stood a woman personifying the world commune.

The most active producer was a network of clubs run by the Petrograd Politprosvet, or Political Education administration. Its artistic director was Piotrovsky, who hired his old colleagues Shcheglov and Shimanovsky. Their system, the United Artistic Circles, used arts instruction to integrate members into Soviet society. This *samodeiatel'nyi* theater was not an imitation of the professional; it had its own esthetics and its own expressive system.[25] It also had a grand social purpose: it was theater "born of the crowd," as Greek tragedy had been born of popular religion, and it could by rights speak for the entire people.[26]

New members joined one of several club circles: theatrical, playwriting, artistic, musical, or political. Initial instruction took place in the individual circle; and the efforts of separate circles were eventually synthesized into the production of a mass spectacle. Work was timed to the calendar of Soviet holidays. To begin, the political circle—which was explicitly the primary circle in the club—chose a theme for the holiday: for example, for Paris Commune Day, the theme might be "From the Paris to the Petrograd Commune." The playwrights then wrote a scenario based on the theme; the theatrical circle put it together with the assistance of the musicians and artists. Each member of the club was given a specific task to be carried out under the supervision of the club director and political circle.[27] Each club in the Petrograd network competed for a central position in the citywide festival. The city had many squares, some on the outskirts, some in the center; and a club's ability to fulfill the tasks set by Politprosvet determined placement and time of performance.

Leftists from the old futurist movement were still enthusiastic about public celebrations, but they worked from a different angle. Their goal was not to unite the nation but to instigate further social change. In January 1923, in collaboration with the national Komsomol, leftists organized a "Komsomol Christmas." When believers exited from their churches for the traditional candlelight procession, they were greeted by Communist youths dressed in pagan costumes who mocked religious superstition and burned religious effigies. Readings from enlightened scientists replaced the scriptures, agit-verses stood in for the old hymns, and modern medicine and technology were forwarded as a substitute for backwardness.[28] In some cities, clubs performed a skit written by the leftist poet Sergei Tretiakov entitled *Neporzach* (a Soviet-style abridgment of the Russian for Immaculate Conception), which subjected the virgin birth of Christ to merciless ridicule.[29] The pious were, needless to say, offended; Communists were rumored to have been murdered in some provincial towns. Lenin himself was discomfited by the hard line at a time of reconciliation, and the practice was discontinued.[30]

The toughest and ultimately most quixotic task taken on by the leftists was to revitalize Soviet holidays. Ideas and practices that were novel during the Civil War had become habitual by the mid-1920s. The main target was demonstrations, which had fallen into an unvarying pattern and become empty forms.[31] One suggestion was to dilute the martial spirit with a dose of carnival laughter: a group of Moscow "Chinamen" carried a traditional carnival dragon; a jazz orchestra marched through

Red Square.³² Still, the artists discovered that the new Moscow did not allow for carnivals: the capital was becoming a modern industrial city, and its winding alleys were giving way to grand thoroughfares. Another leftist suggestion was that rather than hanging up garlands and red banners, which would be taken down the next day and leave the city as dirty and gray as before, artists should devote their holiday work to permanent improvements in the city.³³

Most important was the demand that marchers should once again have a reason, not an obligation, to come to the demonstration. Forced to stand for hours while the parade was organized and then herded before the tribune to shout their "Hurrah!", workers had become bored and annoyed. The leftists proposed reorganizing the demonstration so that it was directed at the marchers, not the spectators—that is, the politicians on the tribune. Placards said little to marchers. They were usually either the images of leaders or slogans; and the practice of giving each marcher only one letter of the slogan had even evolved. Not only did marchers not know which slogan their letters helped constitute, but when they went their separate ways during the day, the slogans collapsed into gibberish. Even when slogans stayed together, they faced forward and were unreadable by the marchers themselves. Artists suggested that banners be held along the length of the marching column, not across, and that columns be marched by one another, not by the tribune. Then, instead of having to read the slogans from a newspaper after the demonstration, marchers could see the placards themselves. The most radical idea was to break down the pattern of movement in the sacred center of Soviet Russia, Red Square. Trooping by the leadership could be expected of slaves, not of workers; why not go through the square in a zigzag pattern, which would mean that no spectator was more important than the marchers and that all marchers could see their comrades? Although avant-gardists were proposing sensible measures for improving holiday demonstrations, they were also trying to remove the centeredness and hierarchy that had crept into festivals in 1920 and that remained forever.

The avant-garde in 1927 did not meet the active resistance it had met in 1918, but the result was the same. NEP was coming to an end in late 1927, and its diffused patterns of culture and politics were soon to be subordinated to the powerful center of the Stalinist state. The center, not the periphery, was the focus of the tenth-anniversary celebration. The avant-garde was invited by the Moscow Soviet to organize the celebration in June; but in July the national government established a

Commission of the Central Executive Committee of the USSR for the Organization and Conduct of the Tenth Anniversary of the October Revolution, the first body in Soviet Russia with authority to regulate festivities throughout the entire country. Its chairman was Podvoisky. The commission issued instructions for the holiday; and preparations were to be supervised by local party organs and the Worker-Peasant Inspectorate.[34]

Local initiative and popular participation were choked off; and in fact spectators were kept as far away from the central celebrations as possible. In Leningrad, the holiday was capped by the largest spectacle there had ever been. In 1920, the Revolution had been the culmination of the show; now, it was the beginning, and the new industrialization program was the climax. Hundreds of thousands of spectators came, but the spectacle took place on the Neva River between the Kirov and Lieutenant Schmidt bridges, which made viewing difficult and mass participation impossible.[35] In Moscow, the celebration was focused on Red Square. Access to the square was severely restricted, and marchers passed by the tribune as they always had. Doubtless, the leadership was not sorry. The holiday came at the moment when the Trotsky-Stalin struggle was reaching a crisis and final resolution. Trotsky's followers had planned a counterdemonstration for the square. It was to be a disappointment. All attention was focused on Lenin's Mausoleum, the ceremonial center of the Soviet Union, atop which stood Stalin and the party leadership; when the counterdemonstration began in a corner of the square, it was drowned out by the hoopla of the marchers and went unnoticed. Stalin had secretly invited a regiment of mounted Georgian Cossacks to the parade; and as the small band of Trotskyists shouted in the corner, the Cossacks charged through the square with swords bared and saluted the tribune. The counterdemonstration fizzled out.[36]

List of Abbreviations

AMI (1971)	*Agitatsionno-massovoe iskusstvo pervykh let oktiabria* (E. Speranskaia, ed.)
AMI (1984)	*Agitatsionno-massovoe iskusstvo: Oformlenie prazdnestv* (I. M. Bibikova and N. I. Levchenko, eds.)
DN	*Delo naroda*
IK	*Iskusstvo kommuny*
IzvPS	*Izvestiia Petrogradskogo soveta*
IzvTsIK	*Izvestiia Tsentral'nogo ispolnitel'nogo komiteta*
KG	*Krasnaia gazeta*
LGAOR	Leningradskii gosudarstvennyi arkhiv oktiabr'skoi revoliutsii
NZh	*Novaia zhizn'*
P	*Pravda*
Pl	*Plamia*
PP	*Petrogradskaia pravda*
PSS	V. V. Maiakovskii, *Polnoe sobranie sochinenii*
RM	*Rabochii mir*
SK	*Severnaia kommuna*
TK	*Teatral'nyi kur'er*
TsGA RSFSR	Tsentral'nyi gosudarstvennyi arkhiv RSFSR
TsGALI	Tsentral'nyi gosudarstvennyi arkhiv literatury i iskusstva
VIMS	*Vechernie izvestiia Moskovskogo soveta*

VO	*Vneshkol'noe obrazovanie*
VT	*Vestnik teatra*
ZI	*Zhizn' iskusstva*
ZPOT	*Zapiski peredvizhnogo-obshchedostupnogo teatra*

Notes

Introduction

1. Thorold Dickinson, *Soviet Cinema* (London: Falcon Press, 1948), pp. 132–33.
2. *Istoriia sovetskogo teatra* (Leningrad: Academia, 1933); *Massovye prazdnestva* (Leningrad: Academia, 1926). See also E. Riumin, *Massovye prazdnestva,* ed. O. M. Beskin (Moscow: GIZ, 1927); O. Tsekhnovitser, *Prazdnestva revoliutsii* (Leningrad: Priboi, 1931). On the artwork, see A. S. Gushchin, *Izoiskusstvo v massovykh prazdnestvakh i demonstratsiiakh* (Moscow: Khudozhestvennoe izdatel'skoe aktsionernoe ob――vo, 1930), and *Khudozhestvennoe oformlenie massovykh prazdnestv v Leningrade, 1918–1931* (Leningrad: Izogiz, 1932); *Massovye prazdnestva v staroi i novoi grafike. Katalog vystavki* (Moscow: Izd. gos. muzeia iziashchnykh iskusstv, 1927); A. Kuznetsova, A. S. Magidson, and Iu. P. Shchukin, *Oformlenie goroda v dni revoliutsionnykh prazdnestv* (Moscow: Gosizdat, 1932).
3. See Rosalinde Sartorti, "Stalinism and Carnival: Organization and Aesthetics of Political Holidays," and Richard Stites, "Stalinism and the Restructuring of Revolutionary Utopianism," in Hans Günther, ed., *The Culture of the Stalin Period* (New York: St. Martin's Press, 1990).
4. Most notable were V. P. Tolstoi, "Materialy k istorii agitatsionnogo iskusstva perioda grazhdanskoi voiny," *Soobshcheniia Instituta istorii iskusstv, Akademiia nauk SSSR*, no. 3 (1953); Iurii Osnos, "U istokov sovetskogo teatra," *Teatral'nyi al'manakh*, no. 2 (1946); P. I. Lebedev, *Sovetskoe iskusstvo v period inostrannoi interventsii i grazhdanskoi voiny* (Moscow: Iskusstvo, 1949); N. Shchekotov, "Iskusstvo khudozhestvennogo oformleniia," *Tvorchestvo*, no. 3 (1938).

5. D. M. Genkin, *Massovye prazdniki* (Moscow: Prosveshchenie, 1975), p. 6.

6. V. I. Brudnyi, *Obriady vchera i segodnia* (Moscow: Nauka, 1968), pp. 164–80.

7. E. Speranskaia, ed., *Agitatsionno-massovoe iskusstvo pervykh let oktiabria* (Moscow: Iskusstvo, 1971); I. M. Bibikova and N. I. Levchenko, comps., *Agitatsionno-massovoe iskusstvo: Oformlenie prazdnestv* (Moscow: Iskusstvo, 1984); V. K. Aizenshtadt, *Sovetskii samodeiatel'nyi teatr* (Kharkov: KhGIK, 1983); T. M. Goriaeva, "Pervaia godovshchina oktiabr'skoi revoliutsii: Dokumenty," *Istoriia SSSR*, no. 6 (1987); *Russkii-sovetskii teatr 1917–1921: Dokumenty i materialy* (Leningrad: Iskusstvo, 1968).

8. Valentina Khodasevich, "Gorod—teatr, narod—akter," *Dekorativnoe iskusstvo SSSR*, no. 11 (1979), and "Massovye deistva, zrelishcha i prazdniki," *Teatr*, no. 11 (1967); Nikolai Petrov, *50 i 500* (Moscow: VTO, 1960); *U istokov* (Moscow: VTO, 1960); N. G. Vinogradov-Mamont, *Krasnoarmeiskoe chudo* (Leningrad: Iskusstvo, 1972).

9. For example, V. S. Aksenov, *Organizatsiia massovykh prazdnikov trudiashchikhsia, 1918–1920* (Leningrad: LGIK, 1974); Brudnyi, *Obriady vchera i segodnia;* A. I. Chechetin, *Istoriia massovykh narodnykh prazdnestv i predstavlenii* (Moscow: Gos. inst. kul'tury, 1976); Genkin, *Massovye prazdniki;* P. P. Kampars and N. M. Zakovich, *Sovetskaia grazhdanskaia obriadnost'* (Moscow: Mysl', 1967); *Massovye prazdniki i zrelishcha* (Moscow: Iskusstvo, 1961); A. I. Mazaev, *Prazdnik kak sotsial'no-khudozhestvennoe iavlenie* (Moscow: Nauka, 1978); V. G. Sinitsyn, ed., *Nashi prazdniki* (Moscow: Politizdat, 1977); V. Aizenshtadt, ed., *Rezhissura i organizatsiia massovykh zrelishch* (Kharkov: KhGIK, 1973); V. A. Rudnev, *Sovetskie prazdniki, obriady, ritualy* (Leningrad: Lenizdat, 1979).

10. See, for instance, Joseph Ben-David and Terry Clark, eds., *Culture and Its Creators: Essays in Honor of Edward Shils* (Chicago: University of Chicago Press, 1977); Sean Wilentz, ed., *Rites of Power: Symbolism, Ritual and Politics since the Middle Ages* (Philadelphia: University of Pennsylvania Press, 1985); David Cannadine and Simon Price, eds., *Rituals of Royalty: Power and Ceremonial in Traditional Societies* (Cambridge: Cambridge University Press, 1987); Roy Strong, *Art and Power: Renaissance Festivals 1450–1650* (Berkeley: University of California Press, 1984). Also: M. M. Bakhtin, *Rabelais and His World*, trans. Helene Iswolsky (Cambridge: MIT Press, 1968); Harvey Cox, *The Feast of Fools* (Cambridge: Harvard University Press, 1969); Eric Hobsbawm and Terence Ranger, eds., *The Invention of Tradition* (Cambridge: Cambridge University Press, 1982); Barbara Babcock, ed., *The Reversible World: Symbolic Inversion in Art and Society* (Ithaca, N.Y.: Cornell University Press, 1978).

11. Mona Ozouf, *Festivals and the French Revolution*, trans. Alan Sheridan (Cambridge: Harvard University Press, 1988); Maurice Agulhon, *Marianne into Battle*, trans. Janet Lloyd (Cambridge: Cambridge University Press, 1981); Lynn Hunt, *Politics, Culture, and Class in the French Revolution* (Berkeley: University of California Press, 1984).

12. See Abbott Gleason, Peter Kenez, Richard Stites, eds., *Bolshevik Culture* (Bloomington: Indiana University Press, 1985); Sheila Fitzpatrick, ed., *Cultural Revolution in Russia, 1928–1931* (Bloomington: Indiana University Press, 1978); Günther, *The Culture of the Stalin Period*.

13. Peter Kenez, *The Birth of the Propaganda State: Soviet Methods of Mass Mobilization, 1917–1929* (Cambridge: Cambridge University Press, 1985); Richard Stites, *Revolutionary Dreams: Utopian Vision and Experimental Life in the Russian Revolution* (New York: Oxford University Press, 1989).
14. Nina Tumarkin, *Lenin Lives! The Lenin Cult in Soviet Russia* (Cambridge: Harvard University Press, 1983).
15. Katerina Clark, *The Soviet Novel: History as Ritual* (Chicago: University of Chicago Press, 1981); Regine Robin, *Le réalisme socialiste: Une esthétique impossible* (Paris: Payot, 1986).
16. Frantishek Déak, "Russian Mass Spectacles," *Drama Review* 19, no. 2 (June 1975).
17. Richard Stites, "Adorning the Russian Revolution: The Primary Symbols of Bolshevism, 1917–1918," *Sbornik*, no. 10 (1984), and "The Origins of Soviet Ritual Style: Symbol and Festival in the Russian Revolution," in Claes Arvidsson and Lars Erik Blomqvist, eds., *Symbols of Power: The Esthetics of Political Legitimation in the Soviet Union and Eastern Europe* (Stockholm: Almqvist & Wiksell, 1987).
18. Christel Lane, *The Rites of Rulers* (Cambridge: Cambridge University Press, 1981); Christopher A. P. Binns, "The Changing Face of Power: Revolution and Accommodation in the Development of Soviet Ceremonial Systems," *Man*, no. 4 (1979), no. 1 (1980).
19. Many sources on the French fêtes were available to Russians, including André Grétry, *Memoires ou essais sur la musique* (Liège: Vaillant-Carmanne, 1914); P. A. Kropotkin, *The Great French Revolution, 1789–1793* (New York: G. P. Putnam, 1909); Julien Tiersot, *Les fêtes et les chants de la Revolution française* (Paris: Hachette et cie, 1908)—in Russian: *Prazdnestva i pesni frantsuzskoi revoliutsii*, trans. K. Zhikhareva (Petrograd: Izd. Parus, 1917).
20. Eugene Zamiatin, *We*, trans. Gregory Zilboorg (New York: Dutton, 1952), pp. 131–32.
21. Lane, *The Rites of Rulers*, pp. 2–3.

Chapter One. The Precursors

1. This description has been condensed from the organizer's account: G. S. Maliuchenko, "Pervye teatral'nye sezony novoi epokhi," in *U istokov*, pp. 285–87. The quotation is from Maliuchenko. I could not find any such article in the *Voronezh Telegraph* for that summer.
2. See A. Ia. Alekseev-Iakovlev, *Russkie narodnye gulianiia*, ed. Evg. Kuznetsov (Leningrad: Iskusstvo, 1948), p. 144. See pp. 100 ff. for descriptions of a number of such productions; for more shows (without descriptions) see the lists in *Istoriia sovetskogo teatra* (Leningrad: Academia, 1933), p. 153, or Nikolai A. Gorchakov, *The Theater in Soviet Russia*, trans. Edgar Lehrman (New York: Columbia University Press, 1957), p. 421, note 77.
3. Iu. A. Dmitriev, *Russkii tsirk* (Moscow: Iskusstvo, 1953), p. 194.
4. Genkin, *Massovye prazdniki*, p. 33. On the celebrations of Nicholas II

and his immediate predecessors, see Richard Wortman, "Moscow and Petersburg: The Problem of the Political Center in Tsarist Russia, 1881–1914," in Wilentz, *Rites of Power*.

5. For the program, see N. N. Vinogradov, ed., *Prazdnovanie 300-letiia tsarstvovaniia Doma Romanovykh v kostromskoi gubernii 19–20 maia 1913 goda* (Kostroma: Gub. tipografiia, 1914).

6. M. A. Chekhov, *Put' aktera* (Leningrad: Academia, 1928), pp. 64–69.

7. See V. V. Vsevolodskii-Gerngross, *Istoriia russkogo teatra* (Leningrad: Teakinopechat', 1929), vol. 1, 360–64. The English reader will find some descriptions in Robert K. Massie, *Peter the Great* (New York: Knopf, 1980), pp. 147–48, 268–71, 740–43.

8. It is described in *Torzhestvuiushchaia Minerva: Obshchenarodnoe zrelishche, predstavlennoe bol'shim maskaradom v Moskve 1763 goda* (Moscow: Imperatorskii Moskovskii universitet, 1763).

9. See Iu. A. Dmitriev, *Mikhail Lentovskii* (Moscow: Iskusstvo, 1978), pp. 194–95. A special illustrated pamphlet was published also: *Vesna krasna*, illustrated by F. O. Shekhtel' (Moscow, 1883).

10. This period is treated in Charles Rougle, "The Intelligentsia Debate in Russia 1917–1918," in Nils Ake Nilsson, ed., *Art, Society, Revolution: Russia, 1917–1921* (Stockholm: Almqvist & Wiksell, 1979). Another discussion of the commission, and of the All-Arts Union, which will presently be discussed, can be found in K. D. Muratova, *M. Gor'kii v bor'be za razvitie sovetskoi literatury* (Moscow: AN SSSR, 1958), pp. 22–50. Although her discussion of leftist artists betrays a certain bias, the archival materials used are of value. A more balanced treatment can be found in V. P. Lapshin, *Khudozhestvennaia zhizn' Moskvy i Petrograda v 1917 godu* (Moscow: Sovetskii khudozhnik, 1983), pp. 73–85.

11. I thank Hubertus Jahn for this information.

12. For the styles of interrevolutionary demonstrations, see Stites, "The Origins of Soviet Ritual Style," pp. 23–29.

13. LGAOR, f. 2551, op. 1, d. 2246.

14. Noted by V. D[esnitsky], "Eshche ne pozdno!" *NZh,* 21 April 1917, p. 2; Peter A. Garvi, *Zapiski Sotsial-Demokrata, 1906–1921* (Newtonville, Mass.: Oriental Research Partners, 1982), p. 266.

15. See Lapshin, *Khudozhestvennaia zhizn'*, pp. 119–24.

16. See Oleg Nemiro, "Prazdnik svobody, vesny i tsvetov," *Neva*, no. 5 (1967), pp. 205–7. More evidence would be needed before this claim could be accepted.

17. *Vo imia svobody. Odnodnevnaia gazeta* (Petrograd: Soiuz deiatelei iskusstv, 25 May 1917). The editor was Sologub.

18. In his *Kollektivnaia refleksologiia* (Petrograd: Kolos, 1921), pp. 176–79, the eminent psychophysiologist Vladimir Bekhterev used the bond campaign as an example of inflamed crowd psychology.

19. A. Rostislavov, "Revoliutsiia i khudozhestvennaia zhizn'," *Rech'*, 26 May 1917, p. 3.

20. The attribution of the performance to Gaideburov's group belongs to S. S. Mokul'skii, "Programma burzhuaznoi revoliutsii v teatre," in *Istoriia*

sovetskogo teatra, p. 50. The description below is taken from L——v, "Teatr i muzyka. Teatr na ulitse," *Rech'*, 30 May 1917, p. 7.

21. See E. M. Bebutova, "Vospominaniia," in *Iz istorii stroitel'stva sovetskoi kul'tury: Moskva 1917–1918 gg.* (Moscow: Mysl', 1964).

22. This People's Art Academy is described in "Khronika," *Put' osvobozhdeniia*, no. 4 (1917), p. 21.

23. P. V. Kuznetsov, "Iskusstvo v 1917 godu," in *Iz istorii*, pp. 314–15.

24. Tiersot, *Prazdnestva i pesni frantsuzskoi revoliutsii*. The translation project was begun before the October Revolution.

25. A. V. Lunacharskii, "O narodnykh prazdnestvakh," *VT*, no. 62 (1920), p. 4.

26. Most notably, A. V. Lunacharskii, "Sotsializm i iskusstvo," in the anthology *Teatr: Kniga o novom teatre* (St. Petersburg: Shipovnik, 1908), and the social-democratic response to this anthology, *Krizis teatra: Sbornik statei* (Moscow: Problemy iskusstva, 1908), in particular V. Friche, "Teatr v sovremennom i budushchem obshchestve."

27. Anatolii Strigalev, "Sviaz' vremen," *Dekorativnoe iskusstvo SSSR*, no. 4 (1978), pp. 1–2.

28. Quoted from account reprinted in Lapshin, *Khudozhestvennaia zhizn'*, p. 389.

29. M. Kuzmin, "Rampa geroizma," *ZI*, 20 November 1918, p. 2.

30. M. Kuzmin, "Tsirk," *ZI*, 4 January 1919, pp. 1–2.

31. The best description is to be found in Iu. Iur'ev, *Zapiski* (Leningrad: Iskusstvo, 1963), pp. 249–69.

32. He had expressed the opinion even before the October Revolution: A. V. Lunacharskii, "Kul'tura sotsializma torzhestvuiushchego i sotsializma boriushchegosia," *NZh'*, 21 June 1917, p. 4. His stand was based more on Hegelianism than cynicism.

33. Romain Rolland, *Le théâtre du peuple* (Paris: Suresnes, 1903). First translated in 1910, then 1919: *Narodnyi teatr*, introduction by Viach. Ivanov (Petrograd-Moscow: Izd. TEO NKP, 1919).

34. For the policy and practices of Proletkult, see Lynn Mally, *Culture of the Future: The Proletkult Movement in Revolutionary Russia* (Berkeley: University of California Press, 1990).

35. See, for instance, Sheldon Cheney, *The Open-Air Theater* (New York: Mitchell Kennerly, 1918), pp. 5 ff.

36. For example, Evg. Bezpiatov, "Teatr pod otkrytym nebom," *Narodnyi teatr*, no. 3–4 (1918), pp. 25–27, or B. Nikonov, "Teatr, blizkii k prirode," *ZI*, 20 May 1919, p. 3.

37. Percy MacKaye, *The Civic Theatre* (New York: Mitchell Kennerly, 1912).

38. Ibid., p. 15.

39. For mention of MacKaye in the Soviet literature, see besides Kerzhentsev's books (referred to in next note): A. A. Gvozdev, "Massovye prazdnestva na zapade," in *Massovye prazdnestva*, pp. 48–50.

40. "Doklad tov. V. Kerzhentseva," in P. I. Lebedev-Polianskii, ed., *Protokoly pervoi vserossiiskoi konferentsii proletarskikh kul'turno-prosvetitel'nykh organizatsii,*

15–20 sent. 1918 g. (Moscow: Proletarskaia kul'tura, 1918). The protocols of the session on theater are translated in William Rosenberg, ed., *Bolshevik Visions: The First Phase of the Cultural Revolution in Soviet Russia* (Ann Arbor, Mich.: Ardis, 1984), pp. 428–35. The following two books were published as practical and theoretical treatises (Kerzhentsev explicitly separated the two): V. Kerzhentsev, *Revoliutsiia i teatr* (Moscow: Dennitsa, 1918) (practical program); and *Tvorcheskii teatr* (five editions from 1918 to 1923; all further citations are from the edition published in Moscow by Gosizdat in 1923). See pp. 28–30 for his discussion of MacKaye and the American festivals.

41. Kerzhentsev, *Tvorcheskii teatr*, p. 23.
42. Ibid., p. 37.
43. Ibid., p. 44.
44. The word was used to translate MacKaye's term into Russian. See Gvozdev, "Massovye prazdnestva na zapade," p. 48.
45. A. A. Mgebrov, *Zhizn' v teatre* (Leningrad: Academia, 1932), vol. 2, p. 43.
46. *Russkii-sovetskii teatr 1917–1921*, p. 338.
47. Mgebrov, *Zhizn' v teatre*, vol. 2, p. 321.
48. "Doklad tov. V. Kerzhentsev," p. 122.
49. Mgebrov, *Zhizn' v teatre*, vol. 2, pp. 322–23. On pp. 321–31 of vol. 2 Mgebrov provides the best description of the declamations, and mine will be based on his account. For a summary of the critical reaction, see the section "Studiia Petrogradskogo Proletkul'ta" in D. I. Zolotnitskii, *Zori teatral'nogo oktiabria* (Leningrad: Iskusstvo, 1976).
50. See *Russkii-sovetskii teatr 1917–1921*, p. 347.
51. Mgebrov, *Zhizn' v teatre*, vol. 2, p. 324. This sort of staging led to accusations of an antirealist bias. Photos of another Proletkult *instsenirovka*, Whitman's *Europe*, are in *Plamia*, 22 September 1918, p. 13.
52. Mgebrov, *Zhizn' v teatre*, vol. 2, pp. 328–29.
53. Ibid., pp. 329–30.
54. The influence of Wagner's pamphlets, which were reprinted in 1918, is discussed in Lars Kleberg, " 'People's Theater' and the Revolution. On the History of a Concept before and after 1917," in Nilsson, ed., *Art, Society, Revolution*.
55. Lunacharskii, "Sotsializm i iskusstvo," in *Teatr*, p. 28.
56. From Richard Wagner, *Prose Works*, trans. William Ashton Ellis (London: Kegan Paul, Trench, Trübner and Co., 1895), vol. 1, p. 90. A Russian translation was published in 1918: *Iskusstvo i revoliutsiia* (Petrograd: LITO Narkomprosa, 1918).
57. Ibid., vol. 1, p. 74.
58. Ibid., vol. 1, p. 34.
59. Ibid., vol. 1, pp. 51–52.
60. Ibid., vol. 1, p. 59.
61. Jean-Jacques Rousseau, *Politics and the Arts: Letter to M. D'Alembert on the Theatre*, trans. Allan Bloom (Glencoe, Ill.: Free Press, 1960), p. 126.
62. Friche, "Teatr v sovremennom i budushchem obshchestve," in *Krizis teatra*, p. 185.

63. Frederick Engels, *The Origin of the Family, Private Property and the State*, trans. Eleanor Burke Leacock (New York: International Publishers, 1972), p. 237. The emphasis is Engels's.
64. See his articles on proletarian culture in A. A. Bogdanov, *Iskusstvo i rabochii klass* (Moscow: Proletarskaia kul'tura, 1918).
65. A. A. Bogdanov, *Red Star: The First Bolshevik Utopia* (Bloomington: Indiana University Press, 1984), pp. 76–79. This work was first published in 1908 and was widely read before and after the Revolution.
66. Lunacharskii, "Sotsializm i iskusstvo," in *Teatr*, p. 30. For the development of his ideas on Wagner, see Bernice Glatzer Rosenthal, "Wagner and Wagnerian Ideas in Russia" in David C. Lange and William Weber, eds., *Wagnerism in European Culture and Politics* (Ithaca, N.Y.: Cornell University Press, 1984), pp. 240–42.
67. N. K. Krupskaia, "Glavpolitprosvet i iskusstvo," *P*, 13 February 1921.
68. For a summary of Ivanov's views of theater, see Lars Kleberg, "Vjaceslav Ivanov and the Idea of Theater," in Lars Kleberg and Nils Ake Nilsson, eds., *Theater and Literature in Russia 1900–1930* (Stockholm: Almqvist & Wiksell, 1984).
69. A. Skriabin, *Pis'ma* (Moscow: Muzyka, 1965), p. 15.
70. See Alfred J. Swan, *Scriabin* (London: John Lane, 1923), pp. 97–111.
71. "Predchuvstviia i predvestiia" (1906), collected in Viacheslav Ivanov, *Po zvezdam* (St. Petersburg: Izd. Ory, 1909), p. 206. See also "Nitsshe i Dionis," in Ivanov, *Po zvezdam*, p. 8, and "The Essence of Tragedy," translated in Laurence Senelick, ed., *Russian Dramatic Theory from Pushkin to the Symbolists* (Austin: University of Texas Press, 1981), pp. 210 ff.
72. "Predchuvstviia i predvestiia," in Ivanov, *Po zvezdam*, pp. 212–13.
73. Viacheslav Ivanov, *Borozdy i mezhi* (Moscow: Musaget, 1916), p. 265.
74. The idea is best expressed in "Kop'e Afeny" (1904), collected in Ivanov, *Po zvezdam*.
75. "Dve stixii v simvolizme" (1908), in Ivanov, *Po zvezdam*, p. 285.
76. "Predchuvstviia i predvestiia," in Ivanov, *Po zvezdam*, p. 218.
77. This view was forwarded notably by M. Gorky: *The Confession*, trans. Rose Strunsky (New York: Frederick A. Stokes, 1909), chs. 14 ff.
78. A. V. Lunacharskii, *Religiia i sotsializm* (St. Petersburg: Shipovnik, 1908–11), vol. 1, p. 16.
79. See the letter from Meyerhold to Briusov in V. E. Meyerhold, *Perepiska, 1896–1939* (Moscow: Iskusstvo, 1976), p. 59.

Chapter Two. Revolution and Festivity

1. *U istokov*, p. 281. The original grammar has been preserved.
2. The following description is based on ibid., pp. 277–80.
3. "Two Tactics of Social Democracy in the Democratic Revolution," in V. I. Lenin, *Collected Works* (Moscow: Progress Publishers, 1960–70), vol. 9, p. 113.

4. Ozouf, *Festivals and the French Revolution*, chs. 6 and 7.

5. Mircea Eliade, *The Sacred and the Profane*, trans. Willard R. Trask (New York: Harcourt and Brace, 1959), particularly ch. 1; Bakhtin, *Rabelais and His World*.

6. Mircea Eliade, *Cosmos and History: The Myth of the Eternal Return*, trans. Willard R. Trask (New York: Harper, 1959), pp. 4–6; see also Eliade, *The Sacred and the Profane*, ch. 1.

7. E. Speranskaia, "Materialy k istorii oformleniia pervykh revoliutsionnykh prazdnestv v Saratove i Nizhnem Novgorode," in *AMI* (1971), p. 141.

8. The Smolny Institute was Bolshevik headquarters during the October uprising.

9. "Monuments Not Made by Human Hands," in K. S. Malevich, *Essays in Art, 1915–1933*, ed. Troels Andersen (London: Rapp & Whiting, 1968), vol. 1, p. 65.

10. See M. L[ev]in, "Miting ob iskusstve," *IK*, 7 November 1918, p. 3.

11. Truman Guy Steffan, ed., *Lord Byron's Cain* (Austin: University of Texas Press, 1968), p. 189.

12. Valerii Briusov, "Nenuzhnaia pravda," *Mir iskusstva*, no. 4 (1902).

13. Translated variously as "stylized," "relativistic," "conditional," and "conventional," it means "agreed on." *Conventional* will be used here, with the reservation that it not have the negative connotation of "routine." See V. Briusov, "Realizm i uslovnost' na stsene," in *Teatr*, translated as "Realism and Convention on the Stage" in Senelick, ed., *Russian Dramatic Theory*, pp. 171–82.

14. Briusov, "Realism," p. 178.

15. V. E. Meyerhold, *Stat'i, pis'ma, rechi, besedy* (Moscow: Iskusstvo, 1968), vol. 1, p. 96.

16. Konstantin Rudnitsky, *Meyerhold the Director*, trans. George Petrov (Ann Arbor, Mich.: Ardis, 1981), pp. 100–101.

17. Meyerhold, *Stat'i*, vol. 1, p. 237.

18. On this point, see Lars Kleberg, "People's Theater and the Revolution: On the History of a Concept before and after 1917," in Nilsson, ed., *Art, Society, Revolution*.

19. V. E. Meyerhold, "The Stylized Theatre," in *Vsevolod Meyerhold on Theatre*, trans. Edward Braun (New York: Hill and Wang, 1969), p. 63.

20. Meyerhold, "The Search for New Forms 1902–1907," in *Vsevold Meyerhold on Theatre*, p. 56. First published in *Teatr*.

21. K. R., *Tsar' Iudeiskii* (St. Petersburg: Tipografiia Ministerstva vnutrennykh del, 1914). This edition has photographs of the production described below. The play was translated into many languages, including English: [Grand Duke] K[onstantin Konstantinovich] R[omanov], *The King of the Jews: A Sacred Drama*, trans. Victor E. Marsden (New York: Funk and Wagnalls, 1914).

22. In late 1920 Soviet critics were still fulminating against the play: "Opium dlia naroda," *VT*, no. 70 (1920), pp. 8–9.

23. *Istoriia sovetskogo teatra*, p. 13.

24. Victor Marsden, who translated the play into English, was also the enthusiastic translator of *The Protocols of the Learned Elders of Zion*, translated from the Russian of Nilus by Victor E. Marsden (London: The Britons, 1923).

25. Dimitri Tiomkin and Prosper Buranelli, *Please Don't Hate Me* (Garden City, N.Y.: Doubleday, 1959), p. 43. The score is included in the Russian edition of the play.

26. Most of the above information was taken from N. N. Gievskii, "Iz teatral'nykh vospominanii," *Novyi zhurnal*, no. 10 (1945), pp. 282–88, 291.

27. On Bakhtin and GIII, see Katerina Clark and Michael Holquist, *Mikhail Bakhtin* (Cambridge: Harvard University Press, 1984), 96–97.

28. Characteristically, a GIII colleague saw the Feast of Fools as an expression of class struggle. See A. A. Gvozdev, *Massovye prazdnestva na zapade* (Petergof, 1926), p. 19.

29. A prominent advocate of festivity's revolutionary potential was Adrian Piotrovsky, a scholar at GIII and leading director of mass spectacles in 1919–20. See, for instance, his "K teorii samodeiatel'nogo teatra," in *Problemy sotsiologii iskusstva* (Leningrad: Academia, 1926).

30. See D. S. Likhachev, A. M. Panchenko, and N. V. Ponyrko, *Smekhovoi mir drevnei Rusi* (Leningrad: Nauka, 1976), pp. 25–35; and Russell Zguta, "Peter I's Drunken Synod of Fools and Jesters," *Jahrbücher für Geschichte Osteuropas* 21, no. 1 (1973), pp. 18–28.

31. Evg. Vakhtangov, *Materialy i stat'i* (Moscow: VTO, 1959), pp. 104–5.

32. V. Smyshliaev, "Opyt instsenirovki stikhotvoreniia Verkharna 'Vosstaniia,'" *Gorn*, no. 2–3 (1919), p. 82.

33. See "The Tragical in Daily Life," in Maurice Maeterlinck, *The Treasure of the Humble*, trans. Alfred Sutro (New York: Dodd, Mead, 1903), pp. 105–9.

34. This information has been culled from a longer description: V. Piast, *Vstrechi* (Moscow: Federatsiia, 1929), pp. 169–80.

35. Mgebrov, *Zhizn' v teatre*, vol. 2, p. 202.

36. From Meyerhold's production notes, in *Vsevolod Meyerhold on Theatre*, p. 143.

37. The history of the problem is discussed by Lars Kleberg, "Sootnoshenie stseny i zritel'nogo zala. K tipologii russkogo teatra nachala XX veka," *Scando-Slavica* 20 (1974).

38. Andrei Bely, "Theater and Modern Drama," in *Teatr*; translated in Senelick, ed., *Russian Dramatic Theory*, p. 158.

39. Ibid., p. 159.

40. Aleksandr Blok, "On Drama," in Senelick, ed., *Russian Dramatic Theory*, p. 110.

41. *Balaganchik*, in Aleksandr Blok, *Sobranie sochinenii* (Moscow: Khudozh. literatura, 1963), vol. 4, p. 20.

42. This period is well documented. See V. V. Sipovskii, "Italianskii teatr pri Anne Ioannovne," *Russkaia starina*, no. 5, June 1900, pp. 593–611; or V. N. Perets, *Italianskie komedii i intermedii, predstavlennye pri dvore imp. Anny Ioannovny v 1733–1735 gg.* (Petrograd: Imp. akademiia nauk, 1917).

43. See T. M. Rodina, *Aleksandr Blok i russkii teatr nachala XX veka* (Moscow: Nauka, 1972), p. 133.

44. In the Foreword to his *Lyrical Dramas*, one of which was *Balaganchik*, in Blok, *Sobranie sochinenii*, vol. 4, p. 434.

45. On prerevolutionary Russian cabarets, see Harold B. Segel, *Turn-of-the-*

Century Cabaret: Paris, Barcelona, Berlin, Munich, Vienna, Cracow, Moscow, St. Petersburg, Zurich (New York: Columbia University Press, 1987).

46. For readers of English there is an excellent monograph on Evreinov: Spencer Golub, *Evreinov: The Theatre of Paradox and Transformation* (Ann Arbor, Mich.: UMI Research Press, 1984).

47. Nikolai Nikolaevich Evreinov, *The Theatre in Life*, trans. Alexander I. Nazaroff (New York: Brentano's, 1927), p. 30.

48. Aleksandr Tairov, *Proklamatsiia khudozhnika* (Moscow: Shlugleit i Bronshtein, 1917), p. 4.

49. See my article on Nietzsche and the Soviet popular theater, "Nietzsche and the Debate on Mass Theater from the Civil War to NEP," in Bernice Glatzer Rosenthal, ed., *Nietzsche in Russia*, vol. 2 (forthcoming).

50. "K prazdniku revoliutsii," *VIMS*, 26 September 1918, p. 3.

51. V. E. Meyerhold, "Voina i teatr," *Birzhevye vedomosti* (evening edition), 11 September 1914, p. 4.

52. P. S. Kogan, "Teatr tribuna," *VT*, no. 2 (1919), see also P. S. Kogan, *V preddverii griadushchego teatra* (Moscow: Pervina, 1921), p. 14.

53. N. N. Evreinov, *V shkole ostroumiia* [unpublished memoirs]. TsGALI, f. 982, op. 1, d. 13, ll. 31–32.

54. The script is in *Liubov' k trem apel'sinam*, no. 6–7 (1914), pp. 19–55.

55. Vladimir Maiakovskii, *Misteriia-Buff, geroicheskoe i satiricheskoe izobrazhenie nashei epokhi, 1918 g*, in V. V. Maiakovskii, *Polnoe sobranie sochinenii* (Moscow: Khudozh. literatura, 1955–61).

56. V. Katanian, *Maiakovskii, literaturnaia khronika* (Leningrad: Sovetskii pisatel', 1948), pp. 90, 102, places it after February; Mayakovsky dates the idea to early fall: "Ia sam," *PSS*, vol. 1, p. 24. Most of the writing was done in 1918: A. Fevral'skii, *Pervaia sovetskaia p'esa* (Moscow: Sovetskii pisatel', 1971), pp. 18 ff.

57. N. Punin, "Kak moglo byt' inache?" *IK*, 12 January 1919, p. 1.

58. RoseLee Goldberg, *Performance: Live Art from 1909 to the Present* (New York: Harry N. Abrams, 1979), pp. 9–10.

59. M. Zagorskii, "Kak reagiruet zritel'," *Lef*, no. 2 (1924), pp. 141–51.

60. Vladimir Markov, *Russian Futurism: A History* (Berkeley: University of California Press, 1968), p. 107.

61. See John E. Bowlt, "The Union of Youth," in George Gibian and H. W. Tjalsma, eds., *Russian Modernism: Culture and the Avant-Garde, 1900–1930* (Ithaca, N.Y.: Cornell University Press, 1976), pp. 177–80, and Markov, *Russian Futurism*, pp. 142–47.

62. On the apocalyptic tendency in prerevolutionary culture, see B. G. Rosenthal, "Eschatology and the Appeal of the Revolution: Merezhkovsky, Bely, Blok," *California Slavic Studies*, no. 2 (1980).

63. As shown in Mayakovsky's sketches, included in the *PSS* text.

64. S. V. Vladimirov, "Maiakovskii," in *Ocherki istorii russkoi-sovetskoi dramaturgii, 1917–1934* (Leningrad: Iskusstvo, 1963), vol. 1, p. 102. For some interesting ideas on the influence of the folk theater on the Russian revolutionary theater, see N. S. Zelentsova, *Narodnyi revoliutsionnyi teatr v Rossii epokhi grazhdanskoi voiny i revoliutsii* (Moscow, 1971).

65. See Edward Braun, *The Theatre of Meyerhold. Revolution and the Modern Stage* (New York: Drama Book Specialists, 1979), p. 150.
66. The recollections of V. N. Soloviev, *Maiakovskomu* (Leningrad: Khudozh. literatura, 1940), p. 149.
67. The Kozlinsky drawings appeared originally in *Oktiabr' 1917–1918. Geroi i zhertvy Oktiabria* (Petrograd: IZO Narkomprosa, 1918); both the drawings and the street paintings are in Mikhail German, ed., *Serdtsem slushaia revoliutsiiu. Iskusstvo pervykh let oktiabria* (Leningrad: Aurora, 1980), plates 148, 94–99.
68. See Rudnitsky, *Meyerhold the Director*, p. 256. Contrary to what historians have claimed, a picture of Malevich's work has survived; see *Novyi zritel'*, 7 November 1927, p. 6.
69. German, ed., *Serdtsem*, plate 305.
70. According to Fevral'skii, *Pervaia sovetskaia p'esa*, p. 73.
71. Alekseev-Iakovlev, *Russkie narodnye gulianiia*, pp. 162–63.
72. For the presence of popular theater in the poem, see B. M. Gasparov and Iu. M. Lotman, "Igrovye motivy v poème *Dvenadtsat*," *Tezisy I Vsesoiuznoi konferentsii "Tvorchestvo A. A. Bloka i russkaia kul'tura XX veka"* (Tartu, 1975), and Iu. M. Lotman, "Blok i narodnaia kul'tura goroda," in *Blokovskii sbornik*, vol. 4 (Tartu: Gos. universitet, 1981).
73. Maiakovskii, *Misteriia-Buff*, p. 212. The passage suffers much in translation.

Chapter Three. The Politics of Meaning and Style

1. "Petrograd 1-e maia," *P*, 4 May 1918, p. 4.
2. *AMI* (1971), p. 13.
3. Gushchin, *Izo-iskusstvo v massovykh prazdnestvakh*, p. 12.
4. Ibid., pp. 12–13.
5. Oleg Nemiro, *V gorod prishel prazdnik* (Leningrad: Aurora, 1973), pp. 15–16.
6. *AMI* (1971), p. 138.
7. *AMI* (1971), pp. 19–20, plates 5–6; *AMI* (1984), plates 36–39; A. Strigalev, "M. V. Dobuzhinskii v revoliutsionnye gody," *Sovetskoe monumental'noe iskusstvo*, no. 75–77 (1979), pp. 244–56.
8. N. P[unin], "K itogam oktiabr' skikh torzhestv," *IK*, 7 December 1918.
9. See *Iz istorii*, pp. 121 ff., for the protocols of some of the planning sessions.
10. A. Chiniakov, *Brat'ia Vesniny* (Moscow: Stroiizdat, 1970), p. 50. See *AMI* (1971), plates 72–92.
11. *Blokovskii sbornik*, vol. 1, p. 332.
12. V. Kerzhentsev, "Peredelyvaite p'esy," *VT*, no. 36 (1919), pp. 6–8.

13. V. Kerzhenstev, "Mozhno li 'iskazhat'' p'esy postanovkoi," *VT*, no. 1 (1919), p. 2.

14. V. Smyshliaev, "Deiatel'nost' teatral'nogo otdela Moskovskogo Proletkul'ta," *VT*, no. 35 (1919), p. 5.

15. N. F., "Novye stsenarii dlia opery Glinki," *VT*, no. 89–90 (1921), pp. 12–13.

16. N. Malkov, "Za krasnyi Petrograd," *ZI*, 5 May 1925, p. 10.

17. For a collection of eyewitness reports, see *Spektakl', zvavshii v boi* (Kiev: Mistetstvo, 1970). For a contemporary view, see L. Nikulin, "Teatr na Ukraine. Pis'mo iz Kieva," *VT*, no. 33 (1919), p. 16.

18. Presumably the opera *Fidelio*, traditionally performed with the "Lenore" overture, which ends in the liberation of political prisoners and a freedom chorus.

19. "Opera S.R.D.," *TK*, 12–14 November 1918, pp. 2–3; "V teatrakh. Opera S.R.D." *IzvTsIK*, 9 November 1918, p. 5. See also Igor Il'inskii, *Sam o sebe* (Moscow: VTO, 1961), pp. 86–88.

20. *AMI* (1971), pp. 99–100. A black-and-white photo of the curtain can be found in René Fülöp-Miller and Joseph Gregor, *The Russian Theatre* (New York: Benjamin Blom, 1930), p. 257. A. Raikhenshtein—"1 maia i 7 noiabria 1918 g. v Moskve," in *AMI* (1971)—provides sufficient evidence for the planning of such a performance for November 1918, but it should be noted that Lentulov dated it to 1923 and claimed the director was Nemirovich-Danchenko: M. Lentulova, *Khudozhnik Aristarkh Lentulov* (Moscow: Sovetskii khudozhnik, 1969), pp. 95–96. Bolshoi Theater archives date the performance to November 1919: *Russkii-sovetskii teatr*, p. 92.

21. Pavel Markov, "Pervye gody," *Teatr*, no. 11 (1957), p. 67; see also "Teatr v oktiabr'skie torzhestva. Bol'shoi teatr," *TK*, 12–14 November 1918, pp. 2–3.

22. Paul Avrich, *Russian Rebels 1600–1800* (New York: Norton, 1976), pp. 265–67.

23. Quoted in Alexander Rabinowitch, *The Bolsheviks Come to Power* (New York: Norton, 1976), p. 277.

24. Lenin, *Collected Works*, vol. 29, p. 331. To add another twist to history, the monument dedicated by Lenin was first proposed by the interrevolutionary Cossack Committee: "Pamiatnik Razinu," *DN*, 30 April 1918, p. 3.

25. *AMI* (1971), pp. 85–86.

26. *AMI* (1984), plate 55.

27. Information on the presentation is sparse. I believe it was a staging of his poem of the same name, published in Moscow in 1918. In 1919 a dramatic text based on the poem was published: Vasilii Kamenskii, *Sten'ka Razin. Kollektivnoe predstavlenie v 9-i kartinakh* (Petrograd, 1919). On November 7, 1918, though, Kamensky did star in a reading of the poem, in a circus from atop a horse: "Grandioznoe zrelishche," *TK*, 29 October 1918, p. 2; Iurii Sobolev, "Sten'ka Razin," *TK*, 12–14 November 1918, p. 3.

28. Fragments of the poem were published as "Chugunnoe zhit'e" in the futurist anthology *Moloko kobylits: sbornik. Risunki, stikhi, proza* (Moscow: Gileia, 1914).

29. Vasilii Kamenskii, *Stikhotvoreniia i poemy* (Moscow: Sovetskii pisatel', 1966), p. 469.
30. See A. I. Klibanov, *Narodnaia sotsial'naia utopiia v Rossii: XIX vek* (Moscow: Nauka, 1978), or Stites, *Revolutionary Dreams*, pp. 14–19.
31. Lunacharskii, *Religiia i sotsializm*.
32. *AMI* (1971), p. 95; *Kuzma Petrov-Vodkin* (Leningrad: Aurora, 1980).
33. *Proletarskie poety pervykh let sovetskoi epokhi* (Leningrad: Sovetskii pisatel', 1959), p. 232; my translation.
34. Pavel Arskii, "Gimn," *Pl*, 12 May 1918, p. 7.
35. B. Shishlo, "Ulitsa revoliutsii," *Dekorativnoe iskusstvo SSSR*, no. 3 (1970), p. 6.
36. Nikolai Petrov, *50 i 500*, pp. 15–16.
37. Viktor Shklovskii, "Soglashateli," in *Khod konia* (Berlin: Helikon, 1923).
38. P. Kozlov, *Legenda o kommunare. P'esa-poema v 5 kartinakh* (Arkhangelsk: Volna, 1923), p. 5. The play actually has only three scenes. Summaries of the text and performance can be found in Mgebrov, *Zhizn' v teatre*, vol. 2, pp. 480–500, and L. Tamashin, *Sovetskaia dramaturgiia v gody grazhdanskoi voiny* (Moscow: Iskusstvo, 1961), pp. 90–94.
39. Kozlov, *Legenda*, pp. 2–3.
40. Ibid., p. 16.
41. Mgebrov, *Zhizn' v teatr*, vol. 2, p. 483.
42. M. Zagorskii, "Legenda o kommunare," *VT*, no. 56 (1920), p. 9.
43. Kozlov, *Legenda*, p. 22.
44. Hunt, *Politics, Culture, and Class in the French Revolution*; Agulhon, *Marianne into Battle*. For a study of the use of a similar approach by Russian revolutionary culture, see Victoria E. Bonnell, "The Representation of Politics and the Politics of Representation," *Russian Review* 47 (1988).
45. This idea was put forward by Maurice Agulhon, "Politics, Images and Symbols in Post-Revolutionary France," in Wilentz, *Rites of Power*, p. 185.
46. *IzvTsIK*, 14 April 1918, p. 3.
47. "Lenin o monumental'noi propagande," in *Literaturnaia gazeta*, no. 4–5 (1933). Reprinted in A. V. Lunacharskii, *Vospominaniia i vpechatleniia* (Moscow: Sovetskaia Rossiia, 1968), p. 199. Lunacharsky recorded his memoirs in 1933, when Lenin's views on art had acquired more sanctity than they had in 1918, and I suspect that his enthusiasm was magnified in the account. For an unexpurgated view of what Lenin thought of the statues (he hated them) and of art in general, see A. V. Lunacharskii, "Lenin i iskusstvo," *Khudozhnik i zritel'*, no. 2–3 (1924), pp. 5–10. Later reprints of this article have been heavily edited.
48. Sergei Eisenstein used footage of these "ceremonies" in *Ten Days That Shook the World*.
49. *Iz istorii*, pp. 38–44.
50. At the dedication of the monument to Blanqui, a brochure with the title *Blanqui: The First Communist Buried Alive* was distributed: "K otkrytiiu pamiatnika Blanki," *ZI*, 4 March 1919, p. 3.
51. See *IzvTsIK*, 2 August 1918. The list given here differs somewhat from that in *Iz istorii*.

52. For a full schedule of the openings, see "K prazdnovaniiu godovshchiny oktiabr'skoi revoliutsii," *P,* 6 November 1918, p. 4. Some of the speeches were amplified by a new invention commissioned by the Central Organizing Bureau: the loudspeaker. See "Liubopytnoe izobretenie," *ZI,* 29 October 1918, p. 7.

53. Robespierre's statue was vandalized on its first night outdoors. This desecration should not have been a surprise: in his opening speech, Lev Kamenev praised Robespierre for "crushing the French counterrevolution with an iron hand and creating a Red Army." "Iz Moskvy," *SK,* 5 November 1918, p. 3.

54. For photos see Hans-Jürgen Drengenberg, *Die sowjetische Politik auf dem Gebiet der bildenden Kunst von 1917 bis 1934* (Wiesbaden: Harrassowitz, 1972); also John E. Bowlt, "Russian Sculpture and Lenin's Plan of Monumental Propaganda," in Henry A. Millon and Linda Nochlin, eds., *Art and Architecture in the Service of Politics* (Cambridge: MIT Press, 1978), pp. 188–191. The Drengenberg book includes a collection of documents relevant to the subject.

55. St. Krivtsov, "Novye pamiatniki," *Iskusstvo,* no. 6 [10] (1918), pp. 7–9; Lunacharskii, *Vospominaniia,* pp. 199, 193; Arthur Ransome, *Six Weeks in Russia in 1919* (London: G. Allen & Unwin, 1919), p. 10; Lunacharskii, *Vospominaniia,* p. 192.

56. Ol'sen, "Otkliki," *Voronezhskii telegraf,* 17 May 1918, p. 3.

57. Quoted in Lunacharskii, *Vospominaniia,* p. 192.

58. Ibid., p. 198. The source is Tommaso Campanella, *The City of the Sun,* trans. Daniel I. Donno (Berkeley: University of California Press, 1981).

59. Thomas More, *Utopia,* trans. Paul Turner (London: Penguin, 1965), p. 106. The passage continues: "But anyone who deliberately tries to get himself elected to a public office is permanently disqualified from holding one."

60. David and neoclassicism were of course not the only French influence. P. Zhilin's poster for the November 7, 1918, festival, *Long Live the Great Anniversary of the Proletarian Revolution. Long Live the Commune,* bears a striking resemblance to Eugène Delacroix's romantic *Liberty Leading the People.* For Zhilin's poster, see Nadezhda Suliaeva, *Revoliutsionnyi prazdnichnyi plakat, 1917–1927* (Leningrad: Khudozhnik RSFSR, 1982).

61. Brudnyi, *Obriady vchera i segodnia,* p. 61.

62. Lunacharsky suggested dating the new era in Russia from the October Revolution rather than from the birth of Christ in an address to students in 1918: TsGA RSFSR, f. 2306, op. 2, d. 224, l. 5.

63. For a discussion of Soviet holidays, see Binns, "The Changing Face of Power," *Man,* no. 4 (1979), pp. 586 ff.

64. "Pereimenovanie ulits," *SK,* 13 November 1918, p. 5. For Moscow, see "Prigotovlenie k oktiabr'skim prazdnestvam," *IzvTsIK,* 23 October 1918.

65. "K godovshchine revoliutsii. *Otdel IZO Narkomprosa,*" *VIMS,* 20 October 1918.

66. Goriaeva, "Pervaia godovshchina," p. 126.

67. "Aviatsionnaia katastrofa," *NZh,* 3 May 1918, p. 3; "Katastrofa s aeroplanom," *DN,* 3 May 1918, p. 2. (These were both opposition newspapers.)

68. "Na otkrytii pamiatnikov," *IzvTsIK,* 5 November 1918, p. 5, and V. Rikhter, "Pervaia godovshchina," in *Vchera i segodnia* (Moscow: Khudozh. literatura, 1960), vol. 1, p. 26.

69. P. D. Mal'kov, *Zapiski komendanta Moskovskogo Kremlia* (Moscow: Molodaia gvardiia, 1961), pp. 134–35.
70. "Chudo na Krasnoi Ploshchadi," *IzvPS*, 3 May 1918, p. 4.
71. See Lane, *The Rites of Rulers*, or Mazaev, *Prazdnik*, for the application of the theory to the history of Soviet festivals. A vast Soviet literature on the subject sprang up in the 1960s and 1970s.
72. A. A. Bogdanov [Malinovskii], *Pervoe maia. Mezhdunarodnyi prazdnik truda* (Petrograd: G. V. Belopol'skii, 1917), p. 9.
73. "Pervoe maia 1918 goda," *Pl*, 12 May 1918; reprinted in Lunacharskii, *Vospominaniia*, p. 212.
74. D. Donskoi, "Khleba i zrelishch. K demonstratsii 1-go Maia, *DN*, 26 April 1918, p. 1; "Chrezvychainoe sobranie upolnomochennykh fabrik i zavodov Petrograda," *DN*, 30 April 1918, p. 4; Veniamin Spavskii, "Tserkov' i pervoe maia," *IzvPS*, 1 May 1918, p. 4; "Anarkhisty o prazdnovanii pervogo maia," *IzvPS*, 1 May 1918, p. 6.
75. "Petrograd," *IzvTsIK*, 1 May 1918.
76. Mazaev, *Prazdnik*, p. 248; I. Rostovtseva, "Uchastie khudozhnikov v organizatsii i provedenii prazdnovaniia 1 maia i 7 noiabria v Petrograde v 1918 g.," in *AMI* (1971), pp. 10–11; Nemiro, *V gorod prishel prazdnik*, p. 7.
77. *AMI* (1971), p. 39.
78. "Prigotovleniia k prazdnestvu pervogo maia," *DN*, 27 April 1918, p. 3.
79. "Rabochaia zhizn'," *DN*, 30 April 1918, p. 4, and 1 May 1918, p. 4; "Rabochie i manifestatsiia," *NZh*, 3 May 1918, p. 3.
80. For the fullest reports, see *DN*, 3 May 1918; *NZh*, 3 May 1918.
81. See "Obzor pechati. Posle pervogo maia," *NZh*, 4 May 1918, p. 1.
82. *Pl*, 12 May 1918.
83. "Velikaia godovshchina. Ob"iazatel'nye postanovleniia tsentral'nogo biuro po organizatsii prazdnestv godovshchiny oktiabr'skoi revoliutsii," *SK*, 1 November 1918, p. 4.
84. A. V. Lunacharskii, "Pervyi pervomaiskii prazdnik posle pobedy," *Krasnaia niva*, no. 18 (1926).
85. This battle has been well documented: see, for example, Bengt Jangfeldt, *Majakovskij and Futurism, 1917–1921* (Stockholm: Almqvist and Wiksell, 1977), pp. 95–98.
86. "K prazdnovaniiu godovshchiny oktiabr'skoi revoliutsii," *P*, 1 November 1918, p. 3.
87. A. Raikhenshtein, "1 maia i 7 noiabria 1918 g. v Moskve," p. 77.
88. From the protocols of a December 10, 1918, TEO meeting. *Russkii-sovetskii teatr*, p. 49.
89. LGAOR, f. 2551, op. 1, dd. 2250 and 2357.
90. Nemiro, *V gorod prishel prazdnik*, p. 7.
91. "Velikaia godovshchina. Ob"iazatel'nye postanovleniia," p. 4; "Podgotovitel'nye raboty," *SK*, 26 October 1918.
92. "Biusty i portrety vozhdei proletariata," *KG*, 30 October 1918.
93. The title is abbreviated here.
94. *P*, 2 November 1918.
95. *PP*, 25 September 1918. Reprinted in Mariia Fedorovna Andreeva,

Perepiska, vospominaniia. Stat'i, dokumenty, vospominaniia o M. F. Andreevoi (Moscow: Iskusstvo, 1961), p. 258.

    96. "Prikaz komiteta po ustroistvu oktiabr'skikh torzhestv," *IzvTsIK*, 5 November 1918, p. 4.

    97. Rikhter, "Pervaia godovshchina," vol. 1, p. 25. I did not believe such munificence possible, but it is confirmed in *P,* 1 November 1918. Extravagance in a time of great deprivation was to remain a feature of Civil War holidays. An extra ration had also been distributed for May Day; yet three days later, the daily ration for all citizens was cut drastically, to one-eighth of a pound: "Moskva bez khleba," *PP,* 4 May 1918, p. 5.

    98. *AMI* (1971), p. 140.

    99. Quoted in Nils Ake Nilsson, "Spring 1918. The Arts and the Commissars," in Nilsson, ed., *Art, Society, Revolution*, p. 45.

    100. *Istoriko-revoliutsionnye pamiatniki SSSR* (Moscow: Politizdat, 1972), pp. 5–6.

    101. Iurii Annenkov, *Dnevnik moikh vstrech* (New York: Inter-language Literary Associates, 1966), vol. 2, p. 265. The quotation should read, "War is the locomotive of history."

    102. *AMI* (1971) credits the work to Lentulov. S. M. Alianskii, "Vstrechi s Blokom," *Novyi mir,* no. 6 (1967), pp. 182–83, credits Annenkov. For a black-and-white photo, see *AMI* (1984), plate 133.

    103. *AMI* (1984), plates 139–40.

    104. Mark Shagal, "Pis'mo iz Vitebska," *IK,* 22 December 1918. Unfortunately, in his enthusiasm Chagall failed to mention what was painted. In his *My Life*, trans. Elisabeth Abbott (New York: Orion Press, 1960), p. 139, he mentions cows and horses; but I expect it was less the subject than the manner that raised the fuss.

    105. See, for instance, Evg. Kuznetsov, "Komissar teatrov," in Andreeva, *Perepiska, vospominaniia,* p. 416.

    106. Ia. Tugenkhol'd, *Iskusstvo oktiabr'skoi epokhi* (Leningrad: Academia, 1930), p. 17.

    107. See *AMI* (1984), plates 24–35. Altman's description of his intent is to be found on pp. 64–65.

    108. Semen Rodov, "Prazdnik Ery," *Gorn,* no. 2–3 (1919), p. 122. Rodov later gained notoriety as a critic with the "Na Postu" (On Guard) group.

    109. "Ukrashenie Petrograda," *ZI,* 9 November 1918, p. 2. Also "K oktiabr'skim torzhestvam," *ZI,* 6 November 1918, p. 3; "Prazdnik oktiabr'skoi revoliutsii,"*IzvTsIK,* 9 November 1918, p. 5; N. Barabanov, "Kartiny oktiabr'skikh prazdnestv," *Vestnik zhizni,* no. 3–4 (1919), pp. 116–20; "Na Krasnoi Ploshchadi," *Vestnik zhizni,* no. 3–4 (1919), p. 118; Leonid Dashkov, "Na prazdnestve revoliutsii," *RM,* 24 November 1918, pp. 30–33. Curiously, futurist work in Kazan also drew praise from local critics: "Proletarskii prazdnik," *Znamia revoliutsii* (Kazan), 10 November 1918.

    110. The negative article most frequently cited is: En. K. [M. F. Andreeva], "Neudachnyi debiut," *ZI,* 6 March 1919. Andreeva was editor of this newspaper. The article, somewhat distorted, is attributed to her in Andreeva, *Perepiska, vospominaniia,* pp. 416–17. Other negative articles are: A. Evgen'ev, "Futuris-

ticheskaia gekuba i proletariat," *Vestnik literatury,* no. 10 (1919); V. Kriazhin, "Futurizm i revoliutsiia," *Vestnik zhizni,* no. 6–7 (1919); Lev Pumpianskii, "Oktiabr'skie torzhestva i khudozhniki Petrograda," *Pl,* 5 January 1919; E. Khersonskaia, "Iz tovarishcheskikh besed o zhivopisi," *Gorn,* no. 2–3 (1919). However, the Pumpiansky article expresses unequivocal praise of the leftist artists. And in the Khersonskaia article no mention is made of the holiday, although the disapproval of decorated houses might be a hint. But Khersonskaia had written another article immediately following the celebration that demanded that easel painting be replaced by the decoration of buildings, which was a futurist slogan: E. Khersonskaia, "O novom tvorchestve. Iz dnevnika liubitelia iskusstv," *Iskusstvo,* No. 6 [10] (1918), pp. 12–13. In addition, the *Gorn* article was followed immediately in the same issue by the Rodov article quoted previously and by another article full of praise: N. Volkov, "Krasnaia Moskva," *Gorn,* no. 2–3 (1919), p. 123. The unfortunate impression one gets is that scholars have not bothered to read the articles they cite.

111. Tamara Karsavina, *Theatre Street* (New York: E. P. Dutton, 1931), p. 327.

112. Andreeva, *Perepiska, vospominaniia,* p. 416. I have seen no other report of anyone receiving such letters, nor have the letters themselves been seen.

113. *AMI* (1984), p. 86. The editors of the collection give the document a faulty date, following I. Matsa, *Sovetskoe iskusstvo za 15 let; Materialy i dokumentatsiia* (Moscow: Ogiz-Izogiz, 1933), p. 37. Matsa changed the date from February 9 to April 9, I assume to make Friche seem the aggressor and IZO the victim in the following events.

114. V. Friche, "Literaturnoe odichanie," *VIMS,* 15 February 1919, p. 1.

115. See, for example, "K godovshchine oktiabr'skoi revoliutsii," *IzvTsIK,* 6 October 1918.

116. O. D. Kameneva, "Pis'mo v redaktsiiu," *VIMS,* 1 March 1919, p. 3.

117. *AMI* (1984), p. 86.

118. "Vladimir Il'ich i ukrashenie krasnoi stolitsy," in V. D. Bonch-Bruevich, *Vospominaniia o Lenine* (Moscow: Nauka, 1965), pp. 380–81. How this statement squares with Krupskaia's recollection that November 7, 1918, was the happiest day of Lenin's life I do not know.

119. A. Talanov, *Bol'shaia sud'ba* (Moscow: Politicheskaia literatura, 1967), pp. 148–49.

120. En. K., "Neudachnyi debiut." Should there by any doubt that the campaign was a Moscow import, see an article with identical complaints and often identical wording: Mikh. Levidov, "Kto nasledniki?" *Ezhenedel'nik pravdy,* 2 March 1919, pp. 13–14.

121. See M. Dobuzhinskii, "Bomba ili khlopushka? Beseda dvukh khudozhnikov," *NZh,* 4 May 1918, p. 3; "Pervoe maia 1918 goda," *DN,* 3 May 1918, p. 2 (including "Den' futurizma i krasnoarmeistva").

122. Andreeva, *Perepiska, vospominaniia,* p. 87.

123. *AMI* (1971), p. 39. The decision to accept IZO's petition was reported in "V Otdele po delam iskusstva i khudozhestvennoi promyshlennosti," *IK,* 6 April 1919, p. 3.

124. Modernists, though, were not banned everywhere: they made impor-

tant contributions in Saratov and other cities, including Odessa, where the poet Max Voloshin and the artist Aleksandra Exter helped direct the festivities: A. Niurenberg, *Vospominaniia, vstrechi, mysli ob iskusstve* (Moscow: Sovetskii khudozhnik, 1969), pp. 7–8.

125. "Ukrashenie k pervomu maia," *IK*, 16 March 1919, p. 4, in *AMI* (1984).

126. "K pervomaiskim torzhestvam," *VT*, no. 22 (1919), pp. 3–4.

127. V. M. Friche, "Znachenie narodnykh prazdnestv," *VIMS*, 11 February 1919, p. 1.

128. Alexei Tolstoy, *Road to Calvary*, trans. Edith Bone (New York: Knopf, 1946), pp. 436–37.

Chapter Four. New Uses for Popular Culture

1. I. I. Vasil'ev-Viaz'min, *Iskusstvo liudnykh ploshchadei* (Moscow: Znanie, 1977), p. 8.

2. A. V. Lunacharskii, "Budem smeiat'sia," in Lunacharskii, *Stat'i o teatre i dramaturgii* (Moscow: Iskusstvo, 1938), pp. 164–65.

3. Fine descriptions of Russian carnival culture can be found in Nekrylova, *Russkie narodnye gorodskie prazdniki, uveseleniia i zrelishcha*, and Alekseev-Iakovlev, *Russkie narodnye gulianiia*. No one should miss the magical description in Alexandre Benois, *Memoirs* (London: Chatto & Windus, 1960), vol. 1, pp. 117–30.

4. Quoted in Dmitriev, *Russkii tsirk*, p. 32.

5. Adolphe L. de Custine, *Journey for Our Time* (Chicago: H. Regnery, 1951), p. 141. Custine noted that the equality was due to a mutual and absolute abasement before the tsar.

6. See Ivan Shcheglov, "Narodnye gulianiia v Moskve," in Shcheglov, *V zashchitu narodnogo teatra* (St. Petersburg: V. Kirshbaum, 1903).

7. "Khronika," *ZI*, 29 April 1919, p. 2.

8. Trotsky, incidentally, would eventually conceive the same notion: see "Vodka, the Church and the Cinema" (1923) in Leon Trotsky, *Problems of Everyday Life, and Other Writings on Culture & Science* (New York: Monad Press, 1973).

9. Aleksandr Benois, "Vykhod iskusstva na ulitsu," *NZh*, 4 June 1917, p. 3.

10. Protocols of the commission can be found in LGAOR, f. 2551, op. 1, dd. 2250, 2357.

11. "K sniatiiu pamiatnika Nikolaiu Nikolaevichu," *ZI*, 15 November 1918, p. 4.

12. See V. A. Nevskii, *Massovaia politiko-prosvetitel'naia rabota revoliutsionnykh let* (Moscow: Gudok, 1925), for a thorough overview of these methods, including their successes and failures.

13. *VT*, no. 22 (1919), p. 3, in *AMI* (1984), p. 93.

14. Mazaev, *Prazdnik*, p. 292.
15. See V. Golovasevich and V. Lashchilin, *Narodnyi teatr na Donu* (Rostov: Rostizdat, 1947), pp. 27–28, 55–58.
16. For descriptions, see "Sud nad Vrangelem," *VT,* no. 72–73 (1920), pp. 16–17; "Obzor agitatsionnogo materiala. Instsenirovka agitatsionnykh sudov," *Vestnik agitatsii i propagandy,* 25 November 1920, pp. 25–27; René Fülöp-Miller, *The Mind and Face of Bolshevism* (New York: Knopf, 1928), pp. 201–2 (with inaccuracies); Kerzhentsev, *Tvorcheskii teatr,* pp. 147–48; and Vsevolod Vishnevskii, "20-letie sovetskoi dramaturgii," *Sovetskie dramaturgi o svoem tvorchestve* (Moscow: Iskusstvo, 1967), pp. 149–50.
17. Kerzhentsev, *Tvorcheskii teatr,* p. 147.
18. Rolland, *Le théâtre du peuple,* pp. 121–24. For the views of Gorky and Lunacharsky, see G. V. Titova, "A. V. Lunacharskii o revoliutsionno-romanticheskom teatre," in *Teatr i dramaturgiia* (Leningrad, 1967), or V. K. Aizenshtadt, *Russkaia sovetskaia istoricheskaia dramaturgiia 1917–1929* (Kharkov: KhGIK, 1969), vol. 1, pp. 27–28.
19. A. V. Lunacharskii, "Kakaia nam nuzhna melodrama" (1919), in Lunacharskii, *Sobranie sochinenii* (Moscow: Khudozh. literatura, 1964), vol. 2, p. 213.
20. *Russkii-sovetskii teatr,* p. 359.
21. Iu. M. Lotman, "Khudozhestvennaia priroda russkikh narodnykh kartinok," in *Narodnaia graviura i fol'klor v Rossii XVII–XIX vv.* (Moscow: Sovetskii khudozhnik, 1976). See also Zelentsova, *Narodnyi revoliutsionnyi teatr,* p. 31.
22. "K oktiabr'skim torzhestvam," *ZI,* 5 November 1918, p. 4.
23. LGAOR, f. 2551, op. 1, d. 2246, l. 6.
24. *U istokov,* pp. 295–96.
25. See "M. Gorkii o kinematografe," *VT,* no. 30 (1919), p. 10, for the original idea.
26. Iu. A. Dmitriev, *Sovetskii tsirk* (Moscow: Iskusstvo, 1963), p. 24.
27. Shklovskii, "Iskusstvo tsirk," in Shklovskii, *Khod konia,* p. 138.
28. For Lunacharsky's views on the conversion of the circus to the new order, see "Zadachi obnovlennogo tsirka" (1919) in A. V. Lunacharskii, *O massovykh prazdnestvakh, estrade i tsirke* (Moscow: Iskusstvo, 1981).
29. Dmitriev, *Sovetskii tsirk,* p. 33.
30. Text translated in Frantishek Déak, "The Agit-Prop and Circus Plays of Vladimir Mayakovsky," *Drama Review* 17, no. 1 (March 1973). Something similar had already been done under different circumstances in the United States: see MacKaye, *The Civic Theatre,* p. 71.
31. For the best descriptions, see Annenkov, *Dnevnik moikh vstrech,* vol. 2, pp. 449–55; Shklovskii, "Dopolnennyi Tolstoi," in Shklovskii, *Khod konia;* and Zolotnitskii, *Zori teatral'nogo oktiabria,* pp. 234–39.
32. N. N[osko]v, "Pervyi vinokur," *ZI,* 24 September 1919, p. 1.
33. Shklovskii, "Dopolnennyi Tolstoi," p. 127.
34. Iu. Annenkov, "Krizis èstrady," *ZI,* 3–4 July 1920, in Zolotnitskii, *Zori teatral'nogo oktiabria,* p. 236. The influence on Eisenstein and his "montage of attractions" would be apparent in a few years.
35. "Vozrozhdenie tsirka," *VT,* no. 9 (1919), pp. 4–5.

36. "Tsirk," *VT*, no. 39 (1919), p. 13.
37. Dmitriev, *Russkii tsirk*, p. 194.
38. TsGALI, f. 2087, op. 1, d. 80, l. 98.
39. E. M. Kuznetsov, *Arena i liudi sovetskogo tsirka* (Leningrad: Iskusstvo, 1947), p. 32.
40. "Vtoroi gos. tsirk," *VT*, no. 44 (1919), p. 7.
41. "Konenkov dlia tsirka," *VT*, no. 44 (1919), pp. 6–7.
42. The figure had been used effectively in posters of the 1905 and 1917 revolutions: Lapshin, *Khudozhestvennaia zhizn'*, pp. 89, 105. And in 1930 Mayakovsky would write a scenario for another circus performance, *Moscow Afire*, using the same formation.
43. "Pervyi gos. tsirk," *VT*, no. 42 (1919), p. 10.
44. D. Samarskii, *Na strazhe mirovoi kommuny* (Rostov: Gosizdat, 1920), p. 5.
45. A tiny theater whose repertory ran to pre-nineteenth-century farces and commedia dell'arte interludes: Cervantes's *The Rival Ladies*, Franz Pocci's *Crocodile and Persia*, Machiavelli's *Mandragola*. See "Moskovskii Balagan," *VT*, no. 8 (1919), p. 6.
46. "K pervomaiskim torzhestvam," *VT*, no. 22 (1919), pp. 3–4, in *AMI* (1984).
47. Vadim Shershenevich, "Tsirk," *Zrelishcha*, no. 2 (1922), p. 15. See also Boris Erdman, "Nepovtorimoe vremia," *Tsirk i estrada*, no. 3–4 (1928), pp. 6–8, or A. V. Lunacharskii, "O tsirkakh," in Lunacharskii, *Stat'i*, pp. 170–72.
48. Historians have ignored Gaideburov's contributions. Unfortunately, the main source for all work on early Soviet festivals has been Piotrovsky, scholar at GIII through the 1920s and 1930s, director of various theaters, and administrator of the Politprosvet theater network. Piotrovsky, who was a brilliant and productive critic, carried something of a vendetta against Gaideburov, partly for ideological reasons, partly for personal reasons. On top of his historiographical elisions, Piotrovsky never hesitated to slander Gaideburov directly: see *Istoriia sovetskogo teatra*, pp. 159–68; A. P[iotrovskii], "Akademicheskii teatr intelligentsii," *ZI*, 20 December 1921, p. 4; "Dovol'no Peredvizhnogo," *ZI*, no. 23 (1923). From his administrative position, Piotrovsky twice succeeded in appropriating the Mobile-Popular Theater's building, the final time when he handed it over to TRAM (Theater of Worker Youth), of which he was administrative patron.
49. This approach was most closely associated with Ivan Shcheglov—for example, "O repertuare narodnogo teatra," in Shcheglov, *V zashchitu narodnogo teatra*.
50. P. P. Gaideburov, "Novye zadachi teatral'nogo instruktorstva," *VO*, no. 2–3 (1919), p. 20.
51. Repertory listings can be found in the appendices of an excellent study: Gaideburov, *Literaturnoe nasledie*.
52. G. A. Khaichenko, *Russkii narodnyi teatr kontsa XIX–nachala XX veka* (Moscow: Nauka, 1975), p. 165.
53. P. P. Gaideburov, "Vsenarodnyi teatr," in Konst. Erberg, ed., *Iskusstvo i narod* (Petrograd: Kolos, 1922).

54. "Nashim budushchim zriteliam" (1918), in Gaideburov, *Literaturnoe nasledie*, p. 224.
55. P. P. Gaideburov, "Novye metody teatral'nogo instruktorstva," *VO*, no. 4–5 (1919), p. 6.
56. P. P. Gaideburov, "Pis'mo k zriteliu. Bez zaglaviia," *ZPOT*, no. 17 (1919), p. 6. Note the reliance on Ivanov's terminology.
57. Osip Mandelstam provides an ironic description in *The Noise of Time*, in *The Prose of Osip Mandelstam*, trans. Clarence Brown (Princeton, N.J.: Princeton University Press, 1965), pp. 98–99.
58. The line is originally from Plutarch and was probably passed on to the Russians by Nietzsche. My description is based mostly on Gaideburov's account in *Literaturnoe nasledie*, pp. 238–39.
59. *Istoriia sovetskogo teatra*, p. 166.
60. Gaideburov, "Novye zadachi," pp. 20–23.
61. "Poezdka v Vitebsk," *ZPOT*, no. 20 (1919), p. 9.
62. Gaideburov, "Novye zadachi."
63. P. P. Gaideburov, "Tvorcheskaia igra. Improvizatsionnyi metod N. F. Skarskoi," *VO*, no. 6–8 (1919), pp. 36–40.
64. A complete course list can be found in "V Institute vneshkol'nogo obrazovaniia," *ZPOT*, no. 24–25 (1919), p. 18.
65. Again, if history has been recorded differently, Piotrovsky and his assistant Avlov (a former lawyer) are at fault. In many publications they propagated the idea that Gaideburov was responsible for the *kulturträger*, or anti-amateur, method of instruction: for example, G. Avlov, *Klubnyi samodeiatel'nyi teatr: Evoliutsia metodov i form*, introduction by A. V. Piotrovskii (Leningrad: Teakinopechat', 1930).
66. A. Mashirov-Samobytnik, "Istoriia Proletkul'ta (1905–1917)," *Voprosy literatury*, no. 1 (1958), pp. 172–76.
67. See S. V. Panina, "Na Peterburgskoi okraine," *Novyi zhurnal*, no. 48–49 (1957).
68. Gaideburov, "Pis'mo k zriteliu," pp. 3–6.
69. See Vinogradov-Mamont, *Krasnoarmeiskoe chudo*, p. 5.
70. Ibid., pp. 13–14.
71. Gaideburov, "Novye zadachi," pp. 22–23.
72. Histories of the group can be found in Vinogradov-Mamont, *Krasnoarmeiskoe chudo*, and in *Istoriia sovetskogo teatra*, pp. 244–50.
73. Fedor Dostoevskii, *Zapiski iz mertvogo doma*, in *Polnoe sobranie sochinenii* (Leningrad: Nauka, 1972), vol. 4, pp. 118–19.
74. English readers can find a good description in Elizabeth Warner, *The Russian Folk Theatre* (The Hague: Mouton, 1977), pp. 127–40.
75. See V. Krupianskaia, "Narodnaia drama (genezis i literaturnaia istoriia)," in *Slavianskii fol'klor* (Moscow: Nauka, 1972).
76. Original accounts can be found in *Istoriia sovetskogo teatra*, pp. 244–46; *Massovye prazdnestva*, pp. 57–60; Vinogradov-Mamont, *Krasnoarmeiskoe chudo*, pp. 26–30; "Pervyi spektakl' dramaticheskoi masterskoi Krasnoi Armii," *IK*, 30 March 1919, p. 4; and "Peterburgskie pis'ma," *VT*, no. 43 (1919), p. 13.

77. The French scholar Nina Gourfinkel called it a *jeu:* see Nina Gourfinkel, *Théâtre russe contemporain* (Paris: La Renaissance du Livre, 1931), p. 129.

78. *Istoriia sovetskogo teatra*, p. 246. The reader may feel free to doubt this figure, which is given by many sources but seems unlikely.

79. Vinogradov-Mamont, *Krasnoarmeiskoe chudo*, p. 22.

80. I have yet to fathom how the seats were arranged. Descriptions suggest that seats faced one of the stages; but that would have forced spectators to constantly swivel back and forth.

81. Vinogradov-Mamont, *Krasnoarmeiskoe chudo*, p. 68.

82. *Massovye prazdnestva*, p. 59.

83. Original accounts can be found in Vinogradov-Mamont, *Krasnoarmeiskoe chudo*, pp. 104–12; "Tret'ii internatsional," *ZI*, 9 May 1919, p. 2; and B. N[ikono]v, "Pod otkrytym nebom," *ZI*, 14 May 1919, p. 1.

84. The obvious precedent was Ivanov's tragedy *Prometheus*, written in 1916 but published only in 1919. Although *The Russian Prometheus* (*Rossiiskii Prometei*) was given wide manuscript circulation, the only text I know of is in TsGALI, f. 2640, op. 1, d. 147. For Vinogradov's vision of "the theater of the future," as declared to Chaliapin, Iurev, Radlov, Petrov-Vodkin, and Aleksei Remizov, see "Khronika," *VT*, no. 43 (1919), p. 14. This vision also reflected Ivanov's influence.

85. Vinogradov-Mamont, *Rossiiskii Prometei*, p. 7.

86. It was scheduled for performance on the November 1919 anniversary: "K oktiabr'skim torzhestvam," *VT*, no. 36 (1919), p. 13.

87. Aleksei Remizov, "Repertuar. III," *ZI*, 5 February 1920, p. 1; *Blokovskii sbornik*, vol. 1, p. 336.

88. V. I. Lenin and A. V. Lunacharskii, *Perepiska, doklady, dokumenty, literaturnoe nasledstvo*, no. 80 (Moscow: Nauka, 1971), pp. 383–85.

89. "Khronika," *ZI*, 17 August 1920, p. 1.

90. "Sverzhenie samoderzhaviia," *Izvestiia arkhangel'skogo gubernskogo revkoma*, 4 May 1920, p. 3.

91. A. Panfilov, *Teatral'noe iskusstvo Urala 1917–1967* (Sverdlovsk: Sredneural'skoe knizhnoe izd., 1967), pp. 34–36.

92. *Istoriia sovetskogo teatra*, p. 250.

93. See *U istokov*, pp. 41–46. To my knowledge, this is one of the few examples of direct political interference in Civil War mass spectacles; and it might have been added to Shcheglov's recollections to meet the political demands of later times.

94. Ibid., pp. 43–45.

95. Vinogradov implies that Piotrovsky removed him from the post by false denunciation: Vinogradov-Mamont, *Krasnoarmeiskoe chudo*, pp. 126–28. Shcheglov just about confirms it: *U istokov*, p. 53. In *ZI*, no. 199–200 (1919), Piotrovsky wrote a strong article against Vinogradov's production of *Overthrow* (*Istoriia sovetskogo teatra*, p. 250). Although these actions would be in line with Piotrovsky's later behavior, it should be noted that weeks after Vinogradov had departed newspapers reported that Piotrovsky was still not part of the studio: "Khronika," *ZI*, 21 November 1919, p. 2.

96. Accounts in Kerzhentsev, *Tvorcheskii teatr*, pp. 124–25; *U istokov*, pp.

66–68; "V Proletkul'te," *ZI*, 28 November 1919, p. 1; "Khronika," *ZI*, 18 December 1919, p. 3; "V Peterburgskom Proletkul'te," *VT*, no. 56 (1920), p. 15. The final episode, *The December Days in Moscow*, was also performed separately: "Instsenirovka dekabr'skogo vosstaniia," *PP*, 18 January 1920, p. 3.

97. For his teaching methods, see D. Shcheglov, "Praktika teatral'nogo dela," *VO*, no. 6–8 (1919), pp. 43–45.

98. The text is in D. Shcheglov, *Spektakl' v klube* (Leningrad: Nachatki znanii, 1925), pp. 81–101. The fact that Shcheglov claims authorship suggests the performance was not as "collective" as claimed.

99. Firsthand accounts can be found in *Istoriia sovetskogo teatra*, pp. 247–48; *Massovye prazdnestva*, pp. 60–61; "Tsirk Chinizelli," *IzvPS*, 24 February 1920, p. 1; "Khronika," *ZI*, 26 February 1920, p. 3; E. Kuznetsov, "Peterburgskie pis'ma," *VT*, no. 56 (1920), p. 15.

100. Tamashin, *Sovetskaia dramaturgiia*, p. 45.

Chapter Five. Transformation by Festival

1. *PP*, 1 January 1920, pp. 3–4.

2. Quoted in M. Z[agorskii], "V sporakh o sovremennom i griadushchem teatre. Na mitinge iskusstv v tsirke," *VT*, no. 48 (1920), pp. 9–10. For a deeper criticism of the *deistvo* theory, see Aleksandr Tairov, *Notes of a Director*, trans. William Kuhlke (Coral Gables, Fla.: University of Miami Press, 1969), pp. 132–42.

3. A. V. Lunacharskii, "O narodnykh prazdnestvakh," *VT*, no. 62 (1920), p. 4.

4. A good summary of the congress can be found in Joachim Paech, *Das Theater der Russischen Revolution* (Kronberg Ts.: Scriptor Verlag, 1974), pp. 95 ff.

5. V. B[ebutov], "O neoutopizme," *VT*, no. 43 (1919), p. 7.

6. Viacheslav Ivanov, "Organizatsiia tvorcheskikh sil narodnogo kollektiva v oblasti khudozhestvennogo deistva," *VT*, no. 44 (1919), p. 3. The resolutions passed by the congress after his address can be found in TsGA RSFSR, f. 628, op. 1, ed. khr. 4, l. 112. For the original speech, see Viacheslav Ivanov, "K voprosu ob organizatsii tvorcheskikh sil narodnogo kollektiva v oblasti khudozhestvennogo deistva," *VT*, no. 26 (1919), p. 4.

7. M. Ch., "Gorodskoe soveshchanie po voprosu o raboche-krest'ianskom teatre," *ZI*, 3 April 1919, p. 1. The quote is from an earlier version of the speech.

8. V. Tikhonovich, "Teatr i estetizatsiia zhizni. II," *VT*, no. 47 (1919), pp. 4–5.

9. TsGA RSFSR, f. 628, op. 1, ed. khr. 4.

10. See TsGA RSFSR, f. 628, op. 1, ed. khr. 4; "Ot slov k delu," *VT*, no. 37 (1919), p. 5. A member of the section claimed that practical work was undertaken for the November 1919 holiday; but a lack of supporting evidence makes

this claim seem doubtful: see Nik. Lvov, "Istoriia pervogo sotsialisticheskogo stsenariia," *VT*, no. 62 (1920), p. 6.

11. "Sektsiia massovykh predstavlenii i zrelishch," *VT*, No. 47 (1919), p. 6. Lvov is something of an enigma; in 1919 he was writing articles as an experienced folk-theater scholar of the Veselovsky school: see Nikolai Lvov, "Narodnye igrishcha v Viatskoi gubernii," *VT*, no. 38 (1919); yet in the 1920s, he was a young enthusiast of mass festivals associated with Communist youth and leftist artistic circles.

12. Doklad fraktsionnyi," in TsGA RSFSR, f. 628, op. 1, ed. khr. 4, ll. 94–95.

13. "Vozzvanie sektsii massovykh predstavlenii zrelishch . . . o sozdanii massovykh narodnykh teatrov," reprinted in *Russkii-sovetskii teatr*, pp. 64–65, from *VT*, no. 50 (1920).

14. An anthology of articles that resulted from these meetings can be found in *Organizatsiia massovykh narodnykh prazdnestv* (Moscow: Gosizdat, 1921). The articles also appeared in various issues of *Vestnik teatra*.

15. "Plan pervogo narodnogo deistva-prazdnestva," *VT*, no. 46 (1919), p. 5.

16. See Victor Turner, *The Anthropology of Performance* (New York: DAJ Publications, 1986), *Dramas, Fields and Metaphors* (Ithaca, N.Y.: Cornell University Press, 1974), and *The Ritual Process* (Chicago: Aldine, 1969); Terry Castle, *Masquerade and Civilization: The Carnivalesque in Eighteenth-Century English Culture and Fiction* (Stanford, Calif.: Stanford University Press, 1986); Victor Turner, ed., *Celebration: Studies in Festivity and Ritual* (Washington, D.C.: Smithsonian Institute Press, 1982); Clifford Geertz, *Negara: The Theatre State in Nineteenth-Century Bali* (Princeton, N.J.: Princeton University Press, 1980); Michel Benamou and Charles Carmello, eds., *Performance in Postmodern Society* (Milwaukee: Center for Twentieth-Century Studies, 1977); John J. MacAloon, ed., *Rite, Drama, Festival, Spectacle* (Philadelphia: ISHI, 1984); and Richard Schechner, *Between Theater and Anthropology* (Philadelphia: University of Pennsylvania Press, 1985).

17. See in particular Hobsbawm and Ranger, eds., *The Invention of Tradition*; Ben-David and Clark, eds., *Culture and Its Creators*, and Wilentz, ed., *Rites of Power*.

18. See Geertz's critique in "Blurred Genres: The Refiguration of Social Thought," in Clifford Geertz, *Local Knowledge* (New York: Basic Books, 1983).

19. A secondhand account from Kerzhentsev, *Tvorcheskii teatr*, pp. 148–49. Firsthand accounts of the ceremonies can be found in Dm. Tolbuzin [its director], "Apofeoz truda. Opyt massovogo deistva," *VT*, no. 66 (1920), p. 16; and Svetlov, "U ploshchadki. Apofeoz truda," *Kommuna* (Samara), 5 May 1920, p. 2.

20. Arthur Holitscher, *Das Theater im revolutionären Russland* (Berlin: Volksbühnen Verlags, 1924), p. 23.

21. See, for example, *Teatr*; Ivanov, *Po zvezdam*; Adrian Piotrovskii, "Prazdnestva kommuny," *PP*, 17 February 1920, p. 1; Vsevolod Vsevolodskii-Gerngross, "Deistvennoe iskusstvo," *ZI*, 11 March 1920, p. 2.

22. Kerzhentsev, *Revoliutsiia i teatr*, pp. 43–44.

23. I. I. Schneider, *Isadora Duncan, the Russian Years* (New York: Harcourt, Brace & World, 1968), pp. 11–13.

24. As recorded in Kerzhentsev, *Tvorcheskii teatr*, pp. 151–52. Another version of the plan is to be found in "Plan pervogo narodnogo deistva-prazdnestva."

25. The point has been made most forcefully about the Bolsheviks by Kenez, *The Birth of the Propaganda State*, pp. 1–3.

26. Lvov, "Istoriia pervogo sotsialisticheskogo stsenariia," p. 7.

27. Years later, Shklovsky was still chuckling over this episode: see Viktor Shklovsky, *Mayakovsky and His Circle*, trans. Lily Feiler (New York: Dodd, Mead, 1972), pp. 169–70.

28. Lvov, "Istoriia pervogo sotsialisticheskogo stsenariia," p. 7. Meyerhold would try this in some of his later productions, in Verhaeren's *Les aubes* and a 1921 production of *Mystery-Bouffe*. The practice, incidentally, was common in nineteenth-century European commercial theater and was standard in Russian *balagans*.

29. This schema is taken from Roger Caillois, *Man, Play and Games*, trans. Meyer Barash (New York: Free Press, 1961). The role of play in culture, first recognized by Schiller, is not a matter of common agreement. Useful approaches come from many sources: Johann Huizinga, *Homo Ludens: A Study of the Play-Element in Culture*, trans. R.F.C. Hull (Boston: Beacon Press, 1949), demonstrated that play was a creator of culture; game playing has been placed in the context of cultural performance by John J. MacAloon, "Olympic Games and the Theory of Spectacle in Modern Societies," in MacAloon, ed., *Rite, Drama, Festival, Spectacle*, and "Sociation and Sociability in Political Celebrations," in Turner, ed., *Celebration*. Perhaps the most important contribution has been by Erving Goffmann, *Frame Analysis: An Essay on the Organization of Experience* (Cambridge: Harvard University Press, 1974), who describes social interaction by an analogy to games and theater.

30. See Evreinov, *The Theatre in Life*.

31. Sometimes translated as *The Chief Thing*. In *Life as Theater: Five Modern Plays* (Ann Arbor, Mich.: Ardis, 1973).

32. Firsthand accounts are in *Istoriia sovetskogo teatra*, p. 278; A. I. Piotrovskii, *Za sovetskii teatr* (Leningrad: Academia, 1925), p. 14; *U istokov*, pp. 87–89; and Ia. Pushchin, "Opyt teatralizatsii voennogo manevra," *ZI*, 26 August 1920, in *Russkii-sovetskii teatr*, pp. 271–72. A complete scenario is in A. I. Piotrovskii, ed., *Krasnoarmeiskii teatr* (Petrograd: Izd. Uprav. Petro. Voen. Okr., 1921), pp. 25–26. I have a suspicion that the Pushchin article was written by Piotrovsky. Dmitry Shcheglov in his memoirs (*U istokov*, pp. 87–89) claims that he was the director; because both he and Piotrovsky never hesitate to slander an old colleague, I cannot be sure which claim is correct. The production itself bears all the marks of Piotrovsky's thinking however.

33. *Russkii-sovetskii teatr*, p. 271.

34. Aleksei Gan, "Bor'ba za massovoe deistvo," *O teatre* (Tver: Tverskoe izd., 1922), p. 74.

35. Aleksei Gan, "Nasha bor'ba," *VT*, no. 67 (1920), pp. 1–2.

36. Aleksei Gan, *Konstruktivizm* (Tver: Tverskoe izd., 1922), p. 1.

37. For a superb history of the movement, see Christina Lodder, *Russian*

Constructivism (New Haven, Conn.: Yale University Press, 1983). Lodder dates the genesis of constructivism to mid-1921.

38. There are many sources for Gan's plan: Kerzhentsev, *Tvorcheskii teatr*, pp. 152–53; Lvov, "Istoriia pervogo sotsialisticheskogo stsenariia"; "Plan prazdnestva pervogo maia," *VT*, no. 51 (1920), also in *AMI* (1984), pp. 101–2; "Pervoe maia. K otchetu sektsii," *VT*, no. 67 (1920), pp. 13–15; and "Plan prazdnovaniia pervogo maia," *ZI*, 24 February 1920, p. 3.

39. *AMI* (1984), pp. 101–2. This "revolutionary" plan sounds suspiciously similar to one used in Voronezh for the November 7, 1918, celebration: see "V provintsii," *IzvTsIK*, 26 October 1918.

40. William Morris, *News from Nowhere* (New York: Monthly Review Press, 1966); Gastev cited in Stites, *Revolutionary Dreams*, p. 150; Lunacharskii, "O narodnykh prazdnestvakh." The idea rests on Bogdanov's aesthetics; and its influence can be seen in some of Trotsky's writings.

41. Ia. Shapirshtein (Lers), "Nashi prazdnestva," *VT*, No. 72–73 (1920), p. 2.

42. See P. Kogan, "Kak organizovat' sorevnovanie mezhdu rabotaiushchimi. Udarnye gruppy truda. Ispol'zovanie sistemy Teilora," *PP*, 7 April 1920, p. 3.

43. See Lev Sosnovskii, "Master Kliuev. K voprosu o proizvodstvennoi propagande," *P*, 24 October 1920, p. 1, and "Ob odnom iz sposobov agitatsii," *P*, 25 November 1920, p. 1.

44. Relevant documents have been collected in *U istokov kommunisticheskogo truda* (Moscow: Izd. sotsial'no-èkonomicheskoi literatury, 1959) and *Krasnyi arkhiv*, no. 82 (1937), pp. 18–40.

45. N. Lenin, "Velikii pochin. O geroizme rabochikh v tylu. Po povodu 'kommunisticheskikh subbotnikov,' " *P*, 28 June 1919.

46. See, for example, R. Arskii, "Nedel'nyi subbotnik," *IzvTsIK*, 21 January 1920, p. 4.

47. "Kommunisticheskie subbotniki," *IzvTsIK*, 11 September 1920, p. 2. In the Soviet and Western literature on *subbotniki*, the notion that most participants were Communists has shown great longevity. This misplaced faith in party workers can be based on only a few sources, most outstandingly V. M. Molotov, ed., *Pervomaiskii sbornik* (Nizhny Novgorod: Nizhegorodskii gub. komitet organizatsii truda, 1920). The claim is discredited by the statistics published in *Pravda* and *Izvestiia* throughout 1920.

48. "O subbotnikakh v derevne," *P*, 4 January 1920, p. 1.

49. G. Prozorov, "Detskie kommunisticheskie subbotniki," *P*, 28 February 1920, p. 2.

50. At least; I stopped counting in June. See *Izvestiia Odesskogo soveta* for that period.

51. Attested to by foreigners both for and against the Soviet regime. See Arthur Holitscher, *Drei Monate in Sowyet Russland* (Berlin: S. Fischer, 1921), pp. 48–59; or Alexander Berkman, *The Bolshevik Myth* (New York: Boni and Liveright, 1925), p. 130. Emma Goldman, however, saw no joy at the same *subbotnik* attended by Berkman: Emma Goldman, *My Disillusionment in Russia*

(New York: Doubleday, Page, 1923), p. 75. Furthermore, the Petrograd press reported that underground literature against *subbotniki* was published by Moscow workers: "Obshchaia kartina pervomaiskikh torzhestv v Moskve," *IzvPS*, 3 May 1920, p. 1. The Moscow papers made no such report.

52. See Ozouf, *Festivals and the French Revolution*, p. 45.

53. Directed by N. N. Arvatov, director of *Tsar Iudeiskii*. Descriptions of the entertainments can be found in *Massovye prazdnestva*, pp. 70–71; "Zrelishcha pervogo maia," *ZI*, 20 April 1920, p. 1; also, *ZI*, 1–3 May 1920, p. 1.

54. For the Mensheviks, see "Novoe pervoe maia"; for the Bolsheviks, L. Trotskii, "Trud i voina," and N. Bukharin, "Prazdnik ili budni"—all on the front page of *P*, 1 May 1920.

55. To those who resented the work, it was useless. There was a funny story going around about a group of Communists who spent an entire *subbotnik* transferring manure from one pile to another. K. Dagel', "Sizifov trud. K vcherashnemu subbotniku," *PP*, 4 April 1920, p. 3.

56. K. Shelavin, *Pervoe maia v Rossii* (Leningrad: Priboi, 1926), pp. 65–67, mentions 165,000 in Petrograd, 350,000 in Moscow, which were huge figures in those days.

57. This became one of the canonical moments of the Lenin cult. It was first reported by L. Sosnovskii, "V Kremle," *P*, 4 May 1920, p. 2. The officially preferred version was Bonch-Bruevich, *Vospominaniia o Lenine*, pp. 249–50. This, the first labor of Lenin, became a popular subject of Soviet painters—for example, M. G. Sokolov's *V. I. Lenin at the Subbotnik* and P. Vasiliev's work of the same title. Authorities also made sure that the "spontaneous event" was recorded on film: see A. Levitskii, *Rasskazy o kinematografe* (Moscow: Iskusstvo, 1964), pp. 194–95. That the incident penetrated the popular consciousness is shown by the large number of jokes about it—most of them involving an inflatable log.

58. A. Kollantai, "Novye zadachi pervogo maia," *P*, 1 May 1920, p. 2.

59. Aksenov, *Organizatsiia*, p. 62; I. A. Aksenov, "Teatr v doroge," in *O teatre*, p. 85.

60. M. Gor'kii, "Put' k shchastiiu," *P*, 1 May 1920, p. 1.

61. Velimir Khlebnikov, *Sobranie proizvedenii* (Leningrad: Izd. pisatelei, 1928), vol. 3, p. 53.

62. N. K., "K prazdnovaniiu pervogo maia," *PP*, 25 April 1920, p. 1.

63. *Massovye prazdnestva*, p. 74.

64. Strigalev, "M. V. Dobuzhinskii v revoliutsionnye gody," p. 252.

65. Gan, "Bor'ba za massovoe deistvo," p. 79.

66. Aksenov, *Organizatsiia*, p. 63.

67. Adrian Piotrovskii, "Imeniny truda," *ZI*, 1–3 May 1920, p. 1.

68. Gourfinkel, *Théâtre russe contemporain*, p. 139.

69. *Pervoe maia* (Leningrad: Izd. Redizdata Puokra, 1924), p. 24.

70. Unfortunately Tiomkin decided to erase the Soviet period from his autobiography, *Please Don't Hate Me*. As organizer of some of the most magnificent festivals, he surely would have been a fine source of information and had much to be proud of.

71. "Khronika," *ZI*, 21 April 1920, p. 1.

72. The following description is drawn from these firsthand accounts: *Istoriia sovetskogo teatra*, pp. 269–71; Piotrovskii, *Za sovetskii teatr*, pp. 10–12; *Russkii-sovetskii teatr*, p. 265; Berkman, *The Bolshevik Myth*, pp. 131–32; E. A. Znosko-Borovskii, *Russkii teatr nachala XX veka* (Prague: Plamia, 1925), pp. 427–30; V. Kerzhentsev, "Massovyi teatr," *VT*, no. 65 (1920), pp. 3–4 (reprinted with confused title in *AMI* (1984), pp. 109–10); Aleksandr Belenson, "Birzhevye vpechatleniia," *ZI*, 4 May 1920, p. 1; Viktor Shklovskii, "O gromkom golose," *ZI*, 8–9 May 1920, p. 2, in Shklovskii, *Khod konia*.

73. Kerzhentsev, *Tvorcheskii teatr*, pp. 136–37. Other scenarios (all with some variations) can be found in Fülöp-Miller, *The Mind and Face of Bolshevism*, pp. 205–8; *Russkii-sovetskii teatr*, pp. 263–64; and "Gimn osvobozhdeniia truda," *IzvPS*, 30 April 1920, p. 1.

74. Richard Stites has noted that festivals were prominent in Russian socialist utopian fiction (they were an embodiment of the ideal city); Stites, *Revolutionary Dreams*, pp. 183–84.

75. Obviously, the Khodynka tragedy of 1896 was still very much in mind. "K ustroistvu spektaklia-pantomimy," *IzvPS*, 24 April 1920, p. 1.

76. Kerzhentsev, "Massovyi teatr."

77. "Pervomaiskaia misteriia—Gimn osvobozhdeniia truda," *IzvPS*, 3 May 1920, p. 2.

78. The scenarios are in *Russkii-sovetskii teatr*, and Kerzhentsev, *Tvorcheskii teatr*, respectively.

79. A. Kugel, "Massovki," *Iskusstvo trudiashchimsia*, no. 1 (1924), pp. 13–15.

80. A favorable opinion was expressed by G[rigory] Zinoviev, "Novoe v nashem pervomaiskom prazdnestve," *P*, 5 May 1920, p. 1; the winter plans were announced in "Khronika," *ZI*, 12 May 1920, p. 1.

81. *Istoriia sovetskogo teatra*, p. 271.

82. P., "Sueslovie," *ZI*, 18 May 1920, p. 4.

83. Shklovskii, "O gromkom golose."

84. From a letter quoted by Evgenii Kuznetsov, "Da zdravstvuet professionalizm!" *ZI*, 15–16 May 1920, p. 1.

85. Clearly, "amateurs" could replace "theater circles"; but because of the use of the term *amateur* by the Adult Education Department, it had negative ideological connotations with radicals.

86. Adr. Piotrovskii, "Teatr vsego naroda. Teatral'nyi kruzhok," *ZI*, 20–21 May 1920, p. 1.

87. Evgenii Kuznetsov, "Armianskaia zagadka," *ZI*, 5 May 1920, p. 1.

88. Konst. Derzhavin, "Moskovskie otkliki," *ZI*, 30 April 1920, p. 1.

89. Viktor Shklovskii, "O psikhologicheskoi rampe," *ZI*, 7 May 1920, p. 1; also in Shklovskii, *Khod konia*.

90. Evgenii Kuznetsov, "Da zdravstvuet professionalizm. Okanchanie," *ZI*, 18 May 1920, p. 1.

91. Sergei Radlov, "Massovye postanovki," in Radlov, *Stat'i o teatre* (Petrograd: Mysl', 1923), p. 41.

92. This interesting fact is brought up in S. L. Tsimbal's introduction to

Adrian Piotrovskii, *Teatr. Kino. Zhizn'*, ed. A. Ia. Trabskii (Leningrad: Iskusstvo, 1969), pp. 6–7.

93. As far as I know, the play, which judging by reviews was one of Gumilev's best, has been lost. It was to be printed in the fourth issue (1920) of *Igra*, which I do not believe ever made it to press. Descriptions can be found in A. L[evinso]n, "Derevo prevrashcheniia," *ZI*, 8 February 1919, p. 1; [P. Morozov], "N. Gumilev. 'Derevo prevrashcheniia.' P'esa dlia detei," 23 September 1918, LGAOR, f. 2551, op. 17, d. 4, l. 151.

94. LGAOR, f. 2551, op. 1, d. 2391, l. 41. See also "Teatr-Studiia," *ZI*, 16 November 1918, p. 4.

95. Sergei Radlov, "Teatr vozrozhdeniia i vozrozhdenie teatra," *ZI*, 12 November 1920, p. 1.

96. LGAOR, f. 2551, op. 1, d. 2137, ll. 3–11; also *Istoriia sovetskogo teatra*, pp. 268–69.

97. Gorchakov, *The Theater in Soviet Russia*, p. 131; on this play, and on the Popular Comedy in general, see Zolotnitskii, *Zori teatral'nogo oktiabria*, p. 249.

98. Konst. Derzhavin, "Iskusstvo tsirka v stsenicheskoi kompozitsii," *ZI*, 1 April 1920, p. 2; see also his "Akter i tsirk," *ZI*, 30 March 1920, pp. 1–2.

99. "Vindzorskie prokaznitsy," *ZI*, 12 November 1920, p. 1.

100. Radlov, *Stat'i o teatre*, pp. 39–44.

101. Evgenii Kuznetsov, "Po povodu," *ZI*, 17 June 1920, p. 1.

102. Emma Goldman, *My Disillusionment in Russia*, pp. 67–73.

103. Adrian Piotrovskii, "Ostrov chudes," *ZI*, 22 June 1920, in Piotrovskii, *Za sovetskii teatr*, p. 21.

104. N. Kuzmin, "Velikoe nachalo," *PP*, 20 June 1920, p. 2.

105. Piotrovskii, "Ostrov chudes," p. 22.

106. Described in H. G. Wells, *Russia in the Shadows* (London: Hodder & Stoughton, 1920), pp. 128–31.

107. Khodasevich, "Gorod—teatr," p. 34.

108. Firsthand sources for the following description are: *Istoriia sovetskogo teatra*, pp. 282–86; *Massovye prazdnestva*, pp. 63–64; Piotrovskii, "Ostrov chudes"; Andreeva, *Perepiska, vospominaniia*, pp. 418–19; Khodasevich, "Massovye deistva, zrelishcha i prazdniki," pp. 12–13; Khodasevich, "Gorod—teatr"; M., "Pervyi amfiteatr," *ZI*, 19–20 June 1920, p. 1; Aleksandr Belenson, "Dva giganta," *ZI*, 23 June 1920; Ievgeny Kuznetsov, "Pod otkrytym nebom. Peterburgskie massovye postanovki," *VT*, no. 71 (1920), in *Russkii-sovetskii teatr*, pp. 266–68; and Alekseev-Iakovlev, *Russkie narodnye gulianiia*. Mazaev, *Prazdnik*, pp. 306–11, although not firsthand, is a fine description.

109. Mazaev, *Prazdnik*, p. 308, following Piotrovsky, believes this is a specific feature of "holiday" theater. However, it should be remembered that it was in Renaissance festivals—another form of holiday theater—that "illusionary" stage designs were first developed.

110. See, for example, "Speshi pana pokrepche vzdut'!", Vlad. Maiakovskii, "ROSTA Window no. 336," Dmitrii Moor, "Krasnyi podarok belomu panu," in German, ed., *Serdtsem*, plates 30, 31, 61. The clichés predated the Revolution by at least a half century.

Chapter Six. Marking the Center

1. Edward Shils, "The Center and Periphery," in his *Center and Periphery: Essays in Macrosociology* (Chicago: University of Chicago Press, 1975), pp. 3–6.
2. Clifford Geertz, "Centers, Kings and Charisma," in Ben-David and Clark, eds., *Culture and Its Creators*, p. 13.
3. Richard Wortman, "Moscow and Petersburg," in Wilentz, ed., *Rites of Power*, pp. 244–76.
4. See, for instance, his critique of Claude Lévi-Strauss in Jacques Derrida, *Writing and Difference*, trans. Alan Bass (Chicago: University of Chicago Press, 1978), or his *Of Grammatology*, trans. Gayatri Chakravorty Spivak (Baltimore: Johns Hopkins University Press, 1976).
5. James W. Hulse, *The Forming of the Communist International* (Stanford, Calif.: Stanford University Press, 1964), p. 35.
6. "Prazdnovanie dnia konstitutsii v Moskve i peredachi znameni Parizhskikh kommunarov," *Leningradskaia pravda*, 8 July 1924, p. 2. "Holy relic" was Zinoviev's phrasing.
7. Günter Nollau, *International Communism and World Revolution* (New York: Praeger, 1961), p. 44.
8. See Robert Lee Wolff, "The Three Romes: The Migration of an Ideology and the Making of an Autocrat," in Henry A. Murray, ed., *Myth and Mythmaking* (Boston: Beacon Press, 1960).
9. J. T. Murphy, *New Horizons* (London: Bodley Head, 1942), p. 139. See also Morris Gordin, *Utopia in Chains* (Boston: Houghton Mifflin, 1926), pp. 89–94.
10. John Reed, "Soviet Russia Now," *Liberator*, December 1920, p. 9.
11. *The Communist International* (Petrograd, 1 May 1919). Available also in Russian, German, and French.
12. German, ed., *Serdtsem*, plates 70, 351.
13. Vladimir Narbut, "Eshche ne vremia . . ." *Izvestiia Odesskogo soveta*, 23 June 1920, p. 1.
14. For descriptions of the demonstrations, see Angelica Balabanoff, *My Life as a Rebel* (New York: Harper, 1938), pp. 258–62; and Mrs. Philip Snowden, *Through Bolshevik Russia* (London: Cassell, 1920), pp. 65 ff. A pictorial record of the festival, with the gaiety of the crowd highly exaggerated, is Boris Kustodiev's painting *Prazdnik v chest' otkrytiia II kongressa Kominterna*. The preliminary sketches for this painting show little such enthusiasm: *AMI* (1984), plate 192.
15. N. Strelnikov, "Giganty," *ZI*, 21 July 1920, p. 1; "Krasnaia Messa," *IzvPS*, 17 July 1920, p. 1.
16. On the ceremony, see Aksenov, *Organizatsiia*, p. 22.
17. "Sud nad zheltym Internatsionalom," *P*, 31 July 1920, p. 1.
18. N. Strelnikov, "Edinyi Internatsional," *ZI*, 29 January 1920; "Khudozhestvennaia zhizn'," *ZI*, 11 February 1920, p. 1.
19. This description is based on the following firsthand accounts: *Istoriia*

sovetskogo teatra, pp. 271–78; Kerzhentsev, *Tvorcheskii teatr*, pp. 139–42; Petrov, *50 i 500*, pp. 188–92; *Russkii-sovetskii teatr*, pp. 268–71; *Massovye prazdnestva*, pp. 66–70; Piotrovskii, *Za sovetskii teatr*, pp. 12–14; Fülöp-Miller, *The Mind and Face of Bolshevism*, pp. 208–10; Lev Nikulin, *Zapiski sputnika* (Moscow: Sovetskaia literatura, 1933), pp. 62–65; Andreeva, *Perepiska, vospominaniia*, pp. 419–20, 435–36; Alfred Rosmer, *Moscow under Lenin*, trans. Ian H. Birchall (New York: Monthly Review Press, 1972), pp. 66–68; Goldman, *My Disillusionment in Russia*, pp. 75–78; *Vtoroi kongress Kommunisticheskogo Internatsionala* (Petrograd: Izd. Kommunisticheskogo Internatsionala, 1920); E. Preobrazhenskii, "Mnogoobeshchaiushchii opyt," *P*, 30 July 1920, p. 1; P. Kudelli, "Novoe zrelishche na portale Fondovoi Birzhi," *PP*, 21 July 1920, p. 2 (also in *AMI* [1984]); Sergei Kozakevich, "V masshtabakh otkrytogo neba," *ZI*, 5 November 1920, p. 1; Aleksandr Belenson, "Vokrug dvukh mirov," *ZI*, 21 July 1920, p. 1; Aleksandr Belenson, "K mirovoi kommune," *ZI*, 23 July 1920, p. 1; Georgii Gur'ev, "Eshche o massovykh postanovkakh," *ZI*, 1 September 1920, p. 1; and Kuznetsov, "Pod otkrytym nebom."

20. G. Kryzhitskii, *K. A. Mardzhanov i russkii teatr* (Moscow: VTO, 1958), p. 116.

21. K. A. Mardzhanov, *Tvorcheskoe nasledie* (Tbilisi: Zaria vostoka, 1958), pp. 107–8.

22. Kerzhentsev, *Tvorcheskii teatr*, pp. 140–42.

23. See *AMI* (1984), plates 186–87. Descriptions in Piotrovskii, *Za sovetskii teatr*, p. 12; and S. Radlov, "Sud'by teatra za vremia revoliutsii," *ZI*, 24 October 1922, p. 1.

24. See also M. Levin, "Miting o khalture," *ZI*, 3 August 1920, p. 1.

25. The same trick had been used by Percy MacKaye in a pageant in Gloucester, Massachusetts, attended by Woodrow Wilson: see MacKaye, *Civic Theatre*, p. 161.

26. "Repetitsiia misterii 'Dva mira,' " *IzvPS*, 17 July 1920, p. 1.

27. Radlov, *Stat'i o teatre*, p. 44.

28. "Okhrana ploshchadi pered birzhei," *PP*, 20 June 1920, p. 2.

29. A similar, though nonelectric, signaling system had been devised by Jacques Louis David for the Fête of Reunion.

30. Radlov, *Stat'i o teatre*, p. 44.

31. A segment of the "score" of the scenario, listing entrances and their accompanying locations, music, and so forth, can be found in *Massovye prazdnestva*, pp. 68–69. See Table 1.

32. Nikulin, *Zapiski sputnika*, p. 63.

33. "K oktiabr'skim torzhestvam," *ZI*, 4–5 November 1919, p. 3.

34. See the march routes in "K pervomu maia," *IzvPS*, 28 April 1918, p. 4.

35. The tribune was the hood of a car. See the photos in *Pl*, 1 May 1918.

36. V. Zhemchuzhnyi, *Kak organizovat' oktiabr'skuiu demonstratsiiu* (Moscow: Gosizdat, 1927), pp. 11–13.

37. "K oktiabr'skim torzhestvam," *ZI*, 1 November 1918, p. 4. Attendance was allowed only for those with a pass. "Ot tsentral'nogo biuro po ustroistvu oktiabr'skikh prazdnestv," *SK*, 6 November 1918, p. 1.

38. "K oktiabr'skim torzhestvam," *ZI*, 5 November 1918, p. 4.

39. "Tsirkuliarnoe obrashchenie Vserossiiskoi tsentral'noi oktiabr'skoi komissii," *Vestnik agitatsii i propagandy*, 19 October 1920, p. 13.
40. "K oktiabr'skim torzhestvam," *ZI*, 23–24 October 1920, p. 1.
41. *PSS*, vol. 3, pp. 168–73.
42. Quoted in Stites, *Revolutionary Dreams*, p. 243.
43. Osip Mandelstam, *The Complete Critical Prose and Letters*, trans. Jane Gray Harris (Ann Arbor, Mich.: Ardis, 1979), p. 170.
44. "K godovshchine oktiabr'skoi revoliutsii," *ZI*, 10 September 1920, p. 1; also, K. N. Derzhavin, "Vziatie Zimnego dvortsa v 1920 g. K 5-letiiu instsenirovki," *ZI*, no. 45 (1925); and Nikulin, *Zapiski sputnika*, p. 81.
45. See "Khronika," *Iskusstvo*, no. 2 [6] (1918), pp. 15–16; N. Punin, "O pamiatnikakh," *IK*, 9 March 1919, p. 2.
46. Viktor Shklovskii, "Pamiatniki russkoi revoliutsii," *ZI*, 28–29 June 1919, p. 2. See similar thoughts in Punin, "O pamiatnikakh," pp. 2–3.
47. N. Punin, *Pamiatnik Tret'emu Internatsionalu* (Petersburg: IZO, 1920); translation from Fülöp-Miller, *The Mind and Face of Bolshevism*, pp. 144–46.
48. "Pamiatnik oktiabr'skoi revoliutsii," *ZI*, 24–25 October 1919, p. 1.
49. "Podgotovka k godovshchine oktiabr'skoi revoliutsii," *IzvTsIK*, 12 September 1920, p. 3.
50. T. M. Goriaeva, "Pervaia godovshchina oktiabr'skoi revoliutsii," *SSSR*, pp. 132–33.
51. "Tretii Internatsional," in *PSS*, vol. 2, p. 43.
52. "Prazdnik v chest' vtorogo kongressa Kommunisticheskogo Internatsionala," *P*, 29 July 1920, p. 1. Another fine description is in Marguerite E. Harrison, *Marooned in Moscow* (New York: George Doran, 1921), pp. 180–83.
53. As far as I know, this is the first instance of a practice familiar to any modern observer who attended a Soviet May Day or November 7 demonstration in Red Square. Films of 1919 demonstrations show marchers filing through the densely packed ranks of spectators: "Moskva. Prazdnovanie pervogo maia 1919 g.," *Kinonedelia*, no. 41 (20 May 1919), pt. II.
54. Vasilii Chibison, "Prazdnik rabochikh," *P*, 29 July 1920, p. 1.
55. Karl Radek, "Organizovannaia massa," *P*, 29 July 1920, supplement, p. 1.
56. TsGALI, f. 2731, op. 1, d. 102.
57. *Sovetskii politicheskii plakat/The Soviet Political Poster 1917–1945* (Moscow: Sovetskii khudozhnik, 1984), poster 15.
58. Accounts of this performance are legion: *Istoriia sovetskogo teatra*, pp. 279–82; N. Evreinov, "Vziatie Zimnego dvortsa," *Krasnyi militsioner*, no. 14 (1920), pp. 4–5—in French: Nicolas Evreinoff, *Histoire du théâtre russes* (Paris: Editions du Chene, 1947), pp. 426–30); Gourfinkel, *Théâtre russe contemporain*, pp. 135–38; Kerzhentsev, *Tvorcheskii teatr*, pp. 142–44; Fülöp-Miller, *The Mind and Face of Bolshevism*, pp. 211–13; Petrov, *50 i 500*, pp. 194–95; *Russkii-sovetskii teatr*, pp. 273–75; Annenkov, *Dnevnik moikh vstrech*, vol. 2, p. 118–28; Piotrovskii, *Za sovetskii teatr*, pp. 16–17; Nikulin, *Zapiski sputnika*, pp. 80–82; Holitscher, *Drei Monat in Sowyet Russland*, pp. 126 ff.; Huntly Carter, *The New Spirit in the Russian Theatre* (London: Brentano, 1929), pp. 143–48; N. D. Volkov, *Teatral'nye vechera* (Moscow: Iskusstvo, 1966), pp. 27–31; Golub,

Evreinov, pp. 195–202; *AMI* (1984), pp. 113–17; "K instsenirovke Vziatiia Zimnego dvortsa," *PP,* 26 October 1920, p. 1; L. Nikulin, "Vos'mogo noiabria 1920 goda," *PP,* 31 October 1920, p. 2; "Na repetitsii instsenirovki 'Vziatie Zimnego dvortsa,' " *PP,* 4 November 1920, p. 2; "Vziatie Zimnego dvortsa. Opyt," *PP,* 7 November 1920, p. 2; "Proletarskoe deistvo. Na instsenirovke 'Vziatie Zimnego dvortsa,' " *PP,* 10 November 1920, p. 2; "Instsenirovka Vziatiia Zimnego dvortsa," *IzvPS,* 28 October 1920, p. 2; "Instsenirovka 'Vziatie Zimnego dvortsa.' Libretto v okonchatel'noi redaktsii," *IzvPS,* 6 November 1920, p. 2; Konst. Derzhavin, "Chudo. K postanovke 'Vziatie Zimnego dvortsa,' " *IzvPS,* 9 November 1920, p. 1; "Vziatie Zimnego dvortsa. Vpechatleniia," *IzvPS,* 9 November 1920, p. 1; Nik. [Evreinov], "Vziatie Zimnego dvortsa," *ZI,* 30–31 October 1920, p. 1; Kozakevich, "V masshtabakh otkrytogo neba"; N. Evreinov, "Vziatie Zimnego dvortsa. Vospominaniia ob instsenirovke v oznamenovanie tret'ei godovshchiny oktiabr'skoi revoliutsii," *ZI,* 4 November 1924, pp. 7–9 (complete version in TsGALI, f. 982, op. 1, d. 31); Derzhavin, "Vziatie Zimnego dvortsa"; "Vziatie Zimnego dvortsa," *VT,* no. 74 (1920), pp. 11–12; and N. Shubskii, "Na ploshchadi Uritskogo. Vpechatleniia Moskvicha," *VT,* no. 75 (1920), pp. 4–5. The idiosyncratic version in Gray-Prokofieva, *The Russian Experiment in Art,* can be ignored.

59. From the libretto, in *Russkii-sovetskii teatr,* p. 272.
60. "K instsenirovke Vziatiia Zimnego dvortsa," *PP,* 26 October 1920.
61. "Chto trebuetsia ot zritelei vo vremia instsenirovki," *PP,* 7 November 1920, p. 4.
62. See Konst. Derzhavin, "O massovykh predstavleniiakh," *IzvPS,* 27 October 1920, p. 2.
63. "K oktiabr'skim torzhestvam," *PP,* 26 October 1920, p. 1. Many thanks to Alma Law for making this film available.
64. This definition is Piotrovsky's: *Za sovetskii teatr,* p. 16.
65. This I assume from the fact that only 600 actors wore make-up: they were most likely the Whites: LGAOR, f. 1000, op. 79, d. 49.

Epilogue

1. A. Agulianskii, "Proletarskie prazdnestva i rabotniki iskusstva," *Vestnik teatra i iskusstva,* 20 December 1921, p. 13.
2. Aksenov, *Organizatsiia,* p. 45.
3. TsGA RSFSR, f. 2313, op. 2, ed. kr. 36.
4. *AMI* (1984), p. 119.
5. V. D. Zeldovich, "Velikolepnii plan," in Lenin and Lunacharskii, *Perepiska,* pp. 663–64.
6. P. M. Kerzhentsev, "Iskusstvo na ulitsu," *Iskusstvo,* no. 3 (1918), p. 12; Vlad. Mass, "Teatral'nyi oktiabr' i futurizm," *VT,* no. 91–92 (1921), p. 4.
7. Zolotnitskii, *Zori teatral'nogo oktiabria,* p. 325.
8. "Revoliutsionnaia poshlost'," *VT,* no. 85–86 (1921), p. 6.

9. Ilya Ehrenburg, *People and Life, 1891–1921* (New York: Knopf, 1962), p. 388.
10. In *Russkaia teatral'naia parodiia XIX–nachala XX veka* (Moscow: Iskusstvo, 1976).
11. L. Arne, "Mirovoi konkurs ostroumiia. Vol'naia komediia," *ZI*, 15 November 1921, p. 1.
12. M. Danilevskii, *Prazdniki obshchestvennogo byta* (Moscow: Doloi negramotnosti, 1927), p. 38.
13. See the following Agit-Prop critiques: Nevskii, *Massovaia politiko-prosvetitel'naia rabota*; and Ia. Shafir, *Gazeta i derevnia* (Moscow: Krasnaia nov', 1924).
14. *U istokov*, pp. 176–77.
15. Tsekhnovitser, *Prazdnestva revoliutsii*, pp. 85–86.
16. TsGALI, f.963, op.1, d.1561.
17. "Moskva," *ZI*, 19 May 1925, p. 22; *Massovye prazdniki i zrelishcha*, p. 12.
18. Samuil Margolin, "Iz tsikla 'neosushchestvlennyi teatr.' 'Bor'ba i pobeda.' Massovoe deistvo Vs. Meierkhol'da," *Ekho*, no. 13 (1923), p. 11.
19. "Spor ob Akvariume," *VT*, no. 89–90 (1921), p. 19.
20. "A Commissar," and "A Meeting with Comrade Podvoisky," in Franklin Rosemont, ed., *Isadora Speaks* (San Francisco: City Lights, 1981), pp. 71–77.
21. "Vsevobuch i iskusstvo," *VT*, no. 78–79 (1921), pp. 24–25.
22. James Riordan, *Sport in Soviet Society: Development of Sport and Physical Education in Russia and the USSR* (Cambridge: Cambridge University Press, 1977), p. 102.
23. Martha Bradshaw, ed., *Soviet Theaters, 1917–1941* (New York: Research Program on the USSR, 1954), p. 25.
24. N. M. Smirnov, "Teatral'naia rabota v klubakh," *Revoliutsionnye vskhody*, no. 7–8 (1920), p. 14.
25. A. Piotrovskii, "K teorii samodeiatel'nogo teatra," in *Problemy sotsiologii iskusstva*, pp. 121–24.
26. *Massovye prazdnestva*, p. 73.
27. See *Edinyi khudozhestvennyi kruzhok. Metody klubno-khudozhestvennoi raboty* (Leningrad: Izd. knizhnogo sektora Gubono, 1924), or Piotrovskii, *Za sovetskii teatr*, pp. 7–9.
28. Poems, songs, slogans, costumes, and games devised for the holiday can be found in several collections published under the title *Komsomol'skoe rozhdestvo* (Tula: Rossiiskii kommunisticheskii soiuz molodezhi, 1923; Moscow: MK RKSM, 1923; Moscow: Krasnaia nov', 1923).
29. "Masterskaia Meierkhol'da," *Lef*, no. 2 (1923), pp. 170–71.
30. William Reswick, *I Dreamt Revolution* (Chicago: Regnery, 1932), p. 164; Lancelot Lawton, *The Russian Revolution, 1917–1926* (London: Macmillan, 1927), p. 417; A. Ivanov, "Komsomol'skoe rozhdestvo," *Rabochii klub*, no. 10–11 (1924), pp. 12–13.
31. Vit. Zhemchuzhnyi, "Protiv obriadov," *Novyi Lef*, no. 1 (1927), p. 45; V. Zhemchuzhnyi, "Demonstratsiia v oktiabre," *Novyi Lef*, no. 5 (1927), pp. 47–48.

32. S[ergei] T[retiakov], "Zapisnaia knizhka. Otsenka khudozhestvennogo oformleniia desiatioktiabria," *Novyi Lef,* no. 10 (1927), pp. 7–8.
33. S. Tretiakov, "Kak desiatiletit'," *Novyi Lef,* no. 4 (1927), p. 37; I. Ch., "Kak ispol'zovali deistvennikov," *Novyi Lef,* no. 10 (1927), p. 10.
34. See *Biulleten' kommissii pri prezidiume TsIK Soiuza SSR po organizatsii i provedeniiu prazdnovaniia 10-letiia oktiabr'skoi revoliutsii,* no. 1 (1927), pp. 3–5.
35. Petrov, *50 i 500,* pp. 195–205.
36. Reswick, *I Dreamt Revolution,* pp. 205–8.

Bibliography

Primary Sources

THEORIES OF CULTURE CURRENT DURING THE REVOLUTION

Belyi, Andrei. *Revoliutsiia i kul'tura.* Moscow: A. Leman i S. I. Sakharov, 1917.

"Beseda s V. E. Meierkhol'dom," *Vestnik teatra,* no. 68 (1920), pp. 3–4.

Bessal'ko, P., and F. Kalinin. *Problemy proletarskoi kul'tury.* Petrograd: Atenei, 1919.

Bezpiatov, Evg. "Teatr pod otkrytym nebom," *Narodnyi teatr,* no. 3–4 (1918), pp. 25–27.

Bogdanov, A. A. [Malinovskii]. *Iskusstvo i rabochii klass.* Moscow: Proletarskaia kul'tura, 1918.

———. *Pervoe maia. Mezhdunarodnyi prazdnik truda.* Petrograd: G. V. Belopol'skii, 1917.

———. *Red Star: The First Bolshevik Utopia.* Edited by Loren R. Graham and Richard Stites. Translated by Charles Rougle. Bloomington: Indiana University Press, 1984.

Br., L. "Teatr pod otkrytym nebom," *Zhizn' iskusstva,* 3 June 1919, p. 4.

Brik, O. M. "Khudozhnik i kommuna," *Izobrazitel'noe iskusstvo,* no. 1 (1919), pp. 25–26.

Briusov, Valerii. "Narodnyi teatr R. Rollana," *Russkaia mysl',* no. 5 (1909).

———. "Nenuzhnaia pravda," *Mir iskusstva,* no. 4 (1902).

Campanella, Tommaso. *The City of the Sun.* Translated by Daniel I. Donno. Berkeley: University of California Press, 1981.

Cheney, Sheldon. *The Open-Air Theater.* New York: Mitchell Kennerly, 1918.
Derzhavin, Konst. "Moskovskie otkliki," *Zhizn' iskusstva,* 30 April 1920, p. 1.
———. "O massovykh predstavleniiakh," *Izvestiia Petrogradskogo soveta,* 27 October 1920, p. 2.
"Dom Igry," *Vestnik teatra,* no. 2 (1919), p. 6.
Dostoevsky, F. M. *Memoirs from the House of the Dead.* Translated by Jessie Coulson. London: Oxford Press, 1956. In Russian: *Zapiski iz mertvogo doma,* in *Polnoe sobranie sochinenii.* Leningrad: Nauka, 1972.
Dramatizatsiia v shkole pervoi stepeni. Moscow: GIZ, 1920.
Dramatizatsiia v shkole vtoroi stepeni. Moscow: GIZ, 1920.
Engels, Frederick. *The Origin of the Family, Private Property and the State.* Translated by Eleanor Burke Leacock. New York: International Publishers, 1972.
Erberg, Konst., ed. *Iskusstvo i narod.* Petrograd: Kolos, 1922.
———, ed. *Iskusstvo staroe i novoe.* Petrograd: Alkonost, 1921.
Evreinov, Nikolai Nikolaevich. *The Theatre in Life.* Translated by Alexander I. Nazaroff. New York: Brentano's, 1927.
[Foregger, N.] "Literaturnaia nedelia," *Vestnik teatra,* no. 43 (1919), pp. 14–15.
Friche, V. M. *Mirovoi krasnyi prazdnik.* Smolensk: Pervaia sovetskaia tipografiia, 1919.
———. "Znachenie narodnykh prazdnestv," *Vechernie izvestiia Moskovskogo soveta,* 11 February 1919, p. 1.
Fuchs, Georg. *Die Schaubühne der Zukunft.* Berlin: Schuster & Loeffler, 1906.
"Futurizm—gosudarstvennoe iskusstvo," *Iskusstvo kommuny,* 29 December 1918, p. 2.
Gaideburov, P. P. "Novye metody teatral'nogo instruktorstva," *Vneshkol'noe obrazovanie,* no. 4–5 (1919), pp. 6–7.
———. "Novye zadachi teatral'nogo instruktorstva," *Vneshkol'noe obrazovanie,* no. 2–3 (1919), pp. 19–23.
———. "Pis'mo k zriteliu. Bez zaglaviia," *Zapiski peredvizhnogo-obshchedostupnogo teatra,* no. 17 (1919), pp. 3–6.
———. "Tvorcheskaia igra. Improvizatsionnyi metod N. F. Skarskoi," *Vneshkol'noe obrazovanie,* no. 6–8 (1919), pp. 36–40.
———. *Zarozhdenie spektaklia.* Petrograd: Izd. Peredvizhnogo teatra Gaideburova i Skarskoi, 1922.
Gan, Aleksei. *Konstruktivizm.* Tver: Tverskoe izd., 1922.
Golovanov, N. "Tolpa na stsene i v zhivopisi," *Narodnyi teatr,* no. 3–4 (1918).
Grétry, André. *Memoires, ou essais sur la musique.* Liège: Vaillant-Carmanne, 1914.
Groshkov, Fedor. "Teatralizatsiia zhizni," *Zhizn' iskusstva,* 22 April 1920, p. 1.
Gurev, Georgii. "Eshche o massovykh postanovkakh," *Zhizn' iskusstva,* 1 September 1920, p. 1.

Gvozdev, A. A. *Massovye prazdnestva na zapade*. Peterhof, 1926.
Gvozdev, A. A., and A. I. Piotrovskii. *Istoriia evropeiskogo teatra*. Leningrad: Academia, 1931.
"Itogi s"ezda po vneshkol'nomu obrazovaniiu," *Vestnik teatra*, no. 29 (1919), pp. 2–3.
Ivanov, Viacheslav. *Borozdy i mezhi*. Moscow: Musaget, 1916.
———. "K voprosu ob organizatsii tvorcheskikh sil narodnogo kollektiva v oblasti khudozhestvennogo deistva," *Vestnik teatra*, no. 26 (1919), p. 4.
———. "Mnozhestvo i lichnost' v deistve," *Vestnik teatra*, no. 62 (1920), p. 5.
———. "Organizatsiia tvorcheskikh sil narodnogo kollektiva v oblasti khudozhestvennogo deistva," *Vestnik teatra*, no. 44 (1919), p. 3.
———. *Po zvezdam*. St. Petersburg: Izd. Ory, 1909.
"K voprosu o peredelkakh," *Vestnik teatra*, no. 33 (1919), p. 7.
Karzhanskii, N. *Kollektivnaia dramaturgiia*. Moscow: Gosizdat, 1922.
———. "Kollektivnaia dramaturgiia. Pis'mo iz Smolenska," *Vestnik teatra*, no. 71 (1920), pp. 6–7.
Kerzhentsev, P. M. "Burzhuaznoe nasledie," *Vestnik teatra*, no. 51 (1920), pp. 2–3.
———. "Kollektivnoe tvorchestvo v teatre," *Proletarskaia kul'tura*, no. 7–8 (1919), pp. 37–41.
———. "Mozhno li iskazhat' p'esy postanovkoi?" *Vestnik teatra*, no. 1 (1919), p. 2.
———. "O professionalizme," *Gorn*, no. 4 (1919), pp. 69–71.
———. "Peredelyvaite p'esy!" *Vestnik teatra*, no. 36 (1919), pp. 6–8.
———. *Pervoe maia i mirovaia revoliutsiia*. Tver: Tsentropechat', 1919.
———. "Pis'mo v redaktsiiu," *Vestnik teatra*, no. 53 (1920), p. 5.
———. "Repertuar proletarskogo teatra," *Iskusstvo*, no. 1 [5] (1918), pp. 5–7.
———. *Revoliutsiia i teatr*. Moscow: Dennitsa, 1918.
———. "Rozn' iskusstva," *Vestnik teatra*, no. 19 (1919), p. 2.
———. "Teatral'nyi muzei," *Vestnik teatra*, no. 48 (1920), pp. 4–5.
———. *Tvorcheskii teatr*. Various publishers, 1918–23 (5 editions).
Khrisanf, Kh. "Narodnye prazdnestva," *Vestnik teatra*, no. 34 (1919), pp. 3–4.
"Klub—masterskaia iskusstv 'Krasnyi Petukh.' Lektsiia Viach. Ivanova," *Vestnik teatra*, no. 1 (1919), p. 2.
Kogan, P. S. "Prazdnik revoliutsii—prazdnik teatra," *Vestnik teatra*, no. 16 (1919), p. 2.
———. "Provozvestniki sotsialisticheskogo teatra," *Vestnik teatra*, no. 62 (1920), p. 3.
———. "Puti proletarskogo teatra," *Vestnik teatra*, no. 27 (1919), pp. 2–3.
———. "Teatr na zakaz," *Vestnik teatra*, no. 66 (1920), pp. 4–5.
———. "Teatr-tribuna," *Vestnik teatra*, no. 2 (1919), pp. 2–3.
———. *V preddverii griadushchego teatra*. Moscow: Pervina, 1921.
Krizis teatra: Sbornik statei. Moscow: Problemy iskusstva, 1908.
Kropotkin, P. A. *The Great French Revolution, 1789–1793*. New York: G. P. Putnam, 1909.
Krupskaia, N. K. "Glavpolitprosvet i iskusstvo," *Pravda*, 13 February 1921.

Kuda my idem? Sbornik statei i otvetov. Moscow: Zaria, 1910.

Kugel, A. "Massovki," *Iskusstvo trudiashchimsia*, no. 1 (1924), pp. 13–15.

———. *Utverzhdenie teatra*. Petrograd: Teatr i iskusstvo, 1923.

Kuzmin, M. "Rampa geroizma," *Zhizn' iskusstva*, 20 November 1918, p. 2.

———. "Tsirk," *Zhizn' iskusstva*, 4 January 1919, pp. 1–2.

Kuznetsov, Evgenii. "Da zdravstvuet professionalizm. Okanchanie," *Zhizn' iskusstva*, 18 May 1920, p. 1.

Lander, K. *Nasha teatral'naia politika*. Moscow: GIZ, 1921.

Lebedev-Polianskii, P. I., ed. *Protokoly pervoi vserossiiskoi konferentsii proletarskikh kul'turno-prosvetitel'nykh organizatsii 15–20 sent. 1918 g*. Moscow: Proletarskaia kul'tura, 1918.

Lenin, N. "Velikii pochin. O geroizme rabochikh v tylu. Po povodu 'kommunisticheskikh subbotnikov,'" *Pravda*, 28 June 1919, p. 1.

L[ev]in, M. "Miting ob iskusstve," *Iskusstvo kommuny*, 7 November 1918, p. 3.

Lunacharskii, A. V. "Budem smeiat'sia," *Vestnik teatra*, no. 58 (1920), pp. 7–8.

———. "Chem dolzhen byt' narodnyi dvorets," *Novaia zhizn'*, 14 September 1917, p. 5.

———. "Chem mozhet byt' narodnyi dvorets," *Novaia zhizn'*, 30 June 1917, p. 3.

———. "Imenem proletariata," *Vestnik teatra*, no. 51 (1920), pp. 3–4.

———. "Kakaia nam nuzhna melodrama?" *Zhizn' iskusstva*, 14 January 1919, pp. 2–3.

———. "Kul'tura sotsializma torzhestvuiushchego i sotsializma boriushchegosia," *Novaia zhizn'*, 21 June 1917, p. 4.

———. *O massovykh prazdnestvakh, èstrade i tsirke*. Moscow: Iskusstvo, 1981.

———. "O narodnykh prazdnestvakh," *Vestnik teatra*, no. 62 (1920), pp. 4–5.

———. *Religiia i sotsializm*. St. Petersburg: Shipovnik, 1908–11.

———. "Revoliutsionnyi teatr. otvet tov. Bukharinu," *Vestnik teatra*, no. 47 (1919), pp. 3–4.

———. *Sobranie sochinenii*. Moscow: Khudozh. literatura, 1963–67.

Lvov, Nikolai. "Narodnye igrishcha v Viatskoi gubernii," *Vestnik teatra*, no. 38 (1919), p. 4.

MacKaye, Percy. *The Civic Theatre*. New York: Mitchell Kennerly, 1912.

Maeterlinck, Maurice. *The Treasure of the Humble*. Translated by Alfred Sutro. New York: Dodd, Mead, 1903.

Malinin, K. "Dramaticheskie kruzhki i teatr budushchego," *Vestnik teatra*, no. 47 (1919), pp. 5–6.

Meierkhol'd, V. E. *Stat'i, pis'ma, rechi, besedy*. Moscow: Iskusstvo, 1968.

———. *Vsevolod Meyerhold on Theatre*. Translated by Edward Braun. New York: Hill and Wang, 1969.

"Miting iskusstv," *Vechernie izvestiia Moskovskogo soveta*, 10 November 1919, pp. 3–4.

"Miting ob iskusstve," *Zhizn' iskusstva*, 22 November 1918, p. 5.

More, Thomas. *Utopia*. Translated by Paul Turner. London: Penguin, 1965.

Morris, William. *News from Nowhere*. New York: Monthly Review Press, 1966.

"Na s"ezde po vneshkol'nomu obrazovaniiu," *Vestnik teatra*, no. 27 (1919), p. 3.
Nietzsche, Friedrich. *The Birth of Tragedy*. Translated by Francis Golffing. New York: Vintage Books, 1967.
Nikonov, B. "Teatr, blizkii k prirode," *Zhizn' iskusstva*, 20 May 1919, p. 3.
Nikulin, L. "O dvukh poliusakh," *Vestnik teatra*, no. 59 (1920), p. 7.
———. "O professionalizme proletariia-khudozhnika," *Vestnik teatra*, no. 19 (1919), pp. 3–4.
O teatre. Tver: Tverskoe izd., 1922.
Organizatsiia massovykh narodnykh prazdnestv. Moscow: Gosizdat, 1921.
"Otkrytie kursov po detskomu teatru," *Vestnik teatra*, no. 27 (1919), p. 7.
"Pechat'," *Vestnik teatra*, no. 59 (1920), p. 8.
Pel'she, R. *Nravy i iskusstvo frantsuzskoi revoliutsii*. Petrograd: Izd. Proletkulta, 1919.
Pervyi vserossiiskii s"ezd po raboche-krest'ianskomu teatru 17–26 noiabria 1919. Moscow: Vestnik teatra, 1920.
Piast, Vl. "Instsenirovka," *Zhizn' iskusstva*, 20 November 1919, p. 1.
Piotrovskii, Adrian. "Prazdnestva kommuny," *Petrogradskaia pravda*, 17 February 1920, p. 1.
———. *Teatr. Kino. Zhizn'*. Edited by A. Ia. Trabskii. Leningrad: Iskusstvo, 1969.
———. "Teatr vsego naroda. Teatral'nyi kruzhok," *Zhizn' iskusstva*, 20–21 May 1920, p. 1.
Plekhanov, G. V. *Ezhegodnyi vsemirnyi prazdnik rabochikh*. Geneva: Sotsial-Demokrat, 1891.
———. *Iskusstvo i obshchestvennaia zhizn'*. Moscow: Izd. Moskovskogo instituta zhurnalistiki, 1922.
Pletnev, V. "O kollektivnom tvorchestve," *Gorn*, no. 5 (1920), pp. 55–59.
"Poezdka v Vitebsk," *Zapiski peredvizhnogo-obshchedostupnogo teatra*, no. 20 (1919), pp. 8–9.
Poletaev, E., and N. Punin. *Protiv tsivilizatsii*. St. Petersburg: 4-ia gos. tip., 1918.
Problemy sotsiologii iskusstva. Leningrad: Academia, 1926.
Punin, N. "Iskusstvo i proletariat," *Izobrazitel'noe iskusstvo*, no. 1 (1919), pp. 8–24.
———. "Kak moglo byt' inache?" *Iskusstvo kommuny*, 12 January 1919, p. 1.
Radlov, Sergei. "Massovye postanovki," *Zhizn' iskusstva*, 21–22 August 1920, p. 1.
———. "O massovykh deistvakh i veshchakh bolee vazhnykh," *Zhizn' iskusstva*, 19 February 1921, p. 1.
———. *Stat'i o teatre*. Petrograd: Mysl', 1923.
"Rezoliutsii Proletkul'tov o proletarskom teatra. Po dokladu V. M. Kerzhentseva," *Vestnik teatra*, no. 19 (1919), p. 4.
Rolland, Romain. *Le théâtre du peuple*. Paris: Suresnes, 1903. In Russian: *Narodnyi teatr*. Introduction by Viach. Ivanov. Petrograd-Moscow: Izd. TEO NKP, 1919.

Rousseau, Jean-Jacques. *Politics and the Arts: Letter to M. D'Alembert on the Theatre.* Translated by Allan Bloom. Glencoe, Ill.: Free Press, 1960.

Shapirshtein, Ia. (Lers) "Nashi prazdnestva," *Vestnik teatra,* no. 72–73 (1920), p. 2.

Shcheglov, D. "Praktika teatral'nogo dela," *Vneshkol'noe obrazovanie,* no. 6–8 (1919), pp. 43–45.

———. *Teatral'no-khudozhestvennaia rabota v klube. Praktika i metodika.* Leningrad: Gubprofsovet, 1926.

Shcheglov, Ivan. *V zashchitu narodnogo teatra.* St. Petersburg: V. Kirshbaum, 1903.

Shklovskii, Viktor. "Drama i massovye predstavleniia," *Zhizn' iskusstva,* 9 March 1921, p. 1.

———. "O psikhologicheskoi rampe," *Zhizn' iskusstva,* 7 May 1920, p. 1.

Slavianova, Z. M. *Raboche-krest'ianskii teatr.* Kazan: Gosizdat, 1921.

Smyshliaev, Val. "Massovyi teatr i iskusstvo," *Vestnik teatra,* no. 62 (1920), pp. 5–6.

———. "O massovom teatre," *Vestnik teatra,* no. 54 (1920), pp. 4–6.

———. "O nekotorykh teatral'nykh terminakh," *Vestnik teatra,* no. 51 (1920), pp. 4–5.

———. *Tekhnika obrabotki stsenicheskogo zrelishcha.* Moscow, 1922.

"Staroe i novoe iskusstvo," *Iskusstvo kommuny,* 5 January 1919, pp. 2–3.

T. "Polegche na povorotakh," *Vestnik teatra,* no. 60 (1920), p. 10.

Tairov, Aleksandr. *Notes of a Director.* Translated by William Kuhlke. Coral Gables, Fla.: University of Miami Press, 1969.

———. *Proklamatsiia khudozhnika.* Moscow: Shlugeit i Bronshtein, 1917.

Teatr: Kniga o novom teatre. St. Petersburg: Shipovnik, 1908.

Teatral'noe delo vneshkol'nika. Petrograd: GIZ, 1919.

Tiersot, Julien. *Les fêtes et les chants de la revolution française.* Paris: Hachette et cie, 1908. In Russian: *Prazdnestva i pesni frantsuzskoi revolutsii.* Translated by K. Zhikhareva. Petrograd: Izd. Parus, 1917. Also: Moscow, 1933, with a new introduction.

Tikhonovich, V. V. *Narodnyi teatr.* Moscow: Magusen, 1918.

———. "Priobshchenie i preodolenie," *Vestnik teatra,* no. 59 (1920), p. 3.

———. *Samodeiatel'nyi teatr.* Vologda: GIZ, 1922.

———. "Teatr i estetizatsiia zhizni. II." *Vestnik teatra,* no. 46–47 (1919).

Trotsky, Leon. *Problems of Everyday Life, and Other Writings on Culture & Science.* New York: Monad Press, 1973.

Trudy vserossiiskogo s"ezda deiatelei narodnogo teatra v Moskve, 27 dek. (1915)–5 ian. (1916). Petrograd, 1919.

V sporakh o teatre: Sbornik statei. Moscow: Kn——vo pisatelei, 1914.

"V studii tsirka," *Vestnik teatra,* no. 15 (1919), p. 7.

"Vozrozhdenie teatra," *Vestnik teatra,* no. 9 (1919), pp. 4–5.

Vsevolodskii-Gerngross, Vsevolod. "Deistvennoe iskusstvo," *Zhizn' iskusstva,* 11 March 1920, p. 2.

Wagner, Richard. *Prose Works.* Translated by William Ashton Ellis. London: Kegan Paul, Trench, Trübner & Co., 1895. In Russian: *Iskusstvo i revoliutsiia.* Petrograd: LITO Narkomprosa, 1918.

"Zadachi narodnogo teatra," *Novaia zhizn'*, 25 May 1917, p. 5.
Zagorskii, M. "Itogi teatral'nogo sezona," *Vestnik teatra*, no. 59 (1920), p. 9.
———. "Kak reagiruet zritel'," *Lef*, no. 2 (1924), pp. 141–51.
Z[agorskii], M. "Na dispute o teatre. Vpechatleniia," *Vestnik teatra*, no. 56 (1920), pp. 9–10.
———. "V sporakh o sovremennom i griadushchem teatre. Na mitinge iskusstv v tsirke," *Vestnik teatra*, no. 48 (1920), pp. 9–10.
Zhemchuzhnyi, V. *Kak organizovat' oktiabr'skuiu demonstratsiiu*. Moscow: Gosizdat, 1927.

EYEWITNESS ACCOUNTS OF RUSSIAN FESTIVALS

Alianskii, S. M. "Vstrechi s Blokom," *Novyi mir*, no. 6 (1967).
Andreeva, Mariia Fedorovna. *Perepiska, vospominaniia. Stat'i, dokumenty, vospominaniia o M. F. Andreevoi*. Moscow: Iskusstvo, 1961.
Annenkov, Iurii. *Dnevnik moikh vstrech*. New York: Inter-language Literary Associates, 1966.
Balabanoff, Angelica. *My Life as a Rebel*. New York: Harper, 1938.
Beatty, Bessie. *The Red Heart of Russia*. New York: Century, 1918.
Bekhterev, V. M. *Kollektivnaia refleksologiia*. Petrograd: Kolos, 1921.
Benois, Aleksandr. *Aleksandr Benua razmyshliaet*. Moscow: Sovetskii khudozhnik, 1968.
Benois, Alexandre. *Memoirs*. London: Chatto & Windus, 1960.
Berkman, Alexander. *The Bolshevik Myth*. New York: Boni and Liveright, 1925.
Bonch-Bruevich, V. D. *Vospominaniia o Lenine*. Moscow: Nauka, 1965.
Chagall, Marc. *My Life*. Translated by Elisabeth Abbott. New York: Orion Press, 1960.
Chekhov, M. A. *Put' aktera*. Leningrad: Academia, 1928.
Crosley, Pauline S. *Intimate Letters from Petrograd*. New York: E. P. Dutton, 1920.
Custine, Adolphe L. de. *A Journey for Our Time*. Chicago: H. Regnery, 1951.
Deich, A. I. *Golos pamiati*. Moscow: Iskusstvo, 1966.
Dukes, Paul. *Red Dusk and the Morrow*. New York: Doubleday, 1922.
Ehrenburg, Ilya. *People and Life, 1891–1921*. New York: Knopf, 1962.
Fülöp-Miller, René. *The Mind and Face of Bolshevism*. New York: Knopf, 1928.
Garvi, Peter A. *Zapiski Sotsial-Demokrata, 1906–1921*. Newtonville, Mass.: Oriental Research Partners, 1982.
Gievskii, N. N. "Iz teatral'nykh vospominanii," *Novyi zhurnal*, no. 10 (1945).
Goldman, Emma. *My Disillusionment in Russia*. New York: Doubleday, Page, 1923.
———. *My Further Disillusionment in Russia*. New York: Doubleday, Page, 1924.
Gordin, Morris. *Utopia in Chains*. Boston: Houghton Mifflin, 1926.

Harrison, Marguerite E. *Marooned in Moscow*. New York: George Doran, 1921.
Holitscher, Arthur. *Das Theater im revolutionären Russland*. Berlin: Volksbühnen Verlags, 1924.
———. *Drei Monat in Sowyet Russland*. Berlin: S. Fischer, 1921.
Houghteling, James L. *A Diary of the Russian Revolution*. New York: Dodd, Mead, 1918.
Karsavina, Tamara. *Theatre Street*. New York: E. P. Dutton, 1931.
Khodasevich, Valentina. "Gorod—teatr, narod—akter," *Dekorativnoe iskusstvo SSSR*, no. 11 (1979).
———. "Massovye deistva, zrelishcha i prazdniki," *Teatr*, no. 11 (1967).
Krupskaia, N. K. *O Lenine*. Moscow: Izd. politicheskoi literatury, 1965.
Lawton, Lancelot. *The Russian Revolution, 1917–1926*. London: Macmillan, 1927.
Lunacharskii, A. V. "Lenin i iskusstvo," *Khudozhnik i zritel'*, no. 2–3 (1924).
———. "Pervyi pervomaiskii prazdnik posle pobedy," *Krasnaia niva*, no. 18 (1926).
———. *Stat'i o teatre i dramaturgii*. Moscow: Iskusstvo, 1938.
———. *Vospominaniia i vpechatleniia*. Moscow: Sovetskaia Rossiia, 1968.
MacKenzie, Frederick. *Russia before Dawn*. London: T. F. Unwin, 1923.
Mal'kov, P. D. *Zapiski komendanta Moskovskogo Kremlia*. Moscow: Molodaia gvardiia, 1961.
Markov, Pavel. "Pervye gody," *Teatr*, no. 11 (1957).
McCullagh, Francis. *A Prisoner of the Reds*. London: J. Murray, 1921.
Mgebrov, A. A. *Zhizn' v teatre*. Leningrad: Academia, 1929–32.
Murphy, J. T. *New Horizons*. London: Bodley Head, 1942.
Nikulin, Lev. *Zapiski sputnika*. Moscow: Sovetskaia literatura, 1933.
Niurenberg, A. *Vospominaniia, vstrechi, mysli ob iskusstve*. Moscow: Sovetskii khudozhnik, 1969.
Petrov, Nikolai. "Massovye revoliutsionnye prazdnestva," *Teatr*, no. 8 (1957).
———. *50 i 500*. Moscow: VTO, 1960.
Radlov, S. E. *Desiat' let v teatre*. Leningrad: Priboi, 1929.
Rafalovich, V. E. *Vesna teatral'naia*. Leningrad: Iskusstvo, 1971.
Ransome, Arthur. *Six Weeks in Russia in 1919*. London: G. Allen & Unwin, 1919.
Reed, John. "Soviet Russia Now," *Liberator*, December 1920.
———. *Ten Days That Shook the World*. New York: Boni and Liveright, 1919.
Reswick, William. *I Dreamt Revolution*. Chicago: H. Regnery, 1932.
Roshal', G. *Kinolenta zhizni*. Moscow: Iskusstvo, 1974.
Rosmer, Alfred. *Moscow under Lenin*. Translated by Ian H. Birchall. New York: Monthly Review Press, 1972.
Rubin, Jacob H. *Moscow Mirage*. London: G. Bles, 1934.
Saylor, Oliver. "Futurists and Others in Famished Moscow: Radical Artists Find New Manners of Expression amid Social Chaos," *Vanity Fair*, September 1919.

Schneider, I. I. *Isadora Duncan, the Russian Years*. New York: Harcourt, Brace & World, 1968.
Shklovskii, Viktor. *Khod konia*. Berlin: Helikon, 1923.
———. *Mayakovsky and His Circle*. Translated by Lily Feiler. New York: Dodd, Mead, 1972.
———. *Zhili-byli*. Moscow: Sovetskii pisatel', 1964.
Sisson, Edgar G. *100 Red Days*. New Haven, Conn.: Yale University Press, 1931.
Smolich, Iu. *Teatr neizvestnogo aktera*. Moscow: Sovetskii pisatel', 1957.
Snowdon, Mrs. Philip. *Through Bolshevik Russia*. London: Cassell, 1920.
Sorokin, Pitirim. *Leaves from a Russian Diary*. London: Hurst & Blackett, 1924.
Spasskii, Iu. "Pervye zrelishcha krasnoi Ukrainy," *Novyi zritel'*, no. 45 (1927).
Spektakl', zvavshii v boi. Kiev: Mistetstvo, 1970.
Tiomkin, Dimitri, and Prosper Buranelli. *Please Don't Hate Me*. Garden City, N.Y.: Doubleday, 1959.
U istokov. Moscow: VTO, 1960.
Vchera i segodnia. Moscow: Khudozh. literatura, 1960.
Vinogradov-Mamont, N. G. *Krasnoarmeiskoe chudo*. Leningrad: Iskusstvo, 1972.
Vishnevskii, Vsevolod. "20-letie sovetskoi dramaturgii," *Sovetskie dramaturgi o svoem tvorchestve*. Moscow: Iskusstvo, 1967.
Volkov, N. D. *Teatral'nye vechera*. Moscow: Iskusstvo, 1966.
Wells, H. G. *Russia in the Shadows*. London: Hodder & Stoughton, 1920.
Wickstead, Alexander. *Life under the Soviets*. London: John Lane, 1928.
Zelenaia ptichka. Petrograd: Petropolis, 1922.
Zetkin, Clara. *Reminiscences of Lenin*. New York: International Publishers, 1934.

CONTEMPORARY PRESS REPORTS

Prerevolutionary

Dimanshtein, S. "Pervoe maia na katorge. Vospominaniia," *Krasnaia gazeta*, 3 May 1919, p. 2.
Meierkhol'd, V. E. "Voina i teatr," *Birzhevye vedomosti* (evening edition), 11 September 1914, p. 4.
Meierkhol'd, V. E., and Iu. M. Bondi. "Ogon'," *Liubov' k trem apel'sinam*, no. 6–7 (1914).
"Pervoe maia," *Izvestiia Petrogradskogo soveta*, 1 May 1918, p. 1.
Pervoe maia v tsarskoi Rossii, 1890–1916 gg.: Sbornik dokumentov. Moscow: OGIZ, 1939.
Shishkov, Viach. "Maevka. Kartinka proshlogo," *Novaia zhizn'*, 20 April 1917, p. 4.
"Teatr A. S. Suvorina," *Teatr i iskusstvo*, 17 August 1914, p. 678.
Vasilich, V. "Dvadtsat' piat' let. Po arkhivnym materialam," *Vechernie izvestiia Moskovskogo soveta*, 30 April 1919, p. 1.

February to October 1917

Benois, Aleksandr. "Vykhod iskusstva na ulitsu," *Novaia zhizn'*, 4 June 1917, p. 3.
"Deiateli iskusstv 'Zaimu svobody,' " *Russkaia volia*, 25 May 1917, p. 5.
D[esnitskii], V. "Eshche ne pozdno!" *Novaia zhizn'*, 21 April 1917, p. 2.
Desnitskii, V. "Nash prazdnik," *Novaia zhizn'*, 18 April 1917, p. 5.
G., I. "1 Maia 1917 g.," *Novaia zhizn'*, 20 April 1917, p. 1.
Gor'kii, M. 'Na ulitse. Vpechatleniia," *Novaia* zhizn', 20 April 1917, p. 1.
"Khronika," *Put' osvobozhdenia*, no. 4 (1917), p. 21.
"Khronika," *Teatr i iskusstvo*, 28 May 1917, p. 373.
"Kreshchenie revoliutsii. Severnoe skazanie," *Put' osvobozhdeniia*, 20 August 1917, p. 5.
[Kugel', A.] Homo Novus. "Zametki," *Teatr i iskusstvo*, 4 June 1917, pp. 396–400.
Lebedev, Mikh. "V den' krasnogo prazdnika. Nabliudeniia," *Novaia zhizn'*, 20 April 1917, p. 1.
L——v. "Teatr i muzyka. Teatr na ulitse," *Rech'*, 30 May 1917, p. 7.
Meierkhol'd, Vsevolod. "Da zdravstvuet zhongler!" *Ekho tsirka*, 14 August 1917, p. 3.
Morskoi, Nikolai. "Dalekoe proshloe," *Tsirk i èstrada*, no. 16 [48] (1928), p. 3.
Pasternak, Boris. "Vesennii dozhd'," *Put' osvobozhdeniia*, 1 October 1917, p. 4 [verse].
R[ostislavo]v, A. "Den' zaima svobody," *Rech'*, 25 May 1917, p. 5.
———. "Den' zaima svobody," *Rech'*, 26 May 1917, p. 6.
Rostislavov, A. "Revoliutsiia i khudozhestvennaia zhizn'," *Rech'*, 26 May 1917, p. 3.
Serebrov, A. "Pust' veiut znamena," *Novaia zhizn'*, 18 April 1917, p. 1.
"Sgorevshii gruzovik 'Zaima svobody,' " *Novaia zhizn'*, 27 May 1917, p. 4.
Sh., A. "Dva shestviia. Iz vospominanii," *Revoliutsionnye vskhody*, no. 5–6 (1920), pp. 6–7.
Sil'vin, M. "Proizkhozhdenie prazdnika," *Novaia zhizn'*, 18 April 1917, p. 1.
"Teatr na ulitse," *Rech'*, 30 May 1917, p. 7.
"V Bol'shom teatre i v derevne," *Novaia zhizn'*, 14 June 1917, p. 1.
"V provintsii," *Novaia zhizn'*, 20 April 1917, p. 1.
[Vengrov, N.] "Pervoe maia," *Novaia zhizn'*, 18 April 1917, p. 1.
Vo imia svobody. Odnodnevnaia gazeta. Petrograd: Soiuz deiatelei iskusstva, 25 May 1917. Includes: V. Leont'ev, "Chto dast russkomu narodu pobeda?"; Anna Akhmatova, "Pamiati 19 iiulia 1914 g."; Fedor Sologub, "Dovol'no likovat' "; Leonid Andreev, "Puti spaseniia"; Teffi, "Ob Ivane Polikarpoviche i Ruble kopeechnom"; Lidiia Lesnaia, "Pis'mo s fronta"; Arkadii Averchenko, "Umnyi medved' "; Aleksei Remizov, "Dar Rysi. Ot egipetskogo mesaika"; Igor Severianin, "Vse—kak odin"; G. V. Plekhanov, "Byt' ili ne byt'?"; Iurii Verkhovskii, "Lazar' "; T. Shchepkina-Kupernik, "K Rossii"; P. Miliukov, "Grazhdanskii ekzamen"; V. Khlebnikov, "Son"; Nina Karatygina, "Khotite-li vystroit' Novuiu Rus' ";

A. Chebotarevskaia, "Kogda zhe nakonets?"; Sasha Chernyi, "Zaem svobody"; S. Esenin, "Est' svetlaia radost' pod sen'iu kustov"; Grig. Petnikov, "Strane."

May Day 1918

"Anarkhisty o prazdnovanii pervogo maia," *Izvestiia Petrogradskogo soveta*, 1 May 1918, p. 6.
Annenkov, Iurii. "Pis'mo v redaktsiiu. O sverzhenii 1 Maia pamiatnikov," *Delo naroda*, 24 April 1918, p. 1.
Arkhangel'skii, V. "Sudnyi den'," *Delo naroda*, 1 May 1918, p. 1.
Arskii, Pavel. "Gimn," *Plamia*, 12 May 1918, p. 7 [verse].
"Aviatsionnaia katastrofa," *Novaia zhizn'*, 3 May 1918, p. 3.
Berg, E. "K 1 Maia," *Delo naroda*, 1 May 1918, p. 1.
Bessal'ko, P. "Tsvety Pervomaia," *Plamia*, 1 May 1918, pp. 4–5 [fiction].
Briusov, Valerii. "Pered maem," *Novaia zhizn'*, 4 May 1918, p. 1.
"Burzhua 1 Maia," *Izvestiia Petrogradskogo soveta*, 4 May 1918, p. 1.
Bystrianskii, V. "Internatsional i 1 Maia," *Plamia*, 1 May 1918, pp. 8–10.
Chadaev, V. "Pervoe maia v Petrograde. Vpechatleniia," *Petrogradskaia pravda*, 3 May 1918, p. 3.
"Chrezvychainoe sobranie upolnomochennykh fabrik i zavodov Petrograda," *Delo naroda*, 30 April 1918, p. 4.
"Chudo na Krasnoi Ploshchadi," *Izvestiia Petrogradskogo soveta*, 3 May 1918, p. 4.
"Den' futurizma i krasnoarmeistva," *Delo naroda*, 3 May 1918, p. 2.
Dobuzhinskii, M. "Bomba ili khlopushka? Beseda dvukh khudozhnikov," *Novaia zhizn'*, 4 May 1918, p. 3.
Donskoi, D. "Khleba i zrelishch. K demonstratsii 1-go Maia," *Delo naroda*, 26 April 1918, p. 1.
[Editorial]. *Voronezhskii telegraf*, 1 May 1918, p. 2.
Il'in, Il'ia. "Pervoe maia," *Plamia*, 1 May 1918, p. 4 [verse].
Ivnev, Riurik. "Vechnoe sluzhenie," *Plamia*, 1 May 1918, pp. 11–13 [fiction].
"Iz Moskvy," *Izvestiia Petrogradskogo soveta*, 3 May 1918, p. 3.
K——. "Pervoe maia. Vpechatleniia ochevidtsa," *Izvestiia Petrogradskogo soveta*, 4 May 1918, pp. 1–2.
"K pervomu maia," *Izvestiia Petrogradskogo soveta*, 28 April 1918, p. 4.
"K pervomu maia," *Izvestiia Petrogradskogo soveta*, 30 April 1918, p. 4.
K——v. "Detskaia manifestatsiia," *Izvestiia Petrogradskogo soveta*, 4 May 1918, p. 2.
"Katastrofa s aeroplanom," *Delo naroda*, 3 May 1918, p. 2.
Kern, N. "Otkrytie dvortsa Proletarskoi kul'tury," *Petrogradskaia pravda*, 3 May 1918, p. 3.
[Kozlinskii, V., V. Lebedev, S. Makletsov, Iv. Puni, Baranov-Rossine, and K. Boguslavskaia]. "Pis'mo v redaktsiiu," *Delo naroda*, 30 April 1918, p. 2.
Kun, Bela. "Dva pervykh maia," *Pravda*, 1 May 1918, p. 1.
Kuzmin, N. "Novaia era," *Petrogradskaia pravda*, 3 May 1918, p. 1.

L., E. "Na ulitsakh," *Delo naroda*, 3 May 1918, p. 2.
L——o, V. "Na ulitsakh pervogo maia," *Voronezhskii telegraf*, 3 May 1918, p. 3.
Laganskii, E. "Zamakhnulis'. Na Isaakevskoi pl.," *Delo naroda*, 28 April 1918, p. 3.
Levidov, M. "Fakty i nastroeniia. Pis'mo iz Moskvy," *Novaia zhizn'*, 8 May 1918, p. 2.
Lunacharskii, A. "Monumental'naia agitatsiia," *Plamia*, 14 July 1918, p. 14.
Lunacharskii, A. V. "Pervoe maia 1918 goda. Eskizy iz zapisnoi knizhki," *Plamia*, 12 May 1918, pp. 2–4.
M., A. "Pervoe maia v Samare," *Nasha zhizn'*, 13 May 1918, p. 2.
Mgeladze, Il. "Togda i teper'," *Petrogradskaia pravda*, 3 May 1918, p. 1.
"Moskva," *Delo naroda*, 30 April 1918, p. 3.
"Moskva," *Delo naroda*, 3 May 1918, p. 2.
"Moskva bez khleba," *Petrogradskaia pravda*, 4 May 1918, p. 5.
"Na Putilovskom zavode," *Delo naroda*, 30 April 1918, p. 4.
"Obukhovskii zavod," *Delo naroda*, 1 May 1918, p. 4.
"Obzor pechati. Posle pervogo maia," *Novaia zhizn'*, 4 May 1918, p. 1.
"Ot organizatsionnoi kommissii po ustroistvu prazdnestv 1 Maia," *Izvestiia Petrogradskogo soveta*, 30 April 1918, p. 1.
"Ot tsentral'noi upravy Petrogradskogo prodovol'stvennogo soveta," *Delo naroda*, 1 May 1918, p. 1.
"Otkrytie dvortsa proletarskoi kul'tury," *Izvestiia Petrogradskogo soveta*, 3 May 1918, p. 5.
"Pamiatnik Razinu," *Delo naroda*, 13 May 1918, p. 3.
"Paskhal'naia torgovlia," *Izvestiia Petrogradskogo soveta*, 26 April 1918, p. 1.
"Pered pervym maia," *Delo naroda*, 27 April 1918, p. 4.
"Pered pervym maia," *Delo naroda*, 28 April 1918, p. 1.
"Pered pervym maia," *Delo naroda*, 1 May 1918, p. 4.
"Pervoe maia," *Izvestiia Petrogradskogo soveta*, 3 May 1918, p. 2.
"Pervoe maia," *Novaia zhizn'*, 1 May 1918, p. 1.
"Pervoe maia," *Novaia zhizn'*, 3 May 1918, p. 3.
"Pervoe maia i agenty burzhuazii sredi proletariata," *Izvestiia Petrogradskogo soveta*, 27 April 1918, p. 2.
"Pervoe maia—prazdnik Tret'ego Internatsionala," *Petrogradskaia pravda*, 1 May 1918, p. 1.
"Pervoe maia v Moskve," *Petrogradskaia pravda*, 3 May 1918, p. 4.
"Pervoe maia v provintsii," *Petrogradskaia pravda*, 3 May 1918, p. 4.
"Pervoe maia 1918 goda," *Delo naroda*, 3 May 1918, p. 2.
"Pervomaiskii prazdnik," *Izvestiia Petrogradskogo soveta*, 3 May 1918, p. 4.
"Pervomaiskii privet iz Voronezha," *Izvestiia Petrogradskogo soveta*, 4 May 1918, p. 2.
"1 Maia 1917 g.—1 Maia 1918 g.," *Novaia zhizn'*, 1 May 1918, p. 1.
"Petrograd," *Izvestiia Tsentral'nogo ispolnitel'nogo komiteta*, 1 May 1918, p. 2.
"Petrograd 1-e Maia," *Pravda*, 4 May 1918, p. 4.
"Podrobnosti pogroma v Vitebske," *Novaia zhizn'*, 4 May 1918, p. 3.
"Posle 1 Maia," *Delo naroda*, 3 May 1918, p. 1.

"Prazdniki Revoliutsii," *Izvestiia Petrogradskogo soveta*. 3 May 1918, p. 1.
"Prazdnovanie Paskhi," *Izvestiia Petrogradskogo soveta*, 1 May 1918, p. 6.
"Prazdnovanie pervogo maia," *Novaia zhizn'*, 1 May 1918, p. 2.
"Prazdnovanie pervogo maia," *Voronezhskii telegraf*, 3 May 1918, p. 3.
"Prazdnovanie pervogo maia v pervom gorodskom raione. Kontsert-miting v klube III Internatsionala," *Izvestiia Petrogradskogo soveta*, 4 May 1918, p. 2.
"Prigotovleniia k prazdnestvu pervogo maia," *Delo naroda*, 27 April 1918, p. 3.
"Proshedshii prazdnik," *Petrogradskaia pravda*, 3 May 1918, p. 1.
"Rabochaia zhizn'," *Delo naroda*, 30 April 1918, p. 4.
"Rabochaia zhizn'," *Delo naroda*, 1 May 1918, p. 4.
"Rabochie i manifestatsiia," *Novaia zhizn'*, 3 May 1918, p. 3.
Rakhmanov, N. "Traur Internatsionala," *Delo naroda*, 1 May 1918, pp. 1–2.
Rakov, D. "Golod," *Delo naroda*, 4 May 1918, p. 1.
S., D. "God nazad," *Delo naroda*, 3 May 1918, p. 2.
Samoilova, K. "Pervomaiskii prazdnik i proletarskaia kul'tura," *Petrogradskaia pravda*, 1 May 1918, p. 2.
Shurupov, G. No title, *Delo naroda*, 3 May 1918, p. 2.
S[oro]kin, Vas. "Pervoe maia v proletarskikh stikhotvoreniiakh," *Petrogradskaia pravda*, 1 May 1918, p. 2.
Spavskii, Veniamin. "Tserkov' i pervoe maia," *Izvestiia Petrogradskogo soveta*, 1 May 1918, p. 4.
"Strel'ba na Nevskom," *Delo naroda*, 3 May 1918, p. 2.
Stroev, V. "Parad," *Novaia zhizn'*, 3 May 1918, p. 1.
"Telegrammy," *Izvestiia Petrogradskogo soveta*, 4 May 1918, p. 3.
"Tseremonial shestviia po ulitsam demonstratsii g. Petrograda 1-go Maia 1918 g.," *Izvestiia Petrogradskogo soveta*, 30 April 1918, p. 1.
"V rabochikh raionakh," *Delo naroda*, 3 May 1918, p. 2.

November 7, 1918

"Attila," *Teatral'nyi kur'er*, 16 October 1918, p. 5.
Babel. "Na Dvortsovoi Ploshchadi," *Zhizn' iskusstva*, 11 November 1918, p. 4.
Barabanov, N. "Kartiny oktiabr'skikh prazdnestv," *Vestnik zhizni*, no. 3–4 (1919), pp. 116–120.
"Biusty i portrety vozhdei proletariata," *Krasnaia gazeta*, 30 October 1918.
"Biusty i portrety vozhdei proletariata," *Zhizn' iskusstva*, 29 October 1918, p. 7.
"Bol'shoi teatr," *Teatral'nyi kur'er*, 17 October 1918, p. 4.
Dashkov, Leonid. "Na prazdnestve revoliutsii," *Rabochii mir*, 24 November 1918, pp. 30–33.
"Godovshchina revoliutsii. Zasedanie Kostromskogo komiteta po organizatsii prazdnovaniia oktiabr'skoi revoliutsii," *Severnyi rabochii* (Kostroma), 4 November 1918.
"Grandioznoe zrelishche," *Teatral'nyi kur'er*, 29 October 1918, p. 2.

"Iz Moskvy," *Severnaia kommuna*, 5 November 1918, p. 3.
"K godovshchine oktiabr'skoi revoliutsii," *Izvestiia Tsentral'nogo ispolnitel'nogo komiteta*, 6 October 1918.
"K godovshchine revoliutsii. Otdel IZO Narkomprosa," *Vechernie izvestiia Moskovskogo soveta*, 20 October 1918.
"K oktiabr'skim torzhestvam," *Krasnaia armiia*, 16 October 1918.
"K oktiabr'skim torzhestvam," *Krasnaia gazeta*, 25 October 1918.
"K oktiabr'skim torzhestvam," *Pravda*, 24 October 1918.
"K oktiabr'skim torzhestvam," *Teatral'nyi kur'er*, 13–14 October 1918, p. 4.
"K oktiabr'skim torzhestvam," *Volia truda*, 24 October 1918.
"K oktiabr'skim torzhestvam," *Zhizn' iskusstva*, 30 October 1918, p. 5.
"K oktiabr'skim torzhestvam," *Zhizn' iskusstva*, 31 October 1918, p. 5.
"K oktiabr'skim torzhestvam," *Zhizn' iskusstva*, 1 November 1918, p. 4.
"K oktiabr'skim torzhestvam," *Zhizn' iskusstva*, 2 November 1918, p. 5.
"K oktiabr'skim torzhestvam," *Zhizn' iskusstva*, 4 November 1918, p. 2.
"K oktiabr'skim torzhestvam," *Zhizn' iskusstva*, 5 November 1918, p. 4.
"K oktiabr'skim torzhestvam," *Zhizn' iskusstva*, 6 November 1918, p. 3.
"K oktiabr'skim torzhestvam," *Voronezhskii krasnyi listok*, 19 October 1918, p. 4.
"K oktiabr'skoi godovshchine," *Izvestiia Olonetskogo ispolkoma*, 15 October 1918.
"K oktiabr'skomu prazdnestvu," *Teatral'nyi kur'er*, 8 October 1918, p. 3.
"K prazdniku oktiabr'skoi revoliutsii," *Pravda*, 20 October 1918.
"K prazdniku revoliutsii," *Golos trudovogo krest'ianstva*, 2 November 1918.
"K prazdniku revoliutsii," *Izvestiia Tsentral'nogo ispolnitel'nogo komiteta*, 25 October 1918.
"K prazdniku revoliutsii," *Pravda*, 24 October 1918.
"K prazdniku revoliutsii," *Vechernie izvestiia Moskovskogo soveta*, 26 September 1918, p. 3.
"K prazdnovaniiu godovshchiny oktiabr'skoi revoliutsii," *Izvestiia Tsentral'nogo ispolnitel'nogo komiteta*, 5 November 1918, p. 3.
"K prazdnovaniiu godovshchiny oktiabr'skoi revoliutsii," *Pravda*, 1 November 1918, p. 3.
"K prazdnovaniiu godovshchiny oktiabr'skoi revoliutsii," *Pravda*, 6 November 1918, p. 4.
"K prazdnovaniiu godovshchiny revoliutsii," *Izvestiia Tsentral'nogo ispolnitel'nogo komiteta*, 13 October 1918.
"K prazdnovaniiu oktiabr'skoi revoliutsii," *Golos trudovoi kommuny*, 16 October 1918.
"K prazdnovaniiu velikoi godovshchiny," *Krasnaia gazeta*, 1 November 1918.
"K proletarskoi Paskhe," *Kommunar*, 31 October 1918.
"K sniatiiu pamiatnika Nikolaiu Nikolaevichu," *Zhizn' iskusstva*, 15 November 1918, p. 4.
"Kamernyi teatr," *Teatral'nyi kur'er*, 24 October 1918, p. 3.
Khersonskaia, E. "O novom tvorchestve. Iz dnevnika liubitelia iskusstv," *Iskusstvo*, no. 6 [10] (1918), pp. 12–13.

"Khronika," *Vremennik teatral'nogo otdela*, no. 1 (1918).
"Khronika," *Zhizn' iskusstva*, 11 November 1918, p. 5.
Kirillov, Vladimir. "Dvenadstat' mesiatsev," *Plamia*, 7 November 1918, p. 10.
Kliuev, Nikolai. "Tovarishch," *Plamia*, 7 November 1918, p. 2 [verse].
Knyshov, P. "O pamiatnikakh oktiabr'skoi revoliutsii," *Vechernie izvestiia Moskovskogo soveta*, 16 October 1918.
Krainyi, Konstantin. "Khudozhestvennye itogi oktiabr'skogo prazdnestva. Oktiabr' 1917 g.–okt. 1918 g.," *Vestnik zhizni*, no. 3–4 (1919), pp. 120–22.
Kremnev, I. "7 noiabria," *Rabochii mir*, 24 November 1918, pp. 33–34.
Kudelli, P. "Kak gotoviatsia kluby k oktiabr'skim prazdnestvam," *Petrogradskaia pravda*, 13 October 1918.
"Kuznetsy kommunizma," *Kommunar*, 1 November 1918.
Levinson, A. "Misteriia-Buff Maiakovskogo," *Zhizn' iskusstva*, 11 November 1918, p. 2.
"Liubopytnoe izobretenie," *Zhizn' iskusstva*, 29 October 1918, p. 7.
Lunacharskii, A. V. "Velikaia godovshchina," *Plamia*, 7 November 1918, pp. 3–4.
Malinin, K. "V teatrakh," *Rabochii mir*, 24 November 1918, pp. 37–39.
Mashkovtsev, N. "God revoliutsii i iskusstvo," *Rabochii mir*, 7 November 1918, pp. 48–52.
———. "Pervaia vsenarodnaia vystavka," *Rabochii mir*, 24 November 1918, pp. 34–36.
Maiakovskii, Vladimir. "Oda Revoliutsii," *Plamia*, 7 November 1918, p. 11 [verse].
Mikhailov, Z. "Ostavit' pamiatnik zhandarmskomu tsariu," *Zhizn' iskusstva*, 1 November 1918, p. 5.
"Misteriia-Buff Maiakovskogo," *Teatral'nyi kur'er*, 16 October 1918, p. 5.
"Misteriia-Buff Maiakovskogo," *Zhizn' iskusstva*, 29 October 1918, p. 4.
"Muzeinyi material oktiabr'skikh torzhestv," *Teatral'nyi kur'er*, 11 October 1918, p. 3.
"Na Krasnoi Ploshchadi," *Vestnik zhizni*, no. 3–4 (1919), p. 118.
"Na otkrytii pamiatnikov," *Izvestiia Tsentral'nogo ispolnitel'nogo komiteta*, 5 November 1918, p. 5.
"Na torzhestve godovshchiny oktiabr'skoi revoliutsii v Kazani," *Znamia revoliutsii* (Kazan), 10 November 1918.
"Nakanune prazdnestv," *Teatral'nyi kur'er*, 25 October 1918, p. 3.
"Nesposobnost' ili nezhelaniia? K oktiabr'skim torzhestvam," *Vechernie izvestiia Moskovskogo soveta*, 16 October 1918.
"O deiatel'nosti kinokomiteta," *Zhizn' iskusstva*, 22 November 1918, p. 5.
"Obshchie raskhody po organizatsii oktiabr'skikh prazdnestv," *Krasnaia gazeta*, 16 October 1918.
Oktiabr' 1917–1918. Geroi i zhertvy Oktiabria. Petrograd: IZO Narkomprosa, 1918.
"Oktiabr'skie dni v Moskve," *Zhizn' iskusstva*, 9 November 1918, p. 2.

"Oktiabr'skie prazdnestva," *Golos trudovogo krest'ianstva,* no. 246 (1918).
"Oktiabr'skie torzhestva," *Teatral'nyi kur'er,* 11 October 1918, p. 3.
"Oktiabr'skii kulich," *Kommunar,* 13 October 1918.
"Opera S.R.D.," *Teatral'nyi kur'er,* 12–14 November 1918, pp. 2–3.
"Ot komiteta po prazdnovaniiu godovshchiny oktiabr'skoi revoliutsii," *Voronezhskii krasnyi listok,* 6 November 1918, pp. 5–6.
"Ot likvidatsionno-material'noi komissii pri tsentral'nom biuro po organizatsii prazdnestv godovshchiny oktiabr'skoi revoliutsii," *Zhizn' iskusstva,* 16 November 1918, p. 2.
"Ot tsentral'nogo biuro po organizatsii prazdnestva v godovshchiny oktiabr'skoi revoliutsii," *Zhizn' iskusstva,* 1 November 1918, p. 2.
"Ot tsentral'nogo biuro po organizatsii prazdnestva v godovshchiny oktiabr'skoi revoliutsii," *Zhizn' iskusstva,* 6 November 1918, p. 2.
"Ot tsentral'nogo biuro po ustroistvu oktiabr'skikh prazdnestv," *Severnaia kommuna,* 6 November 1918, p. 1.
"Otkrytie pamiatnika Karlu Marksu," *Zhizn' iskusstva,* 6 November 1918, p. 2.
"Otkrytie pamiatnikov," *Severnaia kommuna,* 5 November 1918, p. 3.
P., E. "Sozhzhenie kulaka," *Bednota,* 8 November 1918.
"Pereimenovanie ulits," *Severnaia kommuna,* 13 November 1918, p. 5.
"Podgotovitel'nye raboty," *Severnaia kommuna,* 26 October 1918.
Poletaev, Nikolai. "Krasnaia Ploshchad'. 7 noiabria 1918 g.," *Gorn,* no. 2–3 (1919), p. 3 [verse].
———. "Tri lika," *Gorn,* no. 4 (1919), pp. 17–18.
"Prazdnik oktiabr'skoi revoliutsii," *Izvestiia Tsentral'nogo ispolnitel'nogo komiteta,* 9 November 1918, p. 5.
"Prazdnik proletarskikh detei," *Severnaia kommuna,* 12 November 1918, pp. 3–4.
"Prazdnik Velikogo Obnovleniia," *Pravda,* 9 November 1918, p. 3.
"Prazdnovanie godovshchiny oktiabr'skoi revoliutsii na st. Kipelovo," *Izvestiia Vologodskogo gubernskogo ispolkoma sovetov RiKD,* 1 December 1918, p. 3.
"Prigotovleniia k oktiabr'skim prazdnestvam," *Izvestiia Tsentral'nogo ispolnitel'nogo komiteta,* 23 October 1918.
"Prikaz komiteta po ustroistvu oktiabr'skikh torzhestv," *Isvestiia Tsentral'nogo ispolnitel'nogo komiteta,* 5 November 1918, p. 4.
"Proletarskii prazdnik," *Znamia revoliutsii* (Kazan), 10 November 1918.
Pumpianskii, Lev. "Oktiabr'skie torzhestva i khudozhniki Petrograda," *Plamia,* 5 January 1919, pp. 11–16.
P[unin], N. "K itogam oktiabr'skikh torzhestv," *Iskusstvo kommuny,* 7 December 1918.
Punin, N. "O 'Misterii-Buff' Vl. Maiakovskogo," *Iskusstvo kommuny,* 15 December 1918, pp. 2–3.
Rodov, Semen. "Prazdnik Ery," *Gorn,* no. 2–3 (1919), pp. 121–22.
Shagal [Chagall], Mark. "Pis'mo iz Vitebska," *Iskusstvo kommuny,* 22 December 1918.

"Shestvie detei v dni prazdnikov," *Zhizn' iskusstva*, 9 November 1918, p. 3.
Smyshliaev, V. "Opyt instsenirovki stikhotvoreniia Verkharna 'Vosstaniia,' " *Gorn*, no. 2–3 (1919), pp. 82–90.
Sobolev, Iurii. "Sten'ka Razin," *Teatral'nyi kur'er*, 12–14 November 1918, p. 3.
"Soveshchanie Severo-Dvinskoi gubernskoi komissii po ustroistvu prazdnika oktiabr'skoi revoliutsii ot 1-go okt 1916 [sic] goda," *Krest'ianskie i rabochie dumy*, 6 October 1918.
"Teatr v oktiabr'skie torzhestva. Bol'shoi teatr," *Teatral'nyi kur'er*, 12–14 November 1918, pp. 2–3.
"Teatry i zrelishcha v Peterburge i na fronte," *Zhizn' iskusstva*, 29 October 1918, p. 7.
"Tsentral'noe biuro po organizatsii prazdnestv godovshchiny oktiabr'skoi revoliutsii," *Zhizn' iskusstva*, 29 October 1918, p. 1.
"Tseremonial prazdnovaniia godovshchiny oktiabr'skoi revoliutsii," *Severnaia kommuna*, 6 November 1918, p. 1.
Turchaninov. "Pervyi publichnyi vecher Moskovskogo Proletkul'ta," *Gorn*, no. 2–3 (1919), pp. 128–129.
"Ubranstvo Marsova Polia," *Severnaia kommuna*, 24 October 1918.
"Ukrashenie Petrograda," *Zhizn' iskusstva*, 9 November 1918, p. 2.
"Unichtozhenie pamiatnika Robesp'eru," *Severnaia kommuna*, 10 November 1918, p. 3.
"Unichtozhenie pamiatnika Robesp'eru," *Zhizn' iskusstva*, 9 November 1918, p. 3.
"Uvekovechenie pamiati tov. Lenina," *Pravda*, 3 November 1918.
"Uvekovechenie ubranstva krasnogo Peterburga," *Zhizn' iskusstva*, 14 November 1918, p. 3.
"V Astrakhane," *Pravda*, 9 November 1918, p. 4.
"V komitete po ustroistvu prazdnestv v godovshchinu oktiabr'skoi revoliutsii," *Voronezhskii krasnyi listok*, 16 October 1918, p. 4.
"V provintsii," *Izvestiia Tsentral'nogo ispolnitel'nogo komiteta*, 26 October 1918.
"V teatrakh. Opera S.R.D.," *Izvestiia Tsentral'nogo ispolnitel'nogo komiteta*, 9 November 1918, p. 5.
"V Ustiug," *Izvestiia Vologodskogo gubernskogo ispolkoma sovetov RiKD*, 30 October 1918, p. 4.
"Vecher Proletkul'ta," *Izvestiia Tsentral'nogo ispolnitel'nogo komiteta*, 9 November 1918, p. 5.
"Velikaia godovshchina," *Severnaia kommuna*, 23 October 1918.
"Velikaia godovshchina," *Severnaia kommuna*, 3 November 1918, p. 5.
"Velikaia godovshchina. Ob"iazatel'nye postanovleniia tsentral'nogo biuro po organizatsii prazdnestv godovshchiny oktiabr'skoi revoliutsii," *Severnaia kommuna*, 1 November 1918, p. 4.
Volkov, N. "Krasnaia Moskva," *Gorn*, no. 2–3 (1919), p. 123.
"Zasedanie komiteta po ustroistvu prazdnestv v godovshchinu revoliutsii," *Voronezhskii krasnyi listok*, 19 October 1918, p. 4.

Miscellaneous 1918

"Agitatsionnye pamiatniki i otnoshenie k nim soiuza skul'ptorov," *Izobrazitel'noe iskusstvo*, no. 1 (1919), pp. 71–72.
[Brik, O. M., and V. Maiakovskii]. "Letuchii teatr," *Iskusstvo kommuny*, 15 December 1918, p. 3.
Kerzhentsev, P. M. "Iskusstvo na ulitsu," *Iskusstvo*, no. 3 (1918), p. 12.
"Khronika," *Iskusstvo*, no. 2 [6] (1918), pp. 15–16.
"Khronika," *Iskusstvo*, no. 6 [10] (1918), p. 18.
Krivtsov, St. "Novye pamiatniki," *Iskusstvo*, no. 6 [10] (1918), pp. 7–9.
Kuzmin, M. "Tsar' Edip," *Zhizn' iskusstva*, 14 November 1918, p. 3.
"Liubov' i zoloto. Beseda s S. E. Radlovym," *Zhizn' iskusstva*, 26 January 1921, p. 1.
Ol'sen. "Otkliki," *Voronezhskii telegraf*, 4 May 1918, p. 3.
"Pod otkrytym nebom," *Zhizn' iskusstva*, 27 November 1918, p. 5.
Shterenburg, D. P. "Otchet o deiatel'nosti Otdela Izobrazitel'nykh Iskusstv Narkomprosa," *Izobrazitel'noe iskusstvo*, no. 1 (1919), pp. 50–87.
"Teatr-Studiia," *Zhizn' iskusstva*, 16 November 1918, p. 4.

The Futurist Controversy, 1918–19

Brik, O. M. "Nalet na futurizm," *Iskusstvo kommuny*, 9 February 1919, p. 3.
"Druzheskoe," *Vechernie izvestiia Moskovskogo soveta*, 21 February 1919, p. 3.
Evgen'ev, A. "Futuristicheskaia gekuba i proletariat," *Vestnik literatury*, no. 10 (1919), pp. 4–5.
Friche, V. "Literaturnoe odichanie," *Vechernie izvestiia Moskovskogo soveta*, 15 February 1919, p. 1.
———. "Tsitadel' svobodnogo tvorchestva," *Vechernie izvestiia Moskovskogo soveta*, 28 February 1919, p. 1.
Ianov, Gen. "Stil' revoliutsii," *Vestnik teatra*, no. 41 (1919), pp. 5–6.
K., En. [M. F. Andreeva] "Neudachnyi debiut," *Zhizn' iskusstva*, 6 March 1919, p. 2.
Khersonskaia, E. "Iz tovarishcheskikh besed o zhivopisi," *Gorn*, no. 2–3 (1919), pp. 94–95.
Kriazhin, V. "Futurizm i revoliutsiia," *Vestnik zhizni*, no. 6–7 (1919), pp. 71–79.
Levidov, Mikh. "Kto nasledniki?" *Ezhenedel'nik pravdy*, 2 March 1919, pp. 13–14.
Lunacharskii, A. "O polemike," *Zhizn' iskusstva*, 27 November 1918, p. 3.
Men'shoi, A. "Pishcha dukhovnaia," *Vechernie izvestiia Moskovskogo soveta*, 28 February 1919, p. 1.
N., E. "Ob uprekakh khudozhnikam. Otvet tov. Kerzhentsevu. Pis'mo v redaktsiiu," *Vechernie izvestiia Moskovskogo soveta*, 1 March 1919, p. 2.
"O futuristakh," *Izvestiia VTsIK*, 25 February 1919, p. 3.
"Postanovlenie Ispolkoma Petrogradskogo soveta o prazdnovanii pervogo maia," *Severnaia kommuna*, 10 April 1919, p. 1.

Postoronnii. "Dlia naroda ili dlia sebia," *Vechernie izvestiia Moskovskogo soveta*, 18 February 1919, p. 1.
Pumpianskii, Lev. "Iskusstvo i sovremennost'' [10]," *Plamia*, 1 May 1919, pp. 11–12.
P[unin], N. "Goneniia," *Iskusstvo kommuny*, 9 March 1919, p. 2.
Shterenburg, D. P. "Kritikam iz Proletkul'ta," *Iskusstvo kommuny*, 9 February 1919, p. 3.
Stek, K. "Strekochushchu kuznetsu," *Vechernie izvestiia Moskovskogo soveta*, 18 February 1919, pp. 2–3.
Tis. "Literaturnye spekulianty," *Vechernie izvestiia Moskovskogo soveta*, 20 February 1919, p. 1.
"Zaiavlenie po povodu Misteriia-Buff," *Zhizn' iskusstva*, 21 November 1918, p. 4.
"Zhizn' i iskusstvo," *Vestnik teatra*, no. 11 (1919), pp. 4–5.

Red Army Day 1919

"Den' krasnogo podarka," *Vechernie izvestiia Moskovskogo soveta*, 17 February 1919, p. 2.
"Den' Krasnoi Armii," *Vechernie izvestiia Moskovskogo soveta*, 24 February 1919, p. 1.
"Den' Krasnoi Armii," *Zhizn' iskusstva*, 22 February 1919, p. 3.
"Godovshchina Krasnoi Armii," *Vechernie izvestiia Moskovskogo soveta*, 24 February 1919, p. 2.
"K godovshchine Krasnoi Armii," *Izvestiia VTsIK*, 20 February 1919, p. 3.
"K godovshchine Krasnoi Armii," *Izvestiia VTsIK*, 21 February 1919, p. 4.
"Kalendar'," *Vestnik teatra*, no. 7 (1919), p. 7.
Kameneva, O. D. "Pis'mo v redaktsiiu," *Vechernie izvestiia Moskovskogo soveta*, 1 March 1919, p. 3.
Lunacharskii, A. "Krasnyi podarok," *Vestnik teatra*, no. 4 (1919), p. 2.
"Moskva v den' krasnogo podarka," *Vestnik teatra*, no. 9 (1919), p. 3.
"Obzor deiatel'nosti komiteta 'Krasnyi podarok,'" *Izvestiia VTsIK*, 23 February 1919, p. 3.
"Prazdnovanie godovshchiny Krasnoi Armii," *Izvestiia VTsIK*, 25 February 1919, p. 2.
"Prazdnovanie iubileia," *Izvestiia VTsIK*, 23 February 1919, p. 3.
"Rezul'taty konkursa," *Vechernie izvestiia Moskovskogo soveta*, 20 February 1919, p. 3.
"Salamanskii boi," *Zhizn' iskusstva*, 25 February 1919, p. 2.
"Salamanskii boi. Istoricheskaia drama dlia podrostkov v 3 deistviiakh Adriana Piotrovskogo i Sergeia Radlova," *Igra*, no. 3 (1920), pp. 83–122.
"Salamanskii boi. K postanovke v teatre 'Studiia,'" *Zhizn' iskusstva*, 9 April 1919, p. 3.
"V den' godovshchiny Krasnoi Armii," *Zhizn' iskusstva*, 19 February 1919, p. 3.
Zarevoi, Sergei. "Krasnaia Armiia," *Izvestiia VTsIK*, 23 February 1919, p. 1 [verse].

May Day 1919

B., A. "Deti na prazdnike," *Krasnaia gazeta*, 3 May 1919, p. 3.
Borisov, S. "Krasnyi den'. Moskva. Vpechatleniia," *Pravda*, 3 May 1919, p. 1.
The Communist International (Petrograd), 1 May 1919.
"Ekran," *Zhizn' iskusstva*, 24 April 1919, p. 2.
"K dniu 1 Maia," *Severnaia kommuna*, 11 April 1919, p. 2.
"K organizatsii prazdnestv pervogo maia. Ot Petrogradskogo soveta profsoiuzov," *Severnaia kommuna*, 10 April 1919, p. 1.
"K pervomaiskim torzhestvam," *Petrogradskaia pravda*, 1 May 1919, p. 3.
"K pervomaiskim torzhestvam," *Vestnik teatra*, no. 22 (1919), pp. 3–4.
"K pervomaiskomu prazdniku," *Zhizn' iskusstva*, 26 March 1919, p. 3.
"K pervomu maia," *Vechernie izvestiia Moskovskogo soveta*, 26 April 1919, p. 2.
"K pervomu maia," *Vechernie izvestiia Moskovskogo soveta*, 28 April 1919, p. 3.
"K pervomu maia," *Zhizn' iskusstva*, 27 February 1919, p. 2.
"K prazdnovaniiu pervogo maia," *Petrogradskaia pravda*, 30 April 1919, p. 2.
"K prazdnovaniiu pervogo maia," *Zhizn' iskusstva*, 4 April 1919, p. 3.
"Khronika," *Zhizn' iskusstva*, 29 April 1919, p. 2.
"Khudozhestvennaia zhizn'," *Zhizn' iskusstva*, 9 May 1919, p. 2.
"Khudozhestvennaia zhizn'," *Zhizn' iskusstva*, 6 June 1919, p. 2.
Kniazev, Vasilii. "Nasha kolokol'nia. Pervoe maia 1919 g.," *Krasnaia gazeta*, 3 May 1919, p. 2 [verse].
Kormchii, L. "Krasnyi prazdnik. Vpechatleniia," *Krasnaia gazeta*, 3 May 1919, p. 3.
L., V. "Na khodu," *Pravda*, 3 May 1919, p. 1.
L——chi. "Vpechatleniia," *Vestnik teatra*, no. 23 (1919), p. 7.
Loginov, Iv. "Nezabyvaemyi denek," *Krasnaia gazeta*, 3 May 1919, p. 3.
"Moskva," *Zhizn' iskusstva*, 25 April 1919, p. 2.
"Na khudozhestvennoe ubranstvo Peterburga," *Zhizn' iskusstva*, 10–11 May 1919, p. 2.
"Na Krasnoi ploshchadi," *Pravda*, 3 May 1919, p. 1.
Nikulin, L. "Teatr na Ukraine. Pis'mo iz Kieva," *Vestnik teatra*, no. 33 (1919), p. 16.
"Organizatsiia prazdnika," *Vechernie izvestiia Moskovskogo soveta*, 30 April 1919, p. 2.
"Pervoe maia," *Petrogradskaia pravda*, 3 May 1919, p. 2.
"Pervoe maia," *Zhizn' iskusstva*, 1–2 May 1919, p. 2.
"Pervoe maia," *Zhizn' iskusstva*, 3–4 May 1919, p. 3.
"Pervoe maia v Petrograde," *Krasnaia gazeta*, 3 May 1919, p. 2.
"Postanovlenie Ispolkoma Petrogradskogo soveta o prazdnovanii 1-go Maia," *Zhizn' iskusstva*, 11 April 1919, p. 4.
"Prazdnik proletarskoi pobedy," *Vechernie izvestiia Moskovskogo soveta*, 2 May 1919, pp. 3–4.
"Prazdnovanie pervogo maia," *Vechernie izvestiia Moskovskogo soveta*, 3 May 1919, p. 2.

"Prigotovleniia k prazdniku," *Petrogradskaia pravda*, 29 April 1919, p. 2.
"Proletarskii prazdnik," *Zhizn' iskusstva*, 22 March 1919, p. 3.
"Raboty K. S. Mardzhanova," *Vestnik teatra*, no. 39 (1919), p. 10.
Smyshliaev, Val. "Deiatel'nost' teatral'nogo otdela Moskovskogo Proletkul'ta," *Vestnik teatra*, no. 35 (1919), pp. 4–5.
"Teatr pervogo maia v Petrograde," *Vestnik teatra*, no. 26 (1919), pp. 8–9.
"Tseremonial prazdnovaniia pervogo maia," *Petrogradskaia pravda*, 30 April 1919, p. 2.
"Tsirk na ulitsakh," *Vestnik teatra*, no. 23 (1919), p. 8.
"Uchastie Proletkul'ta," *Vestnik teatra*, no. 23 (1919), pp. 7–8.
"Ukrasheniia k pervomu maia," *Iskusstvo kommuny*, 16 March 1919, p. 4.
"V Otdele po delam iskusstva i khudozhestvennoi promyshlennosti," *Iskusstvo kommuny*, 6 April 1919, p. 3.
Vasil'kov. "U krasnykh mogil 1 Maia 1919 g.," *Krasnaia gazeta*, 3 May 1919, p. 2.
Zagorskii, M. "Legenda o kommunare," *Vestnik teatra*, no. 56 (1920), p. 9.

November 7, 1919

"Den' velikoi pobedy. Vtoraia godovshchina oktiabr'skoi revoliutsii," *Vechernie izvestiia Moskovskogo soveta*, 8 November 1919, pp. 1–3.
"Den' velikoi pobedy. Vtoroi den' torzhestva," *Vechernie izvestiia Moskovskogo soveta*, 10 November 1919, p. 3.
"Godovshchina revoliutsii," *Zhizn' iskusstva*, 7–9 November 1919, p. 2.
"Godovshchina revoliutsii," *Zhizn' iskusstva*, 11 November 1919, p. 1.
"K oktiabr'skim torzhestvam," *Pravda*, 6 November 1919, p. 4.
"K oktiabr'skim torzhestvam," *Vestnik teatra*, no. 36 (1919), p. 13.
"K oktiabr'skim torzhestvam," *Zhizn' iskusstva*, 10 October 1919, p. 2.
"K oktiabr'skim torzhestvam," *Zhizn' iskusstva*, 14 October 1919, p. 3.
"K oktiabr'skim torzhestvam," *Zhizn' iskusstva*, 15 October 1919, p. 3.
"K oktiabr'skim torzhestvam," *Zhizn' iskusstva*, 18–19 October 1919, p. 1.
"K oktiabr'skim torzhestvam," *Zhizn' iskusstva*, 4–5 November 1919, p. 3.
"Khudozhestvennaia zhizn'," *Zhizn' iskusstva*, 21 October 1919, p. 2.
"Khudozhestvennaia zhizn'," *Zhizn' iskusstva*, 20 November 1919, p. 1.
"Konenkov dlia tsirka," *Vestnik teatra*, no. 44 (1919), pp. 6–7.
Kuznetsov, E. "Poezdka v Kronshtadt v dni godovshchiny," *Vestnik teatra*, no. 43 (1919), p. 14.
"Na strazhe mirovoi kommuny," *Vechernie izvestiia Moskovskogo soveta*, 11 November 1919, p. 4.
"Pamiatnik oktiabr'skoi revoliutsii," *Zhizn' iskusstva*, 24–25 October 1919, p. 1.
"Pervyi gos. tsirk," *Vestnik teatra*, no. 42 (1919), p. 10.
"Pod grom kanonady," *Vestnik teatra*, no. 39 (1919), p. 12.
"Teatry v dni oktiabr'skikh torzhestv," *Zhizn' iskusstva*, 16 October 1919, p. 1.
"Tseremonial oktiabr'skikh torzhestv," *Vechernie izvestiia Moskovskogo soveta*, 31 October 1919, p. 3.

"Uchastie tsirka v oktiabr'skikh torzhestvakh," *Vestnik teatra*, no. 37 (1919), p. 13.
"Vtoroi gos. tsirk," *Vestnik teatra*, no. 42 (1919), p. 11.
"Vtoroi gos. tsirk," *Vestnik teatra*, no. 44 (1919), p. 7.

Red Army Dramatic Studio (1919)

"Armiia v teatre," *Vestnik teatra*, no. 41 (1919), p. 5.
"Instsenirovka dekabr'skogo vosstaniia," *Petrogradskaia pravda*, 18 January 1920, p. 3.
"Khronika," *Vestnik teatra*, no. 43 (1919), p. 14.
"Khronika," *Zhizn' iskusstva*, 8 May 1919, p. 2.
"Khronika," *Zhizn' iskusstva*, 21 November 1919, p. 2.
"Khronika," *Zhizn' iskusstva*, 18 December 1919, p. 3.
"Khronika," *Zhizn' iskusstva*, 26 February 1920, p. 3.
Kuznetsov, E. "Peterburgskie pis'ma," *Vestnik teatra*, no. 56 (1920), p. 15.
N[ikono]v, B. "Pod otkrytym nebom," *Zhizn' iskusstva*, 14 May 1919, p. 1.
"Otkrytie krasnoarmeiskoi dramaturgicheskoi studii," *Zhizn' iskusstva*, 14 February 1919, p. 3.
"Pervyi spektakl' dramaticheskoi masterskoi Krasnoi Armii," *Iskusstvo kommuny*, 30 March 1919, p. 4.
"Peterburgskie pis'ma," *Vestnik teatra*, no. 43 (1919), p. 13.
"Sverzhenie samoderzhaviia," *Izvestiia arkhangel'skogo gubernskogo revkoma*, 4 May 1920, p. 3.
"Sverzhenie tsarizma," *Krasnaia gazeta*, 3 May 1919, p. 4.
"Tret'ii internatsional," *Zhizn' iskusstva*, 9 May 1919, p. 2.
"Truppa improvizatorov," *Vestnik teatra*, no. 21 (1919), p. 7.
"Truppa improvizatorov," *Zhizn' iskusstva*, 3 April 1919, p. 3.
"Tsirk Chinizelli," *Izvestiia Petrogradskogo soveta*, 24 February 1920, p. 1.
"V masterskoi Krasnoi Armii," *Zhizn' iskusstva*, 9 April 1919, p. 3.
"V Peterburgskom Proletkul'te," *Vestnik teatra*, no. 56 (1920), p. 15.
"V Petrogradskikh teatrakh," *Vestnik teatra*, no. 26 (1919), p. 9.
"V Proletkul'te," *Zhizn' iskusstva*, 28 November 1919, p. 1.

Miscellaneous 1919

"Agitatsionnye doski," *Zhizn' iskusstva*, 9–10 August 1919, p. 1.
Annenkov, Iu. "Krizis èstrady," *Zhizn' iskusstva*, 3–4 July 1920.
Ch[ulkov], G. "Studiitsy i teatr Verkharna," *Vestnik teatra*, no. 15 (1919), p. 7.
Dikson, Konst. "Spektakl' starinnogo teatra," *Vestnik teatra*, no. 22 (1919), p. 7.
Dovol'no Peredvizhnogo," *Zhizn' iskusstva*, no. 23 (1923), p. 1.
Erdman, Boris. "Nepovtorimoe vremia," *Tsirk i èstrada*, no. 3–4 (1928), pp. 6–8.
"Istoriko-revoliutsionnaia biblioteka," *Zhizn' iskusstva*, 26 February 1919, p. 3.

"K otkrytiiu pamiatnika Blanki," *Zhizn' iskusstva*, 4 March 1919, p. 3.
"Kalendar' " (Khar'kov), *Vestnik teatra*, no. 28 (1919), p. 9.
"Kantata," *Zarevo zavodov* (Samara Proletkult), no. 1 (1919), pp. 24–25 [poem written collectively by M. Gerasimov, Sergei Esenin, and Sergei Klychkov].
"Khronika," *Zhizn' iskusstva*, 23 December 1919, p. 1.
"Khudozhestvennaia zhizn'," *Zhizn' iskusstva*, 25 June 1919, p. 1.
"Khudozhestvennaia zhizn'," *Zhizn' iskusstva*, 17 July 1919, p. 1.
"Khudozhestvennye ulichnye plakaty," *Zhizn' iskusstva*, 7 May 1919, p. 1.
Kogan, P. "Sotsialisticheskii teatr v gody revoliutsii," *Vestnik teatra*, no. 40 (1919), p. 3.
Kuzmin, M. "Tsirk," *Zhizn' iskusstva*, 4 January 1919, p. 1–2.
L[evinso]n, A. "Derevo prevrashcheniia," *Zhizn' iskusstva*, 8 February 1919, p. 1.
"M. Gor'kii o kinematografe," *Vestnik teatra*, no. 30 (1919), p. 10.
Malevich, K. "Nerukotvornye pamiatniki," *Iskusstvo kommuny*, 9 February 1919, p. 2.
"Moskovskii Balagan," *Vestnik teatra*, no. 8 (1919), p. 6.
"Na ulitsakh i ploshchadiakh," *Zhizn' iskusstva*, 29–30 May 1919, p. 2.
N[osko]v, N. "Pervyi vinokur," *Zhizn' iskusstva*, 24 September 1919, p. 1.
"Novye tsirkovye pantomimy," *Vestnik teatra*, no. 50 (1920), p. 14.
"Novyi pamiatnik Perovskoi," *Zhizn' iskusstva*, 19–20 July 1919, p. 3.
"Obval pamiatnika Radishchevu," *Zhizn' iskusstva*, 5 February 1919, p. 3.
P[iotrovskii], A. "Akademicheskii teatr intelligentsii," *Zhizn' iskusstva*, 20 December 1921, p. 4.
"Pod vozdeistviem teatra," *Vestnik teatra*, no. 8 (1919), p. 6.
"Postanovlenie," *Zhizn' iskusstva*, 24 January 1919, p. 2.
"Prazdnik kommunisticheskogo internatsionala," *Zhizn' iskusstva*, 7 March 1919, p. 4.
Punin, N. "O pamiatnikakh," *Iskusstvo kommuny*, 9 March 1919, pp. 2–3.
Shershenevich, Vadim. "Tsirk," *Zrelishcha*, no. 2 (1922), p. 15.
Shklovskii, Viktor. "Iskusstvo tsirka," *Zhizn' iskusstva*, 4–5 November 1919, p. 1.
———. "Pamiatniki russkoi revoliutsii," *Zhizn' iskusstva*, 28–29 June 1919, p. 2.
"Sovetskaia konstitutsiia na mramore," *Zhizn' iskusstva*, 25 January 1919, p. 3.
"Torzhestvennoe otkrytie pamiatnika Sof'e Perovskoi," *Iskusstvo kommuny*, 5 January 1919, p. 3.
"Tsirk," *Vestnik teatra*, no. 39 (1919), p. 13.
"Tsirkovaia studiia," *Proletarskaia kul'tura*, no. 9–10 (1919), p. 62.
"V Institute vneshkol'nogo obrazovaniia," *Zapiski peredvizhnogo-obshchedostupnogo teatra*, no. 24–25 (1919), p. 18.
"Vozrozhdenie tsirka," *Vestnik teatra*, no. 9 (1919), pp. 4–5.
Zh., A. "Rabota po-revoliutsionnomu. Kommunisticheskaia subbota," *Pravda*, 17 May 1919, pp. 1–2.

Debate on Worker-Peasant Theater, 1919–20

"Assotsiatsiia pri podotdele RKT," *Vestnik teatra*, no. 46 (1919), p. 15.
B[ebutov], V. "O neoutopizme," *Vestnik teatra*, no. 43 (1919), p. 7.
[Blium]. "U kolybeli sotsialisticheskogo teatra," *Vestnik teatra*, no. 45 (1919), p. 3.
Ch., M. "Gorodskoe soveshchanie po voprosu o raboche-krest'ianskom teatre," *Zhizn' iskusstva*, 3 April 1919, pp. 1–2.
"Disput o RKT," *Vestnik teatra*, no. 43 (1919), p. 3.
"Doklad Alekseia Gana," *Vestnik teatra*, no. 66 (1920), p. 7.
Gan, Aleksei. "Nasha bor'ba," *Vestnik teatra*, no. 67 (1920), pp. 1–2.
———. "O pozitsiiakh vnutrennego fronta RKT," *Vestnik teatra*, no. 67 (1920), pp. 8–9.
[Gan, Aleksei] Aleko. "Obzor faktov," *Vestnik teatra*, no. 67 (1920), pp. 3–4.
Kerzhentsev, P. M. "Bor'ba na s"ezde," *Vestnik teatra*, no. 44 (1919), pp. 5–6.
———. "Bor'ba za sotsialisticheskii teatr," *Proletarskaia kul'tura*, no. 13–14 (1920), pp. 77–79.
———. "Chto na ocheredi," *Vestnik teatra*, no. 45 (1919), p. 4.
K[erzhentsev], P. "Za ili protiv Proletkul'tov. Vpechatleniia s konferentsii," *Vestnik teatra*, no. 15 (1919), pp. 3–4.
Kogan, P. "RKT v gody revoliutsii. Po dannym Sektsii obsledovaniia," *Vestnik teatra*, no. 67 (1920), pp. 11–12.
Lvov, Nikolai. "Cherez teatr k revoliutsii dukha," *Vestnik teatra*, no. 66 (1920), p. 4.
[Lvov], N. "Pervaia sessiia Vserossiiskogo soveta raboche-krest'ianskogo teatra," *Vestnik teatra*, no. 49 (1920), pp. 4–5.
———. "S"ezd po raboche-krest'ianskomu teatru," *Vestnik teatra*, no. 44 (1919), pp. 2–5.
"Plan pervogo narodnogo deistva-prazdnestva," *Vestnik teatra*, no. 46 (1919), p. 5.
Tangens. "Zhizn' operezhaet," *Zhizn' iskusstva*, 9 May 1919, p. 2.
Tikhonovich, V. "Golaia zemlia," *Vestnik teatra*, no. 67 (1920), pp. 2–3.
———. "Nashi raznoglasiia," *Vestnik teatra*, no. 45 (1919), pp. 4–5.
———. "Nazrevshee reshenie," *Vestnik teatra*, no. 68 (1920), pp. 9–10.
———. "Smutnye dni," *Vestnik teatra*, no. 58 (1920), pp. 9–10.
"Vtoraia sessiia soveta raboche-krest'ianskogo teatra," *Vestnik teatra*, no. 57 (1920), p. 4.
"Zhizn' RKT. K rospusku soveta," *Vestnik teatra*, no. 68 (1920), pp. 8–10.

Mass Spectacle and Festival Section (1920)

Bogatyreva, A. P. "Ukazatel' literatury o massovykh zrelishchakh," *Vestnik teatra*, no. 62 (1920), p. 13.
"Disput o massovom deistve," *Vestnik teatra*, no. 49 (1920), pp. 5–6.
Gan, Aleksei. "Massovoe deistvo," *Vestnik teatra*, no. 67 (1920), pp. 12–13.
———. "Massovoe deistvo. Sostiazanie i bor'ba," *Vestnik teatra*, no. 66 (1920), pp. 2–3.
"K pervomaiskim prazdnestvam," *Vestnik teatra*, no. 49 (1920), p. 7.

Kogan, Sofiia. "Muzyka i revoliutsionnye torzhestva," *Vestnik teatra*, no. 62 (1920), pp. 10–11.
Lvov, Nik. "Istoriia pervogo sotsialisticheskogo stsenariia," *Vestnik teatra*, no. 62 (1920), pp. 6–8.
"Ot slov k delu," *Vestnik teatra*, no. 37 (1919), p. 5.
"Pervoe maia. K otchetu sektsii," *Vestnik teatra*, no. 67 (1920), pp. 13–15.
"Plan pervogo narodnogo deistva-prazdnestva," *Vestnik teatra*, no. 46 (1919), p. 5.
"Plan prazdnestva pervogo maia," *Vestnik teatra*, no. 51 (1920), pp. 5–6.
"Plan prazdnovaniia pervogo maia," *Zhizn' iskusstva*, 24 February 1920, p. 3.
"Sektsiia massovykh predstavlenii i zrelishch," *Vestnik teatra*, no. 47 (1919), p. 6.
Shch., A. "O smysle i printsipakh dekorativnogo nachala v massovykh narodnykh predstavleniiakh i zrelishchakh," *Vestnik teatra*, no. 62 (1920), pp. 11–12.
S[myshliaev], V. "Primernyi stsenarii massovogo prazdnestva v otkrytom letnem pomeshchenii," *Vestnik teatra*, no. 62 (1920), pp. 8–10.
"Vozzvanie sektsii massovykh predstavlenii i zrelishch TEO," *Vestnik teatra*, no. 50 (1920), p. 2.

Red Army Day 1920

"Bibliografiia. 'Nedelia krasnogo fronta,'" *Zhizn' iskusstva*, 24 January 1920, p. 3.
"Khronika," *Zhizn' iskusstva*, 26 February 1920, p. 3.
Kuznetsov, E. "Tri postanovki," *Vestnik teatra*, no. 56 (1920), p. 15.
"Obzor agitatsionnogo materiala. Instsenirovka agitatsionnykh sudov," *Vestnik agitatsii i propagandy*, 25 November 1920, pp. 25–27.
"Prazdnovanie vtoroi godovshchiny Krasnoi Armii," *Izvestiia Petrogradskogo soveta*, 24 February 1920, p. 1.
"Sud nad Vrangelem," *Vestnik teatra*, no. 72–73 (1920), pp. 16–17.

May Day 1920

A., P. "Tsar' Edip," *Vestnik teatra*, no. 64 (1920), p. 12.
Almazov. "Pervomaiskie motivy," *Izvestiia Petrogradskogo soveta*, 3 May 1920, p. 1.
B——n, Nik. "Revoliutsionnyi prazdnik drevonasazhdeniia," *Izvestiia Petrogradskogo soveta*, 3 May 1920, p. 1.
Belenson, Aleksandr. "Birzhevye vpechatleniia," *Zhizn' iskusstva*, 4 May 1920, p. 1.
Bukharin, N. "Prazdnik ili budni," *Pravda*, 1 May 1920, p. 1.
Gebs. "Prazdnik truda i radosti," *Izvestiia Petrogradskogo soveta*, 3 May 1920, p. 1.
"Gimn osvobozhdeniia truda," *Izvestiia Petrogradskogo soveta*, 30 April 1920, p. 1.
Gor'kii, M. "Put' k shchastiiu," *Pravda*, 1 May 1920, p. 1.

K., A. "Diskussiia ob Internatsionale," *Izvestiia Petrogradskogo soveta*, 3 May 1920, p. 1.
K., N. "K prazdnovaniiu pervogo maia," *Petrogradskaia pravda*, 25 April 1920, p. 1.
"K itogam pervomaiskogo smotra," *Izvestiia Petrogradskogo soveta*, 3 May 1920, p. 1.
"K pervomu maia," *Zhizn' iskusstva*, 20 February 1919, p. 3.
"K prazdnovaniiu pervogo maia," *Izvestiia Petrogradskogo soveta*, 24 April 1920, p. 1.
"K prazdnovaniiu pervogo maia," *Izvestiia Petrogradskogo soveta*, 30 April 1920, p. 1.
"K prazdnovaniiu pervogo maia," *Petrogradskaia pravda*, 25 April 1920, p. 1.
"K ustroistvu spektaklia-pantomimy," *Izvestiia Petrogradskogo soveta*, 24 April 1920, p. 1.
K[erzhentsev], P. "Iz vpechatlenii pervomaiskogo prazdnika. Po ulitsam," *Vestnik teatra*, no. 64 (1920), pp. 5–6.
Kerzhentsev, P. "Massovyi teatr," *Vestnik teatra*, no. 65 (1920), pp. 3–4.
"Khronika," *Vestnik teatra*, no. 63 (1920), p. 11.
"Khronika," *Zhizn' iskusstva*, 21 April 1920, p. 1.
"Khronika," *Zhizn' iskusstva*, 5 May 1920, p. 1.
"Khudozhestvennaia zhizn'," *Zhizn' iskusstva*, 26 March 1920, p. 1.
"Khudozhestvennaia zhizn'," *Zhizn' iskusstva*, 24 April 1920, p. 3.
Kogan, P. S. "O prazdnovanii pervogo maia," *Vestnik teatra*, no. 62 (1920), pp. 3–4.
Kollantai, A. "Novye zadachi pervogo maia," *Pravda*, 1 May 1920, p. 2.
L., O. "Zhivaia kartina," *Vestnik teatra*, no. 64 (1920), p. 6.
Lenin, N. "Rabota pervomaiskikh subbotnikov," *Izvestiia Petrogradskogo soveta*, 3 May 1920, p. 1.
Molotov, V. M., ed. *Pervomaiskii sbornik*. Nizhny Novgorod: Nizhegorodskii gub. komitet organizatsii truda, 1920.
"Novoe pervoe maia," *Pravda*, 1 May 1920, p. 1.
"Obshchaia kartina pervomaiskikh torzhestv v Moskve," *Izvestiia Petrogradskogo soveta*, 3 May 1920, p. 1.
"Pervoe maia," *Zhizn' iskusstva*, 1–3 May 1920, p. 1.
"Pervoe maia v Moskve," *Vestnik teatra*, no. 62 (1920), pp. 13–14.
"Pervoe maia—vtoroe maia v Samare," *Kommuna* (Samara), 5 May 1920, pp. 1–2.
"Pervomaiskaia misteriia—Gimn osvobozhdeniia truda," *Izvestiia Petrogradskogo soveta*, 3 May 1920, p. 2.
"Pervomaiskie ukrasheniia," *Izvestiia Petrogradskogo soveta*, 3 May 1920, p. 1.
"Pervomaiskie zrelishcha," *Zhizn' iskusstva*, 27 April 1920, p. 1.
"Pervomaiskie zrelishcha," *Zhizn' iskusstva*, 4 May 1920, p. 1.
Piotrovskii, Adrian. "Imeniny truda," *Zhizn' iskusstva*, 1–3 May 1920, p. 1.
"Prazdnik truda i bor'by," *Izvestiia Petrogradskogo soveta*, 30 April 1920, p. 1.
"Prazdnovanie pervogo maia v okrestnostiakh Petrograda," *Izvestiia Petrogradskogo soveta*, 3 May 1920, p. 2.

"Prazdnovanie pervogo maia v Petrograde," *Izvestiia Petrogradskogo soveta*, 3 May 1920, p. 2.
Shklovskii, Viktor. "O gromkom golose," *Zhizn' iskusstva*, 8–9 May 1920, p. 2.
Sosnovskii, L. "V Kremle," *Pravda*, 4 May 1920, p. 2.
Svetlov. "U ploshchadki. Apofeoz truda," *Kommuna* (Samara), 5 May 1920, p. 2.
Tolbuzin, Dm. "Apofeoz truda. Opyt massovogo deistva," *Vestnik teatra*, no. 66 (1920), p. 16.
Trotskii, L. "Trud i voina," *Pravda*, 1 May 1920, p. 1.
"Tseremonial prazdnovaniia," *Petrogradskaia pravda*, 25 April 1920, pp. 2–4.
Zinoviev, G[rigorii]. "Novoe v nashem pervomaiskom prazdnestve," *Pravda*, 5 May 1920, p. 1.
"Zrelishcha pervogo maia," *Zhizn' iskusstva*, 20 April 1920, p. 1.

June to October 1920

Belenson, Aleksandr. "Dva giganta," *Zhizn' iskusstva*, 23 June 1920, p. 1.
———. "K mirovoi kommune," *Zhizn' iskusstva*, 23 July 1920, p. 1.
———. "Vokrug dvukh mirov," *Zhizn' iskusstva*, 21 July 1920, p. 1.
Chibison, Vasilii. "Prazdnik rabochikh," *Pravda*, 29 July 1920, p. 1.
Ionov, Il'ia. "Ostrov otdykha," *Petrogradskaia pravda*, 20 June 1920, p. 2.
"K kongressu III Internatsionala," *Izvestiia Petrogradskogo soveta*, 17 July 1920, p. 1.
"K vtoromu kongressu III Internatsionala. 'Bor'ba dvukh mirov,' " *Petrogradskaia pravda*, 14 July 1920, p. 2.
"K vtoromu kongressu III Internatsionala. Prigotovleniia k torzhestvam," *Petrogradskaia pravda*, 16 July 1920, p. 2.
"Khronika," *Zhizn' iskusstva*, 12 May 1920, p. 1.
"Khronika," *Zhizn' iskusstva*, 10 June 1920, p. 1.
"Khronika," *Zhizn' iskusstva*, 2 July 1920, p. 1.
"Ko dniu vtorogo kongressa III-ego Internatsionala," *Pravda*, 27 July 1920, p. 2.
Kozakevich, Sergei. "V masshtabakh otkrytogo neba," *Zhizn' iskusstva*, 5 November 1920, p. 1.
"Krasnaia Messa," *Izvestiia Petrogradskogo soveta*, 17 July 1920, p. 1.
Kudelli, P. "Novoe zrelishche na portale Fondovoi birzhi," *Petrogradskaia pravda*, 21 July 1920, p. 2.
Kuzmin, N. "Velikoe nachalo," *Petrogradskaia pravda*, 20 June 1920, p. 2.
Kuznetsov, Evgenii. "Armianskaia zagadka," *Zhizn' iskusstva*, 5 May 1920, p. 1.
———. "Da zdravstvuet professionalizm!" *Zhizn' iskusstva*, 15–16 May 1920, p. 1.
———. "Po povodu," *Zhizn' iskusstva*, 17 June 1920, p. 1.
———. "Pod otkrytym nebom. Peterburgskie massovye postanovski," *Vestnik teatra*, no. 71 (1920), pp. 7–8.

———. "Pod otkrytym nebom. Peterburgskie massovye postanovki II," *Vestnik teatra*, no. 72–73 (1920), pp. 14–16.
———. "Pod otkrytym nebom. Peterburgskie massovye postanovki III," *Vestnik teatra*, no. 80–81 (1920), pp. 20–23.
Levin, M. "Miting o khalture," *Zhizn' iskusstva*, 3 August 1920, p. 1.
M. "Pervyi amfiteatr," *Zhizn' iskusstva*, 19–20 June 1920, p. 1.
"Okhrana ploshchadi pered birzhei," *Petrogradskaia pravda*, 20 June 1920, p. 2.
"Otkrytie vtorogo kongressa Kommunisticheskogo Internatsionala," *Pravda*, 20 July 1920, p. 1.
P. "Sueslovie," *Zhizn' iskusstva*, 18 May 1920, p. 4.
Piotrovskii, Adr. "Ostrov chudes," *Zhizn' iskusstva*, 22 June 1920, p. 1.
"Prazdnik v chest' vtorogo kongressa Kommunisticheskogo Internatsionala," *Pravda*, 29 July 1920, p. 1.
Preobrazhenskii, E. "Mnogoobeshchaiushchii opyt," *Pravda*, 30 July 1920, p. 1.
Pushchin, Ia. "Opyt teatralizatsii voennogo manevra," *Zhizn' iskusstva*, 26 August 1920, p. 2.
Radek, Karl. "Organizovannaia massa," *Pravda*, 29 July 1920, supplement, p. 1.
Radlov, S. "Sud'by teatra za vremia revoliutsii," *Zhizn' iskusstva*, 24 October 1922, p. 1.
"Repetitsiia misterii 'Dva mira,' " *Izvestiia Petrogradskogo soveta*, 17 July 1920, p. 1.
Strelnikov, N. "Giganty," *Zhizn' iskusstva*, 21 July 1920, p. 1.
"Sud nad zheltym Internatsionalom," *Pravda*, 31 July 1920, p. 1.
"Ukrasheniia," *Zhizn' iskusstva*, 19–20 June 1920, p. 1.
Vtoroi kongress Kommunisticheskogo Internatsionala. Petrograd: Izd. Kommunisticheskogo Internatsionala, 1920.

November 7, 1920

"Chto trebuetsia ot zritelei vo vremia instsenirovki," *Petrogradskaia pravda*, 7 November 1920, p. 4.
Derzhavin, Konst. "Chudo. K postanovke 'Vziatie Zimnego dvortsa,' " *Izvestiia Petrogradskogo soveta*, 9 November 1920, p. 1.
———. "Massa kak takovaia. Po povodu instsenirovki 'Vziatie Zimnego dvortsa,' " *Zhizn' iskusstva*, 12 November 1920, p. 2.
———. "Teatr na otkrytom vozdukhe," *Zhizn' iskusstva*, 22 October 1920, p. 1.
Derzhavin, K. N. "Vziatie Zimnego dvortsa v 1920 g. K 5-letiiu instsenirovki," *Zhizn' iskusstva*, no. 45 (1925).
Evreinov, N. "Vziatie Zimnego dvortsa," *Krasnyi militsioner*, no. 14 (1920), pp. 4–5.
———. "Vziatie Zimnego dvortsa. Vospominaniia ob instsenirovke v oznamenovanie tret'ei godovshchiny oktiabr'skoi revoliutsii," *Zhizn' iskusstva*, 4 November 1924, pp. 7–9.

[Evreinov], Nik. "Vziatie Zimnego dvortsa," *Zhizn' iskusstva*, 30–31 October 1920, p. 1.
"Instsenirovka 'Vziatie Zimnego dvortsa.' Libretto v okonchatel'noi redaktsii," *Izvestiia Petrogradskogo soveta*, 6 November 1920, p. 2.
"Instsenirovka Vziatiia Zimnego dvortsa," *Izvestiia Petrogradskogo soveta*, 28 October 1920, p. 2.
"K godovshchine oktiabr'skoi revoliutsii," *Zhizn' iskusstva*, 10 September 1920, p. 1.
"K instsenirovke Vziatiia Zimnego dvortsa," *Petrogradskaia pravda*, 26 October 1920, p. 1.
"K oktiabr'skim torzhestvam," *Izvestiia Petrogradskogo soveta*, 28 October 1920, p. 2.
"K oktiabr'skim torzhestvam," *Petrogradskaia pravda*, 26 October 1920, p. 1.
"K oktiabr'skim torzhestvam," *Petrogradskaia pravda*, 4 November 1920, p. 2.
"K oktiabr'skim torzhestvam," *Petrogradskaia pravda*, 5 November 1920, p. 2.
"K oktiabr'skim torzhestvam," *Petrogradskaia pravda*, 6 November 1920, p. 2.
"K oktiabr'skim torzhestvam," *Zhizn' iskusstva*, 23–24 October 1920, p. 1.
"K oktiabr'skoi godovshchine," *Vestnik teatra*, no. 72–73 (1920), p. 24.
"Khronika," *Zhizn' iskusstva*, 5 October 1920, p. 3.
"Khronika," *Zhizn' iskusstva*, 27 October 1920, p. 1.
"Khronika oktiabr'skikh dnei," *Petrogradskaia pravda*, 7 November 1920, p. 2.
"Khudozhestvennaia zhizn'," *Zhizn' iskusstva*, 25–26 September 1920, p. 3.
"Khudozhestvennaia zhizn'," *Zhizn' iskusstva*, 8 October 1920, p. 1.
"Kinematograf i instsenirovka 'Vziatie Zimnego dvortsa,' " *Petrogradskaia pravda*, 4 November 1920, p. 2.
"Na mogile bortsov revoliutsii v Lesnoi," *Izvestiia Petrogradskogo soveta*, 9 November 1920, p. 1.
"Na repetitsii instsenirovki 'Vziatie Zimnego dvortsa,' " *Petrogradskaia pravda*, 4 November 1920, p. 2.
Nikulin, L. "Vos'mogo noiabria 1920 goda," *Petrogradskaia pravda*, 31 October 1920, p. 2.
"Osada Zimnego dvortsa," *Zhizn' iskusstva*, 21–22 September 1920, p. 3.
"Ot komissii po organizatsii oktiabr'skikh torzhestv," *Izvestiia Petrogradskogo soveta*, 26 October 1920, p. 2.
"Parol'noe prikazanie po Petrogradskomu garnizonu No. 315," *Izvestiia Petrogradskogo soveta*, 29 October 1920, p. 2.
"Podgotovka k godovshchine oktiabr'skoi revoliutsii," *Izvestiia Tsentral'nogo ispolnitel'nogo komiteta*, 12 September 1920, p. 3.
"Prazdnovanie oktiabr'skoi godovshchiny," *Vestnik teatra*, no. 70 (1920), p. 14.
"Proletarskoe deistvo. Na instsenirovke 'Vziatie Zimnego dvortsa,' " *Petrogradskaia pravda*, 10 November 1920, p. 2.

Shubskii, N. "Na ploshchadi Uritskogo. Vpechatleniia Moskvicha," *Vestnik teatra*, no. 75 (1920), pp. 4–5.
Smirnov, N. M. "Teatral'naia rabota v klubakh," *Revoliutsionnye vskhody*, no. 7–8 (1920), p. 14.
"Teatr i tret'ia godovshchina," *Vestnik teatra*, no. 72–73 (1920), pp. 5–6.
"Tseremonial prazdnovaniia tret'ei godovshchiny oktiabr'skoi revoliutsii," *Izvestiia Petrogradskogo soveta*, 6 November 1920, p. 1.
"Tsirkuliarnoe obrashchenie Vserossiiskoi tsentral'noi oktiabr'skoi komissii," *Vestnik agitatsii i propagandy*, 19 October 1920, pp. 12–13.
"Ulichnye ukrasheniia," *Zhizn' iskusstva*, 30 November–2 December 1920, p. 2.
"Vneshnii vid goroda," *Izvestiia Petrogradskogo soveta*, 9 November 1920, p. 1.
"Vziatie Zimnego dvortsa," *Vestnik teatra*, no. 74 (1920), pp. 11–12.
"Vziatie Zimnego dvortsa. Opyt," *Petrogradskaia pravda*, 7 November 1920, p. 2.
"Vziatie Zimnego dvortsa. Vpechatleniia," *Izvestiia Petrogradskogo soveta*, 9 November 1920, p. 1.

Miscellaneous 1920

Arne, L. "Mirovoi konkurs ostroumiia. Vol'naia komediia," *Zhizn' iskusstva*, 15 November 1921, p. 1.
Arskii, R. "Nedel'nyi subbotnik," *Izvestiia Tsentral'nogo ispolnitol'nogo komiteta*, 21 January 1920, p. 4.
Dagel', K. "Sizifov trud. K vcherashnemu subbotniku," *Petrogradskaia pravda*, 4 April 1920, p. 3.
Derzhavin, Konst. "Akter i tsirk," *Zhizn' iskusstva*, 30 March 1920, pp. 1–2.
―――. "Iskusstvo tsirka v stsenicheskoi kompozitsii," *Zhizn' iskusstva*, 1 April 1920, p. 2.
―――. "Tsirk," *Zhizn' iskusstva*, 6 August 1920, p. 1.
F., N. "Novye stsenarii dlia opery Glinki," *Vestnik teatra*, no. 89–90 (1921), pp. 12–13.
"Khronika," *Vestnik teatra*, no. 59 (1920), pp. 13–14.
"Khronika," *Zhizn' iskusstva*, 17 August 1920, p. 1.
"Khudozhestvennaia zhizn'," *Zhizn' iskusstva*, 1–2 January 1920, p. 2.
"Khudozhestvennaia zhizn'," *Zhizn' iskusstva*, 11 February 1920, p. 1.
"Khudozhestvennaia zhizn'," *Zhizn' iskusstva*, 2 March 1920, p. 3.
"Khudozhestvennaia zhizn'," *Zhizn' iskusstva*, 11 March 1920, p. 3.
"Khudozhestvennaia zhizn'," *Zhizn' iskusstva*, 7–9 April 1920, p. 2.
"Khudozhestvennyi teatr," *Vestnik teatra*, no. 60 (1920), p. 1.
Kogan, P. "Kak organizovat' sorevnovanie mezhdu rabotaiushchimi. Udarnye gruppy truda. Ispol'zovanie sistemy Teilora," *Petrogradskaia pravda*, 7 April 1920, p. 3.
"Kommunisticheskie subbotniki," *Izvestiia Tsentral'nogo ispolnitel'nogo komiteta*, 11 September 1920, p. 2.
L[vov], N. "Prazdnik ritma," *Vestnik teatra*, no. 65 (1920), pp. 9–10.
Malkov, N. "Za krasnyi Petrograd," *Zhizn' iskusstva*, 5 May 1925, p. 10.

Mass, Vl. "Futurizm i revoliutsiia teatrov," *Vestnik teatra,* no. 57 (1920), pp. 3–4.
Mass, Vlad. "Teatral'nyi oktiabr' i futurizm," *Vestnik teatra,* no. 91–92 (1921), p. 4.
Narbut, Vladimir. "Eshche ne vremia. . . ." *Izvestiia Odesskogo soveta,* 23 June 1920, p. 1 [verse].
"O subbotnikakh v derevne," *Pravda,* 4 January 1920, p. 1.
"Ogosudarstvlenie komissii po organizatsii proletarskikh prazdnikov," *Petrogradskaia pravda,* 27 February 1920, p. 2.
Okskii, N. "Tver'," *Vestnik teatra,* no. 63 (1920), p. 16.
"Opium dlia naroda," *Vestnik teatra,* no. 70 (1920), pp. 8–9.
"Polegche na povorotakh," *Vestnik teatra,* no. 64 (1920), p. 10.
"Prazdnovanie dnia konstitutsii v Moskve i peredachi znameni Parizhskikh kommunarov," *Leningradskaia pravda,* 8 July 1924, p. 2.
Prozorov, G. "Detskie kommunisticheskie subbotniki," *Pravda,* 28 February 1920, p. 2.
Radlov, Sergei. "Teatr vozrozhdeniia i vozrozhdenie teatra," *Zhizn' iskusstva,* 12 November 1920, p. 1.
Remizov, Aleksei. "Repertuar. III," *Zhizn' iskusstva,* 5 February 1920, p. 1.
"Revoliutsionnaia poshlost'," *Vestnik teatra,* no. 85–86 (1921), p. 6.
Sosnovskii, Lev. "Master Kliuev. K voprosu a proizvodstvennoi propagande," *Pravda,* 24 October 1920, p. 1.
———. "Ob odnom iz sposobov agitatsii," *Pravda,* 25 November 1920, p. 1.
Strelnikov, N. "Edinyi Internatsional," *Zhizn' iskusstva,* 29 January 1920, p. 3.
"Sud nad Leninym," *Pravda,* 22 April 1920, p. 2.
"Vindzorskie prokaznitsy," *Zhizn' iskusstva,* 12 November 1920, p. 1.
"Voprosy teatra na Vserossiiskom s"ezde Proletkul'ta," *Vestnik teatra,* no. 71 (1920), pp. 13–14.

NEP Era

Agulianskii, A. "Proletarskie prazdnestva i rabotniki iskusstva," *Vestnik teatra i iskusstva,* 20 December 1921, p. 13.
Biulleten' kommissii pri prezidiume TsIK Soiuza SSR po organizatsii i provedeniiu prazdnovaniia 10-letiia oktiabr'skoi revoliutsii, nos. 1–4 (1927).
Ch., I. "Kak ispol'zovali deistvennikov," *Novyi Lef,* no. 10 (1927), p. 10.
Edinyi khudozhestvennyi kruzhok. Metody klubno-khudozhestvennoi raboty. Leningrad: Izd. knizhnogo sektora Gubono, 1924.
Ivanov, A. "Komsomol'skoe rozhdestvo," *Rabochii klub,* no. 10–11 (1924), pp. 12–13.
Komsomol'skoe rozhdestvo. Moscow: Krasnaia nov', 1923.
Komsomol'skoe rozhdestvo. Moscow: MK RKSM, 1923.
Komsomol'skoe rozhdestvo. Tula: Rossiiskii kommunisticheskii soiuz molodezhi, 1923.
Margolin, Samuil. "Iz tsikla 'neosushchestvlennyi teatr.' 'Bor'ba i pobeda.' Massovoe deistvo Vs. Meierkhol'da," *Ekho,* no. 13 (1923), p. 11.

"Masterskaia Meierkhol'da," *Lef*, no. 2 (1923), pp. 170–71.
"Moskva," *Zhizn' iskusstva*, 19 May 1925, p. 22.
Shafir, Ia. *Gazeta i derevnia*. Moscow: Krasnaia nov', 1924.
"Spor ob Akvariume," *Vestnik teatra*, no. 89–90 (1921), p. 19.
Tretiakov, S. "Kak desiatiletit'," *Novyi Lef*, no. 4 (1927), p. 37.
T[retiakov], S[ergei]. "Zapisnaia knizhka. Otsenka khudozhestvennogo oformleniia desiatioktiabria," *Novyi Lef*, no. 10 (1927), pp. 7–8.
"Vsevobuch i iskusstvo," *Vestnik teatra*, no. 78–79 (1921), pp. 24–25.
Zhemchuzhnyi, V. "Demonstratsiia v oktiabre," *Novyi Lef*, no. 5 (1927), pp. 47–48.
Zhemchuzhnyi, Vit. "Protiv obriadov," *Novyi Lef*, no. 1 (1927), p. 45.

Secondary Sources

THEORIES OF CULTURE

Agulhon, Maurice. *Marianne into Battle*. Translated by Janet Lloyd. Cambridge: Cambridge University Press, 1981.
Babcock, Barbara, ed. *The Reversible World: Symbolic Inversion in Art and Society*. Ithaca, N.Y.: Cornell University Press, 1978.
Bakhtin, M. M. *Rabelais and His World*. Translated by Helene Iswolsky. Cambridge: MIT Press, 1968.
Barthes, Roland. *Mythologies*. Translated by Annette Lavers. New York: Hill and Wang, 1972.
Benamou, Michel, and Charles Carmello, eds. *Performance in Postmodern Society*. Milwaukee: Center for Twentieth-Century Studies, 1977.
Ben-David, Joseph, and Terry Clark, eds. *Culture and Its Creators: Essays in Honor of Edward Shils*. Chicago: University of Chicago Press, 1977.
Burke, Kenneth. *On Symbols and Society*. Edited by Joseph R. Gusfield. Chicago: University of Chicago Press, 1989.
Caillois, Roger. *Man, Play and Games*. Translated by Meyer Barash. New York: Free Press, 1961.
Cannadine, David, and Simon Price, eds. *Rituals of Royalty: Power and Ceremonial in Traditional Societies*. Cambridge: Cambridge University Press, 1987.
Castle, Terry. *Masquerade and Civilization: The Carnivalesque in Eighteenth-Century English Culture and Fiction*. Stanford, Calif.: Stanford University Press, 1986.
Cook, Albert. *Enactment: Greek Tragedy*. Chicago: Swallow Press, 1971.
Cox, Harvey. *The Feast of Fools*. Cambridge: Harvard University Press, 1969.
Derrida, Jacques. *Of Grammatology*. Translated by Gayatri Chakravorty Spivak. Baltimore: Johns Hopkins University Press, 1976.

———. *Writing and Difference*. Translated by Alan Bass. Chicago: University of Chicago Press, 1978.
Durkheim, Emile. *The Elementary Forms of Religious Life*. Translated by Joseph Ward Swain. New York: Macmillan, 1915.
Eco, Umberto, V. V. Ivanov, Monica Rector. *Carnival!* Edited by Thomas A. Sebeok. Berlin: Mouton, 1984.
Eliade, Mircea. *Cosmos and History: The Myth of the Eternal Return*. Translated by Willard R. Trask. New York: Harper, 1959.
———. *The Sacred and the Profane*. Translated by Willard R. Trask. New York: Harcourt and Brace, 1959.
Foucault, Michel. *The Archaeology of Knowledge*. Translated by A. M. Sheridan. New York: Harper & Row, 1972.
Geertz, Clifford. *The Interpretation of Cultures*. New York: Basic Books, 1973.
———. *Local Knowledge*. New York: Basic Books, 1983.
———. *Negara: The Theatre State in Nineteenth-Century Bali*. Princeton, N.J.: Princeton University Press, 1980.
Goffmann, Erving. *Frame Analysis: An Essay on the Organization of Experience*. Cambridge: Harvard University Press, 1974.
Hobsbawn, Eric, and Terence Ranger, eds. *The Invention of Tradition*. Cambridge: Cambridge University Press, 1982.
Huizinga, Johann. *Homo Ludens: A Study of the Play-Element in Culture*. Translated by R. F. C. Hull. Boston: Beacon Press, 1949.
Hunt, Lynn. *Politics, Culture, and Class in the French Revolution*. Berkeley: University of California Press, 1984.
Lotman, Iurii M., Lidiia Ginzburg, and Boris Uspenskii. *The Semiotics of Russian Cultural History*. Ithaca, N.Y.: Cornell University Press, 1985.
MacAloon, John J., ed. *Rite, Drama, Festival, Spectacle*. Philadelphia: ISHI, 1984.
Ozouf, Mona. *Festivals and the French Revolution*. Translated by Alan Sheridan. Cambridge: Harvard University Press, 1988.
Pieper, Joseph. *In Tune with the World: A Theory of Festivity*. New York: Harcourt, Brace & World, 1965.
Schechner, Richard. *Between Theater and Anthropology*. Philadelphia: University of Pennsylvania Press, 1985.
Shils, Edward. *Center and Periphery: Essays in Macrosociology*. Chicago: University of Chicago Press, 1975.
Strong, Roy. *Art and Power: Renaissance Festivals 1450–1650*. Berkeley: University of California Press, 1984.
Turner, Victor. *The Anthropology of Performance*. New York: DAJ Publications, 1986.
———. *Dramas, Fields and Metaphors*. Ithaca, N.Y.: Cornell University Press, 1974.
———. *The Ritual Process*. Chicago: Aldine, 1969.
———, ed. *Celebration: Studies in Festivity and Ritual*. Washington, D.C.: Smithsonian Institute Press, 1982.

Weber, Max. *Max Weber on Charisma and Institution Building.* Edited by S. N. Eisenstadt. Chicago: University of Chicago Press, 1968.
White, Hayden. *Metahistory: The Historical Imagination in Nineteenth-Century Europe.* Baltimore: Johns Hopkins University Press, 1973.
Wilentz, Sean, ed. *Rites of Power: Symbolism, Ritual and Politics since the Middle Ages.* Philadelphia: University of Pennsylvania Press, 1985.

MONOGRAPHS AND TEXTS

Aizenshtadt, V., ed. *Rezhissura i organizatsiia massovykh zrelishch.* Kharkov: KhGIK, 1973.
Aksenov, V. S. *Organizatsiia massovykh prazdnikov trudiashchikhsia, 1918–1920.* Leningrad: LGIK, 1974.
Arkin, D. "Khudozhestvennoe oformlenie narodnykh torzhestv," *Tvorchestvo,* no. 3 (1938).
Arvidsson, Claes, and Lars Erik Blomqvist, eds. *Symbols of Power: The Esthetics of Political Legitimation in the Soviet Union and Eastern Europe.* Stockholm: Almqvist & Wiksell, 1987.
Avlov, G. *Klubnyi samodeiatel'nyi teatr: Evoliutsiia metodov i form.* Leningrad: Teakinopechat', 1930.
Belenson, Aleksandr. *Iskusstvennaia zhizn'.* Petrograd: Strelets, 1921.
Bezpalov, V. F. *Teatry v dni revoliutsii.* Leningrad: Academia, 1927.
Bibikova, I. M., and N. I. Levchenko, comps. *Agitatsionno-massovoe iskusstvo: Oformlenie prazdnestv.* Moscow: Iskusstvo, 1984.
Binns, Christopher A. P. "The Changing Face of Power: Revolution and Accommodation in the Development of Soviet Ceremonial Systems," *Man,* no. 4 (1979), no. 1 (1980).
Brown, Ben W. *Theatre at the Left.* Providence, R.I.: The Booke Shop, 1938.
Brudnyi, V. I. *Obriady vchera i segodnia.* Moscow: Nauka, 1968.
Bulgakov, A., and S. Danilov. *Gosudarstvennyi agitatsionnyi teatr v Leningrade, 1918–30.* Leningrad: Academia, 1931.
Carter, Huntly. *The New Theatre and Cinema of Soviet Russia.* London: Chapman & Dodd, 1924.
Chechetin, A. I. *Istoriia massovykh narodnykh prazdnestv i predstavlenii.* Moscow: Gos. inst. kul'tury, 1976.
Danilevskii, M. *Prazdniki obshchestvennogo byta.* Moscow: Doloi negramotnost', 1927.
Danilov, S. S. *Tridtsat' let v teatre. V. V. Shimanovskii.* Novgorod: Novgorodskoe oblastnoe izd., 1948.
Déak, Frantishek. "The Agit-Prop and Circus Plays of Vladimir Mayakovsky," *Drama Review* 17, no. 1 (March 1973).
———. "Russian Mass Spectacles," *Drama Review* 19, no. 2 (June 1975).
Dobrinskaia, L. "Mesto deistviia—ploshchad'," *Klub i khudozhestvennaia samodeiatel'nost',* no. 22 (1966).

Fevral'skii, A. *Pervaia sovetskaia p'esa*. Moscow: Sovetskii pisatel', 1971.
Genkin, D. M. *Massovye prazdniki*. Moscow: Prosveshchenie, 1975.
Gerasimov, S. "Pervoe prazdnestvo oktiabr'skoi revoliutsii," *Iskusstvo*, no. 7 (1957).
Goriaeva, T. M. "Pervaia godovshchina oktiabr'skoi revoliutsii: Dokumenty," *Istoriia SSSR*, no. 6 (1987).
Gushchin, A. S. *Izo-iskusstvo v massovykh prazdnestvakh i demonstratsiiakh*. Moscow: Khudozhestvennoe izdatel'skoe aktsionernoe ob——vo, 1930.
———. *Khudozhestvennoe oformlenie massovykh prazdnestv v Leningrade, 1918–1931*. Leningrad: Izogiz, 1932.
Istoriia sovetskogo teatra. Leningrad: Academia, 1933.
Iudin, B. V., E. Shchedrin, and S. Belousov. *Massovye prazdnestva*. Moscow: Krest'ianskaia zhizn', 1935.
Kampars, P. P., and N. M. Zakovich. *Sovetskaia grazhdanskaia obriadnost'*. Moscow: Mysl', 1967.
Komitet dlia ustroistva prazdnovaniia 300-letiia Doma Romanovykh. St. Petersburg: Gos. Tipografiia, 1913.
Kuznetsova, A., A. S. Magidson, and Iu. P. Shchukin. *Oformlenie goroda v dni revoliutsionnykh prazdnestv*. Moscow: Gosizdat, 1932.
Lane, Christel. *The Rites of Rulers*. Cambridge: Cambridge University Press, 1981.
Massovye prazdnestva. Leningrad: Academia, 1926.
Massovye prazdnestva v staroi i novoi grafike. Katalog vystavki. Moscow: Izd. gos. muzeia iziashchnykh iskusstv, 1927.
Massovye prazdniki i zrelishcha. Moscow: Iskusstvo, 1961.
Mazaev, A. I. *Prazdnik kak sotsial'no-khudozhestvennoe iavlenie*. Moscow: Nauka, 1978.
Migla, A. *Masu svetku attistibas pirmsakumi*. Riga: M——vo kul'tury LatSSR, 1977.
Moskva teatral'naia. Moscow: Iskusstvo, 1960.
Nemiro, Oleg. "Khudozhestvennoe oformlenie massovykh prazdnikov," *Iskusstvo*, no. 11 (1965).
———. "Lenin i revoliutsionnye prazdniki," *Iskusstvo*, no. 10 [5] (1969).
———. "Ob etom mechtali v ssylkakh," *Nauka i religiia*, no. 11 (1977).
———. "Oformlenie Petrograda k pervoi godovshchine oktiabria," *Iskusstvo*, no. 11 (1964).
———. "Prazdnik svobody, vesny i tsvetov," *Neva*, no. 5 (1967).
———. *V gorod prishel prazdnik*. Leningrad: Aurora, 1973.
Osnos, Iurii. "U istokov sovetskogo teatra," *Teatral'nyi al'manakh*, no. 2 (1946).
Pervoe maia. Leningrad: Izd. Redizdata Puokra, 1924.
Petrova, I. "Khudozhnik teatra i tema revoliutsii," *Dekorativnoe iskusstvo SSSR*, no. 11 (1974).
Piotrovskii, A. I., ed. *Krasnoarmeiskii teatr*. Petrograd: Izd. Uprav. Petro. Voen. Okr., 1921.
———. *Mech mira*. Petrograd, 1921.

———. *Za sovetskii teatr.* Leningrad: Academia, 1925.
Pomerantseva, A. V. *Kalendar' revoliutsionnykh prazdnikov i velikikh godovshchin.* Moscow: Gosizdat, 1927.
Punin, N. *Pamiatnik Tret'emu Internatsionalu.* Peterburg: IZO, 1920.
Riumin, E. *Massovye prazdnestva.* Edited by O. M. Beskin. Moscow: GIZ, 1927.
R[omanov], [Grand Duke] K[onstantin Konstantinovich]. *The King of the Jews: A Sacred Drama.* Translated by Victor E. Marsden. New York: Funk and Wagnalls, 1914.
Rozovskii, M. *Massovye zrelishcha.* Moscow: Sovetskaia Rossiia, 1973.
Rudnev, V. A. *Sovetskie prazdniki, obriady, ritualy.* Leningrad: Lenizdat, 1979.
Russkii-sovetskii teatr 1917–1921: Dokumenty i materialy. Leningrad: Iskusstvo, 1968.
Samarskii, D. *Na strazhe mirovoi kommuny.* Rostov: Gosizdat, 1920.
Shcheglov, D. *Spektakl' v klube.* Leningrad: Nachatki znanii, 1925.
Shchekotov, N. "Iskusstvo khudozhestvennogo oformleniia," *Tvorchestvo,* no. 3 (1938).
Shelavin, K. *Pervoe maia v Rossii.* Leningrad: Priboi, 1926.
Shishlo, B. "Ulitsa revoliutsii," *Dekorativnoe iskusstvo SSSR,* no. 3 (1970).
Sinitsyn, V. G., ed. *Nashi prazdniki.* Moscow: Politizdat, 1977.
Slonimskii, Iu. "V 1918 godu na spektakle 'Misteriia-Buff,' " *Voprosy literatury,* no. 10 (1972).
Speranskaia, E., ed. *Agitatsionno-massovoe iskusstvo pervykh let oktiabria.* Moscow: Iskusstvo, 1971.
Stites, Richard. "Adorning the Russian Revolution: The Primary Symbols of Bolshevism, 1917–1918," *Sbornik,* no. 10 (1984).
———. "The Origins of Soviet Ritual Style: Symbol and Festival in the Russian Revolution." In *Symbols of Power: The Esthetics of Political Legitimation in the Soviet Union and Eastern Europe,* edited by Claes Arvidsson and Lars Erik Blomqvist. Stockholm: Almqvist & Wiksell, 1987.
———. *Revolutionary Dreams: Utopian Vision and Experimental Life in the Russian Revolution.* New York: Oxford University Press, 1989.
Strigalev, A. "M. V. Dobuzhinskii v revoliutsionnye gody," *Sovetskoe monumental'noe iskusstvo,* no. 75–77 (1979).
Strigalev, Anatolii. "Sviaz' vremen," *Dekorativnoe iskusstvo SSSR,* no. 4 (1978).
Suliaeva, Nadezhda. *Revoliutsionnyi prazdnichnyi plakat, 1917–1927.* Leningrad: Khudozhnik RSFSR, 1982.
Tolstoi, V. P. "Iz opyta prazdnichnogo oformleniia gorodov," *Tvorchestvo,* no. 4 (1957).
———. "Materialy k istorii agitatsionnogo iskusstva perioda grazhdanskoi voiny," *Soobshcheniia Instituta istorii iskusstv, Akademiia nauk SSSR,* no. 3 (1953).
Torzhestvuiushchaia Minerva: Obshchenarodnoe zrelishche, predstavlennoe bol'shim maskaradom v Moskve 1763 goda. Moscow: Imperatorskii Moskovskii universitet, 1763.
Tsekhnovitser, O. *Demonstratsiia i karnaval.* Moscow: Doloi negramotnost', 1927.

———. *Prazdnestva revoliutsii*. Leningrad: Priboi, 1931.
Vesna krasna: Allegoricheskoe shestvie, ustroennoe vo vremia narodnogo prazdnika 21 maia 1883 g. na Khodynskom pole M. Lentovskim po sluchaiu sviashchennogo koronovaniia ikh imperatorskikh velichestv. Illustrated by F. O. Shekhtel'. Moscow, 1883.
Vinogradov, N. N., ed. *Prazdnovanie 300-letiia tsarstvovaniia Doma Romanovykh v kostromskoi gubernii 19–20 maia 1913 goda.* Kostroma: Gub. tipografiia, 1914.
Vysochaishe utverzhdennyi poriadok torzhestvennogo prazdnovaniia 100-letiia Borodinskogo srazheniia 26 avg. 1912 g. v sele Borodine. St. Petersburg: Tip. Trenke i Fiusno, 1912.
Zelentsova, N. S. *Narodnyi revoliutsionnyi teatr v Rossii èpokhi grazhdanskoi voiny i revoliutsii.* Moscow, 1971.

GENERAL WORKS

Aizenshtadt, V. K. *Russkaia sovetskaia istoricheskaia dramaturgiia 1917–1929.* Kharkov: KhGIK, 1969.
———. *Sovetskii samodeiatel'nyi teatr.* Kharkov: KhGIK, 1983.
Alekseev-Iakovlev, A. Ia. *Russkie narodnye gulianiia.* Edited by Evg. Kuznetsov. Leningrad: Iskusstvo, 1948.
Alpatov, M. V., and E. A. Gunst. *Nikolai Nikolaevich Sapunov.* Moscow: Iskusstvo, 1965.
Al'pers, B. V. *Teatral'nye ocherki.* Moscow: Iskusstvo, 1977.
Andrianova, K. "K istorii teatra na fronte v period grazhdanskoi voiny," *Trudy gosudarstvennogo tsentral'nogo teatral'nogo muzeia im. A. A. Bakhrushina.* Moscow: Iskusstvo, 1941.
Arena. Teatral'nyi al'manakh. Peterburg: Vremia, 1924.
Arskii, Pavel. *Osvobozhdennyi trud.* Arkhangelsk, 1920.
Arts Council of Great Britain. *Art in Revolution: Soviet Art and Design since 1917.* London: Arts Council, 1971.
Avrich, Paul. *The Russian Anarchists.* Princeton, N.J.: Princeton University Press, 1967.
———. *Russian Rebels 1600–1800.* New York: Norton, 1976.
Bardovskii, A. A. *Teatral'nyi zritel' na fronte v kanun oktiabria.* Leningrad: RTO, 1928.
Barron, Stephanie, and Maurice Tuchman, eds. *The Avant-Garde in Russia, 1910–1930: New Perspectives.* Los Angeles: Museum of Art, 1980.
Beskin, E. *Istoriia russkogo teatra.* Moscow: Gosizdat, 1928.
Bessal'ko, P. *Kamenshchik: Bashnia kommuny.* Petrograd: Izd. Proletkul'ta, 1918.
Blok, A. A. *Dnevniki.* Leningrad: Izd. pisatelei, 1928.
———. *Sobranie sochinenii.* Moscow: Khud. literatura, 1961–1966.
Blokovskii sbornik. 4 vols. Tartu: Gos. universitet, 1972–81.
Boguslavskii, A. O., and V. A. Diev. *Russkaia sovetskaia dramaturgiia, 1917–1935.* Moscow: AN SSSR, 1963.

Bonnell, Victoria E. "The Representation of Politics and the Politics of Representation," *Russian Review* 47 (1988).
Bowlt, John E., ed. and trans. *Russian Art of the Avant-Garde: Theory and Criticism, 1902–1934.* New York: Viking Press, 1976.
Bradby, David, and John McCormick. *People's Theatre.* London: Croom Helm, 1978.
Bradshaw, Martha, ed. *Soviet Theaters, 1917–1941.* New York: Research Program on the USSR, 1954.
Braun, Edward. *The Theatre of Meyerhold. Revolution on the Modern Stage.* New York: Drama Book Specialists, 1979.
Brooks, Jeffrey. *When Russia Learned to Read: Literacy and Popular Literature, 1861–1917.* Princeton, N.J.: Princeton University Press, 1985.
Butnik-Siverskii, B. S. *Sovetskii plakat epokhi grazhdanskoi voiny, 1918–1921.* Moscow: Izd. Vses. knizhnoi palaty, 1960.
Carter, Huntly. *The New Spirit in the Russian Theatre.* London: Brentano, 1929.
Chiniakov, A. *Brat'ia Vesniny.* Moscow: Stroiizdat, 1970.
Clark, Katerina. *The Soviet Novel: History as Ritual.* Chicago: University of Chicago Press, 1981.
Clark, Katerina, and Michael Holquist. *Mikhail Bakhtin.* Cambridge: Harvard University Press, 1984.
Davydova, M. V. *Ocherki istorii russkogo teatral'no-dekoratsionnogo iskusstva XVIII veka–nachalo XX veka.* Moscow: Nauka, 1974.
Dickinson, Thorold. *Soviet Cinema.* London: Falcon Press, 1948.
Dmitriev, Iu. A. *Mikhail Lentovskii.* Moscow: Iskusstvo, 1978.
———. *Russkii tsirk.* Moscow: Iskusstvo, 1953.
———. *Sovetskii tsirk.* Moscow: Iskusstvo, 1963.
Dobuzhinskii, M. V. *Vospominaniia.* New York: Put' zhizn', 1976.
Dostoevsky, Fyodor. *The Devils.* Translated by David Magarshack. London: Penguin, 1953.
Dowd, David. *Pageant-Master of the Republic: Jacques-Louis David and the French Revolution.* Lincoln, Neb.: University of Nebraska, 1948.
Drengenberg, Hans-Jürgen. *Die sowjetische Politik auf dem Gebiet der bildenden Kunst von 1917 bis 1934.* Wiesbaden: Harrassowitz, 1972.
Eastman, Max. *Education and Art in Soviet Russia: In the Light of Official Decrees and Documents.* New York: Socialist Publication Society, 1919.
Efros, A. M. *Portret Natana Al'tmana.* Moscow: Shipovnik, 1922.
Evreinoff, Nicolas. *Histoire du théâtre russe.* Paris: Editions du Chene, 1947.
Fevral'skii, A. *Maiakovskii-dramaturg.* Moscow: Iskusstvo, 1940.
———. "Teatr na fronte grazhdanskoi voiny," *Teatral'nyi al'manakh,* no. 8 (1948).
———. *Zapiski rovesnika veka.* Moscow: Sov. pisatel', 1976.
Filippov, V. *Puti samodeiatel'nogo teatra.* Moscow: GAKhN, 1924.
Fillipov, B. *Aktery bez grima.* Moscow: Sovetskaia Rossiia, 1971.
Fitzpatrick, Sheila. *The Commissariat of Enlightenment: Soviet Organization of Education and the Arts under Lunacharsky, October 1917–1921.* Cambridge: Cambridge University Press, 1970.

———, ed. *Cultural Revolution in Russia, 1928–1931*. Bloomington: Indiana University Press, 1978.
Fülöp-Miller, René, and Joseph Gregor. *The Russian Theatre*. New York: Benjamin Blom, 1930.
Furmanov, Dm. *Sobranie sochinenii*. Moscow: Khudozh. literatura, 1961.
Gaideburov, P. P. *Literaturnoe nasledie*. Edited by Sim. Dreiden. Moscow: VTO, 1977.
German, Mikhail, ed. *Serdtsem slushaia revoliutsiiu. Iskusstvo pervykh let oktiabria*. Leningrad: Aurora, 1980.
Gibian, George, and H. W. Tjalsma, ed. *Russian Modernism: Culture and the Avant-Garde*. Ithaca, N.Y.: Cornell University Press, 1976.
Giliarovskaia, N. *Teatral'no-dekoratsionnoe iskusstvo za 5 let*. Kazan: Izd. kombinata izd——va i pechati, 1924.
Glan, B. "Ob ètom mechtal Gor'kii," *Teatr*, no. 6 (1961).
Gleason, Abbott, Peter Kenez, and Richard Stites, eds. *Bolshevik Culture*. Bloomington: Indiana University Press, 1985.
Goldberg, RoseLee. *Performance: Live Art from 1909 to the Present*. New York: Harry N. Abrams, 1979.
Gollerbakh, E. F., A. Golovin, and L. I. Zheverzheev, eds. *Teatral'no-dekoratsionnoe iskusstvo v SSSR, 1917–1927*. Leningrad: Izd. komiteta vystavki, 1927.
Golovasevich, V., and V. Lashchilin. *Narodnyi teatr na Donu*. Rostov: Rostizdat, 1947.
Golub, Spencer. *Evreinov: The Theatre of Paradox and Transformation*. Ann Arbor, Mich.: UMI Research Press, 1984.
Gorchakov, Nikolai A. *The Theater in Soviet Russia*. Translated by Edgar Lehrman. New York: Columbia University Press, 1957.
Gorky, Maxim. *The Confession*. Translated by Rose Strunsky. New York: Frederick A. Stokes, 1909.
———. *Untimely Thoughts: Essays on Revolution, Culture and the Bolsheviks, 1917–1918*. Translated by Herman Ermolaev. New York: P. S. Eriksson, 1971.
Gourfinkel, Nina. *Théâtre russe contemporain*. Paris: La Renaissance du Livre, 1931.
Gray-Prokofieva, Camilla. *The Russian Experiment in Art, 1863–1922*. London: Thames and Hudson, 1971.
Günther, Hans, ed. *The Culture of the Stalin Period*. New York: St. Martin's Press, 1990.
Gvozdev, A. A., and A. I. Piotrovskii. *Istoriia evropeiskogo teatra*. Leningrad: Academia, 1931.
Hoover, Marjorie L. *Meyerhold: The Art of Conscious Theater*. Amherst: University of Massachusetts Press, 1974.
Hulse, James W. *The Forming of the Communist International*. Stanford, Calif.: Stanford University Press, 1964.
Il'ina, G. I. *Kul'turnoe stroitel'stvo v Petrograde: Oktiabr' 1917–1920 gg*. Leningrad: Nauka, 1982.
Il'inskii, Igor. *Sam o sebe*. Moscow: VTO, 1961.

Istoriia sovetskogo dramaticheskogo teatra. Moscow: Nauka, 1966–71.
Istoriko-revoliutsionnye pamiatniki SSSR. Moscow: Politizdat, 1972.
Iufit, A. Z. *Revoliutsiia i teatr, 1917–1923.* Leningrad: Iskusstvo, 1977.
Iufit, A., ed. *Lenin, revoliutsiia, teatr. Dokumenty i vospominaniia.* Leningrad: Iskusstvo, 1970.
Iurev, Iu. M. *Zapiski.* Leningrad: Iskusstvo, 1963.
Iutkevich, S. *Kontrapunkt rezhissera.* Moscow: Iskusstvo, 1960.
Ivanov, Viacheslav. *Prometei. Tragediia.* Petersburg: Alkonost, 1919.
Iz istorii stroitel'stva sovetskoi kul'tury: Moskva 1917–1918 gg. Moscow: Mysl', 1964.
Jangfeldt, Bengt. *Majakovskij and Futurism, 1917–1921.* Stockholm: Almqvist & Wiksell, 1977.
Kalbouss, George. "From Mystery to Fantasy: An Attempt to Categorize the Plays of Russian Symbolists," *Canadian-American Slavic Studies*, 8, no. 4 (1974).
Kamenskii, A. *Vernisazhi.* Moscow: Sovetskii khudozhnik, 1974.
Kamenskii, Vasilii. *Sten'ka Razin. Kollektivnoe predstavlenie v 9-i kartinakh.* Petrograd, 1919.
———. *Stikhotvoreniia i poèmy.* Moscow: Sovetskii pisatel', 1966.
Kashina-Evreinova, A. *N. N. Evreinov v mirovom teatre XX veka.* Paris, 1964.
Katalog vystavki rabot khudozhnitsy V. M. Khodasevich: 15 let v teatre. Introduction by S. Radlov. Leningrad: Dom teatral'nykh rabotnikov, 1934.
Katanian, V. *Maiakovskii, literaturnaia khronika.* Leningrad: Sovetskii pisatel', 1948.
Kazanskii, B. V. *Metod teatra.* Leningrad: Academia, 1925.
Kenez, Peter. *The Birth of the Propaganda State: Soviet Methods of Mass Mobilization, 1917–1929.* Cambridge: Cambridge University Press, 1985.
Kerzhentsev, P. *Sredi plameni.* Petrograd: Gosizdat, 1921.
Khaichenko, G. A. *Russkii narodnyi teatr kontsa XIX–nachala XX veka.* Moscow: Nauka, 1975.
Khlebnikov, Velimir. *Sobranie proizvedenii.* Leningrad: Izd. pisatelei, 1928–33.
Kleberg, Lars. "Publiczność zjednoczona czy rozbita?" *Dialog*, no. 10 (1979).
———. "Sootnoshenie stseny i zritel'nogo zala. K tipologii russkogo teatra nachala XX veka," *Scando-Slavica* 20 (1974).
———. *Teatern som handling: Sovyetisk avantgardeestetik 1917–1927.* Stockholm: Akademilitt., 1977.
Kleberg, Lars, and Nils Ake Nilsson, eds. *Theater and Literature in Russia 1900–1930.* Stockholm: Almqvist & Wiksell, 1984.
Klibanov, A. I. *Narodnaia sotsial'naia utopiia v Rossii XIX vek.* Moscow: Nauka, 1978.
Knödler-Bunte, E., and G. Erler, eds. *Kultur und Kulturrevolution in der Sowjetunion.* West Berlin, Kronberg Ts.: Aesthetik und Kommunikation Verlag–Scriptor Verlag, 1978.
Kogan, D. *Sergei Iurevich Sudeikin.* Moscow: Iskusstvo, 1974.
Kozlov, P. *Legenda o kommunare. P'esa-poema v 5 kartinakh.* Arkhangelsk: Volna, 1923.
Krasnaia Moskva, 1917–1920 gg. Moscow: Izd. Moskovskogo soveta, 1920.

Krupskaia, N. K. *Pedagogicheskie sochineniia.* Moscow: Izd. APN RSFSR, 1959.

Kryzhitskii, G. K. A. *Mardzhanov i russkii teatr.* Moscow: VTO, 1958.

Kuzma Petrov-Vodkin. Leningrad: Aurora, 1980.

Kuzmin, M., S. Radlov, S. Mokulskii, and A. Movshenson, eds. *Valentina Khodasevich: Sbornik statei.* Leningrad: Academia, 1927.

Kuznetsov, E. M. *Arena i liudi sovetskogo tsirka.* Leningrad: Iskusstvo, 1947.

———. *Tsirk.* Leningrad: Academia, 1931.

———, ed. *Sovetskii tsirk, 1918–1938.* Leningrad: Iskusstvo, 1938.

Lange, David C., and William Weber, eds. *Wagnerism in European Culture and Politics.* Ithaca, N.Y.: Cornell University Press, 1984.

Lapshin, V. P. *Khudozhestvennaia zhizn' Moskvy i Petrograda v 1917 godu.* Moscow: Sovetskii khudozhnik, 1983.

Lebedev, P. I. *Sovetskoe iskusstvo v period inostrannoi interventsii i grazhdanskoi voiny.* Moscow: Iskusstvo, 1949.

Leifert, A. V. *Balagany.* Petrograd: Ezhenedel'nik Petrogradskikh gos. akademicheskikh teatrov, 1922.

Lenin, V. I. *Collected Works.* Moscow: Progress Publishers, 1960–70.

Lenin, V. I., and A. V. Lunacharskii. *Perepiska, doklady, dokumenty.* Literaturnoe nasledstvo, no. 80. Moscow: Nauka, 1971.

Lentulova, M. *Khudozhnik Aristarkh Lentulov.* Moscow: Sovetskii khudozhnik, 1969.

Levitskii, A. *Rasskazy o kinematografe.* Moscow: Iskusstvo, 1964.

Leyda, Jay. *Kino: A History of the Russian and Soviet Film.* New York: Macmillan, 1960.

Life as Theater: Five Modern Plays. Ann Arbor, Mich.: Ardis, 1973.

Likhachev, D. S., A. M. Panchenko, and N. V. Ponyrko. *Smekhovoi mir drevnei Rusi.* Leningrad: Nauka, 1976.

Lisavtsev, E. I. *Novye sovetskie traditsii.* Moscow: Sovetskaia Rossiia, 1966.

Listov, V. *Istoriia smotrit v ob"ektiv.* Moscow: Iskusstvo, 1974.

Lodder, Christina. *Russian Constructivism.* New Haven, Conn.: Yale University Press, 1983.

Lorenz, Richard, ed. *Proletarische Kulturrevolution in Sowjet Russland, 1917–1921.* Munich: Deutscher Taschenbuch Verlag, 1969.

Maiakovskii, V. V. *Polnoe sobranie sochinenii.* Moscow: Khudozh. literatura, 1955–61.

Malevich, K. S. *Essays in Art: 1915–1933.* Edited by Troels Andersen. London: Rapp & Whiting, 1968.

Mally, Lynn. *Culture of the Future: The Proletkult Movement in Revolutionary Russia.* Berkeley: University of California Press, 1990.

Mandelstam, Osip. *The Complete Critical Prose and Letters.* Translated by Jane Gary Harris. Ann Arbor, Mich.: Ardis, 1979.

Mandelstam, Osip. *The Prose of Osip Mandelstam.* Translated by Clarence Brown. Princeton, N.J.: Princeton University Press, 1965.

Mardzhanov, K. A. *Tvorcheskoe nasledie.* Tbilisi: Zaria vostoka, 1958.

Markov, P. A. *Noveishie teatral'nye techeniia.* Moscow: Dom Polenova, 1924.

———. *The Soviet Theater.* New York: G. P. Putnam, 1935.

Markov, Vladimir. *Russian Futurism: A History*. Berkeley: University of California Press, 1968.
Mashirov-Samobytnik, A. "Istoriia Proletkul'ta (1905–1917)," *Voprosy literatury*, no. 1 (1958).
Massie, Robert K. *Peter the Great*. New York: Knopf, 1980.
Matsa, I. *Sovetskoe iskusstvo za 15 let: Materialy i dokumentatsiia*. Moscow: Ogiz-Izogiz, 1933.
Meierkhol'd, V. E. *Perepiska, 1896–1939*. Moscow: Iskusstvo, 1976.
Miklashevskii, K. *La commedia dell'arte, ili teatr italianskikh komediantov*. Petrograd: Sirius, 1917.
Millon, Henry A., and Linda Nochlin, eds. *Art and Architecture in the Service of Politics*. Cambridge: MIT Press, 1978.
Mogilevskii, A. I., V. Filippov, and A. M. Rodionov. *Teatry Moskvy, 1917–1927*. Moscow: GAKhN, 1928.
Mokul'skii, S. S., ed. *Teatral'naia entsyklopediia*. Moscow: Sovetskii entsyklopediia, 1961–1967.
Moloko kobylits sbornik. Risunki, stikhi, proza. Moscow: Gileia, 1914.
Mosse, George L. *Masses and Man*. New York: Howard Fertig, 1980.
Mumford, Lewis. *The City in History*. New York: Harcourt, Brace & World, 1961.
Muratova, K. D. *M. Gor'kii v bor'be za razvitie sovetskoi literatury*. Moscow: AN SSSR, 1958.
Murray, Henry A., ed. *Myth and Mythmaking*. Boston: Beacon Press, 1960.
N. N. Sapunov. Petrograd: Izd. Apollona, 1916.
Narodnaia graviura i fol'klor v Rossii XVII–XIX vv. Moscow: Sovetskii khudozhnik, 1976.
Nekrylova, A. F. *Russkie narodnye gorodskie prazdniki, uveseleniia i zrelishcha: Konets XVIII–nachalo XIX veka*. Leningrad: Iskusstvo, 1984.
Nevskii, V. A. *Massovaia politiko-prosvetitel'naia rabota revoliutsionnykh let*. Moscow: Gudok, 1925.
Neznamov, M. *Stareishii russkii teatr na Urale*. Chkalov: Chkalovskoe izd., 1948.
Nilsson, Nils Ake, ed. *Art, Society, Revolution: Russia, 1917–1921*. Stockholm: Almqvist & Wiksell, 1979.
Nollau, Günter. *International Communism and World Revolution*. New York: Praeger, 1961.
Obzor deiatel'nosti otdela izobrazitel'nykh iskusstv. Petrograd: Narkompros, 1920.
Ocherki istorii Leningrada. Moscow: AN SSSR, 1955–1964.
Ocherki istorii russkogo-sovetskogo dramaticheskogo teatra. Moscow: Izd. AN SSSR, 1954–1961.
Ocherki istorii russkoi-sovetskoi dramaturgii, 1917–1934. Leningrad: Iskusstvo, 1963.
Paech, Joachim. *Das Theater der Russischen Revolution*. Kronberg Ts: Scriptor Verlag, 1974.
Palmier, Jean-Michel. *Lenine, l'art et la révolution*. Paris: Payot, 1975.

Panfilov, A. *Teatral'noe iskusstvo Urala 1917-1967*. Sverdlovsk: Sredne-ural'skoe knizhnoe izd., 1967.
Panina, S. V. "Na Peterburgskoi okraine," *Novyi zhurnal*, no. 48-49 (1957).
Paul, Eden and Cedar Paul. *Proletcult: Proletarian Culture*. New York: Thomas Seltzer, 1921.
Perets, V. N. *Italianskie komedii i intermedii, predstavlennye pri dvore imp. Anny Ioannovny v 1733-1735 gg*. Petrograd: Imp. Akademiia nauk, 1917.
Pervoe maia. Literaturnyi-khudozhestvennyi al'manakh. Leningrad: Izd. Redizdata Puokra, 1924.
Piast, V. *Vstrechi*. Moscow: Federatsiia, 1929.
Pinegina, L. A. *Prazdnichnaia ènergiia mass: Khudozhestvennoe tvorchestvo rabochikh 20-kh godov*. Moscow: Znanie, 1985.
Pozharskaia, M. N. *Russkoe teatral'no-dekoratsionnoe iskusstvo kontsa XIX-nachala XX veka*. Moscow: Iskusstvo, 1970.
Proletarskie poety pervykh let sovetskoi èpokhi. Leningrad: Sovetskii pisatel', 1959.
Rabinowitch, Alexander. *The Bolsheviks Come to Power*. New York: Norton, 1976.
Rakitina, E., ed. *Khudozhnik-stsena-èkran*. Moscow: Sovetskii khudozhnik, 1975.
Red'ko, A. E. *Teatr i èvoliutsiia teatral'nykh form*. Leningrad: Izd. M. i S. Sabashnikovykh, 1926.
Repertuar. Sbornik materialov. Petrograd: Izd. TEO NKP, 1919.
Riordan, James. *Sport in Soviet Society: Development of Sport and Physical Education in Russia and the USSR*. Cambridge: Cambridge University Press, 1977.
Ritm, prostranstvo, vremia v literature i iskusstve. Leningrad: Nauka, 1974.
Robin, Regine. *Le réalisme socialiste: Une esthétique impossible*. Paris: Payot, 1986.
Rodina, T. M. *Aleksandr Blok i russkii teatr nachala XX veka*. Moscow: Nauka, 1972.
Rosenberg, William, ed. *Bolshevik Visions: The First Phase of the Cultural Revolution in Soviet Russia*. Ann Arbor, Mich.: Ardis, 1984.
Rosenthal, B. G. "Eschatology and the Appeal of the Revolution: Merezhkovsky, Bely, Blok," *California Slavic Studies*, no. 2 (1980).
———, ed. *Nietzsche in Russia*. Princeton, N.J.: Princeton University Press, 1986.
Rovinskii, D. A. *Obozrenie ikonopisaniia v Rossii do kontsa XVII veka. Opisaniia feierverkov i illiuminatsii*. St. Petersburg: Suvorin, 1903.
Rudenstine, Angelica, ed. *Russian Avant-Garde Art: The George Costakis Collection*. New York: Harry N. Abrams, 1981.
Rudnitsky, Konstantin. *Meyerhold the Director*. Translated by George Petrov. Ann Arbor, Mich.: Ardis, 1981.
Russkaia teatral'naia parodiia XIX-nachala XX veka. Moscow: Iskusstvo, 1976.
Russkaia-sovetskaia èstrada, 1917-1929. Moscow: Iskusstvo, 1976.

Segel, Harold B. *Turn-of-the-Century Cabaret: Paris, Barcelona, Berlin, Munich, Vienna, Cracow, Moscow, St. Petersburg, Zurich.* New York: Columbia University Press, 1987.

———. *Twentieth-Century Russian Drama: From Gorky to the Present.* New York: Columbia University Press, 1979.

Senelick, Laurence, ed. *Russian Dramatic Theory from Pushkin to the Symbolists.* Austin: University of Texas Press, 1981.

Shiriaeva, P. G. "Iz istorii razvitiia nekotorykh revoliutsionnykh traditsii," *Sovetskaia ètnografiia,* no. 6 (1975).

Sidorov, A. A. *Russkaia grafika za gody revoliutsii.* Moscow: Dom pechati, 1923.

Sipovskii, V. V. "Italianskii teatr pri Anne Ioannovne," *Russkaia starina,* no. 5 (June 1900).

Skorodumov, N. V. *Novyi metod uproshchennykh postanovok: Ustroistvo stseny i dekoratsii.* Moscow: Izd. Sytina, 1913.

Skriabin, A. *Pis'ma.* Moscow: Muzyka, 1965.

Slavianskii fol'klor. Moscow: Nauka, 1972.

Smirnov-Nesvitskii, Iu. *Zrelishche neobychaineishee: Maiakovskii i teatr.* Leningrad: Iskusstvo, 1975.

Soloviev, V. N. *Maiakovskomu.* Leningrad: Khudozh. literatura, 1940.

Sovetskaia kul'tura: Itogi i perspektivy. Moscow: Izd. Izvestii, 1924.

Sovetskii politicheskii plakat / The Soviet Political Poster 1917–1945. Moscow: Sovetskii khudozhnik, 1984.

Sovetskii teatr: K tridtsatiletiiu sovetskogo gosudarstva. Moscow: VTO, 1947.

Stark, E. A. *Starinnyi teatr.* Petrograd: Tret'ia strazha, 1922.

Steffan, Truman Guy, ed. *Lord Byron's Cain.* Austin: University of Texas Press, 1968.

Stepanov, Z. V. *Kul'turnaia zhizn' Leningrada 20-kh–nachala 30-kh godov.* Leningrad: Nauka, 1976.

Stephan, Halina. *"LEF" and the Left Front of the Arts.* Munich: Verlag Otto Sagner, 1981.

Stepun, Fedor. *Byvshee i nesbyvsheesia.* New York: Izd. im. Chekhova, 1956.

———. *Vstrechi.* Munich: T——vo zarubezhnykh pisatelei, 1962.

Swan, Alfred J. *Scriabin.* London: John Lane, 1923.

Talanov, A. *Bol'shaia sud'ba.* Moscow: Politicheskaia literatura, 1967.

Tamashin, L. *Sovetskaia dramaturgiia v gody grazhdanskoi voiny.* Moscow: Iskusstvo, 1961.

Teatr narodov SSSR: Dokumenty i materialy, 1917–1921 gg. Leningrad: Iskusstvo, 1972.

Tezisy Vsesoiuznoi konferentsii "Tvorchestvo A. A. Bloka i russkaia kul'tura XX veka." Tartu, 1975.

Titova, G. V. "A. V. Lunacharskii o revoliutsionno-romanticheskom teatra," in *Teatr i dramaturgiia,* Leningrad, 1967.

Tolstoy, Alexei. *The Road to Calvary.* Translated by Edith Bone. New York: Knopf, 1946.

Tsekhnovitser, O., and I. Erenin. *Teatr Petrushki.* Moscow: Gosizdat, 1927.

Tsinkovich, V., ed. *Pervaia russkaia revoliutsiia i teatr: Materialy i stat'i.* Moscow: Iskusstvo, 1956.
Tugenkhol'd, Ia. *Iskusstvo oktiabr'skoi èpokhi.* Leningrad: Academia, 1930.
Tumarkin, Nina. *Lenin Lives! The Lenin Cult in Soviet Russia.* Cambridge: Harvard University Press, 1983.
U istokov kommunisticheskogo truda. Moscow: Izd. sotsial'no-èkonomicheskoi literatury, 1959.
V. Maiakovskii v vospominaniiakh sovremennikov. Moscow: Goslitizdat, 1963.
Vakhtangov, Evg. *Materialy i stat'i.* Moscow: VTO, 1959.
Vasil'ev-Viaz'min, I. I. *Iskusstvo liudnykh ploshchadei.* Moscow: Znanie, 1977.
Volkov, N. *Meierkhol'd.* Leningrad: Academia, 1929.
Volkova, N. "Materialy Proletkul'ta v TsGALI," *Voprosy literatury,* no. 1 (1958).
Vsevolodskii-Gerngross, V. V. *Istoriia russkogo teatra.* Leningrad: Teakinopechat', 1929.
Vstrechi s Meierkhol'dom. Moscow: VTO, 1967.
Warner, Elizabeth. *The Russian Folk Theatre.* The Hague: Mouton, 1977.
West, James. *Russian Symbolism.* London: Methuen, 1970.
Wiener, Leo. *The Contemporary Drama of Russia.* Boston: Little, 1924.
Zamiatin, Eugene. *We.* Translated by Gregory Zilboorg. New York: Dutton, 1952.
Zguta, Russell. "Peter I's Drunken Synod of Fools and Jesters," *Jahrbücher für Geschichte Osteuropas* 21, no. 1 (1973).
Znosko-Borovskii, E. A. "Bashennyi teatr," *Apollon,* no. 8 (1910).
———. *Russkii teatr nachala XX veka.* Prague: Plamia, 1925.
Zolotnitskii, D. I. *Zori teatral'nogo oktiabria.* Leningrad: Iskusstvo, 1976.
Zorkaia, N. M. *Na rubezhe stoletii: U istokov massovogo iskusstva v Rossii, 1900–1910.* Moscow: Nauka, 1976.

Index

Adaptation. See *Instsenirovka*
Administrator of festivals, 89, 93–94, 108, 111, 185, 193; and futurists, 96–100, 188
Admiralty (Petrograd), 74, 95, 96, 106, 196
Admiralty Square (Petrograd), 105, 106
Adult Education Department. *See under* Narkompros
Aeschylus, 26, 125
Aesthetics. *See* Socialist aesthetics
Agit-Prop, 195
Agit-trial, 110, 172, 181. *See also* Dramatic play; Game playing
Aleksandrinsky Theater (Petrograd), 25
Aleksandrovsky Garden (Moscow), 95
Alekseev, Ivan and Olga, 96, 100
Alekseev-Iakovlev, Aleksei, 16, 70, 128, 129, 130, 172, 173; *Song of the Merchant Kalashnikov*, 107
Aleksei, Crown Prince, 128
Alexander Column (Petrograd), 96, 203
Alexander I, 96
Alexander II, monument to, 82
Alexander III, coronation of (1883), 17; monument to, 82, 157
All-Arts Union (Petrograd, 1917), 18–19
All-Russian Central Committee for October (Celebrations) (Moscow, 1921), 211

Along the Thorny Path to the Stars (Petrograd, 1920), 216
Altman, Nathan, 3, 96, 99, 100, 188, 195, 196, 197
Amateur theater, 133, 135, 136, 216
Anarchism and anarchists, 77, 88, 101
Ancient Theater (Petrograd), 30, 61, 76, 164, 203
Andreev, Leonid, 20; *He Who Gets Slapped*, 111
Andreeva, Maria, 25, 26, 113, 166, 188
Anna Ioannovna (empress), and marriage of dwarf jesters, 55
Annenkov, Iury, 23, 95, 115–16, 157, 165, 168, 203, 204, 205; *First Distiller* (1919), 115–16, 165
Antonov-Ovseenko, Vladimir, 203
Antselovich, 89, 99
Apollonian and Dionysian, 34, 36, 37, 54, 62, 138
Arbatov, Nikolai, 52
Arts Commission (Petrograd, 1917), 18, 19
Arts Department (Moscow Soviet), 94, 98
Arts-Educational Commission (Moscow, 1917), 21
Association of Worker-Peasant and Red Army Theater, 137
Audience, 193, 203; control of, 145–46,

INDEX

Audience (*continued*)
  160, 161, 189; participation, 34, 37,
  51–52, 61, 121, 125–26, 136–37,
  140, 167–68; and propaganda, 10–
  11. See also *Deistvo; Sliianie*
Aurora (battleship), 1, 201, 207
Auto. See *Deistvo*
Avlov, Grigory, 122

Bakhtin, Mikhail, 44, 53–55, 65
Bakhtin, N. N., 124
Bakunin, Mikhail, 77
Balagan. See *under* Fairground entertainments
Balakirev, E. A. (jester), 128
Baltic Factory Theater (Petrograd), 30
Bat (Petrograd cabaret), 60
Battle of Borodino, 100th anniversary of (1912), 17, 63
Beethoven, Ludwig von: *Lenore (Fidelio)*, 76
Beliaev, Iury, 63
Bely, Andrei, 7, 57–58, 64–65, 68, 146
Benois, Aleksandr, 18, 54
Berezovye Rudki (Ukraine), 173
Berlioz, Louis Hector: *Symphonie fantastique*, 133
Bessalko, Pavel, 30, 32
Bezdna, rebellion in (1861), 132
Biblical motifs. See *under* Religion and theater
Bim and Bom (clowns), 114
Björnson, Björnstjerne: *Beyond Human Might*, 49, 120
Blanqui, Jérôme: monument to, 83; *Blockade of Russia* (Petrograd, 1920), 168, 171–74
Blok, Aleksandr, 57–60, 64, 65, 68, 75, 79, 94, 104, 107, 128, 165; *Balaganchik*, 59–60, 104, 111; *Boat*, 113; *Ramses*, 113; *Tristram*, 113; "Twelve," 70
Blokh, Mikhail, 169
Boat (Lodka), 124–25
Bobrishchev-Pushkin, A. V., 117
Boccioni, Umberto, 64
Bogdanov, Aleksandr, 7, 27, 28, 30,35, 38, 88, 151; *Red Star*, 35
Bohemian Club (San Francisco), 27
Bolotnikov, Ivan, 132; monument to, 83

Bolshoi Dramatic Theater (Petrograd), 26, 157, 185
Bolshoi Opera Theater (Petrograd), 164
Bolshoi Theater (Moscow), 72, 76, 95
Bondi, Iury, 63
Book Day (1925), 214
Boy Scouts, 20, 199
Brest-Litovsk, Treaty of, 91, 132
Briusov, Valery, 57
Brutus (Marcus Junius Brutus), monument to, 83
Burliuk, David, 212; *Burning of the Hydra of Counter-Revolution* (Voronezh, 1918), 41
Byron, Lord, 26; *Cain*, 48

Calderón, Pedro, 165; *Adoration of the Cross*, 57–58; *Purgatory of St. Patrick*, 30
Calendar. See Socialist holidays and calendar
Campanella, Tommaso, 7; *City of the Sun*, 84
Capitalist Intrigues. See *Good Men of Versailles*
Carmagnole, 159, 186, 189
Carnivals, 8, 53–55, 58, 59, 97, 105–7; sponsorship of, 8, 16–17, 18, 135
Carousel of Craft-Guilds (Moscow, 1919), 109
Carousels, 106, 107
Catherine the Great, 17, 181; coronation of (1763), 55, 117
Central Organizing Bureau for the October Triumphs (Petrograd, 1918), 94
Central Organizing Committee, 197 (Moscow, 1920); 89 (Petrograd, 1918)
Chagall, Marc, 3, 96
Chaliapin, Fedor, 25, 26, 113, 123, 127
Chamber Theater (Moscow), 62
Charov, I. M., 124
Chastushki, 116
Chekan, Victoria, 30, 57
Chekhov, Anton, 31, 48
Chekhov, Mikhail, 17
Chernyshevsky, Nikolai, 22, 35; monument to, 83
Chopin, Frederic: *Funeral March*, 189
Christianity. See *under* Religion and theater

Chudnovsky, Grigory, 203
Church and theater. *See* Religion and theater
Cinizelli Circus, 15, 16, 25, 41, 114, 132, 166
Circus, 21, 25, 108, 112, 114, 117–18, 209; and theater, 25, 68, 70, 107, 116–17, 167–68, 204; clowns, 68, 114, 116, 165, 167, 172, 209; wrestling, 114–15, 118, 127
Circus Department. *See under* Narkompros
Clowns. *See under* Circus
Comedians' Haven (Petrograd cabaret), 60
Comintern. *See* Third International
Commedia dell'arte, 9, 59, 60–61, 66, 107, 109, 116, 125, 164–67, 172
Commissariat of Education. *See* Narkompros
Commission for Decorating the City (Petrograd, 1918), 89
Commission of the Central Executive Committee of the USSR for the Organization and Conduct of the Tenth Anniversary of the October Revolution (1927), 219
"Conference of the Entente." *See* Krylov: "Quartet"
Conservatory (Petrograd), 157, 185
Constantine, Grand Duke: *King of the Jews*, 52
Constitutional Democrats, 188
Constructivism, 51, 150
Coronation of the Revolution (Samara, 1920), 142
Crooked Mirror (Petrograd cabaret), 157, 185
Curzon, Lord George, 172–73
Cyril and Methodius, 79, 83

David, Jacques-Louis, 44, 84; *Oath of the Tennis Court*, 84
Davydov, Denis, 78
Day of Red Gifts (1919), 99
Decembrists, 12, 132
Degeyter, Felix, 185
Deistvo, 37, 57, 62, 117, 121–22, 128, 135, 137, 140, 143, 150, 151, 156; audience of, 138–39, 147, 161, 167. See also *Sliianie*

Delvary, Georg, 116, 165, 173
Demonstrations and parades, 7, 17–18, 20, 45, 194–95, 199, 218, 219
Department of People's Festivals (Moscow Soviet), 98
Derrida, Jacques, 177
Derzhavin, Konstantin, 164, 166, 203
Dickens, Charles: *Cricket on the Hearth*, 31
Dobuzhinsky, Mstislav, 18, 74, 95, 157
Dostoevsky, Fedor: monument to, 83; *Brothers Karamazov*, 109; *The Possessed*, 31
"Down the Mother Volga," 124
Dramatic play, 109, 124–25, 127–28, 149, 164, 167, 215–16. See also Agit-trial; Game playing
Duncan, Isadora, 27, 215
Durkheim, Emile: *The Elementary Forms of Religious Life*, 145
Durov, Anatoly, 114
Durov, Vladimir, 114, 213

Ehrenburg, Ilya, 114
Eisenstein, Sergei, 30; *Aleksandr Nevsky*, 30; *Ten Days That Shook the World*, 1–2
Ekaterinhof, 105–6
Eliade, Mircea, 44, 45–46, 56, 84
Elizaveta Petrovna (empress), and masques of gender reversal, 55
Engels, Friedrich, 80; monument to, 83, 118; *Origin of the Family, Private Property and the State*, 35
Engineers' Castle (Petrograd), 154, 163
Erdman, Boris, 114
Ermak Timofeevich, 109, 125
Esenin, Sergei, 20; *Eulogy of the Revolution* (Voronezh, 1918), 41
Euripides: *Hippolytus*, 154
Evreinov, Nikolai, 9, 23, 42, 68, 104, 107, 137, 165, 215; and theater as game, 60–62, 122, 148; *1812* (1912), 63; *Main Thing*, 148; *Storming of the Winter Palace* (1920), 200–201, 203, 205, 206; *Three Magi* (1907), 61; *World Contest of Wit*, 213. See also Ancient Theater (Petrograd)

Fairground entertainments, 9, 114, 166; *balagan*, 17, 59, 68, 71, 104, 106, 107, 108, 110, 115; *gulianie*, 104–5, 106, 119; *raek* (peep show), 112

Festival of Federation (Paris, 1790), 154
Festival of Reason (Paris, 1793), 22, 34
Festival of the Supreme Being (Paris, 1794), 23
Festivals. *See* Public celebrations
Feuerbach, Ludwig, 33
Fidman, V., 46; *Filatka and Miroshka's Rivalry*, 124; *Fire of Prometheus* (Petrograd, 1920), 163–64
Field of Mars (Petrograd), 19, 91, 105–7, 154–56, 158, 194, 195
First Congress (Moscow, 1919), 178, 180–81
First International, 77, 149, 151, 178, 185, 186
Fokine, Michel, 52
Fomin, Ivan Alekseevich, 156, 171
Forreger, Nikolai, 113, 118
Free Comedy Theater (Petrograd), 148
Free Theater (Voronezh), 112–13
French Revolution, 12, 23, 46, 51, 84, 85, 110, 112, 159, 200, 209; festivals of, 6, 22–23, 43–44, 140, 154, 160, 212, 214; metric system and calendar of, 85
Friche, Vladimir, 7, 23, 34, 93, 98–99, 140
Fuchs, Georg: *Die Schaubühne der Zukunft*, 37
Futurism and futurists, 64–65, 72, 78, 93, 96–98, 99, 100, 101–2
Fülöp-Miller, René, 4

Gaideburov, Pavel, 20, 49, 119–24, 129, 135
Game playing, 61, 111–12, 122, 124, 126–27, 146–50, 151, 167. *See also* Dramatic play
Gan, Aleksei, 138, 150–51, 156
Garibaldi, Giuseppe, 112
Gastev, Aleksei, 31–32, 151, 152; "We Grow Out of Iron," 31; *Poetry of the Workers' Hammer*, 31
Geertz, Clifford, 176
General Staff Headquarters (Petrograd), 97, 203
Gerasimov, Sergei, 157
German Embassy (Moscow), 102
Gibschmann, Konstantin, 165, 172
GIII. *See* State Institute of Art History
Glavpolitprosvet. *See under* Narkompros

Glazunov, Aleksandr, 52, 185
Glinka, Mikhail: *Ivan Susanin (Life for the Tsar)*, 76
"God-builders," 38, 200
Gogol, Nikolai: *Terrible Vengeance*, 130
Golden King (Moscow, 1920), 144
Goldman, Emma, 169
Goldoni, Carlo, 59
Goleizovsky, Kasian, 114
Golovinskaia, Elena, 122, 124, 165
Good Men of Versailles (Capitalist Intrigues) (Petrograd, 1920), 166
Gorky, Maxim, 18, 25, 26, 38, 48, 110, 111, 113, 120, 127, 135; *History of World Culture*, 113
Gorsky, Aleksandr: *Stenka Razin*, 77
Gozzi, Carlo, 59
GPU. *See* State Political Administration
Granovsky, Aleksei, 25, 157
Guardians of the People's Temperance, 106–7, 119
Gumilev, Nikolai: *Magic Tree*, 165
Gvozdev, Aleksei, 54

Harlequin, 59, 60, 63
Headquarters Arch (Petrograd), 204
Hegel, Georg, 35, 78
Hellenism, 25–26, 33–34, 35–36, 41, 73–74, 125, 209
Hercules, 82
Herder, Johann von, 33, 35
Hofmannsthal, Hugo von: *Everyman*, 25
Holiday of the Defense of Petrograd (Petrograd, 1920), 163
Holiday of the Revolution (1917), 21
Holidays. *See* Socialist holidays and calendar
Hölderlin, Friedrich, 35
Hugo, Victor: *Notre-Dame de Paris*, 54
Hunters' Row (Moscow), 96

Iakhmanov, 89
Iakulov, Georgy, 21
Iberian Chapel (Moscow), 85–86
Igrishche. See Dramatic play
Improvisation, 122, 126, 127, 129, 131, 132, 133, 165. *See also* Skarskaia method
Instructors' Courses for Children's Theater and Festivals (Petrograd), 124
Instsenirovka, 31, 112, 149

Internationale, 159, 161, 181, 185, 187, 205, 206
International Proletarian Political Review (Astrakhan, 1920), 213
International Women's Day, 7
Inundation of Belgium (Petrograd, 1914), 117
Iudenich, General Nikolai, 134, 214
Iurev, Iury, 25, 26, 113, 127; *Macbeth* (1918), 25–26; *Oedipus Rex* (1918), 25–26
Ivan III, 180
Ivan IV (the Terrible), 180
Ivanov, Viacheslav, 7, 51, 54, 65, 71, 101, 104, 123, 131, 138, 140–41, 144, 146; *deistvo,* 37, 62, 135, 136, 137; influence on Gaideburov, 119–20, 122; mystery, 47, 57; myth, 37–38, 143; Nietzschean elements, 36–37; Tower Apartment, 38, 57–58; *Prometheus,* 128
IZO. *See* Narkompros: Arts Section
Izvestiia, 85, 89, 91, 97, 153

Jarry, Alfred: *Ubu Roi,* 65
July Days (Petrograd, 1920), 163

Kaganovich, Lazar, 196
Kalinin, Fedor, 30
Kamenev, Lev, 93; monument to, 195
Kameneva, Olga, 98–99
Kamensky, Vasily, 114; *Stenka Razin—Heart of the People,* 78
Karl Marx Club (Petrograd), 216
Karsavina, Tamara, 97
Kautsky, Karl, 199
Kedril the Glutton, 124
Kemp, Will, 165
Kerensky, Aleksandr, 131, 203–7
Kerzhentsev, Platon, 7, 27–28, 31, 33, 75, 103, 137, 140, 143, 161, 164, 206
Kheraskov, Mikhail, 17
Khlebnikov, Velimir, 65, 107; "Labor Holiday," 155
Khodasevich, Valentina, 171
Khodynka Field (Moscow), 17, 55, 86, 105, 150, 214
Khudozhestvenno-prosvetitel'naia kommissiia (Arts-Educational Commission), 21
Kirillov, Vladimir: "May Day Hymn," 79

Kirov Bridge (Petrograd), 219
Kogan, Petr, 138, 152
Kogan, Sofia, 138
Kolchak, Admiral Aleksandr, 109
Koltsov, Aleksei, monument to, 83
Komissarzhevskaia Theater (Theater of Vera Komissarzhevskaia), 30, 50, 121
Komissarzhevsky, Theodore, 76
Komsomol Christmas (1923), 217
Konenkov, Sergei, 74, 114, 118
Kostroma (1913), 17
Kozlinsky, Vladimir, 68
Kozlov, Petr: *Above Life,* 80; *Legend of the Communard,* 80–81, 108, 213
Krasnoe selo, 149, 206
Kremlin (Moscow), 75, 86, 90, 155, 176, 180, 181
Kropotkin, Petr: *History of the French Revolution,* 23
Kruchenykh, Aleksei: *Victory Over the Sun,* 65–66
Krupskaia, Nadezhda, 36, 108
Krupskaia Institute of Culture (Leningrad), 5
Krylov, Ivan: "Quartet," 76; "Slaughter of the Beasts," 76
Kugel, Aleksandr, 52, 157, 203, 204
Kurmatsep (Master Courses in Scenic Production), 124
Kuzmin, Mikhail, 25
Kuznetsky Bridge (Moscow), 212
Kuznetsov, Pavel, 21, 86, 114, 118, 164; *Stepan Razin on the River Beats Back the Advance of Counter-revolution,* 78

Labor, in socialist society, 35, 81, 152–53, 156, 178, 216
Latvian Riflemen, 86, 114
Lazarenko, Vitaly, 68, 114, 115, 117
Lebedev, N. V., 122, 124
Lebedev, Vladimir: *Apotheosis of the Worker,* 68
Lebedev-Poliansky, Pavel, 30
Lebedeva, Maria, 181
Lenin, Vladimir Il'ich, 25, 28, 42, 77–78, 80, 85, 94, 98, 123, 131, 155, 175, 198, 203, 206, 217; on culture, 27, 72, 104, 108, 136; monument to, 195; "A Great Beginning," 153; "Left-Wing Communism, An Infantile Disorder," 180

Lenin Hills (Sparrow Hills, Moscow), 150, 215, 216
Lenin Mausoleum (Moscow), 180, 198, 219
Lenin monumental plan, 82–84, 94–95, 107, 177, 193–94, 196–97
Lenin Theater (Astrakhan), 213
Lentovsky, Mikhail, 17, 106
Lentulov, Aristarkh, 76, 107
Lermontov, Mikhail: *Song of the Merchant Kalashnikov,* 107
Libakov, M. V., 138; *Liberation* (*see* Beethoven: *Lenore*)
Liberty Bond Day (1917), 18, 19–21, 30, 121, 203, 204
Liebknecht, Karl, monument to, 181
Lieutenant Schmidt Bridge (Petrograd), 219
Ligovsky People's House, 119, 123
Literary Fund (Petrograd), 121
Lithuanian Castle (Petrograd), 23
Litolff, Henri: *Robespierre* (overture), 204
Lloyd George, David, 115
Lobnoe Mesto (Moscow), 77, 118, 198
Lopukhov, Fedor, 107, 157
Louis XIV, 164
Love for Three Oranges (journal), 60
Lubok, 104, 112, 113, 115
Lumet, Louis, 26
Lunacharsky, Anatoly, 7, 8, 25, 30, 72, 78, 82, 108, 120, 128, 136, 138, 212; and festivals, 22–23, 88, 92–93, 103–4, 152; monuments to, 94, 195; Nietzschean elements in work of, 33, 35, 36, 38, 62, 135, 143; on theater, 26, 110–11, 166; *Religion and Socialism,* 79
Luna Park (Petrograd), 63
Lurich, Arthur (wrestler), 25
Luxemburg, Rosa, monument to, 181
Lvov, Nikolai, 138

MacAloon, John, 147
MacKaye, Percy: *Civic Theatre,* 28
Maeterlinck, Maurice, 50, 57, 144; *Death of Tintageles,* 50, 120; *Sister Beatrice,* 49, 50
Magical Accordion (Petrograd, 1920), 166
Maiden's (Devichee) Field (Moscow), 105

Malevich, Kasimir, 21, 47, 49, 65, 70, 138
Maly Opera (Petrograd), 76
Maly Theater, 52 (Petrograd), 78 (Moscow)
Mandelshtam, Osip, 196
March-Route Committee (Moscow, 1920), 197
Mardzhanov, Konstanin, 76, 113, 185, 188, 189, 212; *Fuente ovejuna* (1919), 76, 185; *King Saul* (1920), 185
Marinetti, Emilio, 64
Marseillaise, 20, 23, 159, 204
Marx, Karl, 12, 33, 35, 77, 80, 95, 144, 176, 178, 199, 208; monument to, 83, 84, 118, 195; portraits of, 141
Maslovskaia, S. D., 157
Mass spectacles, 112, 118–19, 127, 129, 163, 204–6, 208, 210, 213–14; and professional participation, 133, 135–136. *See also* Public celebration: theatrical
Master Courses in Scenic Production, 124
Matisse, Henri, 100
Matiushin, Mikhail: *Victory Over the Sun,* 65–66
Mayakovsky, Vladimir, 64, 66, 68, 70, 71, 79, 107, 160, 165, 171, 195, 198; *Mystery-Bouffe,* 43, 63–71, 81, 93, 107, 112, 116, 127, 131; "Ode to Revolution," 101; *The Soviet ABCs,* 114; *Vladimir Mayakovsky: A Tragedy,* 65; *World Wrestling Championship,* 115, 127
May Day, 18, 38, 45, 79, 85, 88, 105, 213; *1903,* 106; *1917,* 18–19, 88, 93, 194; *1918,* 28–32, 62, 73, 75, 80, 82, 86–93, 96, 99, 115, 194; *1919,* 76, 77, 80, 98–100, 106, 109, 127, 129, 134, 198; *1920,* 142, 144, 150, 151, 152, 154, 155, 156–57, 159, 166, 169, 195; *1921,* 211; *1925,* 76
May Day Commission (Moscow, 1923), 211
Mazaev, Anatoly, 5
Melodrama, 110–11, 126, 165–66
Mensheviks, 88, 154
Menzhinskaia, Olga, 98
Merging. See *Sliianie*
Metalworker, 169–70
Metropolitan Hotel (Moscow), 197

INDEX 311

Meyerhold, Vsevolod, 9, 42, 66, 68, 71, 94, 104, 107, 121, 122, 124, 126, 127, 137, 140, 144, 160, 164, 165, 206, 214–15; circus and theater, 116–17; revolution and theater, 62–63; and symbolism, 50, 51, 57–61; *Les Aubes* (1920), 76; *Dithyramb of Electrification* (1921), 215; *Fire* (1914), 63, 164; *Mystery-Bouffe* (1918), 43, 63–71, 128; *Struggle and Victory* (1921), 214–15
Mgebrov, Aleksandr, 20, 25, 30–32, 50, 57, 65, 81, 128
Michelangelo: *David*, 169
Miklashevsky, Konstantin, 107, 165; *Minerva Triumphant*, 17, 117
Mikhailovsky Manège (Petrograd), 106–7, 117
Misheev, N. I., 157
Mobile-Popular Theater (Petrograd), 20–21, 119–124; *Masses,* 121, 122, 124; *Turgenev Evening*, 121
Mobile Theater. *See* Mobile-Popular Theater
Moissi, Sandro, 25
Molière, 103, 165; *Monkey-Informer* (Petrograd, 1920), 166
Monumentalism, 113, 123, 205
Monumental plan. *See* Lenin monumental plan
Monuments, 46–47, 84–85, 86, 99, 169–71, 196
Monument to Liberated Labor (Moscow), 157
Monument to the Third International. *See* Tatlin, Vladimir
Moor, Dmitry, 181
Moralités, 61
More, Thomas, 7; *Utopia*, 84
Morgan, J. P., 166
Morris, William, 47; *News from Nowhere*, 152
Moscow, 177, 180, 181, 197
Moscow Art Theater, 25, 30, 31, 51
Moscow Balagan (theater), 118
Moscow Party Committee: Department of Subbotniki, 153
Moscow Soviet, 62, 93, 94, 98, 99, 218
Moscow Soviet of Soldiers' Deputies (1917), 21
Moscow Soviet of Workers' Deputies (1917), 21

Musical Drama Theater (Petrograd), 63
Mystery play, 25, 47–48, 62, 160, 185, 205, 209; Mayakovsky and, 66, 68; and revolution, 52, 53, 57; symbolism, 9, 37, 49, 59, 61
Mystery of Liberated Labor (Petrograd, 1920), 157–63, 171, 172, 185, 187, 188, 189, 192, 193, 204, 205, 206
Myth, 38, 48, 143–44, 160, 178, 200; and mythmaking, 38, 56, 140, 145, 177; of revolution, 12, 56, 77, 145, 177, 188, 199–200, 205, 206

Napoleon Bonaparte, 160
Narbut, Vladimir, 181
Narkompros (Commissariat of Education), 22, 35, 79, 94, 99, 119, 151; Adult Education Department, 122–23; Arts Section (IZO), 89, 98, 99; Bureau of Mass Festivals, 152; Glavpolitprosvet, 211; Petrograd Politprosvet, 216–17; Petrograd Section, 89; Theater and Spectacle Section of the Northern Commune's Regional Narkompros, 94; Theater Section (TEO), 94, 98, 108; TEO Circus Department, 114, 117, 119; TEO Section for Mass Presentations and Spectacles, 137, 151; TEO Sub-section for Worker-Peasant Theater, 136–37; TEO Sub-section of Worker-Peasant and Red Army Theater, 137; TEO Sub-section on Repertory, 137
Narva Gate (Petrograd), 163
Negotiations of Krasin and Lloyd-George (Berezovye Rudki, 1920), 173
Nemirovich-Danchenko, Vasily, 112
NEP. *See* New Economic Policy
Nevsky Prospect (Petrograd), 85
New Economic Policy, 152, 211
Nezlobin Theater (Petrograd), 52
Nicholas I, 105
Nicholas II, 195; coronation of (1896), 17, 55; monument to, 107
Nicholas II People's House, 106, 111, 126, 127, 130, 165, 168; people's theater, 26–28, 31, 32, 34, 37, 39, 103–4, 209–10
Nietzsche, Friedrich, 7, 36, 62, 65, 138; *Birth of Tragedy*, 36, 54
Nikitin, Ivan, monument to, 83

November 7 celebration, 85; *1918*, 62, 73–74, 76, 78, 83, 85, 91, 93–101, 107, 112, 188, 194, 195, 196, 197, 206; *1919*, 118, 134; *1920*, 76, 195, 196, 200; *1921*, 211; *1927*, 213, 218–19
Novinskoe Field (Moscow), 105

Obelisk to International Revolutionaries (Moscow), 95
Obukhov Factory (Petrograd), 91
Old Man and the Sea (movie), 157
Oprichina, 55
Order of the Red Banner of Labor, 152
Orenburg, 214
Organizing Committee for the October Festivities (Moscow, 1918), 93
Ostrovsky, Aleksandr: *Storm*, 119
Owen, Robert, monument to, 83
Ozouf, Mona, 43–44

Palace Embankment (Petrograd), 156
Palace of the Arts. *See* Winter Palace (Petrograd)
Palace Square (Petrograd), 3, 85, 96, 154–56, 158, 181, 215
Panina, Countess Sofia, 119, 123
Pantaloon, 166
Pantomime, 114, 129, 165
Parades. *See* Demonstrations and parades
Paris Commune, 12, 46, 179–80, 186, 189; monument to, 181
Paris Commune Day, 217
Partition of Russia (Petrograd, 1920), 166
People's Houses, 103, 106, 119
Peredelki. *See under* Tradition, remaking of
Peter the Great, 17, 128, 149; and Most Drunken Council of Fools and Jesters, 17, 55, 128
Petrograd, 177, 196, 197, 203; Lesnaia district, 195; Porokhovye factory district, 129
Petrograd Organizational Bureau (1918), 96
Petrograd Party Committee, 89, 197
Petrograd Pravda, 134
Petrograd Soviet, 19, 89, 94, 98, 99, 169, 195, 201
Petrograd Soviet Day, 7
Petrograd Theater Section (PTO), 93, 108, 111, 112

Petrograd Workers' and Soldiers' Soviets (1917), 18
Petro-Pavlovsk Fortress (Petrograd), 192
Petrov, Nikolai, 148, 185, 203; *Main Thing* (1921), 148
Petrov-Vodkin, Kuzma: *1918 in Petrograd*, 79; *Stepan Razin*, 78
Petrushka, 68, 104, 209
Phidias, 169
Picasso, Pablo, 59
Pierrot, 59, 60, 63, 104
Pilsudski, Jozef, 115
Pinkerton literature, 109, 166
Piotrovsky, Adrian, 4, 54, 122, 131, 132, 149, 156, 163, 166, 185, 216; *Sword of Peace*, 132, 164
Pisarev, Dmitry, 22
Pisemsky, Aleksei, 111
Play. *See* Game playing
Plekhanov, Georgy, 20, 22
Podbelsky, Vadim, 93
Podvoisky, Nikolai, 3, 200, 203, 215, 219
Political Administration of the Petrograd Military District (PUR), 123, 124, 128, 157, 200
Popular Theater. *See* Mobile-Popular Theater
Potemkin, Grigory, 181
Pottecher, Maurice, 26
Pravda, 45, 89, 91, 97, 153, 156
Prokofiev, Sergei, 107
Proletarian Studio of Declamation, 31
Proletkult, 27, 28, 72, 75, 80, 89, 104, 119, 123, 128, 136, 137, 138, 157, 211, 213; Petrograd Literary Studio, 97; Petrograd Proletkult, 129–30, 132, 161; Petrograd Proletkult Studio, 30–32; Proletkult Studio (Moscow), 56–57, 76, 145–46
Proletkult Palace (Petrograd), 30
Prometheus (hymn), 145
Prometheus, 36, 76, 80, 81, 86–88, 128, 144–45
Propaganda: in public events, 8, 10, 105, 113, 120, 141–42, 160–61, 166, 214; monumental (*see* Lenin monumental plan)
PTO (Petrograd Theater Section), 93, 108, 111, 112
Public celebration (outdoors), 9, 19, 21, 27, 42, 51, 73–75, 94–95, 121, 127,

200; and history, 55, 75, 135, 162–63, 200–201, 209, 210; pre-revolutionary, 4–5, 7, 17–18, 38–39, 40–41; as propaganda, 86–88, 92, 137; as show of power, 45, 177, 178; theatrical, 21, 23, 25, 58, 62, 73, 121–22, 123, 127, 137, 140, 150, 168, 208, 209, 210; and theatrical celebrations in the West, 27–28. *See also* Mass spectacles
Puccini, Giacomo: *Tosca*, 76
Pugachev, Emelian, 12, 132
Punin, Nikolai, 47, 64, 74–75, 95
PUR (Political Administration of the Petrograd Military District), 123, 124, 128, 157, 200
Putilov Factory (Petrograd), 91

Rabkrin (Worker-Peasant Inspectorate), 219
Rachilde (Marguerite Eymery Vallette): *Le vendeur de soleil*, 20, 121
Radakov, A. A., 157
Radek, Karl, 199
Radlov, Ernst, 164
Radlov, Sergei, 60, 122, 124, 163, 164, 167, 171, 173, 185, 189, 205
Raskol'niki (religious sectarians), 128
Razin, Stepan, 12, 77–78, 81, 83, 118, 125, 132, 142, 159, 160, 198, 205; monument to, 83
Recollection, 38, 43, 55. *See also* Myth
Red Army, 132–33, 144, 149, 151, 159, 160, 163, 187, 210–11; Northern Army, 195
Red Army Studio, 124–29, 149; *Overthrow of the Autocracy*, 125–28, 131, 132, 147, 166, 206; *Red Year,* 131; *Sword of Peace,* 132–33; *Third International,* 127–28, 147, 178
Red Guard, 200, 203, 206
Red Mass (Petrograd, 1920), 181
Red Navy, 173; Baltic Fleet, 214
Red Square (Moscow), 75, 86, 194, 195, 211, 212, 218, 219
Reed, John, 200
Reinhardt, Max, 25, 157; *Everyman* (1911), 25, 47; *Oedipus Rex* (1911), 25
Religion and theater: Biblical motifs, 56, 63, 66, 68, 81; Christianity, 58, 78, 79, 80, 81, 133, 141, 142, 155, 180, 181; Orthodox ritual, 50, 217
Remizov, Aleksei, 128
Revolution: dramatization of, 2, 11, 44, 125–127, 131–32, 162–63, 202–3, 209, 210; as festival or drama, 30–31, 33, 37, 42, 55, 62–63, 66, 67, 68, 143, 152; place of in history, 12–13, 34, 46, 131–32, 210
Rimsky-Korsakov, Nikolai: monument to, 83; *Maiden of Pskov,* 77; *Sadko,* 189
Ritual and drama, 11, 32, 49–50, 121–22, 124, 139–40, 141, 142–44, 145–46, 160, 181
Robespierre, Maximilien, 23, 34, 44, 85, 205; monument to, 83
Rock Island (Petrograd), 168–71
Roerich, Nikolai, 18
Rolland, Romain, 7, 103, 111; *Le théâtre du peuple,* 23, 26
Romanov dynasty, 105; tercentenary of (1913), 17, 95
Rose Festival (Pasadena), 27
ROSTA (Russian Telegraph Agency), 195
Rousseau, Jean-Jacques, 7, 34, 71, 78, 79, 93, 103; *Consideration of the Government of Poland and Its Reform,* 34; *Letter to M. D'Alembert on the Spectacles,* 34
Rukavishnikov, Ivan, 114, 119; *Political Carousel,* 118
Rus' (Voronezh, 1918), 112–13
Russian Heroes in the Carpatians (Petrograd, 1914), 117
Russian Telegraph Agency (ROSTA), 195

St. Basil's Cathedral (Moscow), 199
St. Isaac's Cathedral (Petrograd), 163
St. Petersburg, 200th anniversary of (1903), 17. *See also* Petrograd
Samara (1920), 142
Samodeiatel'nost', 28, 136, 137, 146, 209, 216
Samson and Delilah, 164
Samson and Delilah (Moscow, 1919), 118
Saratov (1918), 74, 95, 100
Schiller, Johann, 12, 26, 35
Scriabin, Aleksandr, 36, 54, 144; *Mystery,* 36–37; *Prometheus,* 36, 76–77, 128, 144

Sebastopol, 50th anniversary of defense of (1906), 17
Second Congress (Moscow, 1920), 180–85, 198
Second International, 105, 151, 186
Second State Circus (Moscow), 117, 118
Self-government. See *Samodeiatel'nost'*
Semenov Place (Petrograd), 106, 196, 200
Serezhnikov, Vasily, 31
Serge (clown), 165, 172, 173
Severianin, Igor, 20; *Severnaia Kommuna (Northern Commune)*, 89
Shakespeare, William, 12, 26, 103, 165; *Macbeth*, 25
Shcheglov, Dmitry, 122, 129, 130, 132, 216
Shcherbakov, Nikolai, 124
Shchuko, Vladimir, 157
Shekhtel, Fedor, 51
Shershenevich, Vadim, 65, 119
Shevchenko, Taras, monument to, 86–87
Shils, Edward, 176
Shimanovsky, Viktor, 122, 124, 216
Shklovsky, Viktor, 80, 114, 124, 163, 164, 196
Shock-workers, 152
Skarskaia, Nadezhda, 119, 123
Skarskaia method, 122, 125. See also Improvisation
Skobelev, General Mikhail, 82
Skorokhod Factory (Petrograd), 211
Skoropadsky, Hetman, 86
Sliianie, 126, 140, 145
Smashing of Kolchak (1919), 129
Smolny Institute (Petrograd), 1, 46, 83, 105, 194, 195
Smyshliaev, Valentin, 56, 137, 144–46
Social Mystery-Play (Petrograd, 1917), 18
Socialist aesthetics, 21–22, 26–27, 35–36, 98–101, 104; and official taste, 94–95, 98, 99
Socialist holidays and calendar, 7, 85, 88, 89, 97, 152–55, 156, 177, 217, 219
Soiuz deiatelei vsekh iskusstv (All-Arts Union, Petrograd), 18–19
Sologub, Fedor, 19
Soloviev, Vladimir (director), 60, 63, 122, 124, 163–66, 185; *Fire* (1914), 164
Soloviev, Vladimir (philosopher), 164

Somov, Konstantin, 59
Sophocles, 12, 26, 103; *Oedipus Rex*, 25
Sorel, Georges, 38, 135
Soviet of Moscow Art Organizations (1917), 21
Soviet Propaganda Day (1919), 134
Space and time of festivity. See Time and space of festivity
Sparrow Hills (Moscow), 150, 215, 216
Spartacus, 12, 112, 159, 160, 164, 193, 205
Special Assembly of Petrograd Factory and Plant Representatives (Petrograd, 1918), 88
Special Conference for Matters of Art (Petrograd, 1917), 18
Sponsorship of art. See Carnivals: sponsorship of
Spring Is Beautiful (Moscow, 1883), 17
Square of People's Gatherings (Petrograd), 169
Stalin, Joseph, 38, 86, 176, 219
Standing Guard for the World Commune (Moscow, 1919), 118
Stanislavsky, Konstantin, 49, 51, 56, 201
State Institute of Art History (GIII), 4, 54
State Political Administration (GPU), 214
Stenka Razin (movie, 1908), 77
Stepan Razin (game, Moscow, 1930), 216
Stock Exchange (Petrograd), 157, 158, 163, 185, 188
Storming of the Winter Palace (Petrograd, 1920), 1–3, 60, 199–207, 213
Strauss, Johann: *Vienna Waltz*, 189
Stray Dog (Petrograd cabaret), 60
Street decorations, 19, 73, 74, 85, 97–99, 100, 169, 188, 195–96, 198–99; modernist, 89, 91, 95–96, 96–97, 150–51; under NEP, 211, 212–13
Streets: cleanup of, 154–55; in celebrations, 7–8, 96–97, 159, 177, 193–94, 197–98; renaming of, 82, 85, 157, 195
Struggle for the Commune. See Puccini: *Tosca*
Studio-Theater (Petrograd), 165
Subbotnik, 151–56, 169, 178, 187, 195, 216
Sumarokov, Aleksandr, 17, 117

INDEX 315

Summer Garden (Petrograd), 23, 154, 163
Sverdlov, Iakov, 86; monument to, 195
Symbolism/symbolists, 7, 9, 57–60, 78, 80; symbolist theater, 49–51, 104, 119–20, 126

Tableaux vivants, 117–18, 216
Tairov, Aleksandr, 62, 135–36
Taking of Azov, 15, 16, 107, 163, 172
Taking of Rostov and Novocherkassk (1919), 129
Taking of the Bastille (Petrograd, 1920), 163
Tarasov, Aleksandr, 129
Tarzan, 80
Tatlin, Vladimir, 86; *Monument to the Third International,* 196–97
Tauride Palace (Petrograd), 181
Tchaikovsky, Petr, 72; *Swan Lake,* 174
TEO. *See* Narkompros: Theater Section
Terijoki (Finland), 57
Theater of Popular Comedy (Petrograd), 165–68, 172
Theater of Vera Komissarzhevskaia (Petrograd), 30, 50, 121
Theater Square, 95, 197 (Moscow); 78 (Petrograd)
Theatrical-Dramaturgical Studio of the Red Army. *See* Red Army Studio
Théâtre de l'Oeuvre (Paris), 65
Third Congress (Moscow, 1921), 212, 214
Third International, 134, 149, 178, 181, 185, 187, 195, 198, 212
Third Rome (Moscow), 180
Tiersot, Julien: *Les fêtes et les chants de la révolution française,* 22, 41
Tikhonovich, Valentin, 137
Time and space of festivity, 8, 43–44, 48, 55–56, 62, 96, 106, 112, 120, 122, 139, 153, 156, 159, 169, 177; sacred time, 45–46, 48, 49, 51
Tiomkin, Dmitry, 52, 157, 200
Tiutchev, Fedor, monument to, 83
Tolmachev, Nikolai, 99
Tolstoy, Alexei: *Road to Calvary,* 101
Tolstoy, Leo, 48, 103, 111, 115–16; *First Distiller,* 115–16
Tovstonogov, Georgy, 5; *Toward a World Commune* (Petrograd, 1920), 185–93, 206
Tradition, remaking of, 5, 8, 72–74, 79–83, 105; by adapting heroes, 12, 77–78, 83, 86, 112, 132; and carnivals, 107–8, 109; and monuments, 82–84, 95, 96–97, 99; and places, 155–56, 180; by renaming streets, 82, 85, 157, 195; by rewriting classics (*peredelki*), 75–76
Tragedy, 128; as revolutionary genre, 25–26; communist, 111
Treaty of Nystad (1723), festival following, 17
Tretiakov, Sergei: *Neporzach,* 217
Trial of Ataman Buria (traditional game), 109
Trial of the Yellow (Second) International (Petrograd, 1920), 181
Trial of Wrangel (Crimean Station, Kuban region, 1919), 110
Triumph of the (Allied) Powers (Petrograd, 1914), 117
Troitsky Tower (Moscow), 86
Trotsky, Leon, 132, 198, 199, 216, 219; monument to, 195
Tsar Maximilian (folk play), 68
Turgenev, Ivan, 121; *Fathers and Sons,* 121; *Klara Milich,* 121; "The Russian Language," 121; *Spirits,* 121; *A Strange Story,* 121
Turner, Victor, 135, 139–40
Twenty-One Conditions, 180

United Artistic Circles, 216–17
Universal Military Training Corps (Vsevobuch), 212, 215–16
"Unnecessary Truth," 49
Uprising Square (Petrograd), 195
Uritsky, Moisei, monument to, 195
Uritsky Square. *See* Palace Square (Petrograd)
Urvantsov, L. N., 157
Utopianism, 65–66, 68, 78–79

Vacation Island. *See* Rock Island (Petrograd)
Vakhtangov, Evgeny, 56
Varlikh, Hugo, 157, 204
Vaudeville, 59, 107, 112, 115
Vechernie izvestiia (Evening News), 98

Vega, Lope de: *Fuente Ovejuna*, 30, 61, 76
Verhaeren, Emile: monument to, 83; *Les Aubes*, 30, 76; "La Révolte," 56
Vertep (crèche), 70
Vesnin, Aleksandr, 75
Vinogradov-Mamont, Nikolai, 122–29, 133, 144, 147, 149, 166, 177; *Creation of the World*, 128; *Russian Prometheus*, 128
Vitebsk (1918), 3, 96
Vo imia svobody, 20
Voinov, Vladimir, 166, 168
Volkov, Fedor, 17, 117
Volodarsky, V., monument to, 83, 195
Voronezh (1918), 15–16, 40–41, 112–13, 114
Voronezh Opera House, 117
Voronezh Telegraph, 16
Voskresnik, 152
Vsevobuch (Universal Military Training Corps), 212, 215–16
Vsevolodsky-Gerngross, Vsevolod, 122, 136–37

Wagner, Richard, 7, 9, 26, 28, 30, 33, 35–36, 47, 58, 80, 88, 101, 103, 136; *Art and Revolution*, 33; *Art-Work of the Future*, 33, 35; *Götterdämmerung*, 181; *Lohengrin*, 159, 189
Wanderers, The, 100
War against White Poland (Petrograd, 1920), 163
Weber, Max, 176
Whitman, Walt, 31, 41
William of Orange, 112
Wilson, Woodrow, 115
Winckelmann, Johann, 35
Winter Palace (Petrograd), 1, 74, 194, 195, 201; Heraldic Hall, 115; Hermitage Hall, 52
Women's Death Battalion, 201, 206
Worker-Peasant Inspectorate (Rabkrin), 219
Workers' Soviet Opera (Moscow), 76
World of Art, 18, 59
World-Wide October (Moscow, 1928), 216
Wrangel, Baron N. N., 107
Wrangel, General Petr, 110, 115
Wrestling. *See under* Circus

Zamiatin, Evgeny: *Fires of St. Dominic*, 113; *We*, 9
Zhizn' iskusstva (The Life of Art), 98
Zielinski, Tadeusz, 164
Zimin Theater. *See* Workers' Soviet Opera
Zinoviev, Grigory, 88–89, 94, 180, 181; monument to, 195
Znamenskaia Square (Petrograd). *See* Uprising Square

Compositor:	Huron Valley Graphics, Inc.
Text:	10/13 Galliard
Display:	Galliard
Printer:	Braun-Brumfield, Inc.
Binder:	Braun-Brumfield, Inc.

OHIO UNIVERSITY LIBRARY
Please return this book as soon as you have
finished   to avoid a fine it must
                 late stamped b